## Advance praise for *Criminal Juries in the 21st Century*

"Recognizing that the jury system imagined in the late 18th century reflects a mere shadow of what contemporary juries face, Cynthia Najdowski and Margaret Stevenson, and the impressive experts they assembled, have done much to move the scholarship of juries into the here-and-now. This must-read book tackles important issues playing out in today's courtrooms including those relevant to LGBQT individuals, implicit biases, testilying, neuroscientific evidence, video recordings, and many more significant challenges. Using engaging real-world cases to illustrate issues, this book is destined to become the go-to classic for those who study, appeal to, or sit on juries."

—*Allison Redlich, PhD, Professor of Criminology,*
*Law and Society, George Mason University*

"Najdowski and Stevenson's *Criminal Juries in the 21st Century* reflects a contemporary and thorough review of psychological science applied to the jury system. The editors brought together an all-star cast of scholars, including psychologists and law professors, to review the scientific and policy issues associated with classic research issues such as juror selection and bias as well as modern and emerging issues such as jury use of ubiquitous video recordings and neuroscience evidence. Each chapter provides an in-depth review of the contemporary issues and research. The contributions of the volume as a whole are elegantly summarized and integrated in the final chapter by Shari Seidman Diamond. This volume will be immensely useful to the newest and the more seasoned followers of jury science."

—*Brian L. Cutler, PhD, University of Ontario*
*Institute of Technology*

"Written by a terrific mix of seasoned and emerging jury scholars, the chapters in this volume provide a comprehensive exploration of how recent shifts in societal attitudes and ongoing technological developments influence the work of the criminal jury. Readers are sure to come away with new insights that will invigorate their investigations into jury behavior."

—*Margaret Bull Kovera, PhD, John Jay*
*College of Criminal Justice, CUNY*

"Cynthia Najdowski and Margaret Stevenson have brought together an impressive set of new and established scholars to explore the key challenges facing 21st century criminal juries. From concerns about lingering racism and implicit bias to questions about the impact of cutting-edge technologies, this volume masterfully interweaves actual cases, social science research, and legal analysis. The result is a highly useful compendium of what we know and what we still need to learn to help future juries navigate these challenges."
—*Edie Greene, PhD, Professor, Department of Psychology,*
*University of Colorado Colorado Springs*

# Criminal Juries in the 21st Century

# American Psychology-Law Society Series

# Criminal Juries in the 21st Century

*Contemporary Issues, Psychological Science, and the Law*

*Edited by*

Cynthia J. Najdowski
and
Margaret C. Stevenson

OXFORD
UNIVERSITY PRESS

Oxford University Press is a department of the University of Oxford. It furthers
the University's objective of excellence in research, scholarship, and education
by publishing worldwide. Oxford is a registered trade mark of Oxford University
Press in the UK and certain other countries.

Published in the United States of America by Oxford University Press
198 Madison Avenue, New York, NY 10016, United States of America.

CIP data is on file at the Library of Congress
ISBN 978-0-19-065811-3

To my children Jake, Katarina, and Benjamin, loving little darlings who are yet as mighty as the forces of nature and even more fundamental in my view, and my husband Jeff, the center of our universe.

—C. J. N.

To my husband Emmett, who is a vital and constant pillar of love and support, and to my children George and Edward, who are the sources of my passions and inspirations.

—M. C. S.

For all those who strive to ensure the jury system meets our high ideals for achieving criminal justice, the defendants and victims who have faith in this important democratic institution, and every citizen who has ever served in the role of juror.

—C. J. N. and M. C. S.

# Contents

# Series Foreword

This book series is sponsored by the American Psychology-Law Society (AP-LS). AP-LS is an interdisciplinary organization devoted to scholarship, practice, and public service in psychology and law. Its goals include advancing the contributions of psychology to the understanding of law and legal institutions through basic and applied research; promoting the education of psychologists in matters of law and the education of legal personnel in matters of psychology; and informing the psychological and legal communities and the general public of current research, educational, and service activities in the field of psychology and law. AP-LS membership includes psychologists from the academic, research, and clinical practice communities as well as members of the legal community. Research and practice is represented in both the civil and criminal legal arenas. AP-LS has chosen Oxford University Press as a strategic partner because of its commitment to scholarship, quality, and the international dissemination of ideas. These strengths will help AP-LS reach its goal of educating the psychology and legal professions and the general public about important developments in psychology and law. The focus of the book series reflects the diversity of the field of psychology and law, as we publish books on a broad range of topics.

In the latest book in the series, *Criminal Juries in the 21st Century: Contemporary Issues, Psychological Science, and the Law*, Cynthia Najdowski and Margaret Stevenson have edited a series of chapters authored by top scholars that weave together research on various understudied and cutting-edge topics related to the intersection of psychological research and criminal jury decision-making. By using actual criminal cases that exemplify the issues being discussed in each of these chapters, the research is relevant to real-world contexts where discussions of current issues related to societal attitudinal shifts, technological advances, and how juror experiences affect the structure, function, and performance of the modern criminal jury ensue.

Najdowski and Stevenson have curated a collection of 12 chapters, divided into three parts: Societal changes in attitudes and the implications for jury selection and decision-making (five chapters: jury selection, death penalty, gender and sexuality, implicit bias, and the aftermath of Ferguson); technological changes and challenges, new sources of influence on juror decisions (five chapters: media exposure, Internet and social media, surveillance and sousveillance, video recordings of interrogations, and neuroscience); and emotion and the contemporary jury (two chapters: emotion and motivation, jury service). In addition, introductory and conclusory chapters set the stage and wrap up the discussions, providing an easy framework for the reader and summarizing relevant themes across the chapters.

*Criminal Juries in the 21st Century: Contemporary Issues, Psychological Science, and the Law* presents a comprehensive and detailed analysis of issues most relevant to the modern-day jury system. Scholars, researchers, policymakers, and practitioners will undoubtedly find that this book has the potential to help shape the future of interactions with criminal juries and the legal system.

Patricia A. Zapf
Series Editor

# Acknowledgments

We are very grateful to Patricia Zapf and Sarah Harrington for supporting our project; Patricia Breault, Jordan Buechler, Sean Houlihan, Carolyn Solomine, and Ar'Reon Watson for their research assistance; all of the scholars whose elegant and insightful analyses of the criminal jury system are the very heart of this volume; our mentors who continue to show us the way to do interdisciplinary work to improve the administration of justice; and, last, and anything but least, our families and friends for their love, support, and encouragement.

# Contributors

Iris Blandón-Gitlin, PhD
Department of Psychology
California State University,
    Fullerton

Brian H. Bornstein, PhD, MLS
Department of Psychology
University of Nebraska–Lincoln

Lindsey M. Cole, PhD
Department of Psychology
Oklahoma City University

Tarika Daftary-Kapur, PhD
Justice Studies, College of
    Humanities and Social Sciences
Montclair State University

Shari Seidman Diamond, JD, PhD
School of Law
Northwestern University and
    American Bar Foundation

Neal R. Feigenson, JD
School of Law
Quinnipiac University

Jennifer L. Groscup, JD, PhD
Department of Psychology
Scripps College

Catherine M. Grosso, JD
College of Law
Michigan State University

Valerie P. Hans, PhD
Cornell Law School
Cornell University

Colin Holloway, JD
Department of Psychology
University of Nebraska–Lincoln

Amelia Courtney Hritz, JD
Department of Human
    Development
Cornell University

**Shelby Hunter, MS**
Department of Psychology
University of Alabama

**Monica K. Miller, JD, PhD**
Department of Criminal Justice
University of Nevada, Reno

**Amelia Mindthoff, MA**
Department of Psychology
Florida International University

**Cynthia J. Najdowski, PhD**
School of Criminal Justice
University at Albany

**Barbara O'Brien, JD, PhD**
College of Law
Michigan State University

**Steven D. Penrod, JD, PhD**
Department of Psychology
John Jay College of Criminal Justice

**Anna Roberts, JD**
School of Law
Seattle University

**Caisa Elizabeth Royer, JD**
Department of Human
   Development
Cornell University

**N. J. Schweitzer, PhD**
School of Social and Behavioral
   Sciences
Arizona State University

**Christina O. Spiesel, MA**
School of Law
Yale University
Quinnipiac University

**Margaret C. Stevenson, PhD**
Department of Psychology
University of Evansville

**Sarah A. Trescher, MA**
Department of Psychology
University of Nevada, Reno

**Jillian M. Ware, MS**
School of Social and Behavioral
   Sciences
Arizona State University

**Richard L. Wiener, PhD, MLS**
Department of Psychology
University of Nebraska–Lincoln

**Jordan Blair Woods, JD, PhD**
School of Law
University of Arkansas–Fayetteville

# 1

# Criminal Juries in the 21st Century

## A Case-Study Introduction to Contemporary Issues

*Margaret C. Stevenson and Cynthia J. Najdowski*

The jury is often celebrated as an important symbol of American democracy. Yet, much has changed since 1791 when the Sixth Amendment guaranteed all citizens the right to a jury trial in criminal prosecutions. Psychological and legal scholars have empirically evaluated many claims about the strengths and limitations of the jury system. Now, scientific attention is focusing on new challenges that are faced by the contemporary jury. The overarching goals of this volume are to identify important understudied topics that arise when jurors decide criminal cases and discuss how cutting-edge psychological research can guide efforts to improve the modern criminal jury system in light of contemporary challenges. It is the first volume to provide an in-depth examination of current issues related to societal shifts in relevant attitudes, challenges stemming from technological advances, and what we know about the human experience of serving as a juror. Each of these sets of issues is relevant to understanding the structure, functioning, and performance of today's juries.

The authors of the chapters in this volume, who are all leading experts in their respective fields, explore various topics related to psychology and modern criminal juries. Specifically, the first part of this book reviews recent societal shifts in attitudes and their potential impact on the demographic and ideological composition of the criminal jury and, in turn, the jury's ability to make fair and just decisions. The second part of the book considers how recent technological advances have generated new sources of influence on jurors' evaluations of evidence and decision-making. The final part of the book examines how emotions impact the jury decision-making process and individual citizens' experiences of serving as jurors. As such, this volume offers a unique and broad view of criminal juries to increase awareness about a range of issues that impact jurors' decision-making in criminal cases and, thus, are in need of theoretical, scientific, and legal attention.

In this introductory chapter, we orient the reader to the contemporary hot-button issues and research to be reviewed by presenting actual cases that exemplify each topic. Chapter authors refer to the cases, underscoring the applied significance of the work reviewed throughout the volume. In particular, each chapter illustrates how theoretically and methodologically sound psychological and legal research can inform our understanding of the criminal jury system, emphasizes the importance of developing evidence-based law and practice, provides recommendations for reforms and improvements, and highlights avenues for future exploration.

First, however, to ensure readers are familiar with the various strategies used to gain information about juries, we briefly review the four methodological approaches typically used to learn about jury decision-making (for an in-depth review, see DeMatteo & Anumba, 2009). First, archival analyses of actual criminal cases allow researchers to code a wide variety of factors (e.g., the racial composition of the jury, presence of neuroimaging evidence) and examine whether those factors enhance or diminish the likelihood of certain outcomes, such as conviction or the imposition of particular sentences. A second type of methodology involves collecting and analyzing the rich content of detailed surveys and interviews conducted with actual jurors after being excused from service or at the conclusion of their trials. A third methodological approach involves field research, which allows researchers to observe jurors during actual trials. Some courts have even allowed researchers to manipulate variables and observe their effects on actual jurors (e.g., Hannaford, Hans, & Munsterman, 2000) or to video record and analyze actual jury deliberations (e.g., Diamond, Murphy, & Rose, 2012). The final method used to study juror and jury decision-making involves controlled mock trial experiments, in which researchers simulate the trial experience for individuals who have been asked to imagine they were serving as jurors in a real case. In such studies, researchers manipulate one or two elements of the simulated trial while holding all other elements constant.

On the one hand, archival analysis of actual jury verdicts, posttrial interviews with jurors, and field research are high in ecological validity because their results can be assumed to generalize to real-world trials. However, they are limited in internal validity because they lack experimental control, precluding researchers' ability to make causal inferences about the relations between variables. On the other hand, mock trial experiments are high in internal validity and allow researchers to isolate the impact the manipulated variables have on juror or jury decision-making, but they frequently suffer from threats to ecological validity. For instance, mock trial research often includes (a) samples of undergraduate students rather than jury-eligible community members, (b) short written summaries of trials rather than lengthy trial transcripts or video recordings of real trials, and (c) assessment of individual juror verdicts rather than group-level outcomes produced by jury deliberation. There is a great deal of scholarly debate regarding whether researchers should prioritize ecological validity or internal validity in mock trial research (see Kovera & Austin, 2016). Although some scholars argue for enhanced ecological validity in mock trial experimentation (e.g., Krauss & Lieberman, 2017), others argue that the emphasis on ecological versus internal validity should be guided by whether the researcher's goals are aimed toward legal application versus theory development (Koehler & Meixner, 2017). Understanding the basic strengths and limitations of jury research methodology will facilitate a better understanding of the chapters in this volume, each of which provides an integrated and critical review of relevant research, as well as recommended directions for future research, as reviewed next.

## Societal Changes in Attitudes: Implications for Jury Selection and Decision-Making

The first part of this volume is focused on recent societal attitudinal shifts and their implications for jury selection, perceptions, and decision-making. Specifically, to what extent is the jury system keeping pace with societal attitudes? The authors of chapters in this part explore the possibility that criminal jury proceedings are informed (or misinformed) by real or perceived changes in public attitudes and also review cutting-edge psychological research that is making its way into the courts.

### Jury Selection: The Challenge of Ensuring Jury Racial Diversity

The volume begins by exploring the enforceability of the U.S. Supreme Court decision in *Batson v. Kentucky* (1986), which determined that it is unlawful to use peremptory challenges to strike prospective jurors on the basis of their race or ethnicity. That is, while attempting to seat a jury that is favorable to one's side, neither prosecuting nor defense attorneys are permitted to exclude citizens from service just because they are members of a racial or ethnic minority group. Yet research suggests that prospective juror race nonetheless drives attorney decision-making during the jury selection process today (see Sommers & Norton, 2008), and claims of *Batson* violations are notoriously hard to prove. Consider the following case, which occurred mere months after the 1986 *Batson* decision. Queen Madge White, a 79-year-old White woman, was found dead in her apartment and Timothy Foster, an African American man, later confessed and was convicted for her murder (*Foster v. State*, 1988). Nearly three decades later, the U.S. Supreme Court ruled that the prosecutors had intentionally exercised peremptory challenges against Black jurors due to their race (*Foster v. Chatman*, 2016). The evidence was compelling: In the prosecutors' list of prospective jurors, each Black citizen's name was highlighted in green, and there was an accompanying legend indicating that green signified the citizen was Black. Moreover, on a second list of prospective jurors who had survived voir dire (the preliminary questioning of potential jurors used to determine who will be seated on the jury), there were "Ns" (i.e., an abbreviation for "no") next to the names of each of the Black citizens, reflecting the prosecutors' preferences about whom to strike. As a result of the prosecutorial team's deliberate efforts, not a single Black citizen served on the jury.

*Foster* is a compelling and unique case for a number of reasons. First, although it took over 30 years to wind its way through the courts, it is among the few cases to have successfully adjudicated a charge of intentionally striking jurors based on race, perhaps only because the evidence was so well documented, straightforward, and unequivocal. Rarely has it been so clear that race formed the basis of the decision to exclude prospective jurors from jury service. Why are such claims so difficult to prove? Why has the *Batson* decision failed to effectively support the seating of diverse juries? In Chapter 2, Barbara O'Brien and Catherine Grosso explore the answers to these questions, evaluating practices that may contribute to the underrepresentation of minorities on contemporary juries as well as reforms that may counter the problem.

### Does Declining Death Penalty Support Compromise Fairness in Capital Jury Trials?

Attorneys' race-based decision-making during jury selection may contribute to the underrepresentation of minorities on juries, but this disparity is also fueled in capital cases by racial differences in death penalty support (Cover, 2016). In fact, support for capital punishment is related to not only race but also gender, age, education, political ideology, and religion (Oliphant, 2016). Capital juries are biased along all of these domains because of the process used to seat juries in capital cases, which is known as "death qualification." This point is illustrated clearly in the recent case of Dzhokhar Tsarnaev, the Boston Marathon bomber. Tsarnaev's jury was composed predominantly of middle-aged White men and women. Indeed, only one of the 18 jurors was a minority group member (O'Neil & Moghe, 2015). Why? Jurors are considered to be "qualified" or eligible to serve on a capital case only if their attitudes toward the death penalty would not prevent them from complying with the law (i.e., rendering a sentence of death or life as consistent with the evidence presented during trial). Although death-qualification questions during voir dire systematically exclude citizens with certain demographic characteristics from serving as capital jurors, the process does not violate constitutional law technically because the citizens are excluded due to their attitudes toward the death penalty and not their demographics. Yet, it has the same deleterious effect of reducing jury diversity.

In Chapter 3, Amelia Hritz, Caisa Royer, and Valerie Hans review the implications of using death qualification to identify eligible jurors for capital jury decision-making. Indeed, even aside from the differences in race, gender, age, education, political ideology, and religion noted previously, death-qualified jurors differ from non-death-qualified jurors in myriad ways that have the potential to shape legal decisions. For instance, those who support the death penalty, compared to those who do not, are more likely to convict in the first place (e.g., Ellsworth, 1993) as well as subsequently more likely to impose capital punishment (e.g., O'Neil, Patry, & Penrod, 2004). The recent death sentence rendered in the Tsarnaev case could be construed as evidence of these downstream consequences. Hirtz and colleagues also discuss evidence that support for capital punishment has declined (Oliphant, 2016), as well as the potential effects this attitude shift may have on the administration of justice in capital jury cases.

## Biases Affecting LGBTQ Individuals in the Courtroom

Although most research exploring social group bias within the criminal justice system has focused on race, ethnicity, and gender, more recent work is focusing on other marginalized citizens, including members of the lesbian, gay, bisexual, transgender, and queer (LGBTQ) community who face unique challenges in criminal court. In Chapter 4, Jordan Blair Woods explores the limited but emerging body of research on biases that arise and affect LGBTQ citizens when they fill various roles within the criminal justice system (i.e., as jurors, victims, defendants, or witnesses).

For instance, Woods reviews provocation defenses that are used to justify the victimization of LGBTQ individuals. Consider the case involving Michael Magidson and Jose Merel, who were convicted and sentenced to life in prison for the brutal murder of Gwen Araujo in 2005 (Fraley, 2016). Notably, the 17-year-old victim in this case, Gwen (formerly Eddie) Araujo, was biologically male but identified and portrayed herself as a girl. The defendants were alleged to have beaten Araujo with their fists, cans, and a frying pan before finally strangling her to death upon discovering that they had just had sex with someone who was actually male rather than female. That is, the defendants invoked what is known as a "trans panic defense," arguing that they were merely guilty of manslaughter, not murder, because they had been provoked by the enraging discovery of Araujo's hidden biological sex. Although the first jury deadlocked, the second jury appeared to have been influenced by the trans panic defense arguments, convicting Magidson and Merel of the lesser charges of second-degree murder and acquitting them altogether of a hate crime. Woods considers Gwen Araujo's case in light of evidence that conservative but not liberal jurors are influenced by such provocation defenses (Salerno et al., 2015). Woods discusses the potential for jurors' biases to lead to unfair judgments in cases involving LGBTQ individuals, considers research regarding identifying LGBTQ biases among jurors' during voir dire, and explores whether certain laws (e.g., shield laws) might improve justice for this population.

## Interventions to Curb Juror Implicit Bias
## in Criminal Trials

In light of substantial evidence that bias negatively affects perceptions and case judgments for members of disadvantaged groups, efforts toward the development of interventions designed to curb bias have increased (e.g., Lee, 2015). Yet research reveals that jurors are swayed not only by explicit bias but also by bias that falls below the threshold of awareness and which jurors do not realize needs correction. In one recent case, such implicit bias was acknowledged by court officials. On August 31, 2015, New Jersey's Appellate Division of the Superior Court ruled that the defendants' right to an impartial jury and fair trial had been violated due to juror implicit racial bias (*State v. Brown*, 2015). The case involved two Black men, Rashon Brown and Malik Smith, who were convicted of carjacking. During the second day of deliberations, one juror allegedly shared with two fellow jurors that she recently noticed the presence of two Black men in her neighborhood, which made her nervous because she suspected they had some connection to the current case. Those two jurors encouraged her to report her concerns to a court officer. Later, the trial judge interviewed each juror about her own racial bias. Each juror indicated that she could remain impartial, and all jurors remained on the jury. The appellate court reversed this decision, stating that the juror's inference of "a sinister conspiratorial purpose from a facially innocuous event, based only on the race of the participants . . . revealed a deeply-rooted, latent racial bias that required her removal from the jury" (p. 881).

The appellate court's decision in *State v. Brown* is evidence that theory and research regarding implicit bias have begun to penetrate judicial decision-making. Indeed, the prolific body of work on implicit bias has begun to make its way into the courtroom via expert testimony (Sommers, 2010) and to affect policy. For instance, in 2016, the American Bar Association passed a resolution recommending that jurors be educated about implicit bias and how to prevent it from impacting their decisions (Laird, 2016). In Chapter 5, Anna Roberts discusses interventions designed to educate jurors about how implicit bias could influence their perceptions and judgments (e.g., jury instructions, expert witness testimony) as well as whether the interventions are effective at reducing the influence of implicit bias on juror decision-making.

## Jurors' Perceptions of Police as Criminal Trial Witnesses
## or Defendants

Another way in which jurors might be biased in their decision-making relates to police officer testimony. Police officers often appear in court as witnesses in cases that they helped bring into the justice system, but little is known about whether jurors are biased to either believe or disbelieve them. In Chapter 6, Lindsey Cole reviews research showing that potential jurors tend to perceive police officer testimony as more reliable and legitimate than lay eyewitness testimony (e.g., Hans, Kaye, Dann, Farley, & Albertson, 2011).

Even so, Black and Hispanic individuals may perceive police witnesses to be less credible than do Whites, given that minorities generally have lower confidence and trust in the police (Tyler, 2005). This is exemplified by a 2016 criminal case, in which a racially diverse jury of five Black jurors, six White jurors, and one mixed-race juror decided the fate of a Black man charged with stabbing another Black man during an altercation over the victim's alleged $40 debt to the defendant. The juror of mixed ethnicity happened to be Jay Newton-Small, a correspondent for *TIME* magazine. She described that she and the White jurors received the police officers' evidence and testimony unquestioningly. In contrast, Newton-Small (2016, para. 9) wrote: "Most of the black jurors were clear that they did not believe the evidence presented to us. . . . they found it perfectly reasonable to doubt the testimony of the officers who investigated."

Indeed, the divergent racial perspectives produced such an acrimonious climate during deliberations that one Black juror requested to be excused from jury duty—and her request was granted. Still, jury deliberations remained contentious, with several White jurors advocating for a conviction of felony aggravated assault pitted against Black jurors who were opposed to that outcome. The jury finally compromised, finding the defendant guilty of misdemeanor simple assault.

Experiences like Newton-Small's (2016) highlight the relations between juror race, perceived police legitimacy, and jury case decisions. Cole explores these issues by reviewing evidence that jurors' perceptions of police and court legitimacy affect their case decisions. She also considers how recent attention to police use of excessive and deadly force against Black men, women, and children and the resulting Black Lives Matter movement might be impacting both Black and White jurors' attitudes toward police and the justice system. Such changing attitudes could make it simultaneously harder to prosecute cases that rest on police officer testimony and easier to prosecute cases of police misconduct.

## Technological Changes and Challenges: New Sources of Influence on Juror Decisions

The second part of this volume reviews the impact of recent technological advances on the criminal jury's primary function of evaluating evidence. The proliferation of crime-relevant media and its widespread dissemination via the Internet and social media has numerous implications for jurors. In addition, contemporary jurors must evaluate and weigh new forms of videographic and scientific evidence while rendering judgments. Chapters in this part explore these issues.

## Is There Empirical Evidence that Media Affects Juror Decision-Making?

Attorneys sometimes claim that the *CSI Effect* leads jurors to expect quality scientific evidence that provides unequivocal insight regarding the causes of crimes (Wise, 2009). The concern is that crime dramas like *CSI* and *Law and Order* overemphasize the role of scientific evidence in court cases and may lead jurors to be overly skeptical even when there is overwhelming nonscientific evidence pointing to a defendant's guilt. Illustrating this phenomenon is Casey Anthony's highly publicized trial in 2011, in which jurors determined whether Anthony murdered her two-year-old daughter. Circumstantial evidence implicating Anthony in the crime was compelling, but the prosecutors lacked DNA evidence linking Anthony to the duct tape that was used to suffocate her toddler. Indeed, there was no forensic evidence of any kind in the case. The jury ultimately acquitted Anthony, leading psychological and legal scholars to question the potential power of a CSI Effect to influence jury decision-making (e.g., Hoffmeister, 2011).

It is also possible that popular culture has a broader cultivation effect on jury decision-making. That is, like the supposed CSI Effect, does exposure to other sources of popular culture (e.g., news, reality-based programs) lead jurors to require a heightened burden of scientific proof to convict? Alternatively, does crime-relevant media exposure lead jurors to be overly impressed by questionable forensic evidence (e.g., bite mark evidence)? Does such media exposure influence other aspects of the jury process? Jennifer Groscup addresses these questions in Chapter 7. For instance, she reviews studies showing that exposure to media depicting the justice system, including *CSI* and reality court shows like *Judge Judy*, changes jurors' expectations for and perceptions of forensic scientific evidence (e.g., DNA) as well as how jurors react to courtroom players (e.g., judges, attorneys). Groscup puts the research into context by exploring how the media impacts juror decision-making, how concerns about this impact have led to changes in courtroom practice, and possible legal reforms that might effectively mitigate its influence in trials.

## Pre- and Midtrial Publicity in the Age of the Internet

Technological advances in media have generated widespread concerns about not only a broader cultivation effect but also an increased risk that jurors will be exposed to and influenced by trial-specific media. Widespread and instant access to news reports and public opinion from websites, social media, and user-driven sources (e.g., "Reddit") creates opportunities for jurors to be exposed to potentially biasing publicity, both before trials begin and while they are in progress. The complexities associated with jurors having unmitigated access to the Internet are illustrated in the case of John Goodman, a multimillionaire polo player known for his family wealth and success in the air conditioning industry (Duret, 2014; Joseph, 2014; Shammas, 2015). In 2012, Goodman was convicted of manslaughter for the death of 23-year-old Scott Wilson, which resulted from a hit-and-run accident Goodman caused while under the influence of alcohol. Due to juror misconduct (e.g., a juror failed to disclose a conflict of interest during voir dire), however, Goodman was granted a new trial in 2014. Goodman requested a change of venue for the second trial to avoid being tried by jurors who might have been exposed to extensive local media coverage of his case, but his request was denied. During the voir dire process, the judge discovered that one member of the jury pool, 23-year-old Travis Van Vliet, had Googled the case, learned it was a retrial, and shared that information with another prospective juror. Van Vliet was charged with contempt of court, to which he pled no contest, resulting in a sentence of community service. To prevent the remaining seated jurors from learning the details of the original trial, they were sequestered during the 19-day retrial, living in a Palm Beach Gardens resort where they were denied access to the television and phones and were constantly monitored by uniformed guards, who even escorted the jurors to the bathroom. Even so, one alternate juror was caught using an iPad in his room, allegedly to read about sports. The parties agreed to move forward with the case, however, and Goodman was again convicted of manslaughter.

In Chapter 8, Tarika Daftary-Kapur and Steven Penrod review research pertaining to the issues highlighted by the Goodman case. For example, what do we know about jurors' use of the Internet and social media and its potential impact on their ability to evaluate criminal cases fairly? What do attorneys and judges do to counteract such use? Are those strategies effective? Answers to these questions are critical for understanding the impact of emerging technologies on jurors' exposure to pretrial and midtrial publicity and its influence on their decision-making.

### Jury Decision-Making in a Video Era

It is also increasingly likely that jurors will encounter video and photographic evidence while serving on criminal trials. The nation is increasingly under video surveillance, as evidenced by the fact that New York City saw the number of public surveillance cameras surge by 581% between 1998 and 2005 (New York Civil Liberties Union, 2006). Video sousveillance is on the rise, as well, as there is a growing trend for citizens to document their lives and experiences on portable recording devices. Thus there is need for a deeper understanding of jurors' reactions to video evidence from the kinds of understudied contexts that have been the subject of recent controversies, like the police killing of Samuel DuBose on July 19, 2015 (Sanchez, 2017). The police officer, Raymond Tensing, was wearing a bodycam when he pulled DuBose over and began questioning him. After requesting that DuBose exit his car, DuBose began putting his car into drive. At that moment, Officer Tensing reached in and grabbed DuBose's seat belt with his left hand, simultaneously drew his revolver with his right hand, and then shot DuBose in the head.

In Chapter 9, Neal Feigenson and Christina Spiesel discuss how the bodycam footage of this incident, viewed by the jury, might have contributed to a jury deadlock and subsequent mistrial. The authors also evaluate the strengths and weaknesses of surveillance and sousveillance video evidence and discuss recent research on jurors' responsiveness to visual evidence. Topics covered include jurors' beliefs about the reliability of video evidence, biases that could influence jurors' ability to evaluate the probative value of video evidence, jurors' ability to reconcile events recorded from multiple perspectives (e.g., recordings from police sources versus citizens), and the potential for gruesome crimes captured in videos and photographs to elicit emotion-based decision-making. The research reviewed highlights numerous potential issues that warrant further consideration to ensure that video evidence is used in ways that facilitate rather than impede the jury's ability to administer justice.

### Do Electronic Recordings Help Jurors Recognize Coercive Influences in Interrogations?

Another type of video evidence that jurors may be exposed to is video-recorded interrogations. Indeed, in recognition of the role that false confessions play in leading to wrongful convictions, it has been recommended that all criminal interrogations be video recorded from beginning to end to document the process by which suspects decide to confess (Kassin et al., 2010). Can jurors accurately evaluate video-recorded coerced confessions? Consider the 2009 case in which Adrian Thomas was convicted of killing his infant son (*People v. Thomas*, 2009). Although there was evidence that the infant had died from a bacterial infection, police had obtained a video-recorded confession from Thomas in which he demonstrated how he supposedly killed his son by throwing him onto a bed in frustration. The interrogation was highly coercive, including police minimization techniques, false promises of leniency, the introduction of details by the detectives, and threats to the well-being of Thomas's infant and wife. Moreover, Thomas was interrogated over the course of two days, all while he was extremely emotionally distressed. The New York Court of Appeals later ruled that Thomas's confession was coerced and inadmissible as evidence and ordered a second trial. Thus the jurors in the 2014 retrial did not see the video recorded confession evidence. They ultimately acquitted Thomas of the crime (*People v. Thomas*, 2014).

The results of the retrial suggest that the jurors in the original trial were not able to accurately identify and evaluate the coercive interrogation techniques used to elicit the confession. This is consistent with a growing body of work that suggests that a variety of factors influence the extent to which jurors' perceive an interrogation to be coercive, such as whether the camera focuses equally on the police interrogator and suspect (e.g.,

Lassiter, Geers, Handley, Weiland, & Munhall, 2002) or the social identity of the suspect (e.g., Pickel, Warner, Miller, & Barnes, 2013). In Chapter 10, Iris Blandón-Gitlin and Amelia Mindthoff review the literature on the usefulness of electronically recorded interrogations in assisting jury decision-making, calling for future research exploring the potential for procedural safeguards (e.g., expert testimony) to improve jurors' understanding of the issues at hand.

## The Impact of Neuroscientific Evidence on Jury Decision-Making

Technological advances have changed not only the types of media and video evidence to which jurors may be exposed but also the types of psychological evidence that are presented. As the field of neuroscience continues to advance by bounds, more and more jurors are asked to evaluate neuroscientific evidence, including elaborate depictions of defendants' brains created by functional magnetic resonance imaging. This kind of evidence challenges long-standing notions regarding free will and criminal culpability. Shelby Hunter, Nick Schweitzer, and Jillian Ware explore the prevalence and strategic use of neuroscientific evidence in criminal cases in Chapter 11. They also review research aimed at understanding the impact of neuroscientific evidence on jurors' perceptions of defendants' culpability and, ultimately, their verdicts, highlighting untested empirical questions.

These issues are nicely illustrated by the 2013 federal case in which Steven Northington was convicted for having killed two men who were cooperating with the FBI to bring down a drug ring with which the defendant was allegedly involved (*United States v. Northington*, 2013). During the sentencing phase of Northington's capital trial, his defense attorney, William Bowe, argued that "his brain doesn't function like ours. It means when he makes a decision, he doesn't do it like you or me. It's broken" (Kelkar, 2016, para. 11). The jurors viewed images of Northington's brain, revealing brain growth deficiencies that the defense claimed stemmed from his prenatal exposure to drugs and alcohol, childhood abuse, and homelessness. The defense introduced the brain images to prove that Northington was intellectually disabled—a finding that would render a death sentence cruel and unusual (*Atkins v. Virginia*, 2002).

Critics of the introduction of neuroscientific testimony in courts emphasize the limitations of applying group-level research toward the analysis of a single individual's brain. Relevant to the topic at issue, they also worry that jurors—typically novices at evaluating the validity of neuroscience—will be unduly persuaded by seemingly sophisticated medical technology that has yet to be fully empirically vetted. The neuroscientific evidence appears to have had a mitigating influence in Northington's case: The jurors unanimously voted for a life sentence over a death sentence. This case illustrates the potential powerful influence of neuroscientific evidence on juror decisions.

## Emotion and the Contemporary Jury

Although historically neglected in the field of psychology and law, increasingly more scholarly attention has been given in recent years to the role of emotion in jury decision-making. Thus, the final part of this volume explores the role of emotion in jury decision-making and the overall emotional impact of criminal jury service on contemporary jurors.

### The Role of Emotion in Jury Decision-Making

In Chapter 12, Colin Holloway and Richard Wiener review the burgeoning area of work aimed at understanding how emotion influences jury decision-making, highlighting what we know from the research literature as well as what issues remain to be explored. The authors apply the research they review to a case that evoked a great deal of juror emotion—the high-profile 2017 case involving the famous comedian and actor Bill Cosby and his alleged sexual assault victim, Andrea Constand (Bowley, Perez-Pena, & Hurdle, 2017). For the past several years, a cloud of controversy involving multiple accusations has covered Cosby. The original 2017 criminal trial involved accusations that he drugged and sexually assaulted Constand in 2004. The case ended in a mistrial because two jurors did not convict, but a retrial resulted in a conviction in April of 2018.

Holloway and Wiener unpack the effect the emotional testimony in the Cosby case might have had on the jury's failure to reach a verdict in the initial trial. The authors review a number of theoretical models to explain how emotion impacts jury decision-making (e.g., affect-as-feedback, appraisal theory) and apply those models to understand jurors' decisions in the Cosby mistrial. For instance, the authors explore the possibility that jurors might have been motivated to render a particular verdict based on their expectations about how the verdict would affect their own emotional experiences. They also consider how disgust reactions stemming from the norm-violating crime of sexual assault might have caused jurors to evaluate the evidence in line with a predetermined conclusion that Cosby was guilty. Holloway and Wiener also offer practical suggestions the courts could take (e.g., emotion regulation training) to enable jurors to be better equipped to comply with judicial instructions mandating that they be rational, unemotional decision-makers when rendering verdicts.

### How Does Jury Service Impact Jurors?

Considering the types of emotional testimony and evidence jurors may be exposed to, it is not surprising that they sometimes have strong emotional reactions during trial, as well as long after the verdict is rendered. Illustrating this point is the recent case involving James Holmes, who opened fire in a Colorado movie theater. Jurors in that case deliberated for 12 hours, ultimately convicting Holmes for shooting and killing 12 people and injuring 70 others (*People v. James Holmes*, 2012). Jurors have recounted the terror and horror of listening to witness accounts of the gunshot wounds and viewing detailed gruesome photographic evidence of bloody dead bodies, including the bullet-riddled body of a six-year-old girl. Jurors convicted Holmes of many charges but sentenced him to life in prison rather than death, citing evidence of the defendant's mental illness. Some jurors now struggle with this decision, which was met with cries from victims in the courtroom ("Jurors Who Oversaw James Holmes Case," 2016). One juror claimed to have cut her hair because she was worried that victims in the community might recognize her. Others report suffering from posttraumatic stress disorder and recurring nightmares. Several jurors sought therapy to cope with the general anxiety they continued to experience, coupled with intrusive flashbacks and images from the trial. These jurors have kept in touch since the trial, forming a support group for one another.

In Chapter 13, Sarah Trescher, Monica Miller, and Brian Bornstein examine the emotional toll that jury service takes on jurors. Specifically, the authors review evidence that participating in certain criminal cases (e.g., those involving particularly heinous crimes) and certain aspects of participation (e.g., deliberation) can be stressful for jurors. In particular, they discuss the implications for technology to exacerbate or mitigate juror stress, as well as possible remedies that have the potential to enhance positive attitudes toward jury duty and, in turn, increase the likelihood that citizens will fulfill their civic obligations when called upon to do so again in the future.

## Conclusion

Finally, in Chapter 14, Shari Diamond reviews the major themes covered throughout the volume, including the challenges that evolving attitudes and modern advances in technology and science raise for contemporary juries who are tasked with the emotionally taxing responsibility of administering justice in criminal cases. Also, Diamond highlights areas in which future research is needed. Implications for jury reform are discussed, with a focus on reforms that are supported by empirical evidence from theoretically and methodologically rigorous research and designed to improve jury performance.

As readers will see, this volume examines various issues that modern juries face and how psychological research can inform practice to improve justice within the jury system. Shifts in societal attitudes can have significant implications for who is seated on criminal juries and how jurors respond to evidence. Moreover, jury decision-making is inevitably influenced by technological advancements, which may have unanticipated effects on jurors in criminal trials with respect to how they perceive and evaluate evidence. The growing body of research on emotion also has important implications for understanding how jurors make decisions as well as the immediate and long-term psychological impacts of jury service. A careful examination of the issues reviewed in this volume has the potential to inform law and policy related to criminal trials, improve the experience for jurors, and, ultimately, facilitate justice.

## References

Atkins v. Virginia, 536 U.S. 304, 122 S. Ct. 2242, 153 L. Ed. 2d 335 (2002).

Batson v. Kentucky, 476 U.S. 79 (1986).

Bowley, G., Perez-Pena, R., & Hurdle, J. (2017, June 17). Bill Cosby's sexual assault case ends in a mistrial. *The New York Times*. Retrieved from https://www.nytimes.com

Cover, A. P. (2016). The eighth amendment's lost jurors: Death qualification and evolving standards of decency. *Indiana Law Journal, 92*, 113–156.

DeMatteo, D., & Anumba, N. (2009). The validity of jury decision-making research. In J. D. Lieberman & D. A. Krauss (Eds.), *Jury psychology: Social aspects of trial processes* (pp. 1–23). Surrey, UK: Ashgate.

Diamond, S. S., Murphy, B., & Rose, M. R. (2012). The kettleful of law in real jury deliberations: Successes, failures, and next steps. *Northwestern University Law Review, 106*, 1537–1608.

Duret, D. (2014, October 10). Contrite jailed juror gets stern lecture from judge in Goodman case. *Palm Beach Post*. Retrieved from http://www.mypalmbeachpost.com/news/contrite-jailed-juror-gets-stern-lecture-from-judge-goodman-case/WlGcrM5r9v1PdaY4mxpqwK/

Ellsworth, P. C. (1993). Some steps between attitudes and verdicts. In R. Hastie (Ed.), *Inside the juror: The psychology of juror decision making* (pp. 42–64). New York: Cambridge University Press.

Foster v. Chatman, 136 S. Ct. 1737, 578 U.S., 195 L. Ed. 2d 1 (2016).

Foster v. State, 374 S.E.2d 188, 258 Ga. 736 (1988).

Fraley, M. (2016, October 4). Gwen Araujo murder 14 years later: Transgender teen's killers face parole. *The Mercury News*. Retrieved from http://www.mercurynews.com/2016/10/14/the-murder-of-gwen-araujo/

Hannaford, P. L., Hans, V. P., & Munsterman, G. T. (2000). Permitting jury discussions during trial: Impact of the Arizona Reform. *Law and Human Behavior, 24*, 359–382. doi:10.1023/A:1005540305832

Hans, V. P., Kaye, D. H., Dann, B. M., Farley, E. J., & Albertson, S. (2011). Science in the jury box: Jurors' comprehension of mitochondrial DNA evidence. *Law and Human Behavior, 35*, 60–71. doi:10.1007/s10979-010-9222-8

Hoffmeister, T. (2011, July 7). Did "CSI" effect sway Anthony jury? *CNN*. Retrieved from http://www.cnn.com/2011/OPINION/07/06/hoffmeister.anthony.jury/

Joseph, C. (2014, October 10). Potential juror in John Goodman retrial arrested before trial begins. *Broward Palm Beach New Times*. Retrieved from http://www.browardpalmbeach.com/news/potential-juror-in-john-goodman-retrial-arrested-before-trial-begins-6473067

Jurors who oversaw James Holmes case haunted by trial testimony and burden of decision. (2016, January 11). *Daily News*. Retrieved from http://www.nydailynews.com/life-style/health/ jurors-oversaw-james-holmes-case-haunted-trial-article-1.2493112

Kassin, S. M., Drizin, S. A., Grisso, T., Gudjonsson, G. H., Leo, R. A., & Redlich, A. D. (2010). Police-induced confessions: Risk factors and recommendations. *Law and Human Behavior, 34*, 49–52. doi:10.1007/s10979-010-9217-5

Kelkar, K. (2016, January 17). Can a brain scan uncover your morals? *The Guardian*. Retrieved from https://www.theguardian.com/science/2016/jan/ 17/can-a-brain-scan-uncover-your-morals

Koehler, J. J., & Meixner, J. J. (2017). Jury simulation goals. In M. B. Kovera (Ed.), *The psychology of juries* (pp. 161–183). Washington, DC: American Psychological Association.

Kovera, M. B., & Austin, J. L. (2016). Identifying juror bias: Moving from assessment and prediction to a new generation of jury selection research. In C. Willis-Esqueda & B. H. Bornstein (Eds.), *The witness stand and Lawrence S. Wrightsman, Jr.* (pp. 75–94). New York: Springer Science.

Krauss, D. A., & Lieberman, J. D. (2017). Managing different aspects of validity in trial simulation research. In M. B. Kovera (Ed.), *The psychology of juries* (pp. 185–205). Washington, DC: American Psychological Association.

Laird, L., (2016, September 16). ACLU sues Kansas City school district for handcuffing a crying 7-year-old. *ABA Journal*. Retrieved from http://www. abajournal.com/news/article/family_aclu_sues_kansas_city_school_ district_for_handcuffing_crying_seven_y/

Lassiter, G. D., Geers, A. L., Handley, I. M., Weiland, P. E., & Munhall, P. J. (2002). Videotaped interrogations and confessions: A simple change in camera perspective alters verdicts in simulated trials. *Journal of Applied Psychology, 87*, 867–874. doi:10.1037/0021-9010.87.5.867

Lee, C. (2015). A new approach to voir dire on racial bias. *UC Irvine Law Review, 5*, 843–872.

New York Civil Liberties Union. (2006). *Who's watching? Video camera surveillance in New York City and the need for public oversight*. Retrieved from http://www.nyclu.org/files/publications/nyclu_pub_whos_watching.pdf

Newton-Small, J. (2016, August 18). What my week of jury duty taught me about race. *TIME*. Retrieved from http://time.com/4448516/jury-duty-race/

Oliphant, B. (2016, September 29). *Support for death penalty lowest in more than four decades*. Pew Research Center. Retrieved from http://www.pewresearch.org/fact-tank/2016/09/29/ support-for-death-penalty-lowest-in-more-than-four-decades/

O'Neil, A., & Moghe, S. (2015, March 4). Tsarnaev jury cuts across class, but not race. *CNN*. Retrieved from http://www.cnn.com/2015/03/03/us/ boston-bombing-trial/

O'Neil, K. M., Patry, M. W., & Penrod, S. D. (2004). Exploring the effects of attitudes toward the death penalty on capital sentencing verdicts. *Psychology, Public Policy, and Law, 10*, 443–470. doi:10.1037/1076-8971.10.4.443

People v. Thomas, 19 N.Y.3d 1105, (2009).

People v. Thomas, 8 N.E.3d 308 (2014).

Pickel, K. L., Warner, T. C., Miller, T. J., & Barnes, Z. T. (2013). Conceptualizing defendants as minorities leads mock jurors to make biased evaluations in retracted confession cases. *Psychology, Public Policy, and Law, 19*, 56–69. doi:10.1037/a0029308

Salerno, J. M., Najdowski, C. J., Bottoms, B. L., Harrington, E., Kemner, G., & Dave, R. (2015). Excusing murder? Conservative jurors' acceptance of the gay-panic defense. *Psychology, Public Policy, and Law, 21*, 24–34. doi:10.1037/law0000024

Sanchez, R. (2017, June 23). Ray Tensing retrial: Mistrial declared 2nd time after jury deadlocks. *CNN.* Retrieved from http://www.cnn.com/2017/06/23/us/cincinnati-ray-tensing-retrial/index.html

Shammas, B. (2015, January 20). Goodman juror contempt of court case postponed. *Sun Sentinel.* Retrieved from http://www.pressreader.com/usa/sun-sentinel-broward-edition/20150120/281925951407039

Sommers, S. R. (2010). What we do (and don't) know about race and jurors. *The Jury Expert, 22*(4), 1–9.

Sommers, S. R., & Norton, M. I. (2008). Race and jury selection: Psychological perspectives on the peremptory challenge debate. *American Psychologist, 63*, 527–539. doi:10.1037/0003-066X.63.6.527

State v. Brown, 121 A.3d 878, 442 N.J. Super. 154 (2015).

The People of the State of Colorado v. James Holmes, 12CR1522 (2012).

Tyler, T. R. (2005). Policing in black and white: Ethnic group differences in trust and confidence in the police. *Police Quarterly, 8*, 322–342. doi:10.1177/1098611104271105

United States of America v. Steven Northington, Criminal Action No. 07-550-03 (2013)

Wise, J. (2009). Providing the *CSI* treatment: Criminal justice practitioners and the CSI Effect. *Current Issues in Criminal Justice, 21*, 383–399.

# PART I

## SOCIETAL CHANGES IN ATTITUDES

*Implications for Jury Selection and Decision-Making*

# 2

# Jury Selection in the Post-*Batson* Era

*Barbara O'Brien and Catherine M. Grosso*

In *Batson v. Kentucky* (1986), the US Supreme Court renewed its efforts to eliminate the influence of race on jury selection. Many years earlier, the Court recognized the importance of fair and nondiscriminatory jury selection to the conduct of fair and just trials. It had also become clear even then that inclusive jury participation was necessary to protect the reputation of the justice system. Yet broad participation in juries requires that the jury selection process be fair and race neutral.

Jury selection involves two distinct reviews of potential jurors during which neutrality might be compromised. First, a trial judge should remove any potential juror for "cause" if there is evidence that the juror cannot be impartial and follow the judge's instructions (see, e.g., N.C. Gen. Stat. § 15A-1212 [2009]). There is no limit to the number of jurors who may be removed for cause, but the basis for doing so must be explicit and fall within specific categories relating to the juror's fitness to serve (e.g., pre-existing opinions about the case, a relationship with one of the parties). Second, each party may peremptorily remove or "strike" a limited number of potential jurors for any reason other than race or gender, and typically without explanation. While each review serves the well-established purpose of ensuring a fair and unbiased jury, each has the potential to limit diversity among jurors in a way that is detrimental to the criminal justice system.

To address racial discrimination in the second stage of review, the Court set forth a three-part test in *Batson* for establishing that race improperly motivated a peremptory strike. A party raising a *Batson* challenge must first establish a prima facie case of intentional discrimination by offering evidence that the prosecutor used peremptory strikes to exclude potential jurors because of their race. If the trial judge finds that the evidence establishes a prima facie case, the prosecutor must provide a race-neutral explanation for the strike decisions at issue. The proffered explanation must offer more than a bare assertion of good faith but need not present a compelling reason or one that impacts members of all races evenly. The trial court must then determine whether the proffered reason reflected genuine grounds for the strike or merely a pretext for racial discrimination (*Miller-El v. Dretke*, 2005; *Snyder v. Louisiana*, 2008). Trial courts rarely reject these reasons as disingenuous or "pretextual" (see Bellin & Semitsu, 2011; Melilli, 1996; *Miller-El v. Dretke*, 2005 [Thomas, dissenting]).

We are aware of no study directly assessing *Batson*'s effectiveness in countering consideration of race in jury selection, such as by comparing strike rates against Black jurors in trials before *Batson* was decided to those that came after the decision. Yet the consistency of researchers' findings of racial disparities in studies spanning several decades after the decision suggests, at least, that *Batson* has not been especially successful in purging consideration of race from jury selection (see Baldus, Woodworth, Zuckerman, Weiner, & Broffitt, 2001; Grosso & O'Brien, 2012). A substantial body of scholarship analyzes the reasons for the failure. At the bottom line, the difficulty of detecting instances of racial bias—whether deliberate or unconscious—has led many to conclude that the *Batson* regime is ineffective (see O'Brien & Grosso, 2011a). Some have noted the humiliation suffered when qualified jurors appear for jury service only to be excluded in a situation that appears to be driven by race (Equal Justice Initiative, 2010) or the stigma of being excluded from participation in one of the fundamental components of the democratic system (Marder, 1995; Rose, 2005).

Many scholars and some judges have called for an outright abolition of peremptory strikes (see Grosso & O'Brien, 2012). Others have suggested modifying the *Batson* regime, such as by reducing the number of peremptories available to each side to limit the opportunity for discrimination (Adams & Lane, 1998; Ogletree, 1993; Wilson, 2009).

Abolition seems unlikely, however, and rather than questioning the relative value of the peremptory challenge itself, the Court has focused on perfecting *Batson*. Supreme Court decisions in recent years try to reinforce the *Batson* framework by more readily recognizing claims and clarifying and expanding the evidence relevant to *Batson*'s three-part test for establishing that race motivated a peremptory strike (*Snyder v. Louisiana*, 2008). The Court recognizes *Batson*'s shortcomings and has agreed to review a steady stream of claims alleging race discrimination in the exercise of peremptory strikes. Additionally, the Court seems more likely to rule in favor of criminal defendants in these cases than in any other context (see *United States v. Armstrong*, 1996; *McCleskey v. Kemp*, 1987). In *Foster v. Chatman* (2016), the Supreme Court again reaffirmed its commitment to protecting the equal protection rights of prospective jurors.

In this chapter, we review the evidence that *Batson* has failed to protect potential jurors from race-based strikes and the reasons for this failure. First, we review briefly the process of summoning and selecting a jury. We argue that even though enforcing *Batson* effectively is critical to the fairness and integrity of the system, its capacity to ensure diverse representation on juries is limited by the stages of jury selection that precede it. Then we present some of the costs of discrimination to jury decision-making. Next, we present the evidence that racial discrimination persists despite the Court's best efforts to eradicate it in *Batson* and its progeny. Finally, we discuss *Batson*'s design flaws. Specifically, we discuss the psychological mechanisms that make enforcing *Batson* so hard, including how the process of jury selection itself may reinforce racial bias.

## Placing Peremptories in Context

Despite the Court's efforts to give it teeth, there is only so much *Batson* can do to mitigate the pernicious influence of race in the jury selection process. Even if trial courts were to rigorously enforce *Batson* when parties challenge a peremptory strike as motivated by race, that opportunity comes only after a long process of jury selection has unfolded. Citizens must be identified, successfully summoned, reviewed for basic qualifications, arrive for service, and survive removals for cause before facing peremptory strikes (Vidmar & Hans, 2007). From the opposite view, by the time a party can exercise a peremptory strike against a potential juror, these steps—each with its own pitfalls and opportunities for race to influence the process—have already taken place.

Indeed, historically, this process has excluded significant portions of the population on the basis of race, gender, and social class (Diamond & Ryken, 2013). Laws no longer exclude qualified citizens, but inadvertent jury summons practices and life's practical challenges continue to lead to the underrepresentation of minorities and indigent people on juries. Ongoing reform seeks to address these limitations. Expanding and verifying summons lists can make them more inclusive and insure that they reach the prospective jurors (Munsterman, Hannaford-Agor, & Whitehead, 2006). Jury pay can be modified to compensate fully for lost work hours (Quilty, 2015). These efforts have expanded the representativeness of juries, but reform efforts continue.

Consider *Foster v. Chatman* (2016). The Court found that the state struck potential jurors on the basis of race, relying not only on the fact that the state struck all four African American venire members but also on the prosecutor's notes that left little doubt that race was a foremost consideration in the prosecution's strikes. Yet several things had to happen to reach the point where there were only four Black venire members eligible to serve on Foster's jury in the first place.

To begin with, the county had to create a jury summons list to call potential jurors to the courthouse. The City of Rome and Floyd County governments, where Foster's trial took place, use voter registration and driver's license records to identify potential jurors (Ga. Code Ann. §15-12-40.1). Not everyone complies with the summons, however. Some citizens choose not to come or do not understand the summons; others never receive the summons because they have moved and changed addresses (Berris, 2011). Still others, including students, caregivers, and the elderly, are statutorily exempt (Ga. Code Ann. §15-12-1.1). In Georgia, as in many jurisdictions, felons are ineligible to serve as jurors (§15-12-40; Kalt, 2003). Research has shown that several of these rules and practices disproportionally limit participation of racial and ethnic minorities (see Gau, 2016; Kalt, 2003).

Among those who do show up for jury duty, many will be excused from service. Trial judges often excuse jurors for whom service may impose an undue economic hardship, or those who must care for small children or elderly parents. In addition, a trial judge should remove any potential juror for "cause" if there is evidence that the juror cannot be impartial and follow the judge's instructions (see, e.g., N.C. Gen. Stat. §15A-1212). Judges may remove any number of potential jurors for cause, but the basis for doing so must be explicit and fall within specific categories relating to the juror's fitness to serve (e.g., pre-existing opinions about the case, a relationship with one of the parties). Thus other potential jurors in Foster's case might have been excused because they knew interested parties, already knew too much about the case, or held opinions that prevented them from being impartial (§15-12-133).

Some jurors were likely excused because they did not believe in the death penalty (see Chapter 3 of this volume), and, because the state sought the death penalty against Foster, those potential jurors' beliefs rendered them unfit for service (*Wainwright v. Witt*, 1985).

The overwhelming majority of studies on cause challenges focus on the impact of "death qualifying" capital jurors under *Wainwright v. Witt* (1985), in which the Supreme Court endorsed the dismissal from capital juries of potential jurors who oppose the death penalty and would not impose a death sentence. Some research suggests that such challenges for cause also may diminish diversity (e.g., Eisenberg, 2017; Fitzgerald & Ellsworth, 1984; Rose & Diamond, 2008; see Chapter 3 of this volume). In an unpublished pilot study of cause removals in Cumberland County, North Carolina (O'Brien & Grosso, 2011b), we found that although people of different races were removed at about the same rate (49% of non-Blacks versus 52% of Blacks), the reasons for removal varied by race. More Black potential jurors were removed for anti-death penalty views (46% of the Black jurors removed for cause had this characteristic, compared to only 16% of non-Blacks removed for cause). A higher percentage non-Black jurors (versus Black jurors) were removed for having formed an opinion about the case (13% versus 5%; see also Eisenberg, 2017).

Only after the trial judge has had the opportunity to remove jurors for cause, each party may peremptorily strike a limited number of prospective jurors for any reason other than race, and usually without justification. While each of these stages of review is intended to ensure a fair and unbiased jury, each has the potential to limit diversity among jurors in a way that harms the criminal justice system. If the winnowing process—the composition of the summons list, the response to those summons, and excusals for cause—is not race neutral in both intent and impact, then *Batson* starts from a deficit and cannot be expected to ensure racial diversity on juries.

## Discrimination in the Exercise of Peremptory Challenges

The importance of heterogeneity in juries has been well-documented. Broad participation in the judicial process legitimizes the criminal justice system in the public's view (see, e.g., Ellis & Diamond, 2003; King, 1994; McDougall, 1970). Including a range of people and perspectives on a jury may make it more likely that the public will view a particular verdict as legitimate (Ellis & Diamond, 2003; Marder, 1995). Scholars have documented a strong relation between perceptions of fairness and those of legitimacy (Ellis & Diamond, 2003; MacCoun & Tyler, 1988). Conversely, excluding people based on group identity undermines the criminal justice system's foundational ideals, such as representativeness, individuality, citizen participation, and equal access (Ellis & Diamond, 2003; Hoffman, 1997; Marder, 1995; Underwood, 1992).

Jury heterogeneity may enhance the fact-finding process by diversifying the perspectives and values considered in deliberation, and this may improve the reliability of verdicts (see Ellis & Diamond, 2003; Ellsworth, 1989; McDougall, 1970; Sommers, 2006). Individual jurors undoubtedly bring personal biases with them into the courtroom. Yet forming an impartial jury is possible by ensuring that a variety of backgrounds and experiences are included (Ellis & Diamond, 2003). For example, some research suggests selecting diverse juries may mitigate the risk of certain biases among White jurors. This is especially true in cases in which race is not expressly at issue, and thus racial bias is more likely to be implicit and thus go unchallenged (Sommers & Ellsworth, 2000, 2001). Similarly, the presence of diverse groups that include members with competing biases may mitigate juror biases (Bernard, 1979; Zeisel & Diamond, 1976).

The Supreme Court has long recognized the importance of diversity and grappled with barriers to achieving racial diversity in juries (e.g., juries exist "to guard against the exercise of arbitrary power" [*Taylor v. Louisiana*, 1975, p. 530]; juries must not be "the organ of any special group or class" [*Glasser v. United States*, 1942, p. 86]; see also *Casteneda v. Partida*, 1977; *Duren v. Missouri*, 1979). Jurors, the Court asserted, "should be selected as individuals, on the basis of individual qualifications, and not as members of a race" (*Swain v. Alabama*, 1965, p. 204 [quoting *Cassell v. Texas*, 1950, p. 286]). The Court elaborated on this view in *Batson v. Kentucky* (1986) when it noted that purposefully excluding people from jury service based on their race undermines public confidence in the justice system. The Court later clarified that excluding jurors because of their race harmed not only the defendant but the wrongly excluded jurors as well (*Powers v. Ohio*, 1991), and that defense counsel are held to the same standard as the prosecution

(*Georgia v. McCollum*, 1992). The Supreme Court has extended the doctrine to prohibit gender-based strikes (*J.E.B. v. Alabama*, 1994), and some lower courts have prohibited strikes based on religious affiliation (*United States v. Brown*, 2003; see also Liepold, 1998) and sexual orientation (*SmithKline Beecham Corporation [GSK] v. Abbott Laboratories*, 2014; see also Chapter 4 of this volume).

Despite the clear constitutional prohibition against consideration of race in strike decisions, literature in both law reviews and social science journals demonstrates that improper factors continue to play a role (e.g., Baldus et al., 2001; Grosso & O'Brien, 2012; Rose, 1999; Turner, Lovell, Young, & Denny, 1986). Studies of discrimination in the exercise of peremptory challenges can be divided into several groups. The first set we present reviews experimental and mock jury studies. The second turns to studies of jury selection in actual trials. The final section reviews research on appellate decisions reviewing *Batson* rulings.

### Experimental and Mock Jury Studies

A significant body of experimental work in mock jury selection suggests that race plays a role in jury selection (see Sommers & Norton, 2008, for a review). Even before *Batson*, several studies demonstrated the importance of race in decision-making. For example, Hayden, Senna, and Seigel (1978) examined the types of information relevant to prosecutorial decision-making in voir dire (i.e., the questioning of prospective jurors) among 20 randomly selected prosecutors from four Boston-area counties. They gave prosecutors categories of information about potential jurors for two hypothetical cases, one involving a Black defendant and the other a White defendant. Prosecutors could seek information about potential jurors from one category at a time and then decide whether to strike the juror or to seek more information. Prosecutors typically sought information about potential jurors' gender, age, residence, occupation, demeanor, and appearance. In the case involving the Black defendant, however, prosecutors sought information on race of the venire member significantly more often than they did in the case involving the White defendant. This research highlights how defendant race might shape prosecutors' perceptions and decisions about which jurors are likely to be sympathetic to the defendant.

The relevance of race persists after *Batson*. Sommers and Norton (2007) presented three samples of participants—college students, law students, and trial attorneys—with the facts of a criminal case involving a Black defendant. They told participants to assume the role of the prosecutor and that they had only one peremptory strike left in deciding which of two prospective jurors to strike. Each of the prospective jurors had qualities that pretesting suggested would be troubling to prosecutors: one was a journalist who had investigated police misconduct and the other expressed skepticism about statistics relevant to forensic evidence that the state would offer. The researchers randomly assigned participants to one of two conditions: one in which the first prospective juror was Black and the second White, and another in which the races of the prospective jurors were reversed.

Within each sample, participants challenged the Black juror more often than the White juror, regardless of whether the juror was presented as the journalist or the statistics skeptic. Yet, when asked to explain their strike decision, the participants almost never mentioned race. Rather, they tended to offer the first juror's experience writing about police misconduct when striking him and the second juror's skepticism about statistics when striking him. Race-neutral reasons were easy to generate, but clearly race was driving participants' decision-making.

In another study, Kerr, Kramer, Carroll, and Alfini (1991) showed attorneys videotaped voir dire of mock jurors in a criminal case involving a Black defendant and assigned them the role of prosecutor, defense attorney, or judge. They asked participants to rate the desirability of the potential jurors and to indicate which ones they would strike. Attorneys assigned to the role of prosecutor were far more likely to strike Black prospective jurors than jurors of another race, but no such pattern was found for participants assigned to the roles of defense attorney or trial judge.

The artificial nature of studies that examine jury selection in experimental settings limits their generalizability. Their strength, however, is that researchers have greater control over the variables in question, enabling identification of causal factors. When considered in tandem with the research on jury selection in real trials set forth next, these studies offer substantial evidence that race plays a significant role in jury selection.

### Studies Examining Jury Selection in Actual Trials

Anecdotal evidence of discrimination also exists. In a 1986 training video, for example, Philadelphia prosecutor Jack McMahon emphasized the importance of striking certain kinds of jurors, such as "Blacks from low-income areas" and Blacks who are "real educated" (as cited in Baldus et al., 2001). Documents presented in *Foster v. Chatman* (2016), discussed later, also provided direct evidence of discrimination. Only a handful of published studies, however, have examined how parties strike jurors in actual trials. Every study of which we are aware—both before and after *Batson*—found substantial disparities in both prosecutorial and defense use of peremptory challenges (Baldus et al., 2001; Grosso & O'Brien, 2012; Rose, 1999; Turner et al., 1986).

In one pre-*Batson* study, Turner and colleagues (1986) examined strikes by both the prosecution and defense in 12 felony trials in one Louisiana parish from 1976 to 1981. The authors compared the percentage of struck jurors who were Black (44%) to the percentage of the population in the Louisiana parish that was Black at the time of the study (18%) and inferred from this 26-point disparity that jury selection was not race neutral.

The post-*Batson* picture is not much better. Rose (1999) examined peremptory strike decisions in 13 noncapital felony trials in North Carolina. Prosecutors used 60% of their strikes against Black jurors, who comprised only 32% of the venire. But defense attorneys were not exercising their strikes in a racially neutral manner either: They used 87% of their strikes against White jurors, who made up 68% of the venire.

Baldus and colleagues (2001) examined strike decisions over a 17-year period in 317 Philadelphia County capital murder trials. They found that prosecutors struck on average 51% of the Black jurors they had the opportunity to strike, compared to only 26% of comparable non-Black jurors. Defense strikes exhibited a nearly identical pattern in reverse: Defense counsel struck only 26% of the Black jurors they had the opportunity to strike, compared to 54% of comparable non-Black jurors.

A major strength of Baldus et al.'s (2001) Philadelphia study was the inclusion of race-neutral factors about jurors that might bear on a party's decision to strike. One possible explanation for racial disparities in strike rates is that race is associated with other race-neutral factors that drive strike decisions. This is a common response to findings of racial disparities in strike rates. For example, when the *Dallas Morning News* reported that prosecutors excluded eligible Black potential jurors at more than twice the rate of their White counterparts, Bill Hill, the Dallas County district attorney, explained, "[t]he statistics may show we strike more Blacks, but it's not because they're Black, it's because for one reason or another, they [prosecutors] don't think they are going to be fair and impartial" (McGonigle, Becka, Lafleur, & Wyatt, 2005, p. 1A).

If members of one race are disproportionately less supportive of the death penalty (see Chapter 3 of this volume), for example, prosecutors' disproportionately high strike rates against that group may be driven by group members' views rather than their race. Controlling for various race-neutral factors that may bear on the decision to strike allows researchers to rule out at least some alternative explanations of racial disparities. In the Baldus et al. (2001) study in Philadelphia, the disparate effect of race on jury selection held even when the authors controlled for various nonracial characteristics of the jurors, such as age, occupation, education, and certain responses to questions asked in voir dire.

Similarly, we found that prosecutors in 173 North Carolina capital cases between 1990 and 2010 exercised peremptory challenges against Black potential jurors at twice the rate as jurors of other races, even after controlling for alternative grounds for removal (Grosso & O'Brien, 2012). Previous analysis of these cases formed the basis of four claims for relief under the North Carolina Racial Justice Act of 2009 (the RJA Study; see, e.g., Robertson, 2012). These claims, while initially successful, were remanded on procedural grounds in 2015 and are being reheard (*North Carolina v. Augustine et al.*, 2015; *North Carolina v. Robinson*, 2015).

Most recently, Eisenberg (2017) studied jury selection in 35 South Carolina cases that ended in a death sentence from 1997 to 2012. Of those, she was able to determine the race of the prospective jurors in 24 cases. Her results were consistent with studies from other jurisdictions finding substantial racial disparities in how parties use their peremptory strikes. Prosecutors struck relatively more Black eligible venire members, and defense attorneys did the opposite.

## Studies Analyzing Appellate Decisions Reviewing *Batson* Claims

One reason *Batson* has done little to curb race-based strikes may be the ease with which parties can generate race-neutral explanations for strike decisions, as suggested by experimental studies (see, e.g., Sommers & Norton, 2007). Indeed, analyses of appellate decisions reveal that courts commonly accept reasons proffered to justify strikes based on little more than stereotyping and guesswork. Melilli (1996) analyzed all published *Batson* decisions from 1986 to 1993. He concluded that the explanations were based on stereotypes and, to a lesser extent, attorneys' intuition about how a potential juror would view the evidence. Some of them bordered on the absurd, such as that the potential juror had a similar build to the defendant, or that the juror watched science fiction programs on television. Bellin and Semitsu (2011) conducted a similar study. Like Melilli, they also cited examples of absurd explanations and concluded that the reasons courts often find acceptably race neutral may merely obfuscate race discrimination. They surveyed all published and unpublished federal decisions from 2000 to 2009 that reviewed state or federal trial courts' denials of *Batson* challenges. Based on their review of these 269 decisions, they reported that their "most revealing discovery was the substantial list of acceptable reasons that could conceivably implicate a juror's likelihood of being impartial but were likely to disproportionately impact specific racial or ethnic groups" (p. 1092).

Three studies examined how North Carolina courts implement *Batson* and concluded that the significant deference the North Carolina Supreme Court gives to trial courts weakened *Batson*'s impact. Schwartz (1991) analyzed the first five years of *Batson* appeals and found that "neither the North Carolina Supreme Court nor the North Carolina Court of Appeals ever ha[d] held for the defendant on the merits of a *Batson* claim" (p. 1535). In particular, Schwartz documents the court's almost total deference to prosecutors' proffered explanations justifying strikes. Hitchcock (2006) reached a similar conclusion when she analyzed North Carolina Supreme Court rulings in the 61 capital cases involving a *Batson* claim between 1986 and 2005. In almost every case, the court deferred to the trial court "because *Batson* determinations often turn on the credibility of the prosecutor's stated reasons for the objectionable challenges" (p. 1344). Such findings suggest that the easily generated race-neutral explanations for race-motivated peremptory challenges are likely to be convincing to judges who are required to consider their merit. Hitchcock further noted the court's reluctance to look to statistical evidence to establish a prima facie case of race discrimination, its rigid demand for a perfect match in comparing jurors, and its unwillingness to delve into claims of disparate questioning. The most recent research, by Pollitt and Warren (2016), reviews the universe of 114 *Batson* appeals decided by the North Carolina Supreme Court and finds that the court continues to deny substantive *Batson* claims. In three cases, the court found procedural errors, but ultimately these cases were affirmed.

Thus while through *Batson* and its progeny the Supreme Court has established a framework to limit the consideration of race in the exercise of peremptory challenges, the research suggests that it continues to play a role. We have come some distance from overtly racist laws seen in *Strauder v. West Virginia* (1880), which explicitly limited qualifications for jury service to White men. Nevertheless, race continues to influence attorneys' peremptory challenge decisions via multiple (and nonmutually exclusive) processes. More research is needed to understand how these processes operate in jury selection. General evidence suggests, however, that both stereotypes and prejudice work to maintain the influence of race on perception and judgment (Sommers & Norton, 2008). The lore of jury selection includes many racial stereotypes (*Miller-El v. Dretke*, 2005, collecting examples), including assumptions that Black jurors would be more lenient toward Black defendants (*Batson v. Kentucky*, 1986). Prosecutors may strike Black prospective jurors because they buy into these stereotypes and believe it will help them win (see, e.g., Johnson, 2016; Stevenson & Friedman, 1994), or because they harbor unconscious biases that lead them to question and perceive these potential jurors differently from their White counterparts.

## *Batson's* Design Flaws

A number of factors limit *Batson*'s potential to render the jury selection process race neutral. As noted, *Batson* is limited by the fact that it applies only at the tail end of a process with many opportunities for race to influence the process of forming a jury. Other issues stem from the nature of the test itself, which is designed to ferret out intentional discrimination even though bias can manifest in ways far more subtle than overt racial animus. Most attorneys strongly deny any suggestion that they engage in intentional discrimination (*North Carolina v. Robinson*, Transcript of Closing Argument, 2012). Significant psychological research, however, suggests that racial bias can operate below the level of conscious awareness to affect people's perceptions and behaviors (Devine, 1989; Fiske, 1998; see Chapter 5 of this volume for a discussion of interventions designed to prevent such bias from influencing juror decision-making). As a result, a party who is subconsciously influenced by a juror's race might nevertheless offer in good faith a race-neutral reason for a strike. Next we review some other important design flaws and provide examples of how they impact jury selection.

## The Uniquely Personal Nature of a *Batson* Objection

Trial lawyers are used to hearing objections to their conduct. They try to introduce evidence or pursue a line of questioning that their adversaries argue is improper. They respond, the judge rules, and (usually) no one takes it personally. *Batson*, on the other hand, is personal. The party challenging a strike decision is accusing the other lawyer of not only judging the potential juror based on his or her race but also of lying about it.

The judge who sustains a *Batson* objection is making a legal finding not about something relatively academic like the admissibility of a piece of evidence but about the lawyer's true intentions and credibility. There are other situations when a judge must assess the intentions of a lawyer, such as in ruling on whether the prosecutor goaded the defense into seeking a mistrial (e.g., *Oregon v. Kennedy*, 1982), or determining whether the destruction of potentially exculpatory evidence was done in bad faith (e.g., *Arizona v. Youngblood*, 1988). But such instances are rare and require egregious misconduct to warrant relief for the defendant making such allegations.

Making a *Batson* objection is hard, even for trial attorneys used to objecting to the opposing party's conduct. In the North Carolina litigation in which the RJA Study was presented, four death-row defendants presented significant statistical and other documentary evidence showing that race was a factor in jury selection. Yet, in closing argument, the prosecutor described the statistical study showing pronounced racial disparities in capital jury selection as "[d]esperate, illogical, overreaching, assuming, nonsensical, slanderous, incomplete, wholly unconvincing, insulting, offensive, McCarthyist" (*North Carolina v. Golphin et al.*, 2012, p. 56). Explaining his reference to McCarthy, he stated that "[b]ut now it's not calling folks a communist. They're calling them racist" (p. 57).

The tension that arises when one party accuses another of acting with racial bias is real. And sustaining an objection—particularly against a lawyer who frequently appears in the judge's courtroom—is likely even more uncomfortable. In *Foster v. Chatman* (2016), the prosecutor not only vehemently denied considering race in selecting a jury, despite appalling smoking-gun evidence to the contrary (e.g., an investigator's note to the prosecutor stating, "If it comes down to having to pick one of the black jurors, [this one] might be okay," p. 4), but demanded an apology for the mere accusation. The Court did not share the state's indignation, finding instead that "the contents of the prosecution's file . . . plainly belie the State's claim that it exercised its strikes in a 'color-blind' manner" (p. 1755). These prosecutors are not repeat players before the Supreme Court. It might be much easier for all-too-human trial judges in a local trial court (who must continue to work with a prosecutor in the very trial for which the jury is being selected) to appease the umbrage rather than call it out.

## The Ease of Producing Race-Neutral Reasons to Strike (Black) People

Despite—or perhaps because of—the discomfort that a meaningful discussion of race causes, *Batson*'s requirements are often viewed as a meaningless ritual (Price, 2009) or a technicality that imposes a few hoops to jump through. The prosecution's files in *Foster* included a note about the benefits of getting at least one Black person on the jury "to avoid the appearance of a lynch mob" (*Foster v. Chatman*, Joint Appendix, Vol. 1, 2015, Transcript of Direct Examination of Mr. Steve Lanier, p. 103). A similar attitude came to light in the RJA litigation. The defendants offered into evidence a handout distributed at a trial advocacy course offered at a North Carolina Conference of District Attorneys training conference. The handout was titled "*Batson* Justifications: Articulating Juror Negatives," and it provided a standard list of reasons that would satisfy *Batson*'s second prong requiring the striking party to offer a race-neutral reason for the strike.

Recall that the only thing required to rebut a challenge is a genuine race-neutral reason—it need not be a good reason, just truthful. In fact, even a "silly or superstitious reason" will suffice, so long as it is truthful (*Purkett v. Elem*, 1995, p. 768). Even when race-neutral justifications are true, however, they may be motivated by prosecutors' discriminatory intentions (Sommers & Norton, 2007). And the only reason a list of justifications would come in handy is if the real motivation for the strike is not actually race neutral. Yet North Carolina prosecutors relied on the *Batson* justifications handout. For example, the prosecutor in one of the RJA defendants' trials recited these reasons almost verbatim in responding to a *Batson* objection (*North Carolina v. Golphin et al.*, 2012).

## The Voir Dire Process as an Exercise in Confirming Stereotypes

The RJA Study documented stark racial disparities, but prosecutors met the defendant's case with earnest claims that race does not enter their minds when picking a jury (*North Carolina v. Robinson*, Transcript of Closing Argument, 2012). As noted, there are many reasons to think that attorneys' clear preference for jurors of a certain race operates in ways far more subtle than overt racial bias. Moreover, the voir dire process itself may create a structure that reinforces unconscious bias and facilitates the easy production of race-neutral reasons sufficient to satisfy *Batson*'s third prong. As Melilli (1996) argued, evaluating people on the basis of stereotypes is an inherent aspect of the peremptory challenge system. The peremptory challenge system allows lawyers and litigants to impose these stereotypes upon the jury selection process without articulating these potentially offensive and divisive prejudices. (p. 447)

Substantial social psychological evidence supports the possibility that people—including prosecutors, defense counsel, and judges—harbor stereotypes about race that bear on people's attractiveness as jurors (Fitzgerald & Ellsworth, 1984; Lynch & Haney, 2011; Rector, Bagby, & Nicholson, 1993; Sweeney & Haney, 1992). These stereotypes about which demographic groups are more or less likely to convict and ultimately sentence a defendant to death operate as a starting hypothesis that informs how they collect information during the voir dire process (see Fiske, 1998; Johnston & McCrae, 1994; Snyder & Swann, 1978).

Judges and lawyers who begin the voir dire process with a hypothesis already in place about a potential juror's attitudes and beliefs are vulnerable to confirmation bias. Confirmation bias is the tendency to support a hypothesis by seeking consistent evidence while minimizing inconsistent evidence (Nickerson, 1998). This kind of bias can lead to testing a hypothesis in a way that is likely to support it (Klayman & Ha, 1987) or to search for new information in a biased or biasing manner (Friedrich, 1993; Frey, 1986; Jonas, Schultz-Hardt, Frey, & Thelen, 2001). Confirmation bias may lead police investigating a crime to focus on information consistent with the guilt of their lead suspect and to minimize evidence pointing in a different direction (O'Brien, 2009; see Simon, 2012, for a review). Confirmation bias is not deliberate (Gibson, Sanbonmatsu, & Posavac, 1997) and can present even when someone has no motivation to prefer a particular hypothesis (Klayman & Ha, 1987).

Psychologists have also demonstrated that this phenomenon can serve to reinforce stereotypes. Stereotypes are categorizations that allow people to process information efficiently and to generate hypotheses about how members of a particular group are likely to think and behave (Macrae, Milne, & Bodenhausen, 1994). This efficiency, however, comes at a cost in that it can lead perceivers to relegate their targets to caricatures, and these perceptions are often resistant to disconfirming information (Bodenhausen, Todd, & Becker, 2007; Todd, Galinsky, & Bodenhausen, 2012).

There are several mechanisms at work in maintaining stereotypes (see Todd et al., 2012, for a review). One stereotype maintenance process particularly relevant in the voir dire context involves the solicitation and interpretation of information. People often seek information that confirms rather than disconfirms what they expect based on the stereotype they hold (Fiske, 1998; Johnston & McCrae, 1994; Snyder & Swann, 1978). Moreover, to the extent perceivers receive stereotype-inconsistent information, they often seek to reconcile it with what they expect to see or otherwise minimize its value (Todd et al., 2012). In other words, the stereotypes they hold are the hypotheses they seek to test and influence the information they seek and how they interpret it (Bodenhausen, 1988).

If this process is at work when attorneys select jurors, a pre-existing belief about whether a potential juror is likely to favor or disfavor the prosecution or the defense will influence the discourse—namely the line and tone of examination—that takes place during voir dire. Otis, Greathouse, Kennard, and Kovera (2014) found evidence for this process when they examined how law students' and attorneys' lay theories about potential jurors' demographic characteristics and their attitudes affected how they questioned the jurors and the conclusions they drew. They found that the hypothesis they were asked to test, as well as the questions they asked, biased the conclusions they drew from their questioning of potential jurors.

If attorneys start with the hypothesis that Black jurors are more likely to have experiences and attitudes that would undermine their willingness to convict or impose certain sentences, and if attorneys act consistently with research in other domains that shows that people often search for evidence that confirms rather than disconfirms an initial hypothesis, we should observe disparities not only in whom they choose to strike or pass but also in how they question jurors. This tendency would undermine not only the fairness of the process by contributing to racial disparities but also its accuracy by skewing the evaluation of fitness for jury service.[1]

Capital jury selection is particularly fertile ground for stereotyping. Prosecutors frequently argue that race disparities in the exercise of peremptory strikes arise because Black citizens are more likely to oppose the death penalty (see Chapter 3 of this volume; Baldus et al., 2001; *North Carolina v. Robinson*, 2012, Transcript of Closing Argument). Although there is empirical support for that generalization (Cochran & Chamlin, 2006; Fitzgerald & Ellsworth, 1984; Unnever & Cullen, 2007a, 2007b), controlling for death penalty attitudes did not substantially mitigate the race disparities in the RJA Study (Grosso & O'Brien, 2012). We found that while the expression of death penalty reservations greatly increased the odds that a prosecutor would strike potential jurors of any race, Black jurors with that characteristic were still significantly more likely to be struck than their non-Black counterparts expressing similar views. Among people who expressed hesitation about the death penalty, the prosecution passed (i.e., declined to strike) disproportionally more non-Black potential jurors (26%) than Black potential jurors with such reservations (10%).

Preconceived notions about racial differences in support for the death penalty may contribute to differences in questioning of potential jurors and thus strike decisions. We have observed differences in transcripts with respect to how Black and non-Black jurors are questioned about this topic (O'Brien, Grosso, & Taylor, 2017). Consider, for instance, the following exchange between a prosecutor and a White juror about his views on the death penalty:

*Prosecutor*: Do you have feelings about either [a life or death sentence]?

*Juror*: I'm kind of against the death penalty, but it's in our system.

*Prosecutor*: Can you tell me a little about what makes you feel that way?

*Juror*: I don't know. Just—I mean to kill somebody seems wrong. But if somebody killed somebody . . . they could get the death penalty if that's what the finding was.

*Prosecutor*: If I'm hearing you correctly, it sounds like you're opposed to killing, period. And that if you were a jury member, even though you were generally opposed to killing, you could consider both possible punishments?

*Juror*: Yes, sir.

*Prosecutor*: And you could vote for the death penalty even though you're not really in favor of it, if that's the law . . . You could still vote for it?

*Juror*: Yes, sir.

The prosecutor passed this juror but struck the Black juror whose exchange with the prosecutor appears in the following transcript:

*Prosecutor*: Could you tell me what your thoughts or feelings are about both of those punishments, life imprisonment without parole and the death penalty?

*Juror*: I believe if you commit a crime you deserve your punishment. And if it's the death penalty, I think you should get it. I really—I don't feel it's right, but if it's the law, it's the law. That's how I feel.

*Prosecutor*: So personal preferences, as opposed to what the law is, you don't feel that the death penalty is an appropriate punishment?

*Juror*: Um, I . . .

*Prosecutor*: Or I shouldn't say that it's "appropriate." You just don't think it's right to have the death penalty?

*Prosecutor*: From your personal point of view, regardless of what the law . . . is, do you think that you have some personal reservation about the death penalty?

*Juror*: No.

*Prosecutor*: If you had your druthers, would you rather not sit on a case where the death penalty might be an appropriate punishment or might be a punishment that you had to consider?

*Juror*: It wouldn't matter.

The prosecutor is faced with very similar assertions by jurors in the very same case: They personally do not favor the death penalty but believe that the law must be followed regardless of their personal beliefs. The prosecutor follows up these assertions, however, with quite different tactics.

In the first instance, the prosecutor engages in a process known as "rehabilitation" of the first juror, providing the juror through leading questions with an answer that reconciles the juror's discomfort with capital punishment with the prospect of imposing it. The prosecutor focuses on the juror's stated respect for the law as it stands. In response to the second juror, however, the prosecutor focuses on the juror's personal beliefs and suggests that she would prefer not to serve. The starkness of the disparate approach in this example suggests that there may also be more subtle disparities in the process of questioning jurors around death penalty reservations (see O'Brien et al., 2017).

*Batson*, however, seeks to remedy only intentional discrimination. If the defense had challenged the prosecutor's decision to strike the Black venire member from the exchange excerpted here, the prosecutor could have easily proffered the venire member's statement "I don't feel it's right" as a race-neutral reason for the strike. The judge need not find that this is a good reason, just an honest one, and it quite likely would be honest. If the prosecutor approached this conversation expecting the venire member to oppose the death penalty, then any hesitation she expressed simply confirmed what he already believed. The prosecutor may be wrong that race played no role in his decision, but a court would be hard-pressed to find that he was lying.

## Conclusion

In *Foster v. Chatman* (2016), the Court once again emphasized its commitment to eradicating race discrimination in jury selection. It rightly denounced the prosecutor's unambiguous consideration of race when selecting Foster's capital jury. But as Justice Kagan noted during oral argument, "Isn't this as clear a *Batson* violation as a court is ever going to see?" (*Foster v. Chatman*, Transcript of Oral Argument, 2015, pp. 30–31). Rarely will the evidence of discrimination be as well documented as it was in this case, where the prosecutor's files included notes about the undesirability of jurors who belong to a "Black church" or which juror to accept "if it comes down to having to pick one of the black jurors" (p. 1745).

More typically, such notes will not exist, and if they do, the defense will never see them. They may not exist because the prosecutor knows better than to write down her or his thoughts, or just as likely, because she or he is not consciously considering race in selecting the jury. But that does not mean that race is not influencing the prosecutor's decisions—both in how the voir dire conversations unfold and who to strike. *Batson*, unfortunately, has done little to counter these instances of race discrimination, despite the Court's best efforts to strengthen it.

No simple solutions exist to remedy the stubborn persistence of racial bias in jury selection, but there are a few measures that could be taken to strengthen *Batson*'s protections. First, simply reducing the number of peremptory challenges available to the parties necessarily limits the opportunities for biased decision-making (see Grosso & O'Brien, 2012). Second, in light of the Court's commitment to enforcing *Batson*, parties should feel emboldened to object to their opponents' use of peremptory strikes when they appear to be driven in some part by race. Being proactive requires not only having the courage to raise a *Batson* challenge but also being prepared with information about the history of racially biased jury selection in opposing counsel's prior cases. Moreover, trial judges need to cope with the discomfort that may arise from confronting attorneys accused of being racially motivated in their use of peremptory strikes. Finally—and related to our second point—complete and accurate data about the jury selection process should be recorded and made available as a matter of course. Fair and racially neutral jury selection is a matter of public interest, and trial courts have a duty to preserve and provide access to basic data about who serves on juries, who is excused, and by whom (Grosso & O'Brien, 2017). Mounting meaningful challenges to race-based jury selection requires access to information over time to establish patterns that may not be obvious in an isolated case.

## Note

1. Prosecutors are also, indubitably, influenced by the prospect of having to explain their reasons for striking a Black juror if the defense raises a *Batson* challenge. This concern might cause them to ask more questions of any Black juror they consider striking than they would ask similarly situated White jurors, as it is very unlikely they will face a *Batson* objection for striking White jurors.

## References

Adams, E. S., & Lane, C. J. (1998). Constructing a jury that is both impartial and representative. *New York University Law Review, 73*, 703–764.

Arizona v. Youngblood, 488 U.S. 51 (1988).

Baldus, D. C., Woodworth, G. G., Zuckerman, D., Weiner, N. A., & Broffitt, B. (2001). The use of peremptory challenges in capital murder trials: A legal and empirical analysis. *University of Pennsylvania Journal of Constitutional Law, 3*, 3–169.

Batson v. Kentucky, 476 U.S. 79 (1986).

Bellin, J., & Semitsu, J. P. (2011). Widening Batson's net to ensnare more than the unapologetically bigoted or painfully unimaginative attorney. *Cornell Law Review, 96*, 1075–1130.

Bernard, J. L. (1979). Interaction between the race of the defendant and that of jurors in determining verdicts. *Law & Psychology Review, 5*, 103–111.

Berris, K. A. (2011). Appearance rates of potential jurors who confirm, postpone, or fail to respond to the jury summons: Are postponed jurors saying "no" or "not now"? *Drake Law Review, 59,* 549–667.

Bodenhausen, G. V. (1988). Stereotypic biases in social decision making and memory: Testing process models of stereotype use. *Journal of Personality and Social Psychology, 55,* 726–737. doi:10.1037/0022-3514.55.5.726

Bodenhausen, G. V., Todd, A. R., & Becker, A. P. (2007). Categorizing the social world: Affect, motivation, and self-regulation. In B. H. Ross & A. B. Markman (Eds.), *Psychology of learning and motivation: Categories in use* (Vol. 47, pp. 123–155). New York: Academic Press.

Cassell v. Texas, 339 U.S. 282 (1950).

Casteneda v. Partida, 430 U.S. 482 (1977).

Cochran, J. K., & Chamlin, M. B. (2006). The enduring racial divide in death penalty support. *Journal of Criminal Justice, 34,* 85–99. doi:10.1016/j.jcrimjus.2005.11.007

Devine, P. G. (1989). Stereotypes and prejudice: Their automatic and controlled components. *Journal of Personality and Social Psychology, 56,* 5–18. doi:10.1037/0022-3514.56.1.5

Diamond, S. S., & Ryken, A. (2013). The modern American jury: A one hundred year journey. *Judicature, 96,* 315–322.

Duren v. Missouri, 439 U.S. 357 (1979).

Eisenberg, A. M. (2017). Removal of women and African-Americans in jury selection in South Carolina capital cases, 1997–2012. *Northeastern University Law Journal, 9,* 299–345.

Ellis, L., & Diamond S. S. (2003). Race, diversity, jury composition: Battering and bolstering legitimacy. *Chicago-Kent Law Review, 78,* 1033–1058.

Ellsworth, P. C. (1989). Are twelve heads better than one? *Law and Contemporary Problems, 52,* 205–224.

Equal Justice Initiative. (2010, August). *Illegal race discrimination in jury selection: A continuing legacy.* Retrieved from http://eji.org/reports/illegal-racial-discrimination-in-jury-selection.

Fiske, S. T. (1998). Stereotyping, prejudice, and discrimination. In D. T. Gilbert, S. T. Fiske, & G. Lindzey (Eds.), *The handbook of social psychology* (4th ed., pp. 357–414). New York: McGraw-Hill.

Fitzgerald, R., & Ellsworth, P. C. (1984). Due process vs. crime control: Death qualifications and jury attitudes. *Law and Human Behavior, 8,* 31–51. doi:10.1007/BF01044350

Foster v. Chatman, No. 14-8349, Joint Appendix, Vol. 1 (2015).

Foster v. Chatman, No. 14-8349, Transcript of Oral Argument (2015).

Foster v. Chatman, 136 S.Ct. 1737 (2016).

Frey, D. (1986). Recent research on selective exposure to information. In L. Berkowitz (Ed.), *Advances in experimental social psychology* (pp. 41–80). New York: Academic Press.

Friedrich, J. (1993). Primary error detection and minimization (PEDMIN) strategies in social cognition: A reinterpretation of confirmation bias phenomena. *Psychological Review, 100,* 298–319. doi:10.1037/0033-295X.100.2.298

Ga. Code Ann. §15-12-40 (2017).

Ga. Code Ann. §15-12-40.1 (2017).

Ga. Code Ann. §15-12-133 (2017).

Gau, J. M. (2016). A jury of whose peers? The impact of selection procedures on racial composition and the prevalence of majority-white juries. *Journal of Crime and Justice*, *39*, 75–87. doi:10.1080/0735648X.2015.1087149

Georgia v. McCollum, 505 U.S. 42 (1992).

Gibson, B., Sanbonmatsu, D. M., & Posavac, S. S. (1997). The effects of selective hypothesis testing on gambling. *Journal of Experimental Psychology: Applied*, *3*, 126–142. doi:10.1037/1076-898X.3.2.126

Glasser v. United States, 315 U.S. 60, 86 (1942).

Grosso, C. M., & O'Brien, B. (2012). A stubborn legacy: The overwhelming importance of race in jury selection in 173 post-*Batson* North Carolina capital trials. *Iowa Law Review*, *97*, 1531–1560.

Grosso, C. M., & O'Brien, B. (2017). A call to criminal courts: Record rules for *Batson*. *Kentucky Law Review*, *105*, 651–670.

Hayden, G., Senna, J., & Siegel, L. (1978). Prosecutorial discretion in peremptory challenges: An empirical investigation of information use in the Massachusetts jury selection process. *New England Law Review*, *13*, 768–791.

Hitchcock, A. S. (2006). Recent development, "deference does not by definition preclude relief": The impact of *Miller-El v. Dretke* on *Batson* review in North Carolina capital appeals. *North Carolina Law Review*, *94*, 1328–1356.

Hoffman, M. B. (1997). Peremptory challenges should be abolished: A trial judge's perspective. *University of Chicago Law Review*, *64*, 809–871. doi:10.2307/1600312

J.E.B. v. Alabama, 511 U.S. 127 (1994).

Johnson, V. B. (2016). Arresting *Batson*: How striking jurors based on arrest records violates *Batson*. *Yale Law and Policy Review*, *34*, 387–419.

Johnston, L. C., & Macrae, C. N. (1994). Changing social stereotypes: The case of the information seeker. *European Journal of Social Psychology*, *24*, 581–592. doi:10.1002/ejsp.2420240505

Jonas, E., Schulz-Hardt, S., Frey, D., & Thelen, N. (2001). Confirmation bias in sequential information search after preliminary decisions: An expansion of dissonance theoretical research on selective exposure to information. *Journal of Personality and Social Psychology*, *80*, 557–571. doi:10.1037/0022-3514.80.4.557

Kalt, B. C. (2003). The exclusion of felons from jury service. *American University Law Review*, *53*, 65–189.

Kerr, N. L., Kramer, G. P., Carroll, J. S., & Alfini, J. J. (1991). On the effectiveness of voir dire in criminal cases with prejudicial pretrial publicity: An empirical study. *American University Law Review*, *40*, 665–701.

King, N. J. (1994). The effects of race-conscious jury selection on public confidence in the fairness of jury proceedings: An empirical puzzle. *American Criminal Law Review*, *31*, 1177–1201.

Klayman, J., & Ha, Y. (1987). Confirmation, disconfirmation, and information in hypothesis testing. *Psychological Review*, *94*, 211–228. doi:10.1037/0033-295X.94.2.211

Liepold, A. D. (1998). Constitutionalizing jury selection in criminal cases: A critical evaluation. *Georgetown Law Journal*, *86*, 945–1010.

Lynch, M., & Haney, C. (2011). Mapping the racial bias of the White male capital juror: Jury composition and the "empathic divide." *Law and Society Review, 45*, 69–101. doi:10.1111/j.1540-5893.2011.00428.x

MacCoun, R., & Tyler, T. R. (1988). The basis of citizens' perceptions of the criminal jury: Procedural fairness, accuracy, and efficiency. *Law and Human Behavior, 12*, 333–352. doi:10.1007/BF01044389

Macrae, C. N., Milne, A. B., & Bodenhausen, G. V. (1994). Stereotypes as energy-saving devices: A peek inside the cognitive toolbox. *Journal of Personality and Social Psychology, 66*, 37–47. doi:10.1037/0022-3514.66.1.37

Marder, N. S. (1995). Beyond gender: Peremptory challenges and the role of the jury. *Texas Law Review, 73*, 1041–1138.

McCleskey v. Kemp, 481 U.S. 279, 107 S. Ct. 1756, 95 L. Ed. 2d 262 (1987).

McDougall, H. A. (1970). The case for Black juries. *Yale Law Journal, 79*, 531–550.

McGonigle, S., Becka, H., Lafleur, J., & Wyatt, T. (2005, August 21). A process of juror elimination: Dallas prosecutors say they don't discriminate, but analysis shows they are more likely to reject Black jurors. *Dallas Morning News*, 1A.

Melilli, K. J. (1995-1996). *Batson* in practice: What we have learned about *Batson* and peremptory challenges. *Notre Dame Law Review, 71*, 447–503.

Miller-El v. Dretke, 545 U.S. 231 (2005).

Munsterman, G. T., Hannaford-Agor, P. L., & Whitehead, G. M. (eds.) (2006). *Jury trial innovations* (2nd ed). Williamsburg, VA: National Center for State Courts.

Nickerson, R. S. (1998). Confirmation bias: A ubiquitous phenomenon in many guises. *Review of General Psychology, 2*, 175–220. doi:10.1037/1089-2680.2.2.175

North Carolina Racial Justice Act, N.C. Gen. Stat. § 15A-2011-2012 (2009).

North Carolina v. Augustine et al., 368 N.C. 594, 780 S.E.2d 552 (2015).

North Carolina v. Golphin et al. Transcript of Record, Vol. IX, at 56, No. 97 CRS 47314-15 (2012).

North Carolina v. Robinson. Cumberland County, Superior Court Division, No. 91 CRS 23143 (2012).

North Carolina v. Robinson. Transcript of closing argument, Racial Justice Act Hearing, Vol. XIII (2012).

North Carolina v. Robinson, 368 N.C. 596, 780 S.E.2d 151 (2015).

O'Brien, B. (2009). Prime suspect: An examination of factors that aggravate and counteract confirmation bias in criminal investigations. *Psychology, Public Policy, and Law, 15*, 315–334. doi:10.1037/a0017881

O'Brien, B., & Grosso, C. M. (2011a). Confronting race: How a confluence of social movements convinced North Carolina to go where the *McCleskey* court wouldn't. *Michigan State Law Review, 2011*, 463–504.

O'Brien B., & Grosso, C.M. (2011b). *Pilot study of cause removals in Cumberland County, North Carolina.* Unpublished manuscript, College of Law, Michigan State University, East Lansing.

O'Brien, B., Grosso, C. M., & Taylor, A. P. (2017). Examining jurors: Applying conversation analysis to voir dire in capital cases, a first look. *Journal of Criminal Law and Criminology, 107*, 687–732.

Ogletree, C. J. (1993). Beyond justifications: Seeking motivations to sustain public defenders. *Harvard Law Review, 106*, 1239–1294.

Oregon v. Kennedy, 456 U.S. 667 (1982).

Otis, C. C., Greathouse, S. M., Kennard, J. B., & Kovera, M. B. (2014). Hypothesis testing in attorney-conducted voir dire. *Law and Human Behavior, 38*, 392–404. doi:10.1037/lhb0000092

Pollitt, D. R., & Warren, B. P. (2016). Thirty years of disappointment: North Carolina's remarkable appellate Batson record. *North Carolina Law Review, 94*, 1957–1994.

Powers v. Ohio, 499 U.S. 400 (1991).

Price, M. J. (2009). Performing discretion or performing discrimination: Race, ritual, and peremptory challenges in capital jury selection. *Michigan Journal of Race & Law, 15*, 57–107.

Purkett v. Elem, 514 U.S. 765 (1995).

Quilty, K. J. (2015). The unrecognized right: How wealth discrimination unconstitutionally bars indigent citizens from the jury box. *Cornell Journal of Law and Public Policy, 24*, 567–589.

Rector, N. A., Bagby, R. M., & Nicholson, R. (1993). The effect of prejudice and judicial ambiguity on defendant guilt ratings. *Journal of Social Psychology, 133*, 651–659. doi:10.1080/00224545.1993.9713920

Robertson, C. (2012, April 21). Bias used to move a man off death row. *The New York Times*, A1.

Rose, M. R. (1999). The peremptory challenge accused of race or gender discrimination? Some data from one county. *Law and Human Behavior, 23*, 695–702. doi:0.1023/A:1022393506784

Rose, M. R. (2005). A dutiful voice: Justice in the distribution of jury service. *Law and Society Review, 39*, 601–633.

Rose, M. R., & Diamond, S. S. (2008). Judging bias: Juror confidence and judicial ruling on challenges for cause. *Law and Human Behavior, 42*, 513–549. doi:10.1111/j.1540-5893.2008.00350.x

Schwartz, P. J. (1991). Equal protection in jury selection? The implementation of *Batson v. Kentucky* in North Carolina. *North Carolina Law Review, 69*, 1533–1577.

Simon, D. (2012). *In doubt: The psychology of the criminal justice process.* Cambridge, MA: Harvard University Press.

*SmithKline Beecham Corporation (GSK) v. Abbott Laboratories*, 740 F.3d 471 (9th Cir. 2014).

Snyder, M., & Swann, W.B. (1978). Hypothesis testing processes in social interaction. *Journal of Personality and Social Psychology, 36*, 1202–1212. doi:10.1037/0022-3514.36.11.1202

Snyder v. Louisiana, 552 U.S. 472 (2008).

Sommers, S. R. (2006). On racial diversity and group decision-making: Identifying multiple effects of racial composition on jury deliberations. *Journal of Personality and Social Psychology, 90*, 597–612. doi:10.1037/0022-3514.90.4.597

Sommers, S. R., & Ellsworth, P. C. (2000). Race in the courtroom: Perceptions of guilt and dispositional attributions. *Personality and Social Psychology Bulletin, 26*, 1367–1379. doi:10.1177/0146167200263005

Sommers, S. R., & Ellsworth, P. C. (2001). White juror bias: An investigation of racial prejudice against Black defendants in the American courtroom. *Psychology, Public Policy, and Law, 7*, 201–229. doi:10.1037/1076-8971.7.1.201

Sommers, S. R., & Norton, M. I. (2007). Race-based judgments, race-neutral justifications: Experimental examination of peremptory use and the Batson challenge procedure. *Law and Human Behavior, 31,* 269–273. doi:10.1007/s10979-006-9048-6

Sommers, S. R., & Norton, M. I. (2008). Race and jury selection: Psychological perspectives on the peremptory challenge debate. *American Psychologist, 63,* 527–539. doi:10.1037/0003-066X.63.6.527

Strauder v. West Virginia, 100 U.S. 303 (1880).

Stevenson, B. A., & Friedman, R. E. (1994). Deliberate indifference: Judicial tolerance of racial bias in criminal justice. *Washington and Lee Law Review, 51,* 509–527.

Swain v. Alabama, 380 U.S. 202 (1965).

Sweeney, L. T., & Haney, C. (1992). The influence of race on sentencing: A meta-analytic review of experimental studies. *Behavioral Sciences & the Law, 10,* 179–195. doi:10.1002/bsl.2370100204

Taylor v. Louisiana, 419 U.S. 522, 530 (1975).

Todd, A. R., Galinsky, A. D., & Bodenhausen, G. V. (2012). Perspective taking and stereotype maintenance. *Social Cognition, 30,* 94–108. doi:10.1521/soco.2012.30.1.94

Turner, B. M., Lovell, R. D., Young, J. D., & Denny, W. F. (1986). Race and peremptory challenges during voir dire: Do prosecution and defense agree? *Journal of Criminal Justice, 14,* 61–69. doi:10.1016/0047-2352(86)90027-9

Underwood, B. D. (1992). Ending race discrimination in jury selections: Whose right is it anyway? *Columbia Law Review, 92,* 725–774.

United States v. Armstrong, 517 U.S. 456 (1996).

United States v. Brown, 352 F.3d 654 (2d. Circuit 2003).

Unnever, J. D., & Cullen, F. T. (2007a). Reassessing the racial divide in support for capital punishment: The continuing significance of race. *Journal of Research in Crime and Delinquency, 44,* 124–158. doi:10.1177/0022427806295837

Unnever, J. D., & Cullen, F. T. (2007b). The racial divide in support for the death penalty: Does White racism matter? *Social Forces, 85,* 1281–1301. doi:10.1353/sof.2007.0058

Vidmar, N., & Hans, V. P. (2007). *American juries: The verdict.* Amherst, NY: Prometheus Books.

Wainwright v. Witt, 469 U.S. 412, 424 (1985).

Wilson, A. (2009). The end of peremptory challenges: A call for change through comparative analysis. *Hastings International and Comparative Law Review, 31,* 363–378.

Zeisel, H., & Diamond, S. S. (1976). The jury selection in the Mitchell-Stans conspiracy trial. *Law and Social Inquiry, 1,* 151–174. doi:10.1111/j.1747-4469.1976.tb00954.x

# 3

# Diminishing Support for the Death Penalty

## *Implications for Fair Capital Case Outcomes*

### Amelia Courtney Hritz, Caisa Elizabeth Royer, and Valerie P. Hans

In the American justice system, there is no time when the jury has a more important role than during a capital trial. In most other sentencing contexts, while juries may decide the guilt of a criminal defendant, the applicable punishment is decided by either a judge or a statute. In contrast, capital defendants face a bifurcated trial in which the jury plays a significant role in determining both guilt and punishment. The jury's power and authority in capital cases ensures a vital role for the community in the decision about whether a defendant should be executed.

The Sixth Amendment gives criminal defendants the right to an "impartial jury of the state and district wherein the crime shall have been committed" (U.S. Const. amend. VI). The Founding Fathers entrusted the criminal jury to introduce the conscience of the community into the criminal justice system. Without the institution of the jury, the activities of the criminal justice system would be the sole province of government actors; legislators pass the laws, prosecutors decide whether to bring criminal charges, and judges preside over trials and determine most criminal sentences. The jury system allows members of the community to decide the facts of a case and, during the sentencing phase of a capital trial, whether the defendant should receive the death penalty. These judgments are not exclusively legal determinations. Instead, they depend importantly upon social norms and the community's sense of morality. The criminal jury reflects the idea that members of the community, not the government, are better able to judge whether a defendant has violated community standards and morality (Carroll, 2014; Royer, 2017). The criminal jury injects the voice of the community into the criminal justice system, acting as a check on the government's power and preventing government overreach. In order for the jury to be a voice for the community, however, the jury must be representative of the community. A representative jury also increases legitimacy of verdicts by improving public confidence in the legal system (Ellis & Diamond, 2003). This protection becomes especially important when the most serious of penalties is at stake.

In this chapter, we present and analyze the current state of law and research on the capital jury. First, we present the legal framework for capital jury selection and research on the "death-qualified" jury, whose members are eligible to serve in a capital case. We also discuss research showing that the death-qualification process skews the composition of the capital jury so that it fails to represent the community. Next, we discuss the contemporary death penalty in the United States, noting the challenge that comes from declining support for capital punishment and the need to select representative capital juries. We highlight two case studies which demonstrate how death qualification can create a jury that is unrepresentative of the community: Dzhokhar Tsarnaev in Boston, Massachusetts, and Dylann Roof in Charleston, South Carolina. Finally, we conclude by discussing the implications of the current trends in support for the death penalty and research on capital juries.

## The Death-Qualification Process

In the vast majority of death penalty cases, a jury decides whether the defendant receives the death penalty or a life sentence. Who among the nation's citizens should decide the ultimate punishment? What is the relevance of prospective jurors' attitudes and views about capital punishment, including a person's willingness to send a defendant to death row? These questions have engaged legal thinkers and psychological researchers for many decades (e.g., Haney, 1984a; Summers, Hayward, & Miller, 2010; Yelderman, Miller, & Peoples, 2016).

It has been routine for over half a century for judges and lawyers to question prospective jurors about their attitudes to ensure that they are eligible to serve as jurors in capital trials—a process known as "death qualification." Potential jurors must always be willing and able to follow the law to qualify to serve on capital cases, and courts anticipated that some would object to being involved in deciding a death penalty case, whether for religious, political, or other reasons. The trial judge may remove a prospective juror for cause when the judge concludes that the individual is biased or otherwise incapable of serving as a fair and impartial factfinder.

In one early case, *Witherspoon v. Illinois* (1968), the judge stated near the start of the voir dire process, "Let's get these conscientious objectors out of the way, without wasting any time on them" (p. 514). In Witherspoon's case, 47 prospective jurors, about half the jury pool, were quickly eliminated through challenges for cause, despite the fact that only five of them made specific statements that they would be unable, as the law required, to vote in favor of a death sentence under any circumstances. Most of the others who expressed reservations were quickly removed without extensive follow-up questioning.

The jury chosen for the case convicted Witherspoon and sentenced him to death.

When Witherspoon's case was reviewed by the US Supreme Court, his lawyers offered some preliminary data suggesting that removing prospective jurors with concerns about the death penalty could have increased the likelihood of his conviction. They cited three unpublished research studies that they argued demonstrated that death penalty supporters were more conviction prone. The Court was unconvinced by this modest body of empirical evidence relating to guilt judgments: "The data adduced by the petitioner . . . are too tentative and fragmentary to establish that jurors not opposed to the death penalty tend to favor the prosecution in the determination of guilt" (*Witherspoon v Illinois*, 1968, p. 517). However, the Court did end up reducing Witherspoon's sentence to life imprisonment due to concern about the overbroad removal of all who expressed any doubt about capital punishment. The Court noted that "in 1966, approximately 42% of the American public favored capital punishment for convicted murderers, while 47% opposed it and 11% were undecided" (n. 16). The Court reasoned that at a time when more than half of the nation opposes the death penalty, a jury from which all those with even mild opposition to capital punishment were removed would be "uncommonly willing to condemn a man to die" (p. 521).

The *Witherspoon* decision changed the way that capital juries are selected. Individuals with reservations about the death penalty but who say they can follow the law and consider it are no longer automatically removed (Gross, 1984; Hans & Vidmar, 1986). Additionally, the decision spurred empirical research on capital juries. The National Association for the Advancement of Colored People (NAACP) Legal Defense Fund heard in *Witherspoon* an open invitation to make the empirical case that death-qualified juries were more conviction-prone. They recruited social science researchers to test the impact and operation of death penalty attitudes on conviction likelihood. Phoebe Ellsworth, Craig Haney, and their collaborators undertook a series of studies to examine the operation and impact of death penalty attitudes on jury composition and jury decision-making (see Haney, 1984a, for discussion).

One of the first discoveries of the research was that selecting juries on the basis of their death penalty attitudes has dramatic effects on the demographic composition of the jury (see also Chapter 2 of this volume). Death penalty attitudes are linked to individual characteristics such as race, ethnicity, gender, age, socioeconomic status, and religion: Racial and ethnic minorities, women, younger and poorer individuals, and Catholics are significantly less likely than others to support capital punishment and to say that they could deliver a death sentence (Fitzgerald & Ellsworth, 1984). Fitzgerald and Ellsworth asked the following question in a 1979 poll of 811 jury-eligible residents in Alameda, California: "Is your attitude toward the death penalty such that as a juror you would never be willing to impose it in any case, no matter what the evidence was, or would you consider voting to impose it in at least some cases?" Respondents who answered that they would never impose the death penalty were identified as those who would be excluded under *Witherspoon*. These included a subgroup of respondents who said that their death penalty views were so strong that if chosen as a juror, they would not be able to decide guilt fairly. Fitzgerald and Ellsworth removed this subgroup of "nullifiers" and then compared the demographic makeup of the remaining *Witherspoon*-excludable respondents with the respondents who were death-qualified. The comparisons between these groups revealed that Black prospective jurors would be much more likely to be excluded from capital juries on the basis of their death penalty attitudes: 26% of Black respondents said they would never be able to impose a death sentence compared to 17% of non-Black respondents. Similarly, more women (21%) expressed opposition to giving a death sentence than men (13%).

Contemporary surveys observe similar race and gender disparities in attitudes toward capital punishment (Oliphant, 2016; Summers et al., 2010; Yelderman et al., 2016). Research has shown that, compared to White potential jurors, Black potential jurors are more likely to be removed for cause due to an unwillingness to enforce the death penalty (Eisenberg, Hritz, Royer, & Blume, 2017). Over half of Black and Hispanic Americans oppose the death penalty (63% and 50%, respectively) compared to only 35% of White Americans (Oliphant, 2016). This racial disparity could be explained by an expected likelihood to empathize with the defendant as an in-group member, given the fact that the death penalty targets Black defendants at unrepresentatively higher rates than White defendants (*McCleskey v. Kemp*, 1987; Royer et al., 2014). Black defendants are three times more likely to end up on death row than White defendants (Death Penalty Information Center [DPIC], 2018b). Similarly, women are less likely than men to support the death penalty for someone convicted of murder: 45% of women oppose the death penalty compared to 38% of men (Oliphant, 2016). Women are also more likely than men to be removed for cause due to their unwillingness to enforce the death penalty (Eisenberg, 2017; Eisenberg et al., 2017). Given these statistics, it is not surprising that capital juries, which tend to overrepresent men, are more likely to return a death sentence verdict than a verdict of life (Lynch & Haney, 2011).

Death penalty attitudes are also related to age and income. Support for the death penalty increases with age, with only 42% of Americans between the ages of 18 and 29 supporting the death penalty compared to 50% of Americans aged 65 and older (Oliphant, 2016). Similarly, death penalty support increases with socioeconomic status; poorer people are more likely than their more affluent counterparts to say that they could not give a death sentence (Fitzgerald & Ellsworth, 1984). Religious affiliation is likewise linked to death penalty attitudes, with Catholics disproportionately likely to be removed for cause on account of their opposition to capital punishment (Summers et al., 2010). Thus capital juries selected under the *Witherspoon* standard are likely to fall far short of fully representing the range of individuals in a community compared to the community at large or even juries in other types of cases.

Of equal significance is the fact that death penalty attitudes are part of a cluster of attitudes and views about crime and justice. Fitzgerald and Ellsworth (1984) found striking differences reflecting the tendency of *Witherspoon*-excludables to be more due process oriented compared to death penalty supporters, who were more likely to espouse crime control views. For instance, excludable survey participants were more apt than death-qualified participants to say that it is better for society to let some guilty defendants go free than to risk convicting the innocent (63% versus 44%). In contrast, death-qualified participants were more likely to agree that the insanity plea is a loophole (78% versus 59%) and to express distrust in defense attorneys (73% versus 65%). Thus death-qualified participants were more punitive than *Witherspoon*-excludables, favoring strict enforcement of the law and harsh punishment and being less likely to consider mercy.

Subsequent studies have confirmed the crime control-due process attitude clusters of death-qualified and excludable individuals (for a review, see Yelderman et al., 2016). Death-qualified jurors, as compared to non-death-qualified jurors, hold more favorable attitudes toward crime victims, have more negative attitudes toward defendants, see themselves as more similar to victims, and perceive the defendant's chances of rehabilitation in prison to be less likely (Yelderman et al., 2016). Interpretation of aggravating and mitigating circumstances also differs, with death-qualified individuals giving aggravating factors more credence and mitigating factors less weight compared to those who would be excluded because of their death penalty views (Yelderman et al., 2016). These interrelated attitudes indicate that defendants whose cases are being heard by death-qualified juries face an up-hill battle at both the guilt and penalty phases of capital trials.

Additionally, the death-qualification process may exclude potential jurors who are able to empathize with the defendant. In general, people tend to empathize more easily with members of their in-group (Haegerich & Bottoms, 2000; Johnson et al., 2002). For example, women tend to empathize more with other women than with men, and Black people tend to empathize more strongly with other Black people than with White people (Johnson et al., 2002; Lynch & Haney, 2015). In-group empathy also extends to shared experiences. For example, people empathize most with others who have experienced similar trauma or who have similar socioeconomic status (McKeever, 2015). Jurors who feel similar to a defendant are more lenient in finding guilt and in sentencing than jurors who view the defendant as an outgroup member (Haegerich & Bottoms, 2000; Johnson et al., 2002). Because the death-qualification process is more likely to exclude certain types of jurors (e.g., Black potential jurors; Eisenberg et al., 2017), the resulting jury may be less able to empathize with certain types of defendants (e.g., Black defendants). In addition, White men, who are less likely to be excluded through death qualification, are more likely to empathize with other White men (Lynch & Haney, 2015). This effect is likely to be magnified because White men tend to assert more authority in deliberations compared to other race-gender groups (Lynch & Haney, 2015). Death qualification may also remove potential jurors who express a general willingness to empathize with a capital defendant. This is another reason that death qualification creates more punitive juries, because jurors who feel empathy for a defendant tend to be less punitive and make more decisions based on all the facts of the case compared to jurors who lack empathy for the defendant (Archer, Foushee, Davis, & Aderman, 1979; Haegerich & Bottoms, 2000; Johnson et al., 2002; Plumm & Terrance, 2009).

Analysis of the impact of death qualification bears out the concerns related to increased punitiveness. In an early mock jury experiment, Cowan, Thompson, and Ellsworth (1984) presented a videotaped mock homicide trial to individuals. Death-qualified mock jurors (78%) were more likely than excludable mock jurors (53%) to vote guilty in the noncapital homicide case. Views of the evidence differed, too, with death-qualified jurors finding the testimony of prosecution witnesses more believable. In another study, death-qualified jurors were more apt than excludables to convict in schizophrenia-based insanity defense cases, although no differences occurred when the insanity defense was based on mental retardation or epilepsy (Ellsworth, Bukaty, Cowan, & Thompson, 1984). Thompson, Cowan, Ellsworth, and Harrington (1984) found that the relations between death penalty attitudes and willingness to convict could be mediated by both differing interpretations of evidence and differing thresholds for conviction. In their study, compared to excludables, death-qualified mock jurors interpreted evidence in a way that was more favorable to the prosecution; they also had a lower threshold for conviction.

Subsequent studies have borne out the link between death qualification and conviction proneness too. A meta-analysis of 14 studies (Allen, Mabry, & McKelton, 1998), including the studies described earlier, confirmed the positive relationship between favorable death penalty attitudes and willingness to convict. Allen and colleagues estimated that a pro-death penalty attitude translates into a 44% increase in the likelihood of conviction. Combining the Allen et al. meta-analysis results with findings from five later studies on the topic, Yelderman et al. (2016) concluded that the evidence of a link between death qualification and conviction proneness is reliable and substantial.

Haney (1984b, 2005) identifies one additional consequence of death qualification: The selection process itself may lead jurors to become more conviction prone and more likely to sentence an individual to death. Being questioned about one's willingness to give a death sentence, Haney theorized, may predispose jurors to expect a conviction. Entertaining the idea of giving a death sentence may increase their willingness to do it. To test the process effect, Haney had participants watch a videotape of a mock voir dire. Half the participants saw a voir dire that included death-qualification questions; the other half did not. In line with predictions, those who watched the death qualification rated the likelihood of the defendant's guilt as higher, estimated the judge's belief in the defendant's guilt as higher, and were more likely to think a death sentence was appropriate compared to those who had not seen the death-qualification questions (Haney, 1984b). In effect, through the jury selection procedure in capital trials, jurors are "reoriented with a pro-death penalty mental framework" (Yelderman et al., 2016, p. 42).

## The Current Relationship Between American Juries and the Death Penalty

As discussed in the previous section, the death-qualification process appears to create less diverse juries that are also more crime control oriented and conviction prone. But are capital juries still fulfilling their role of representing their community in the criminal justice system and preventing government overreach? In recent years, popular support for and use of the death penalty has declined (DPIC, 2018c). However, the localized nature of criminal sentencing and the death-qualification process may prevent this shift in community sentiment from being represented during capital trials. In this section, we describe the current relationship between the community, which the jury is meant to represent, and the death penalty. First, we review the latest trends in public support for the death penalty, and, second, we examine the role of the jury in capital cases.

### Declining Public Support for the Death Penalty

The United States currently has a complicated relationship with the death penalty. The federal government and 31 states maintain the death penalty as a possible sanction for qualifying murders. In the last five years, some states have abolished capital punishment, while voters in other jurisdictions have reinforced their support. Recently, legislatures in New Mexico (2009), Illinois (2011), Connecticut (2012), and Maryland (2013) abolished the death penalty and replaced it with the sentence of life without the possibility of parole (National Conference of State Legislatures, 2017). In 2016, the US Supreme Court struck down Florida's capital statute on constitutional grounds in *Hurst v. Florida*, and the Supreme Court of Delaware followed that decision by holding that its state capital punishment law was unconstitutional in *Rauf v. State*. In contrast, in 2016, voters in California chose to retain the death penalty, and voters in Nebraska reinstated that state's death penalty law one year after the Nebraska legislature had repealed it. In a similar vein, voters in Oklahoma supported a measure declaring that the death penalty was not cruel and unusual under the state constitution (Sarat, 2016).

Despite these crosscurrents in individual states, the use of the death penalty has declined dramatically, with both death sentences and executions reaching historic lows in 2016. Thirty-one people were sentenced to death that year, the lowest number since the Supreme Court reinstated the death penalty in 1976. In addition, only 20 people were executed, the lowest number since 1991 (DPIC, 2018c). This trend continued in 2017, with 39 people sentenced to death and 23 executions, the second-lowest numbers in a quarter century (DPIC, 2018c). Thus, while the majority of US jurisdictions retain capital punishment, few states actively sentence people to death, and even fewer execute people on death row. As a result, the death penalty is extremely localized. In 2016, two states, Georgia and Texas, carried out 80% of the country's executions (DPIC, 2018c). Death sentences are even localized within states. Most death sentences arise out of a very small number of counties (Baumgartner, 2010; Liebman & Clarke, 2011; Smith, 2012). Between 1973 and 1997, of 3,143 total counties in the United States, 66 counties imposed close to half of all death sentences (Blume & Vann, 2016; *Glossip v. Gross*, 2015). Fifteen counties enforced 30% of total executions since 1976. Furthermore, out of 2,400 chief prosecutors in the United States, just five are responsible for one out of every seven people on death row (Swarns, 2016).

Support for the death penalty has fluctuated over time: It rose from the 1930s to the 1950s, with a peak of 68% support in 1953, then it decreased to a low of 42% support in 1966, and rose again to its all-time high of 80% support in 1994 (Gallup, n.d.). For the last 10 years, public support for the death penalty has been decreasing (Oliphant, 2016). In 2016, public support for capital punishment reached lows not seen since the time of *Witherspoon v. Illinois* (1968), 40 years ago. A Pew poll found that about half of Americans (49%) support the death penalty for a defendant who is convicted of murder, while just under one-half (42%) oppose the death penalty (Oliphant, 2016). A poll by Gallup also found that death penalty support is decreasing and has reached the lowest level of support since 1972, with 60% of people in favor and 37% opposed (Jones, 2016). These numbers are strikingly different than in the mid-1990s when 80% of Americans favored the death penalty and only 13% opposed it (Gallup, n.d.). There are many possible explanations for the national decrease in support for the death penalty, including the widespread publicity about exonerations through DNA and other evidence, increased awareness about the cost of the death penalty, increased concern about discrimination in the criminal justice system, and the availability of life without the possibility of parole as a sentencing option (DPIC, 2018c; Gross, 1998).

While national support for the death penalty is declining, support still varies greatly across counties. Polls conducted in California and Nebraska before the 2016 referendums illustrate this trend. A January 2016 poll of 1,003 registered voters in California revealed that 60% of residents in inland counties favored speeding up the state's execution process and 37% favored replacing the death penalty with life without parole (DiCamillo, 2016). In contrast, 44% of residents in the coastal counties favored speeding up the process and 51% favored replacing it. A 2016 poll of 600 registered voters in Nebraska found that support for the death penalty varied across congressional districts, with 64% of residents of the Third District supporting the death penalty (23% opposed), compared to 56% supporting it in the First District (32% opposed) and 55% in support in the Second District (36% opposed) (Vote Repeal Staff, 2016). The Third District of Nebraska is mostly rural and one of the most Republican districts in the country; in contrast, the First and Second districts are mostly urban and include the cities of Omaha and Lincoln. The varying support for capital punishment is a clear explanation for the localized nature of its use, as counties elect prosecutors who determine whether to seek death sentences.

As discussed previously, support for the death penalty is also divided across political and demographic lines. The California poll found that the groups in favor of speeding up executions included Republicans (73%), White non-Hispanic people (52%), men (51%), people aged 50 to 64 (54%), and Protestant and non-Catholic Christians (58%). Groups that favored replacing it with life without parole included Democrats (60%), African American people (61%), Latino people (54%), people aged 18 to 39 (51%), Catholics (52%), and non-Christian religious people (62%). The Nebraska poll showed similar political and demographic trends to the California poll. These demographic patterns are in line with the previously discussed relations between individual characteristics and death penalty opposition found in research on death-qualified juries.

As noted by the US Supreme Court, "a jury that must choose between life imprisonment and capital punishment can do little more—and must do nothing less—than express the conscience of the community on the ultimate question of life or death" (*Witherspoon v. Illinois*, 1968, p. 519). The jury will internalize the community's conscience when the jury is representative of the state and district in which the crime was committed. There is no constitutional provision that requires juries to be made up of a fair cross-section of the community, but there are precedents which suggest that a fair cross-section is an important part of the criminal jury (e.g., *Ballew v. Georgia*, 1978; *Taylor v. Louisiana*, 1975). The possibility of a fair cross-section is jeopardized by the process of death qualification, which requires the removal of potential jurors who are unwilling to impose the death penalty or who would automatically impose death (see earlier discussion). This will affect representativeness with respect to political ideology, race, gender, and religion. It could even affect the representativeness of certain attitudes and personality characteristics. In places where more people oppose the death penalty, the effect of death qualification will be heightened. The Supreme Court recognized this problem almost 50 years ago in *Witherspoon*: "in a nation less than half of whose people believe in the death penalty, a jury composed exclusively of such people cannot speak for the community . . . such a jury can speak only for a distinct and dwindling minority" (*Witherspoon v. Illinois*, 1968, pp. 519–520).

Two cases illustrate how death qualification can produce a disconnect between the jury and the community. The first is Dzhokhar Tsarnaev, who faced the death penalty for the bombing of the Boston Marathon in 2013 (Seelye, 2015a). The crime struck the heart of Boston, occurring during one of its most famous and well-attended events. The bomb explosions killed three people and injured an estimated 264 others. Although Massachusetts does not have the death penalty, Tsarnaev was eligible for the death penalty because he was charged with federal crimes.

Multiple polls conducted after the crime showed that the majority of Boston residents disapproved of sentencing Tsarnaev to death and favored a life sentence. A poll conducted during the trial revealed that only 27% favored death whereas 62% favored life for Tsarnaev (Seelye, 2015c). It was questionable whether the jury deciding the case would reflect the same perspective, because death qualification excludes jurors who are not willing to impose the death penalty. During jury selection, over 1,000 potential jurors filled out a 28-page questionnaire with questions ranging from thoughts on capital punishment and immigration policies in America to education in computer science (*United States v. Tsarnaev*, Document 1178, 2015; Wolff, 2015). The judge and attorneys questioned 256 of the potential jurors individually during 21 days of voir dire and eventually removed 181 potential jurors for cause (Boeri & Sobel, 2015). In Tsarnaev's case, many jurors were removed for bias from pretrial publicity (see Chapter 8 of this volume for a discussion of issues related to this topic). Despite the defense's assertion that a local Boston jury could not be fair, the judge asserted that he would be able to find enough impartial jurors within the city of Boston in order to hold the trial (Abramson, 2015). But if the jury is meant to introduce the conscience of the community into the criminal justice system, the relevant question is not whether there were enough unbiased people in the city of Boston who were willing to consider sentencing Tsarnaev to death but whether that group would be representative of the community. From the pool of 75 death-qualified jurors, the state and defense exercised 23 peremptory challenges each, and finally 12 jurors and 6 alternates were seated. These jurors were all White, with one man of Iranian descent (Seelye, 2015b). Tsarnaev's lawyers objected to the jury's composition because it was significantly more White and older than the population in Boston, but the trial judge overruled the objection. Tsarnaev was convicted at his trial. After 14 hours of deliberation, the jury sentenced Tsarnaev to death, even though the majority of Boston residents, including the victims, preferred a different outcome. Tsarnaev is one of nine people currently on federal death row (14.75% of the total federal death row) who were sentenced in states without their own death penalty (DPIC, 2016).

The second case which highlights a disconnect between an impacted community and a seated jury is that of Dylann Roof. In 2015, Dylann Roof, a 21-year-old White man, opened fire during a bible study group at the historic Emanuel African Methodist Episcopal Church in Charleston, South Carolina (Hersher, 2016). The massacre left nine Black parishioners dead. Roof later claimed that his intention was to start a race war, because he believed that Black people were taking over the world (Rogo, 2016). Both the federal government and the state of South Carolina made the decision to pursue the death penalty against Roof, who was charged with 33 federal hate crimes and the murders. Jury selection for Roof's federal trial resulted in a jury composed of two Black women, eight White women, one Black man, and one White man (Rogo, 2016). This jury was slightly unrepresentative of the county, with an overrepresentation of women (83% women on the jury compared to 52% in Charleston County; US Census Bureau, 2015). Unlike Tsarnaev's jury, the racial demographics were similar to the county, with Black people comprising 25% of the jury compared to 28% of Charleston County.

Although there was a national outcry for Roof to receive the death penalty, the local community was split across racial lines. Only 31% of Black South Carolina residents believed that Roof should be sentenced to death, compared to 64% of White residents (Blinder, 2016; Cope, 2016). Similarly, several Black activists publically opposed the death penalty in Roof's case. The NAACP Legal Defense and Educational Fund announced its opposition of the death penalty for Roof, arguing that the death penalty has "not only failed to serve the Black community well, [but also] has failed to serve any community well," and "[s]upporting the death penalty for Mr. Roof means supporting the use of a punishment that will continue to be inflicted on people who are nothing like him" (Swarns, 2016, para. 11). In fact, many family members of Roof's victims also opposed the federal government's choice to pursue the death penalty (Blinder, 2016). For example, during the trial, the sister-in-law of one of his victims prayed for his soul to be saved, testifying, "If at any point before you are sentenced and you're in prison and you want me to come and pray with you, I will do that" ("Charleston Church Shooting," 2017, para. 11).

These perspectives do not necessarily suggest that the Charleston community felt empathy for Roof himself but rather that empathy can exist for capital defendants in general. The sentiment from those speaking out against capital punishment for Roof was that the death penalty is cruel and unusual, no matter who the defendant is. Black South Carolinians were not only less in favor of the death penalty for Roof, but they also were more distrustful of the state's use of force and of the criminal justice system as a whole (Cope, 2016). Ta-Nehisi Coates (2016), a national correspondent for *The Atlantic* who publically criticized the government for seeking the death penalty against Roof, wrote that "killing Roof, like the business of the capital punishment itself, ensures that innocent people will be executed" (para. 6). The death-qualification process likely eliminates all potential jurors who voice similar beliefs, including distrust of the government's use of force or concern that the death penalty leads to execution of innocent people. Furthermore, the death-qualification process is designed to eliminate those potential jurors whose general sense of empathy toward capital defendants causes them to feel unable to enforce the death penalty. Removing those potential jurors creates a more punitive jury as a whole, as the evidence suggests (see prior discussion regarding death qualification). Therefore, even though the death-qualification process in Roof's case did not lead to a jury that was composed disproportionately of Whites and men as research would lead us to expect, the jury was still likely to be more death prone than the community as a whole. In fact, despite opposition from the community impacted by Roof's crimes, the jury recommended that Roof be sentenced to death after only a three-hour deliberation (Blinder & Sack, 2017).

## The Expanding Role of the Capital Jury

While support for the death penalty is declining, along with the ability to seat a jury that is representative of its community, the US Supreme Court has maintained the importance of the jury in capital and other criminal cases "to guard against a spirit of oppression and tyranny on the part of rulers" (*Apprendi v. New Jersey*, 2000, p. 477). The Court has noted that for centuries, "trial by jury has been understood to require that the truth of every accusation . . . should afterwards be confirmed by the unanimous suffrage of twelve of the defendant's equals and neighbours" (*Apprendi v. New Jersey*, 2000, p. 477, citing Blackstone, 1769, p. 343).

Recent US Supreme Court decisions emphasize that the capital jury must play an integral role in the enforcement of the death penalty for the punishment to remain constitutional. For example, in *Ring v. Arizona* (2002), the Court held that the jury must unanimously find the factors that make a defendant eligible for the death penalty; this decision means that judges cannot have singular responsibility of decision-making in a capital jury trial. Although this decision showed a commitment to the capital jury, the Court did not reach the question of whether a jury must make the *final* sentencing decision. Thus the decision left open the constitutionality of hybrid sentencing models. In a hybrid sentencing scheme, juries typically make a recommended sentence which the judge can overturn. Therefore, the judge is making the final decision, albeit after input from the jury. Following *Ring*, several states changed their capital statutes to give juries the binding decision. Three states with active capital punishment systems, however, retained their hybrid schemes: Delaware, Florida, and Alabama. In all other states that actively use capital punishment, juries have the exclusive power to decide whether a defendant should be executed.

There are several reasons why a state may want a judge to have the ultimate power to decide whether a defendant should receive the death penalty. Judges are seen as both less likely to be swayed by emotion and more likely to be strict (Shapiro, 2004). For example, Delaware made the change to a hybrid sentencing model after a jury refused to sentence a high-profile defendant to death, leading to public outcry (Hans et al., 2015). Other research, however, suggests that judges and juries tend to make similar decisions and rely upon similar information when making those decisions (Guthrie, Rachlinski, & Wistrich, 2001, 2007), and what differences that do exist may fall apart once a jury has gone through death qualification (Ellsworth et al., 1984).

Judges appear to be more prone than juries to decide that defendants deserve to die. A study by the authors and others that examined the death penalty in Delaware found that when judges as opposed to juries made the ultimate decision, capital cases were significantly more likely to result in the death penalty (Hans et al., 2015). These Delaware judges were almost all White men, but men and women judges did not significantly differ in death sentencing rates. There were not enough non-White judges for a statistical comparison, however. In Alabama, judges enforced the death penalty when the jury had recommended a life sentence in 95 cases, but judges gave a life sentence when the jury recommended death in only 9 cases (*Woodward v. Alabama*, 2013). In the 1980s, cases in Florida showed the same asymmetric pattern, with 89 judicial overrides of life sentence recommendations and no judicial overrides of death sentence recommendations. However, there have been no judicial overrides of life-sentence recommendations in Florida since 1999 (*Woodward v. Alabama*, 2013).

In 2013, the Supreme Court denied a petition for certiorari asking whether the hybrid sentencing model used in Alabama was constitutional (*Woodward v. Alabama*, 2013). In a passionate dissent, Justice Sotomayor questioned whether judge sentencing in capital trials was constitutional, given the unusual usage of this method, and whether, given this power, the judge oversteps the Sixth Amendment requirement that juries find the facts that make a defendant eligible for the death penalty (*Woodward v. Alabama*, 2013; see also Hans et al., 2015).

The Supreme Court scrutinized hybrid sentencing again three years later in *Hurst v. Florida* (2016). Writing for the majority this time, Justice Sotomayor held that Florida's hybrid scheme, in which the jury offers an advisory sentence, violated the right to a trial by jury, stating "[a] jury's mere recommendation is not enough" (p. 619). Following *Hurst*, the Florida Supreme Court noted in order for a Florida judge to sentence a defendant to death, first juries must find all the facts that make a defendant eligible for a death sentence and they must unanimously recommend the death sentence (*Hurst v. State*, 2016). The Delaware Supreme Court held that Delaware's hybrid sentencing model was unconstitutional, which has left the state without a way to impose the death penalty (*Rauf v. State*, 2016; Reyes, 2016). Following these judicial decisions, the Alabama legislature passed and the governor signed a bill eliminating its hybrid approach to the death penalty (Faulk, 2017). Now, Alabama juries will have the last word on whether the defendant will be sentenced to death. However, just 10 of 12 jurors must agree to recommend death in Alabama, in contrast to the unanimity requirement in other states. Whether a future Court decision will find that capital juries must be unanimous in recommending a death sentence is unclear. But what is certain is that capital juries must decide that a defendant is eligible for a death sentence, and they play an important role in deciding whether a defendant should receive the death penalty or not. Given that public support for capital punishment is declining, however, it is increasingly likely that death sentences will be handed down by juries that do not represent the community at large.

## Conclusion

With support for the death penalty reaching historic lows, the difference between a death-qualified jury and the community is likely to be especially pronounced. Not only will a death-qualified jury be qualitatively different in the representation of characteristics such as political beliefs, race, gender, religion, and ability to empathize with the defendant, but it will also over-represent the community's support for capital punishment. Thus the death-qualified jury is unlikely to be able to fully introduce the conscience of the community into the criminal justice system and will be more likely to convict the defendant and impose a death sentence. At the very least, death qualification calls into question the legitimacy of the federal capital jury when the jurors are drawn from a state that does not support capital punishment. In these situations, it is unlikely that the capital jury will represent the community's feelings about the death penalty, as seen during the Tsarnaev trial. Future research should explore the effect of localized support for capital punishment on death-qualification procedures. How do counties that actively use capital punishment differ in public support for capital punishment from the surrounding counties and the state as a whole? How does community support for capital punishment change after legislatures remove the option of capital punishment?

Another important area for future research is the influence of race and gender on empathy in capital jury decision-making. More research examining when jurors empathize with defendants and when they empathize with victims could help us better understand juror decision-making. This research could further examine the role that race and gender play in the effects of victim impact evidence or certain jury instructions (e.g., asking jurors to be objective and focus only on the facts), which would inform policy decisions to allow or prohibit these practices, especially in capital jury trials.

The death-qualification research generated by *Witherspoon v. Illinois* (1968) has shown that the death-qualification process skews the composition of the capital jury in a way that is disloyal to the country's current relationship with the death penalty. With public support of capital punishment reaching lows not seen since the time of *Witherspoon* and the Supreme Court placing added importance on the role of the jury in capital cases, one might extrapolate that the capital jury could play an important role in further reducing or even eliminating the use of the death penalty. It is unlikely, however, that growing national anti-death penalty sentiment will reduce death penalty implementation, given that death-qualification proceedings produce capital juries who are unrepresentative of the population (i.e., atypically pro-death penalty). Diminishing national support for the death penalty puts societal sentiment at odds with current law and policy. As Justice Douglas argued in *Witherspoon*, "why should not an accused have the benefit of that controlling principle of mercy in the community?" (p. 528). If the capital jury does not speak for the people, the purpose of the criminal jury is lost.

## References

Abramson, J. (2015, January 7). Room for debate: When a local jury won't do. *The New York Times*. Retrieved from http://www.nytimes.com/roomfordebate/2015/01/07/when-a-local-jury-wont-do?nl=opinion&emc=edit_ty_20150108

Allen, M., Mabry, E., & McKelton, D. M. (1998). Impact of juror attitudes about the death penalty on juror evaluations of guilt and punishment: A meta-analysis. *Law and Human Behavior, 22*, 715–731. doi:10.1023/A:1025763008533

Apprendi v. New Jersey, 530 U.S. 466 (2000).

Archer, R. L., Foushee, H. C., Davis, M. H., & Aderman, D. (1979). Emotional empathy in a courtroom simulation: A person-situation interaction. *Journal of Applied Social Psychology, 9*, 275–291. doi:10.1111/j.1559-1816.1979.tb02711.x

Ballew v. Georgia, 435 U.S. 223, 98 S. Ct. 1029, 55 L. Ed. 2d 234 (1978).

Baumgartner, F. R. (2010). The geography of the death penalty. Death Penalty Info. Retrieved from http://www.deathpenaltyinfo.org/documents/Baumgartner-geography-of-capital-punishment-oct-17-2010.pdf

Blackstone, W. (1769). *Commentaries on the laws of England*. Oxford: Clarendon Press.

Blinder, A. (2016, November 26). U.S. seeks death for Charleston shooting suspect. Victims' families prefer mercy. *The New York Times*. Retrieved from https://nyti.ms/2k1sgkJ

Blinder, A., & Sack, K. (2017, January 10). Dylann Roof is sentenced to death in Charleston church massacre. *The New York Times*. Retrieved from https://nyti.ms/2jF0s8q

Blume, J. H., & Vann, L. S. (2016). Forty years of death: The past, present, and future of the death penalty in South Carolina (still arbitrary after all these years). *Duke Journal of Constitutional Law & Public Policy, 11*, 183–254.

Boeri, D., & Sobel, Z. (2015, March 3). Judge's quest to find a "fair and impartial" Tsarnaev jury in Boston finally comes to a close. *WBUR News*. Retrieved from http://www.wbur.org/news/2015/03/03/tsarnaev-jury-boston-judge-otoole

Carroll, J. E. (2014). Nullification as law. *The Georgia Law Journal, 102*, 579–635.

Charleston church shooting: Angry forgiving families confront Dylann Roof at sentencing hearing. (2017, January 11). *Chicago Tribune*. Retrieved from http://www.chicagotribune.com/news/nationworld/ct-dylann-roof-death-sentence-20170111-story.html

Coates, T. (2016, May 26). Killing Dylann Roof. *The Atlantic*. Retrieved from http://www.theatlantic.com/politics/archive/2016/05/dylann-roof-death-penalty/484274/?utm_source=atlfb

Cope, C. (2016, June 11). Most SC blacks say Dylann Roof should get life without parole. *The State*. Retrieved from http://www.thestate.com/news/politics-government/politics-columns-blogs/the-buzz/article83131927.html

Cowan, C. L., Thompson, W. C., & Ellsworth, P. C. (1984). The effects of death qualification on jurors' predisposition to convict and the quality of deliberation. *Law and Human Behavior, 8*, 53–79. doi:10.1007/BF01044351

Death Penalty Information Center. (2018a). *Federal death penalty*. Retrieved from http://www.deathpenaltyinfo.org/federal-death-penalty

Death Penalty Information Center. (2018b). *National statistics on the death penalty and race*. Retrieved from http://www.deathpenaltyinfo.org/race-death-row-inmates-executed-1976?scid=5&did=184#racestat

Death Penalty Information Center. (2018c). The death penalty in 2017: Year end report. Retrieved from http://www.deathpenaltyinfo.org/YearEnd2017

DiCamillo, M. (2016). *Californians sharply divided about what to do with the state's death penalty law* (The Field Poll Release No. 2528). Retrieved from https://www.scribd.com/document/295638776/Field-Poll-californians-sharply-divided-about-what-to-do-with-the-state-s-death-penalty-law

Eisenberg, A. M. (2017). Removal of women and African-Americans in jury selection in South Carolina capital cases, 1997–2012. *Northeastern University Law Journal, 9*, 299–345.

Eisenberg, A. M., Hritz, A. C., Royer, C. E., & Blume, J. H. (2017). If it walks like systematic exclusion and quacks like systematic exclusion: Follow-up essay on removal of women and African-Americans in jury selection in South Carolina capital cases, 1997–2014. *South Carolina Law Review, 68*, 373–390.

Ellis, L., & Diamond, S. S. (2003). Race, diversity, and jury composition: Battering and bolstering legitimacy. *Chicago-Kent Law Review, 78*, 1033–1058.

Ellsworth, P. C., Bukaty, R. M., Cowan, C. L., & Thompson, W. C. (1984). The death-qualified jury and the defense of insanity. *Law and Human Behavior, 8*, 81–93. doi:10.1007/BF01044352

Faulk, L. (2017, April 11). Alabama Gov. Kay Ivey signs bill: Judges can no longer override juries in death penalty cases. *AL.com*. Retrieved from http://www.al.com/news/birmingham/index.ssf/2017/04/post_317.html

Fitzgerald, R., & Ellsworth, P. C. (1984). Due process vs. crime control: Death qualification and jury attitudes. *Law and Human Behavior, 8*, 31–51. doi:10.1007/BF01044350

Gallup (n.d.). *Death penalty*. Retrieved from http://www.gallup.com/poll/1606/death-penalty.aspx

Glossip v. Gross, 135 S. Ct. 2726 (2015).

Gross, S. R. (1984). Determining the neutrality of death-qualified juries: Judicial appraisal of empirical data. *Law and Human Behavior, 8*, 7–30. doi:10.1007/BF01044349

Gross, S. R. (1998). Update: American public opinion on the death penalty—It's getting personal. *Cornell Law Review, 83*, 1448–1475.

Guthrie, C., Rachlinski, J. J., & Wistrich, A. J. (2001). Inside the judicial mind. *Cornell Law Review, 86*, 777–830.

Guthrie, C., Rachlinski, J. J., & Wistrich, A. J. (2007). Blinking on the bench: How judges decide cases. *Cornell Law Review, 93*, 1–44.

Haegerich, T. M., & Bottoms, B. L. (2000). Empathy and jurors' decisions in patricide trials involving child sexual assault allegations. *Law and Human Behavior, 24*, 421–448. doi:10.1023/A:1005592213294

Haney, C. (1984a). Editor's introduction. Special issue: Death qualification. *Law and Human Behavior, 8*, 1–6. doi:10.1007/BF01044348

Haney, C. (1984b). On the selection of capital juries: The biasing effects of the death-qualification process. *Law and Human Behavior, 8*, 121–132. doi:10.1007/BF01044355

Haney, C. (2005). *Death by design: Capital punishment as social psychological system*. New York: Oxford University Press.

Hans, V. P., Blume, J. H., Eisenberg, T., Hritz, A. C., Johnson, S. L., Royer, C. E., & Wells, M. T. (2015). The death penalty: Should the judge or the jury decide who dies? *Journal of Empirical Legal Studies, 12*, 70–99. doi:10.1111/jels.12065

Hans, V. P., & Vidmar, N. (1986). *Judging the jury*. New York: Plenum.

Hersher, R. (2016, November 7). Jury selection postponed in trial of church shooting suspect Dylann Roof. *NPR*. Retrieved from http://www.npr.org/sections/thetwo-way/2016/11/07/501001947/jury-selection-postponed-in-trial-of-church-shooting-suspect-dylann-roof

Hurst v. Florida, 136 S. Ct. 616 (2016).

Hurst v. State, 202 So. 3d 40 (Fla. 2016).

Johnson, J. D., Simmons, C. H., Jordan, A., MacLean, L., Taddei, J., Thomas, D., . . . Reed, W. (2002). Rodney King and O.J. revisited: The impact of race and defendant empathy induction on judicial decisions. *Journal of Applied Psychology, 32*, 1208–1223. doi:10.1111/j.1559-1816.2002.tb01432.x

Jones, J. M. (2016, October 25). U.S. death penalty support at 60%. *Gallup*. Retrieved from http://www.gallup.com/poll/196676/death-penalty-support.aspx?g_source=Death%20penalty&g_medium=search&g_campaign=tiles

Liebman, J. S., & Clarke, P. (2011). Minority practice, majority's burden: The death penalty today. *Ohio State Journal of Criminal Law, 9*, 255–351.

Lynch, M., & Haney, C. (2011). Mapping the racial bias of the White male capital juror: Jury composition and the "empathetic divide." *Law & Society Review, 45*, 69–102. doi:10.1111/j.1540-5893.2011.00428.x

Lynch, M., & Haney, C. (2015). Emotion, authority, and death: (Raced) negotiations in mock capital jury deliberations. *Law & Social Inquiry, 40*, 377–405. doi:10.1111/ lsi.12099

McCleskey v. Kemp, 481 U.S. 279 (1987).

McKeever, R. (2015). Vicarious experience: Experimentally testing the effects of empathy for media characters with severe depression and the intervening role of perceived similarity. *Health Communications, 30*, 1122–1134. doi:10.1080/10410236.2014.921969

National Conference of State Legislatures. (2017, February 2). *States and capital punishment*. Retrieved from http://www.ncsl.org/research/civil-and-criminal-justice/death-penalty.aspx

Oliphant, B. (2016, September 29). *Support for death penalty lowest in more than four decades*. Pew Research Center. Retrieved from http://www.pewresearch.org/fact-tank/2016/09/29/support-for-death-penalty-lowest-in-more-than-four-decades/

Plumm, K. M., & Terrance, C.A. (2009). Battered women who kill: The impact of expert testimony and empathy induction in the courtroom. *Violence Against Women, 15*, 186–205. doi:10.1177/1077801208329145

Rauf v. State, 145 A.3d 430 Del. (2016).

Ring v. Arizona, 536 U.S. 584 (2002).

Reyes, J. M. (2016, August 2). Top court: Delaware's death penalty law unconstitutional. *Delaware Online*. Retrieved from http://www.delawareonline.com/story/news/local/2016/08/02/court-delawares-death-penalty-law-unconstitutional/87963012/

Rogo, P. (2016, December 8). Dylann Roof jury selection revealed as trial begins. *Essence*. Retrieved from http://www.essence.com/news/dylan-roof-jury-selection-revealed-death-penalty-trial

Royer, C. E. (2017). Legislative intent and failed attempts: Why lawmakers should codify jury nullification. *Cornell Law Review, 102*, 1399–1428.

Royer, C. E., Hritz, A. C., Hans, V. P., Eisenberg, T., Wells, M. T., Blume, J. H., & Johnson, S. L. (2014). Victim gender and the death penalty. *University of Missouri-Kansas City Law Review, 82*, 429–464.

Sarat, A. (2016, November 14). A comeback for the death penalty? *CNN Opinion*. Retrieved from http://www.cnn.com/2016/11/14/opinions/comeback-for-death-penalty-opinion-sarat/

Seelye, K. Q. (2015a, May 15). Dzhokhar Tsarnaev given death penalty in Boston marathon bombing. *The New York Times*. Retrieved from https://nyti.ms/2otWpuB

Seelye, K. Q. (2015b, March 3). Jurors chosen for Dzhokhar Tsarnaev's trial in Boston marathon bombings. *The New York Times*. Retrieved from https://nyti.ms/2sivunw

Seelye, K. Q. (2015c, March 23). Most Boston residents prefer life term over death penalty in marathon case, poll shows. *The New York Times*. Retrieved from https://nyti.ms/2rjWXYL

Shapiro, M. R. (2004). Reevaluating the role of the jury in capital sentencing after *Ring v. Arizona. New York University Law Review, 59*, 633–666.

Smith, R. J. (2012). The geography of the death penalty and its ramifications. *Boston University Law Review, 92*, 227–289.

Summers, A., Hayward, R. D., & Miller, M. K. (2010). Death qualification as systematic exclusion of jurors with certain religious and other characteristics. *Journal of Applied Social Psychology, 40*, 3218–3234. doi:10.1111/j.1559-1816.2010.00698.x

Swarns, C. (2016, November 7). Dylann Roof shouldn't get the death penalty. *The New York Times*. Retrieved from https://nyti.ms/2jGZ5TK

Taylor v. Louisiana, 419 U.S. 522 (1975).

Thompson, W. C., Cowan, C. L., Ellsworth, P. C., & Harrington, J. C. (1984). Death penalty attitudes and conviction proneness: The translation of attitudes into verdicts. *Law and Human Behavior, 8*, 95–113. doi:10.1007/BF01044353

U.S. Census Bureau (2015). *QuickFacts: Charleston County, South Carolina*. United States Census. Retrieved from http://www.census.gov/quickfacts/table/PST045215/45019

United States v. Tsarnaev, 13-10200-GAO (Mass. Dist. Ct. 2015) (No. 1178).

Vote Repeal Staff. (2016). *New poll confirms Nebraskans support keeping the death penalty by 2-1 margin*. Retrieved from http://www.voterepeal.com/new-poll-confirms-nebraskans-support-keeping-the-death-penalty-by-2-1-margin/

Witherspoon v. Illinois, 391 U.S. 510 (1968).

Wolff, J. (2015, March 24). Is a little technical knowledge a dangerous thing? Why the Tsarnaev juror questionnaire screened for computer scientists. *Slate*. Retrieved from http://www.slate.com/articles/technology/future_tense/2015/03/tsarnaev_juror_selection_questionnaire_screened_for_computer_scientists.html

Woodward v. Alabama, 571 U.S. 405 (2013).

Yelderman, L. A., Miller, M. K., & Peoples, C. D. (2016). Capital-izing jurors: How death qualification relates to jury composition, jurors' perceptions, and trial outcomes. In B. H. Bornstein & M. K. Miller (Eds.), *Advances in psychology and law* (Vol. 2, pp. 27–54). Cham, Switzerland: Springer International. doi:10.1007/978-3-319-43083-6_2

# 4

## LGBTQ in the Courtroom

### How Sexuality and Gender Identity Impact the Jury System

*Jordan Blair Woods*

Lesbian, gay, bisexual, transgender, and queer (LGBTQ) individuals have recently achieved significant advances in recognition of their rights and legal protections at the federal, state, and local levels. For instance, in *Obergefell v. Hodges* (2015), the US Supreme Court recognized the constitutional right of same-sex couples to marry. Approximately 20 states and the District of Columbia also have antidiscrimination laws that offer protections on the basis of sexual orientation and gender identity in the areas of employment, housing, and public accommodations (Movement Advancement Project, 2017b). In spite of this progress, however, LGBTQ communities still commonly face discrimination and marginalization in vital spheres of everyday life, including employment, housing, public accommodations, and education (Human Rights Watch, 2016; Mallory & Sears, 2015, 2016a, 2016b).

The criminal justice system is another important domain in which LGBTQ people have achieved significant progress, yet still face obstacles that compromise legitimacy and fairness within the system (Mogul, Ritchie, & Whitlock, 2011). The purpose of this chapter is to provide an overview of the relevant challenges linked to sexuality and gender identity in the criminal jury system. As I discuss, there is a dearth of empirical research on LGBTQ people's experiences in criminal courts and, in particular, on how anti-LGBTQ biases can influence jury deliberations and case outcomes. Although there is a need for more empirical research, existing studies describe several ways in which LGBTQ people experience bias and discrimination in criminal courts, whether as jurors, victims, defendants, or witnesses.

### Historical Background

The challenges that LGBTQ people face today in criminal courts are by no means recent phenomena. Rather, as this section briefly discusses, these challenges are connected to at least two major historical factors that have shaped LGBTQ people's treatment in the US criminal justice system over time (Woods, 2017). The first is the long history of criminalizing LGBTQ people for their sexual orientation or gender identity, same-sex sexual conduct, or gender-nonconforming expressions. The second is the tense historical relationship between LGBTQ communities and the psychology and mental health professions.

## LGBTQ Identity as a Criminal Status

Until 1961, every state criminalized sodomy (Eskridge, 2008). Although sodomy laws took different forms, they were disproportionately applied and enforced in ways that targeted LGBTQ people (and in particular lesbians and gay men; Eskridge, 2008). These inequalities facilitated stereotypes and popular images of LGBTQ people as criminals (Chauncey, 1994). Beyond sodomy laws, transgender people were further targeted under local ordinances that prohibited cross-dressing and other gender-nonconforming behaviors (Capers, 2008). These ordinances rested on ideas that transgender and gender-nonconforming people were frauds and threats to public order for violating gender norms (Dunlap, 1979).

The trend to decriminalize sodomy laws began in 1961, mostly as a result of over 20 states adopting the American Law Institute's Model Penal Code in full or in part during the 1970s (Eskridge, 2008; Hunter, 1992). The momentum to decriminalize sodomy laws and their application to LGBTQ people, however, encountered a major setback in 1986 with the US Supreme Court's decision in *Bowers v. Hardwick* (1986). In *Hardwick*, the Court upheld the constitutionality of Georgia's sodomy law. The decision had the broader consequence of temporarily halting federal challenges to sodomy laws that then existed in over 20 states (Leslie, 2005). In addition, some state courts relied on the *Hardwick* decision to uphold the constitutionality of their own state sodomy statutes (Eskridge, 2008; Leslie, 2005).

Several other states, however, eliminated sodomy laws or the application of these laws to same-sex intimate partners through state legislation and state court decisions between *Hardwick* and *Lawrence v. Texas* (2003)—the next major US Supreme Court case involving sodomy laws decided in 2003 (Leslie, 2005; NeJaime, 2011). By the time that *Lawrence* reached the Court, only 13 states criminalized sodomy (Carpenter, 2012). The *Lawrence* decision overruled *Hardwick* and invalidated these remaining laws as they applied to private consensual sex between two adults (whether same sex or opposite sex; Strader, 2011).

In spite of *Lawrence*, about a dozen states have not repealed and thus still have criminal sodomy laws on the books that prohibit private consensual nonprocreative sex (Christensen, 2014). Recent cases have been reported of police officers applying these remaining laws against LGBTQ people in discriminatory and constitutionally suspect ways (Christensen, 2014; Hoppe,

2016). These incidents continue to create tension and conflict when LGBTQ people interact with or enter the criminal justice system today.

## LGBTQ Identity as a Mental Illness

In the 1940s, emerging ideas about psychopathy coincided with a growing consensus in the US psychiatric profession that homosexuality was a mental illness (Schmeiser, 2013). Illustrating the influence of this consensus, homosexuality was listed as a mental disorder in the 1952 edition of the American Psychiatric Association's *Diagnostic and Statistical Manual of Mental Disorders* (DSM; Bayer, 1981). At that time, homosexuality was viewed in the profession to encompass both nonheterosexual sexual identities and non-cisgender[1] gender identities (King, 1981).

The dominant view in the psychology and mental health professions that homosexuality and gender nonconformity were mental illnesses paralleled important changes in how LGBTQ people were treated under the law (Woods, 2017). Between the 1940s and early-1970s, over half of the states enacted "sexual psychopath laws," which facilitated the incarceration and involuntary civil commitment of LGBTQ people (D'Emilio, 1998). Some sexual psychopath laws allowed for any person who was charged with a crime and deemed a "sexual psychopath" by a jury to be handed over to the state's department of public health until that person was "cured" of the purported condition (Freedman, 2006). Other laws allowed for the psychiatric commitment of "sexual psychopaths," perhaps indefinitely, regardless of whether their targets were charged with a crime.

As written, sexual psychopath laws could conceivably apply to a variety of sex crimes (e.g., rape, prostitution, child molestation) as well as noncriminal sexual disorders (Freedman, 2006). These laws, however, were disproportionately enforced against LGBTQ people in ways that reinforced stereotypes of them as sexual predators and to such an extent that the phrase "sexual psychopath" became culturally associated with homosexuality (Canaday, 2008; Freedman, 2006). In order to avoid criminal prosecution under existing sodomy laws, many LGBTQ people reluctantly underwent invasive and harmful psychiatric treatments that were directed to change their sexual orientation or gender identity (Bayer, 1981; Stein, 1988).

Homosexuality was removed from the DSM in 1973 (Bayer, 1981). Many states also began to repeal their sexual psychopath laws in the early 1970s (James, Thomas, & Foley, 2008). Both of these legal reforms were associated with declining views among psychology and mental health professionals that homosexuality was a mental illness (Bayer, 1981). Scholars have identified at least two factors which contributed to this shift (Woods, 2017). The first factor was a growing body of psychological research that offered empirical justification to denounce pathological conceptions of homosexuality. The studies of Alfred Kinsey and Evelyn Hooker were especially influential in this regard (Hooker, 1965, 1958, 1957, 1956, 1955; Kinsey, Pomeroy,

& Martin, 1953, 1948). Their research revealed that same-sex sex was more common than the public assumed and concluded that there was no inherent connection between homosexuality and mental illness symptoms (Murray, 2015; Woods, 2017).

The second factor was the rise of lesbian and gay social movements. Early movements in the 1950s prioritized eliminating the stigma of disease attached to homosexuality (Bayer, 1981; D'Emilio, 1998). Organizations—such as the Mattachine Society and the Daughters of Bilitis—provided forums for experts to present research debunking the idea that homosexuality was a mental disease (Bayer, 1981). In the 1960s, many lesbian and gay activists embraced a more radical political strategy, which paralleled other growing counterculture movements at the time (e.g., the Civil Rights Movement, anti-Vietnam war protests; D'Emilio, 1998). Radical activists joined at the American Psychiatric Association's annual convention in 1971 to protest for the removal of homosexuality from the DSM (Bayer, 1981; D'Emilio, 1998). These protests inspired more critical conversations on the profession's stance toward homosexuality, culminating in the removal of homosexuality from the DSM in 1973 (Bayer, 1981).

It is important to acknowledge that these advances helped to reduce the stigma against homosexuality in the psychology and mental health professions, but they did not apply more broadly to gender identity. In 1980, "gender identity disorders" were included in the DSM (Barry, Farrell, Levi, & Vanguri, 2016). Those labels remained in the DSM until 2013, when the American Psychiatric Association changed "gender identity disorders" to "gender dysphoria." This revision was intended to avoid stigmatizing transgender people who sought gender-reaffirming medical care and to better characterize their experiences (American Psychiatric Association, 2013).

Although the relationship between LGBTQ communities and the psychology and mental health professions has improved over time, this tense history still translates into problems for LGBTQ people in the criminal justice system, affecting both their trust in the system and biases that arise when they come into contact with it. Having sketched this historical background, I now turn to discuss the limited available research on LGBTQ fairness in criminal courts today.

## A Survey of Empirical Studies on LGBTQ Fairness in the Courts

Although several scholars have discussed how anti-LGBTQ biases can permeate courts (Boso, 2013; Brower, 2011; Shay, 2014; Young, 2011), only three studies to date have systematically examined the issue. Importantly, each of these studies examines experiences of anti-LGBTQ bias in both criminal and civil cases. This broad scope illustrates a need for greater systematic study of LGBTQ fairness in criminal courts specifically.

In the most recent study, Lambda Legal (2014) conducted a national online survey of 2,376 LGBTQ individuals and people living with HIV about their mistreatment in the courts. Forty-three percent of the eligible respondents had been involved in the court system in the previous five years as an attorney, juror, party to a legal case, or witness. Of those 965 court-involved respondents, 19% reported hearing a judge, attorney, or other court employee make negative comments about their own or another person's sexual orientation or gender identity. Notably, certain subgroups of respondents heard negative comments at higher rates than the overall sample, including respondents with physical or mental disabilities (24%), low-income respondents (28%), respondents of color (30%), transgender and gender-nonconforming respondents (33%), and transgender and gender-nonconforming respondents of color (53%). These findings illustrate the complexities and important role of intersectionality when approaching issues surrounding anti-LGBTQ bias in the courts (Carbado & Moran, 2008).

Moreover, of the 965 court-involved respondents, 16% reported having their own sexual orientation or gender identity raised when it was irrelevant to the case at hand. Eleven percent reported that their sexual orientation or gender identity was disclosed in court against their will. Notably, certain subgroups of respondents also reported these issues at higher rates than the overall sample, including respondents with physical or mental disabilities (25% irrelevant disclosure, 16% "outed" in court against their will), low-income respondents (28% irrelevant disclosure, 20% outed), respondents of color (25% irrelevant disclosure, 14% outed), and transgender and gender-nonconforming respondents (26% irrelevant disclosure, 21% outed).

Trends also emerged in the Lambda Legal study based on respondents' different roles in court. Among the 965 court-involved respondents, 19% were attorneys, 44% were jurors, 61% were parties to a case, and 21% were witnesses (some respondents had multiple contacts with courts in different roles). Of the attorneys, 32% reported hearing discriminatory language about their own or someone else's sexual orientation or gender identity, compared to 12% of the jurors, 22% of the parties, and 28% of the witnesses. Witnesses, however, were the most likely role group to report having their sexual orientation or gender identity raised when it was irrelevant to the case (30%), compared to attorneys (13%), jurors (7%), and parties (24%).

Prior to the Lambda Legal study, only two studies had systematically examined the experiences of LGBTQ individuals in US courts. Both studies were released in 2001 and focused on sexual orientation bias only. The first study examined sexual orientation fairness in California state courts (Judicial Council of California, 2001). The California study consisted of a survey of two groups of participants: (a) 1,225 lesbian and gay court users recruited with the help of national and local lesbian and gay organizations and (b) 1,525 California court employees (both heterosexual and nonheterosexual). The survey asked lesbian and gay court users about their most recent contact with California state courts, as well as one other significant contact since 1990 in which sexual orientation became an issue. One limitation of the study was that of the 1,525 court employee respondents, only 64 identified as lesbian, gay, or bisexual.

Of the lesbian and gay court-user respondents, almost half believed that the courts were not providing for the fair treatment of lesbians or gay men, and 56% experienced or observed a negative comment or action toward lesbians or gays. Of the court-user respondents who had a contact with the courts in which sexual orientation became an issue, 56% did not want to state their sexual orientation, 29% believed that someone else stated their sexual orientation without their approval, and 25% felt forced to state their sexual orientation against their will. Of importance, 38% felt threatened in the courtroom setting because of their sexual orientation.

Of the court-employee respondents, one in five heard derogatory comments or language toward lesbians or gay men in open court, most often · by judges, lawyers, or court employees. In settings other than open court, 32% of the court-employee respondents heard ridicule or jokes, 28% heard negative comments, and 21% heard derogatory comments toward lesbians or gay men. In addition, lesbian and gay court-employee respondents were almost four times more likely to report experiencing negative actions or comments based on sexual orientation compared to heterosexual court-employee respondents.

The second study focused on New Jersey state courts and found similar challenges surrounding sexual orientation bias (New Jersey Supreme Court Task Force on Sexual Orientation Issues, 2001). The New Jersey study consisted of a survey that was publicized through court employee rosters, attorney magazines and bar associations, and lesbian and gay organizations and newspapers. Of the 2,594 respondents, 1,917 identified their sexual orientation (93% reported being heterosexual, 6% lesbian or gay, and <1% bisexual). Most of the respondents who identified their relationship to the court were court employees.

The New Jersey study found that lesbian and gay respondents were almost seven times more likely than heterosexual respondents to report experiences or observations of sexual orientation bias against lesbian or gay litigants or witnesses. Offensive jokes or remarks about lesbians and gays were by far the most common forms of reported bias. Moreover, compared to heterosexual respondents, lesbian and gay respondents were more likely to believe that sexual orientation bias affected the judicial process. In particular, 61% of lesbian and gay respondents who were involved in the litigation process believed that sexual orientation bias affected the outcome in the cases they observed or in which they participated, compared to 6% of heterosexual respondents. Those disparities were consistent across criminal, civil, and family cases. Based on these findings, the task force concluded that sexual orientation bias had the capacity to negatively affect case outcomes, discourage people from using the courts, and undermine public confidence in the judiciary.

Although each of these studies has limitations, they offer a foundation for understanding how anti-LGBTQ bias can affect LGBTQ people who come into contact with the courts as prospective jurors, victims of crime, and criminal defendants. Next, I shift gears to focus on anti-LGBTQ juror bias in these more specific contexts.

## LGBTQ-Related Challenges in Criminal Jury Selection

The Sixth Amendment to the US Constitution guarantees all criminal defendants the right to trial by an "impartial jury" (U.S. Const. amend. VI). The US Supreme Court has interpreted "impartial jury" in two ways: first, as one composed of jurors who can "conscientiously and properly" apply the law to the facts of the case (*Lockhart v. McCree*, 1986, p. 184) and, second, as a jury that is drawn from a venire that constitutes a fair cross section of the community (*Taylor v. Louisiana*, 1975).

A defendant's constitutional right to trial by an impartial jury is safeguarded by the process of "voir dire" (Babcock, 1975). During voir dire, prosecutors and defense attorneys can question prospective jurors and object to them serving on the jury. This section discusses three challenges surrounding voir dire and the fair treatment of LGBTQ people in criminal courts: (a) whether LGBTQ topics are relevant when questioning prospective jurors, (b) the validity of considering a prospective juror's sexual orientation or gender identity during jury selection, and (c) best practices to identify and combat prospective jurors' anti-LGBTQ biases.

### Questioning Prospective Jurors on LGBTQ Topics

There are several situations in which prosecutors or defense attorneys might wish to ask prospective jurors about their views on LGBTQ issues or attitudes toward LGBTQ people. One situation is when LGBTQ issues are centrally related to the criminal charges in a case (Young, 2011). For instance, if a case involves an anti-LGBTQ hate crime, then the prosecution may wish to ask prospective jurors about LGBTQ-related topics in order to expose possible biases against the victim. Another situation is when LGBTQ issues are not centrally related to the criminal charges but the evidence or questioning of the parties or witnesses could reveal that the victim, the defendant, or a witness identifies as LGBTQ (Shay, 2014). In these situations, criminal attorneys may wish to question prospective jurors about LGBTQ-related topics in order to prevent anti-LGBTQ bias from affecting how jurors perceive evidence or testimony, jury deliberations, or the verdict.

In addition, anti-LGBTQ bias in jury selection is relevant when LGBTQ people appear as prospective jurors (for discussion of discriminatory jury selection practices, see also Chapter 2 of this volume). In criminal cases involving LGBTQ defendants, the question of whether LGBTQ individuals should be part of, or excused from, a criminal jury goes to the very heart of what it means to have a trial by an impartial jury of one's peers. As discussed in the next section, in most jurisdictions there are no legal restrictions against objecting to prospective jurors serving on a jury based on their LGBTQ identity.

### Legal Issues Surrounding LGBTQ Identity and Jury Selection

There are two types of challenges that are available to prosecutors and defense attorneys during voir dire, as noted in Chapter 2. The first level of screening jurors involves challenges "for cause." At this stage, prospective jurors are questioned and excused if a judge concludes that they are unqualified to serve on the jury, do not have the capacity to evaluate trial testimony, or will not apply the law fairly and impartially (Lee, 2015). Although the number of challenges for cause is unlimited in a given case, those challenges can only be exercised on these limited grounds.

Some courts have concluded that prosecutors and defense attorneys may challenge, and that judges may excuse, prospective jurors for cause when anti-LGBTQ biases would interfere with their ability to weigh evidence fairly and impartially (Shay, 2014). Other courts have upheld a judge's decision to reject challenges for cause when the judge concluded that a prospective juror would be able to put their anti-LGBTQ attitudes aside and weigh the evidence fairly and impartially (Young, 2011). Those decisions usually involve practices of "rehabilitative questioning," during which judges simply ask prospective jurors who have expressed anti-LGBTQ attitudes whether they could be impartial if the case involved an LGBTQ victim, defendant, or witness (Shay, 2014). As long as jurors indicate that they can remain impartial and the judge is persuaded, then they can be selected for the jury, although it remains unclear whether jurors can actually remain impartial in those cases.

The second level of screening jurors involves peremptory challenges. Generally, there is a set number of peremptory challenges that prosecutors and defense attorneys may use in a given case. Unlike challenges for cause, peremptory challenges require no justification (Miller, 2014). For this reason, concerns about discriminatory uses of peremptory challenges in both LGBTQ and non-LGBTQ contexts have been a long-standing issue in litigation and scholarship (Shay, 2014; Young, 2011; see also Chapter 2 in this volume).

As reviewed by O'Brien and Grosso in Chapter 2, in *Batson v. Kentucky* (1986), the US Supreme Court held that a peremptory challenge is unconstitutional if it is used to exclude a juror on the basis of race. In *J.E.B. v. Alabama ex rel. T.B.* (1994), the Court extended *Batson*'s holding to invalidate peremptory challenges on the basis of gender. To date, the Court has not yet addressed whether *Batson* also applies to prohibit peremptory challenges on the basis of a prospective juror's sexual orientation or gender identity. In

2014, however, the US Court of Appeals for the Ninth Circuit became the first federal appellate court to extend *Batson* to prohibit peremptory challenges on the basis of sexual orientation (*SmithKline Beecham Corporation v. Abbott Laboratories*, 2014). Importantly, the Ninth Circuit's holding only applies to federal criminal and civil cases in the nine states within its jurisdiction. A few state courts and four state legislatures (California, Colorado, Minnesota, and Oregon) have also barred peremptory challenges on the basis of sexual orientation (Maddera, 2016). In March 2017, members of both the US Senate and the House of Representatives reintroduced a federal bill that would prohibit excluding individuals from serving on federal juries on the basis of their sexual orientation or gender identity (LGBT Bar, 2017). Nonetheless, these challenges remain valid in most federal and state courts today (Maddera, 2016; Shay, 2014).

## Identifying and Combating Prospective Jurors' Anti-LGBTQ Biases

There is a dearth of empirical research on how anti-LGBTQ biases may shape jury selection. Nonetheless, questioning prospective jurors on LGBTQ topics can pose many challenges. For instance, asking prospective jurors about their sexuality or gender identity may trigger privacy concerns, especially because it is not always obvious whether a juror identifies as LGBTQ (Lynd, 1998; Shay, 2014). In some cases, questioning jurors on LGBTQ topics may "out" a victim, defendant, or witness against his or her will (Young, 2011). Such questioning may also make prospective LGBTQ or LGBTQ-friendly jurors vulnerable to peremptory challenges (Overland, 2009; Young, 2011).

Other challenges stem from the fact that anti-LGBTQ juror bias can manifest in different ways (Stawiski, Dykema-Engblade, & Tindale, 2012). On this issue, Lee (2008) created a three-category typology of jurors who hold sexual orientation bias, which can also apply to gender identity bias. In Category 1 ("explicit homophobes"), jurors are not shy to voice their disapproval of LGBTQ people and issues during voir dire. In Category 2 ("closet homophobes"), jurors are aware that they hold anti-LGBTQ attitudes but refrain from expressing them in court. In Category 3 ("implicit homophobes"), jurors believe in LGBTQ equality but hold unconscious biases that disadvantage LGBTQ people (for further discussion of jurors' implicit biases, see Chapter 5 of this volume).

Given these different categories, it is unclear which questioning method most effectively identifies and combats prospective jurors' anti-LGBTQ biases. Scholars and practitioners, however, have advanced and applied three different questioning methods. Under the first method, criminal attorneys ask jurors "hard" (or pointed) questions about their feelings toward LGBTQ people and controversial LGBTQ topics. This method responds most to the "explicit homophobes" category in Lee's (2008) typology. To illustrate how this method works, attorneys might ask prospective jurors direct questions about LGBTQ people and controversial LGBTQ topics along the following lines: "What are your feelings about same-sex marriage?"; "Do you believe the hate crimes law should apply to issues regarding sexuality and gender identity?"; and "If I held up a picture of two men kissing, would it make you uncomfortable?" (Shay, 2014, p. 418).

Overland (2009) argues that one major drawback of this first method is that pointed questions may expose LGBTQ-friendly jurors and make them vulnerable to peremptory challenges. He thus recommends a second questioning method, under which criminal attorneys ask jurors "soft" questions about noncontroversial LGBTQ topics, such as, "Would you feel bothered if a gay or lesbian couple moved in next door to you?"; "Do you think employers should be able to refuse to hire someone because of his or her sexual orientation?"; and "Would you feel bothered if you had to work closely with someone who was gay or lesbian?" (see Overland, 2009, p. 3). Based on his own research, Overland estimates that between 10% to 20% of jurors would answer "yes" to these questions.

Given their focus on the "explicit homophobe" category, it is unclear whether either the "hard" or "soft" questioning method helps to identify jurors in the "closet homophobe" or "implicit homophobe" categories of Lee's (2008) typology. The third questioning method, based on Sherrod and Nardi's (1998) research, addresses this issue. Sherrod and Nardi asked a representative sample of over 3,500 adults across 15 states "proxy" questions about their demographic background, lifestyle, and attitudes. Some examples included, "Do you have any close friends who are gay or lesbian?"; "Politically, are you liberal, middle-of-the-road, or conservative?"; "Do you think the world would be a better place if more people followed old-fashioned values?"; "What is your religion?"; and "What is your highest level of education?" (Sherrod & Nardi, 1998, pp. 36–37). In general, the most homophobic potential jurors did not have any close friends who were gay or lesbian, thought the world would be a better place if people followed old-fashioned values, were politically conservative, and attended religious services weekly or tried to attend services every week. Based on their findings, Sherrod and Nardi concluded that a proxy questioning method may help to identify likely homophobic jurors, regardless of whether those jurors have explicit or implicit anti-LGBTQ biases.

Future studies are necessary to evaluate which of these three questioning methods most effectively combats anti-LGBTQ juror biases in general or whether one method is better suited to identify a particular type of anti-LGBTQ biased juror over another. Future research is also needed to clarify the extent to which anti-LGBTQ bias affects juror perceptions of evidence and testimony and whether jury deliberations and case outcomes are fairer when anti-LGBTQ biased jurors are disqualified from serving on criminal juries. Although these important questions surrounding the process of identifying anti-LGBTQ biased jurors remain open, I now turn to evaluate what happens when those jurors are permitted to serve on criminal juries.

## The Gay and Trans "Panic" Defenses

One topic surrounding anti-LGBTQ juror bias that has received a consider-able amount of attention in the literature is the use of gay and trans "panic" defenses (Dressler, 1995; Lee, 2013, 2008; Lee & Kwan, 2014; Strader et al., 2015; Wodda & Panfil, 2015). These defenses allow perpetrators of anti-LGBTQ murders to receive a reduced charge and sentence, or even avoid con-viction altogether, by asking a jury to find that the victim's actual or perceived sexual orientation or gender identity was partially or wholly to blame for the killing (Woods et al., 2016).

The gay and trans panic defenses are rooted in antiquated ideas that ho-mosexuality and gender nonconformity are mental illnesses (Lee, 2013). The term "homosexual panic disorder" was initially coined in the 1920s to de-scribe the mental state of World War I veterans who resisted and feared same-sex desire (Wodda & Panfil, 2015). In the 1960s, defense attorneys began to use gay panic concepts as a defense strategy to claim that their clients who killed LGBTQ victims acted in a state of "panic" after the victims purportedly made unwanted sexual advances (Lee, 2008). According to research from the Williams Institute, a research institute on LGBT law and public policy at UCLA School of Law, the gay and trans panic defenses have appeared in published court opinions in approximately half of the states (Woods et al., 2016). It is difficult, however, to track exactly how often defendants have used, and continue to raise, these defenses because most criminal trials in state courts do not result in published opinions (Bernstein, 2015). Rather, most published opinions are from appellate courts, and defendants are not likely to appeal verdicts when gay or trans panic defenses are successful.

Notably, the gay and trans panic defenses are not freestanding defenses (American Bar Association [ABA], Criminal Justice Section, 2013). Rather, defendants use gay and trans panic concepts to support existing defense theories of provocation, diminished capacity, or self-defense (Lee, 2013). With regard to provocation, defendants argue that the discovery or poten-tial disclosure of the victim's LGBTQ identity reasonably drove them to kill in the heat of passion (ABA, Criminal Justice Section, 2013). For diminished capacity, defendants argue that the discovery or potential disclosure of the victim's LGBTQ identity drove them into a temporary mental disturbance in which they panicked and killed the victim. Finally, with regard to self-defense, defendants argue that the discovery or potential disclosure of a victim's LGBTQ identity caused them to have a reasonable belief that they were in immediate danger of serious bodily harm. All three manifestations of the gay and trans panic defenses enable jurors to rely on their anti-LGBTQ beliefs when evaluating evidence and deciding case outcomes.

Historically, courts have taken a leading role in curbing the use of gay and trans panic defenses. In 2006, however, California enacted the Gwen Araujo Justice for Victims Act, which was the first piece of state legislation to address the "panic" defenses (Wodda & Panfil, 2015). This groundbreaking law gave judges in California state courts the authority to instruct jurors that anti-LGBTQ bias should not affect the jury's deliberations or verdict.

The California law was named after Gwen Araujo, whose brutal murder at the age of 17 helped to bring public attention to anti-transgender violence and the panic defenses. Araujo's killing involved four men at a house party in October 2002 (Wodda & Panfil, 2015). Araujo had been sexually intimate with two of the men, and after she refused to have vaginal intercourse, the men became suspicious that Araujo's birth sex was male. After learning that this was the case, the two men and two of their friends severely beat and strangled Araujo, hit her over the head with a can and a shovel, tied her wrists and ankles, wrapped her in a bedsheet, and dropped her body off at a campground 100 miles away.

The four men were charged with Araujo's murder (*People v. Merel*, 2009). One of the men pleaded guilty to a lesser charge of voluntary manslaughter in exchange for his testimony against the other defendants. The other three defendants were charged with first-degree murder and committing a hate crime. At trial, two of the defendants raised the trans panic defense, arguing that they killed Araujo in the heat of passion after discovering they had been sexually intimate with another "man." Illustrating the success of this form of provocation defense, the jury was unable to reach a verdict on whether the defendants were guilty of first-degree or second-degree murder, resulting in a mistrial. At the retrial, the jury appeared to accept the trans panic defense, convicting two of the defendants on a lesser charge of second-degree murder and acquitting them of the hate crime. The jury was unable to reach a verdict as to the third defendant, who later pleaded guilty to the lesser charge of voluntary manslaughter.

In light of unjust outcomes like the Araujo case, some recent reforms have been introduced to curb the gay and trans panic defenses. In 2013, the ABA approved a resolution calling for federal, state, local, and tribal governments to eliminate the gay and trans panic defenses through legislation (ABA, Criminal Justice Section, 2013). In 2014, California became the first state to do so by amending the definition of voluntary manslaughter under the California Penal Code (Woods et al., 2016). Specifically, as a result of that amendment, for the purpose of determining sudden quarrel or heat of passion in California, provocation is not objectively reasonable if it "resulted from the discovery of, knowledge about, or potential disclosure of the victim's actual or perceived gender, gender identity, gender expression, or sexual orientation" (California Penal Code Section 192[f][1]). Since then, similar legislation has been enacted in Illinois and advocated for or introduced in several other states (Dart, 2018). The gay and trans panic defenses, however, remain valid in most jurisdictions today.

Only a few empirical studies have examined how gay and trans panic concepts affect jury decision-making (Plumm, Terrance, Henderson, & Ellingson, 2010; Ragatz & Russell, 2010; Salerno et al., 2015). In one study, Ragatz and Russell examined the influence of a defendant's sex and sexual orientation, as well as mock jurors' sex, on juror decision-making in cases involving heat-of-passion killings. The researchers asked an online sample of over 450 participants to evaluate a homicide scenario which involved a defendant killing his or her partner after learning that the partner had an affair. The scenario was then manipulated based on the defendant's sex and sexual orientation. Generally, participants rated straight defendants higher in terms of satisfying the legal elements of the provocation defense or mitigating circumstances compared to nonheterosexual defendants. Participants also rated lesbian defendants lowest of any defendant group to satisfy the legal elements of the provocation defense or mitigating circumstances. Based on their findings, Ragatz and Russell concluded that jurors may be more inclined to find that straight defendants qualify for a lesser criminal charge in heat-of-passion killings compared to gay or lesbian defendants.

Salerno et al.'s (2015) more recent study evaluated the connection between gay panic provocation defenses and jurors' political orientation. The study involved a multiethnic sample of 74 men and women who were eligible for jury service. The researchers randomly assigned participants to evaluate either a gay panic scenario that involved a victim's same-sex sexual advance or a provocation scenario that did not have gay panic-related facts. Conservative participants were significantly less punitive when the defendant claimed to have acted out of gay panic compared to the non-gay-panic scenario. Facts involving gay panic, however, did not sway liberal jurors. The researchers explained these differences in terms of the participants' moral outrage. They argued that conservative jurors were less morally outraged toward a defendant who killed in response to a same-sex sexual advance than in response to reasons that did not involve gay panic. Conversely, the same-sex sexual advance did not reduce liberal jurors' moral outrage toward that defendant.

Given their potential to shape juror decision-making and unjust outcomes, scholars have advanced different ideas to combat gay and trans panic concepts in court. Lee (2008) offers a more critical take on eliminating the defenses entirely. While acknowledging that gay and trans panic defenses are problematic, Lee argues that if the defenses were eliminated, then defense attorneys would find subtler ways to get the same biased ideas across to the jury. Those subtler arguments may be more difficult to counter in court than explicitly homophobic or transphobic ideas and remarks. In Lee's (2013) view, the better prosecutorial strategy is to ferret out people who hold anti-LGBTQ biases during jury selection and then use direct language and exercises during opening and closing arguments to confront gay and trans panic arguments.

In addition, Strader and colleagues (2015) recently proposed a "shield" rule that would limit evidence used in trials where defendants assert gay or trans panic defenses. The shield rule would specifically bar evidence relating to (a) the victim's sexual conduct beyond the case, (b) the victim's sexual orientation or gender identity for the purpose of showing that it incited or related to the crime, and (c) reputation or opinion evidence offered to show that the victim's other sexual conduct or LGBTQ identity incited or related to the killing. The authors argue that one possible benefit of this proposed shield rule is its broad applicability to a range of criminal cases. The rule could not only apply in murder cases where defendants raise gay or trans panic defenses but also in cases where defendants use gay or trans panic concepts to support defenses for other crimes (e.g., assault or battery). Along these lines, I now shift focus to evaluate how anti-LGBTQ bias can affect jury decision-making in criminal contexts that do not necessarily involve panic defenses or the killing of LGBTQ victims.

## Anti-LGBTQ Juror Bias in Other Criminal Contexts

This section discusses anti-LGBTQ juror bias in three other specific criminal contexts: (a) hate crimes, (b) intimate partner violence (IPV), and (c) sexual offenses. The limited available studies describe how anti-LGBTQ juror bias can pose challenges for both LGBTQ victims and defendants in cases involving these crimes.

### Hate Crimes

A long line of research documents how LGBTQ people have historically suffered, and are still victims of, hate-motivated violence at disproportionately high rates (Grant, Mottet, & Tanis, 2011; Herek, 2009; Stotzer, 2009). As of May 2018, only 17 states and the District of Columbia have a hate crime law that includes both sexual orientation and gender identity, and 13 states have a hate crime law that covers only sexual orientation (Movement Advancement Project, 2017a). According to recent official crime data, over 1,300 people reported being victims of anti-LGBTQ hate crime to law enforcement in 2016 (US Department of Justice, 2017). This figure accounted for almost 20% of all hate crimes reported to the FBI that year. These official statistics likely underestimate the true extent of the problem because many LGBTQ victims do not report hate crimes to the police due to their distrust of law enforcement and the criminal justice system more generally (Rubenstein, 2004; Woods, 2008). This distrust is related to the historical mistreatment of LGBTQ identity under the criminal law and in the psychology and mental health professions, as discussed previously.

The few studies on jury decision-making in anti-LGBTQ hate crime cases focus on sexual orientation only and describe how sexual orientation bias can influence juror perceptions of victim blame (Cramer, Wakeman, Chandler, Mohr, & Griffin, 2013; Plumm et al., 2010). For instance, Plumm and colleagues asked mock jurors to evaluate an anti-gay hate crime scenario, which varied based on the location of the crime (specifically, whether the incident took place at a local or a gay bar) and whether the crime involved "provocation" (specifically, whether the victim put his arm around and asked the defendant to dance after buying the defendant a drink). Mock jurors who were more supportive of the gay community were less likely to attribute blame to the victim. Moreover, participants who evaluated the gay bar scenario were more likely to place blame on the defendant and less likely to place blame on the victim. Regardless of location, mock jurors who evaluated the "provocation" scenario were more likely to attribute blame to the victim. Based on these findings, the researchers concluded that extralegal factors surrounding sexual orientation (e.g., jurors' previously held attitudes, the crime location, whether the crime involved "provocation") can shape juror perceptions in anti-gay hate crime cases.

Although more research is needed, especially with regard to juror bias and anti-transgender hate crime, these challenges surrounding juror bias are part of a broader pattern of obstacles that anti-LGBTQ hate crime victims may face before the cases go to trial, if they ever do. For instance, prosecutors may decide not to prosecute anti-LGBTQ violence as hate crimes because of the difficult evidentiary burden of proving hateful motives (Woods, 2008). Heavy caseloads may also deter prosecutors from pursuing hate crime charges or push them to offer plea bargains, in which a defendant agrees to plead guilty to a lesser charge in exchange for dropping the hate crime charge (Anti-Defamation League, 2017). Accordingly, combating anti-LGBTQ juror bias is one of many needed steps to address challenges that anti-LGBTQ hate crime victims commonly face in the criminal justice system.

### Intimate Partner Violence

IPV is common within LGBTQ communities, but it is often overlooked and misunderstood (Brown & Herman, 2015; Messinger, 2014). The few existing studies that examine juror decision-making in LGBTQ-related IPV cases describe how anti-LGBTQ biases and gendered assumptions can shape how jurors perceive evidence and testimony (Poorman, Seelau, & Seelau, 2003; Wasarhaley, Lynch, Golding, & Renzetti, 2015). In a recent study, Wasarhaley and colleagues found that gender stereotypes about defendants and victims of IPV may disadvantage lesbians involved in IPV cases, which, in turn, could discourage lesbian victims of IPV from seeking protection in the courts.

This conclusion is consistent with other literature describing how distrust of law enforcement and lack of confidence in the courts may dissuade LGBTQ victims of IPV from reporting incidents and seeking state protection (Eaton, et al., 2008; Goodmark, 2013). It is important to recognize, however, that these problems go well beyond juror bias. For instance, many state statutes are silent as to whether victims of same-sex IPV qualify for civil protection orders, and a few states disqualify victims of same-sex IPV from obtaining them (ABA, 2014). Scholars have also noted that LGBTQ victims of IPV who are also parents may fear that judges will terminate their parental rights after seeking state protection (Hardesty, Oswald, Khaw, & Fonseca,

2011). Therefore, anti-LGBTQ juror bias is only one, yet an important and underexplored, challenge that LGBTQ people may experience in IPV cases.

## Sexual Offenses

As discussed earlier, the previous consensus among psychology and mental health professionals that homosexuality was a mental illness reinforced stereotypes of LGBTQ people as sexual predators (Freedman, 2006). Although this consensus has since declined, damaging stereotypes of LGBTQ people as sexual predators still persist and facilitate the criminalization of LGBTQ people for various sexual offenses. Three common examples include child sexual abuse, rape, and public lewdness (Hill, 2000; Meidinger, 2012; Wiley & Bottoms, 2009).

Several studies discuss how anti-LGBTQ biases can influence juror decision-making in child sexual abuse cases (Stawiski et al., 2012; Wiley & Bottoms, 2009, 2013). In one leading study, Wiley and Bottoms (2009) found that participants were more likely to convict defendants of child sexual abuse who they perceived to be gay versus straight. Moreover, participants assigned a higher degree of guilt, less credibility, and more responsibility to gay versus straight defendants. In a later study, Wiley and Bottoms (2013) found that mock jurors who held more negative beliefs about homosexuality were more willing to accept stereotypes of gay men as sexual molesters. Those who were more religious were also more likely to make judgments in favor of the prosecution when the defendants were gay (Wiley & Bottoms, 2013).

Fewer studies have examined the role of anti-LGBTQ juror bias in cases involving rape and sexual assault of adult victims. In one study, Hill (2000) found that participants attributed the highest guilt ratings in cases involving gay male defendants who were accused of raping heterosexual male victims. Conversely, participants attributed the lowest guilt in cases involving gay male defendants accused of raping gay male victims. One possible explanation for these findings is that oversexualized stereotypes of gay men may influence how jurors perceive the culpability of defendants and the seriousness of the crimes. Along these lines, other studies have found that mock jurors are more likely to attribute blame to LGBTQ sexual assault victims and view crimes against them as less serious (Davies & Hudson, 2011; Davies & Rogers, 2006).

With regard to public lewdness, there is little to no data on LGBTQ-related arrests, convictions, and sentences. Scholars, however, have documented a long history of undercover police officers using sex sting operations to target gay as well as non-gay-identified men who have same-sex sex (Carpenter, 2012; Eskridge, 2008). These stings continue today and have recently resulted in lawsuits and verdicts against police departments for discriminatory conduct (Queally & Branson-Potts, 2016). Many of these cases never go to trial because the arrestees accept plea bargains in order to avoid public exposure and humiliation (Woods, 2009). But anti-LGBTQ juror bias can affect the cases that do reach a jury. In many jurisdictions, a defendant cannot successfully raise an entrapment defense if the jury concludes that the defendant was "predisposed" to commit the crime (Gilden, 2016). To determine predisposition, jurors may consider a gay sting defendant's character and reputation, which opens avenues for jurors to base their decisions on anti-LGBTQ biases (Woods, 2009).

## Conclusion

There is a limited but emerging body of research on biases that arise and affect juror decision-making when LGBTQ people are involved in criminal cases, whether as jurors, victims, defendants, or witnesses. More empirical studies and data are needed to offer a more comprehensive understanding of how anti-LGBTQ biases shape criminal jury selection, juror perceptions, and case outcomes. Although many open questions remain, what we know from existing research illustrates how challenges linked to sexuality and gender identity in criminal courts can compromise legitimacy and fairness in the criminal justice system.

## Note

1. "Cisgender" is a term used to describe individuals whose gender identity matches their sex assigned at birth (Herman, 2014).

## References

American Bar Association, Criminal Justice Section. (2013). *Resolution 113A and Report*. Retrieved from http://lgbtbar.org/wp-content/uploads/sites/6/2014/02/Gay-and-Trans-Panic-Defenses-Resolution.pdf

American Bar Association. (2014). *Domestic Violence Civil Protection Orders by State*. Retrieved from http://www.americanbar.org/content/dam/aba/administrative/domestic_violence1/Resources/statutorysummarycharts/2014%20CPO%20Availability%20Chart.authcheckdam.pdf

American Psychiatric Association. (2013). *Gender dysphoria*. Retrieved from https://perma.cc/T2LH-8245

Anti-Defamation League. (2017). *Hate crimes data collection and prosecutions FAQ*. Retrieved from http://www.adl.org/combating-hate/hate-crimes-law/c/hate-crimes-faq.html?referrer=https://www.google.com/#.WJqyQWQrKL8

Babcock, B. A. (1975). Voir dire: Preserving "its wonderful power." *Stanford Law Review, 27*, 545–565.

Barry, K. M., Farrell, B., Levi, J. L., & Vanguri, N. (2016). A bare desire to harm: Transgender people and the equal protection clause. *Boston College Law Review, 57*, 507–582.

Batson v. Kentucky, 476 U.S. 79 (1986).

Bayer, R. (1981). *Homosexuality and American psychiatry: The politics of diagnosis.* New York: Basic Books.

Bernstein, L. (2015). Custom in the courts. *Northwestern University Law Review, 110,* 63–113.

Boso, L. A. (2013). Urban bias, rural sexual minorities, and the courts. *UCLA Law Review, 60,* 562–637.

Bowers v. Hardwick, 478 U.S. 186 (1986).

Brower, T. (2011). Twelve angry—and sometimes alienated—men: The experiences and treatment of lesbians and gay men during jury service. *Drake Law Review, 59,* 669–706.

Brown, T. N. T., & Herman, J. L. (2015). *Intimate partner violence and sexual abuse among LGBT people.* Los Angeles, CA: The Williams Institute.

California Penal Code Section 192(f)(1) (2014).

Canaday, M. (2008). Heterosexuality as a legal regime. In M. Grossberg & C. Tomlins (Eds.), *The Cambridge history of law in America* (Vol. III, pp. 442–471). New York: Cambridge University Press.

Capers, I. B. (2008). Cross dressing and the criminal. *Yale Journal of Law & the Humanities, 20,* 1–30.

Carbado, D. W., & Moran, R. F. (2008). The story of law and American racial consciousness: Building a canon one case at a time. *UMKC Law Review, 76,* 851–883.

Carpenter, D. (2012). *Flagrant conduct: The story of* Lawrence v. Texas. New York: W. W. Norton.

Chauncey, G. (1994). *Gay New York: Gender, urban culture, and the making of the gay male world, 1890–1940.* New York: Basic Books.

Christensen, A. K. (2014). Equality with exceptions? Recovering *Lawrence*'s central holding. *California Law Review, 102,* 1337–1368.

Cramer, R. J., Wakeman, E. E., Chandler, J. F., Mohr, J. J., & Griffin, M. P. (2013). Hate crimes on trial: Judgments about violent crime against gay men. *Psychiatry, Psychology, and Law, 20,* 202–215. doi:10.1080/13218719.2011.633488

Dart, T. (2018, May 12). After decades of "gay panic defence" in court, US states slowly begin to ban tactic. *TheGuardian.com.* Retrieved from https://www.theguardian.com/us-news/2018/may/12/gay-panic-defence-tactic-ban-court

Davies, M., & Hudson, J. (2011). Judgments toward male and transgendered victims in a depicted stranger rape. *Journal of Homosexuality, 58,* 237–247. doi:10.1016/j.avb.2006.01.002

Davies, M., & Rogers, P. (2006). Perceptions of male victims in depicted sexual assaults: A review of the literature. *Aggression and Violent Behavior, 11,* 367–377. doi:10.1016/j.avb.2006.01.002

D'Emilio, J. (1998). *Sexual politics, sexual communities: The making of a homosexual minority in the United States, 1940–1970* (2nd ed.). Chicago: University of Chicago Press.

Dressler, J. (1995). When "heterosexual" men kill "homosexual" men: Reflections on provocation law, sexual advances, and the "reasonable man" standard. *Journal of Criminal Law and Criminology, 85,* 726–763.

Dunlap, M. C. (1979). The constitutional rights of sexual minorities: A crisis of the male/female dichotomy. *Hastings Law Journal, 30,* 1131–1149.

Eaton, L., Kaufman, M., Fuhrel, A., Cain, D., Cherry, C., Pope, H., & Kalichman, S. C. (2008). Examining factors co-existing with interpersonal violence in lesbian relationships. *Journal of Family Violence, 23,* 697–705. doi:10.1007/s10896-008-9194-3

Eskridge, W. N. (2008). *Dishonorable passions: Sodomy laws in America 1861–2003.* New York: Viking.

Freedman, E. B. (2006). "Uncontrolled desires": The response to the sexual psychopath, 1920–1960. In E. B. Freedman, *Feminism, sexuality, and politics: Essays* (pp. 121–139). Chapel Hill: University of North Carolina Press.

Gilden, A. (2016). Punishing sexual fantasy. *William and Mary Law Review, 58,* 419–491.

Goodmark, L. (2013). Transgender people, intimate partner abuse, and the legal system. *Harvard Civil Rights-Civil Liberties Law Review, 48,* 51–104.

Grant, J., Mottet, L. A., Tanis, J., with Harrison, J., Herman, J. L., & Keisling, M. (2011). *Injustice at every turn: A report of the national discrimination survey.* Washington, DC: National Center on Transgender Equality and National Gay and Lesbian Task Force.

Hardesty, J. L., Oswald, R. F., Khaw, L., & Fonseca, C. (2011). Lesbian/bisexual mothers and intimate partner violence: Help seeking in the context of social and legal vulnerability. *Violence against Women, 17,* 28–46. doi:10.1177/1077801209347636

Herek, G. M. (2009). Hate crimes and stigma-related experiences among sexual minority adults in the United States: Prevalence estimates from a national probability sample. *Journal of Interpersonal Violence, 24,* 54–74. doi:10.1177/0886260508316477

Herman, J. L. (2014). *Best practices for asking questions to identify transgender and other gender minority respondents on population-based surveys.* Los Angeles, CA: GenIUSS Group.

Hill, J. M. (2000). The effects of sexual orientation in the courtroom: A double standard. *Journal of Homosexuality, 39,* 93–111. doi:10.1300/J082v39n02_05

Hooker, E. (1955). Inverts are not a distinct personality type. *Mattachine Review, 1,* 20–22.

Hooker, E. (1956). A preliminary analysis of group behavior of homosexuals. *Journal of Psychology, 42,* 217–225. doi:10.1080/00223980.1956.9713035

Hooker, E. (1957). The adjustment of the male overt homosexual. *Journal of Projective Techniques, 21,* 18–31. doi:10.1080/08853126.1957.10380742

Hooker, E. (1958). Male homosexuality in the Rorschach. *Journal of Projective Techniques, 22,* 33–54. doi:10.1080/08853126.1958.10380822

Hooker, E. (1965). Male homosexuals and their "worlds." In J. Marmor (Ed.), *Sexual inversion: The multiple roots of homosexuality* (pp. 83–107). New York: Basic Books.

Hoppe, T. (2016). Punishing sex: Sex offenders and the missing punitive turn in sexuality studies. *Law & Social Inquiry, 41,* 573–594. doi:10.1111/lsi.12189

Human Rights Watch. (2016). *"Like walking through a hailstorm": Discrimination against LGBT youth in US schools.* Retrieved from https://www.hrw.org/sites/default/files/report_pdf/uslgbt1216web_2.pdf

Hunter, N. D. (1992). Life after Hardwick. *Harvard Civil Rights-Civil Liberties Law Review, 27,* 531–554.

James, N., Thomas, K. R., & Foley, C. (2008). *Civil commitment of sexually dangerous persons.* New York: Nova Science.

J.E.B. v. Alabama ex rel. T.B., 511 U.S. 127 (1994)

Judicial Council of California. (2001). *Sexual orientation fairness in the courts: Final report of the sexual orientation subcommittee of the Judicial Council's Access and Fairness Advisory Committee.* San Francisco, CA: Author. Retrieved from http://www.courts.ca.gov/documents/sexualorient_report.pdf

King, D. (1981). Gender confusions: Psychological and psychiatric conceptions of transvestism and transsexualism. In K. Plummer (Ed.), *The making of the modern homosexual* (pp. 155–183). Totowa, NJ: Barnes and Noble Books.

Kinsey, A. C., Pomeroy, W. B., & Martin, C. E. (1948). *Sexual behavior in the human male.* Philadelphia, PA: W. B. Saunders.

Kinsey, A. C., Pomeroy, W. B., & Martin, C. E. (1953). *Sexual behavior in the human female.* Philadelphia, PA: W. B. Saunders.

Lambda Legal. (2014). *Protected and served? Survey of LGBT/HIV contact with police, courts, prisons, and security.* New York: Author. Retrieved from http://www.lambdalegal.org/protected-and-served

Lawrence v. Texas, 539 U.S. 558 (2003).

LGBT Bar. (2017). *The Jury ACCESS Act and Juror Non-discrimination Act prevent discrimination in jury selection based on sexual orientation or gender identity.* Retrieved from http://lgbtbar.org/what-we-do/programs/jury-access-act/

Lee, C. (2008). The gay panic defense, *UC Davis Law Review, 42,* 471–566.

Lee, C. (2013). Masculinity on trial: Gay panic in the criminal courtroom. *Southwestern Law Review, 42,* 817–831.

Lee, C. (2015). A new approach to voir dire on racial bias. *UC Irvine Law Review, 5,* 843–872.

Lee, C., & Kwan, P. (2014). The trans panic defense: Masculinity, heteronormativity, and the murder of transgender women. *Hastings Law Journal, 66,* 77–132.

Leslie, C. R. (2005). *Lawrence v. Texas* as the perfect storm. *UC Davis Law Review, 38,* 509–544.

Lockhart v McCree, 476 U.S. 162 (1986).

Lynd, P. R. (1998). Juror sexual orientation: The fair cross-section requirement, privacy, challenges for cause, and peremptories. *UCLA Law Review, 46,* 231–288.

Maddera, J. C. (2016). Batson in transition: Prohibiting peremptory challenges on the basis of gender identity or expression. *Columbia Law Review, 116,* 195–235.

Mallory, C., & Sears, B. (2015). *Evidence of employment discrimination based on sexual orientation and gender identity: An analysis of complaints filed with state enforcement agencies, 2008-2014.* Los Angeles, CA: The Williams Institute.

Mallory, C., & Sears, B. (2016a). *Evidence of discrimination in public accommodations based on sexual orientation and gender identity: An analysis of complaints filed with state enforcement agencies, 2008-2014.* Los Angeles, CA: The Williams Institute.

Mallory, C., & Sears, B. (2016b). *Evidence of housing discrimination based on sexual orientation and gender identity: An analysis of complaints filed with state enforcement agencies, 2008–2014.* Los Angeles, CA: The Williams Institute.

Meidinger, M. H. (2012). Peeking under the covers: Taking a closer look at prosecutorial decision-making involving queer youth and statutory rape. *Boston College Journal of Law & Social Justice, 32,* 421–451.

Messinger, A. M. (2014). Marking 35 years of research on same-sex intimate partner violence: Lessons and new directions. In D. Peterson & V. R. Panfil (Eds.), *Handbook of LGBT communities, crime, and justice* (pp. 65–85). New York: Springer.

Miller, E. J. (2014). Permissive justification. *Indiana Law Review. 47,* 689–737.

Mogul, J. L., Ritchie, A. J., & Whitlock, K. (2011). *Queer (in)justice: The criminalization of LGBT people in the United States.* Boston: Beacon Press.

Movement Advancement Project. (2017a). *Hate crime laws.* Retrieved from http://www.lgbtmap.org/equality-maps/hate_crime_laws

Movement Advancement Project. (2017b). *Non-discrimination laws.* Retrieved from http://www.lgbtmap.org/equality-maps/non_discrimination_laws

Murray, M. (2015). *Griswold*'s criminal law. *Connecticut Law Review, 47,* 1045–1073.

NeJaime, D. (2011). Winning through losing. *Iowa Law Review, 96,* 941–1012.

New Jersey Supreme Court. (2001). *Final report of the Task Force on Sexual Orientation Issues.* Trenton, NJ: Author.

Obergefell v. Hodges, 135 S.Ct. 2584 (2015).

Overland, S. (2009). Strategies for combating anti-gay sentiment in the courtroom. *The Jury Expert, 21*(2), 1–5.

People v. Merel, 2009 WL 1314822, No. A113056 (2009).

Plumm, K. M., Terrance, C. A., Henderson, V. R., & Ellingson, H. (2010). Victim blame in a hate crime motivated by sexual orientation. *Journal of Homosexuality, 57,* 267–286. doi:10.1080/00918360903489101

Poorman, P. B., Seelau, E. P., & Seelau, S. M. (2003). Perceptions of domestic abuse in same-sex relationships and implications for criminal justice and mental health responses. *Violence and Victims, 18,* 659–669. doi:10.1891/vivi.2003.18.6.659

Queally, J., & Branson-Potts, H. (2016, April 26). Judge slams gay sex stings by Long Beach police, calling them discriminatory. *LA Times.* Retrieved from http://www.latimes.com/local/lanow/la-me-ln-gay-sex-stings-police-discriminatory-20160429-story.html

Ragatz, L. L., & Russell, B. (2010). Sex, sexual orientation, and sexism: What influence do these factors have on verdicts in a crime-of-passion case? *The Journal of Social Psychology, 150,* 341–360. doi:10.1080/00224540903366677

Rubenstein, W. B. (2004). The real story of U.S. hate crime statistics: An empirical analysis. *Tulane Law Review, 78,* 1213–1246.

Salerno, J. M., Najdowski, C. J., Bottoms, B. L., Harrington, E., Kemner, G., & Dave, R. (2015). Excusing murder? Conservative jurors' acceptance of the gay-panic defense. *Psychology, Public Policy, and Law, 21,* 24–34. doi:10.1037/law0000024

Schmeiser, S. R. (2013). The ungovernable citizen: Psychopathy, sexuality, and the rise of medico-legal reasoning. *Yale Journal of Law & Humanities, 20,* 163–240.

Shay, G. (2014). In the box: Voir dire on LGBT issues in changing times. *Harvard Journal of Law & Gender, 37,* 407–457.

Sherrod, D., & Nardi, P. M. (1998). Homophobia in the courtroom: An assessment of biases against gay men and lesbians in a multiethnic sample of potential jurors. In G. M. Herek (Ed.), *Stigma and sexual orientation: Understanding prejudice against lesbians, gay men, and bisexuals* (pp. 24–38). Thousand Oaks, CA: SAGE.

SmithKline Beecham Corporation v. Abbott Laboratories, 740 F.3d 471, 9th Cir. (2014).

Stawiski, S., Dykema-Engblade, A., & Tindale, R. S. (2012). The roles of shared stereotypes and shared processing goals on mock jury decision making. *Basic and Applied Social Psychology, 34,* 88–97. doi:10.1080/01973533.2011.637467

Stein, T. S. (1988). Theoretical considerations in psychotherapy with gay men and lesbians. *Journal of Homosexuality, 15,* 75–95. doi:10.1300/J082v15n01_07

Stotzer, R. L. (2009). Violence against transgender people: A review of United States data. *Aggression and Violent Behavior, 14,* 170–179. doi:10.1016/j.avb.2009.01.006

Strader, J. K. (2011). *Lawrence*'s criminal law. *Berkeley Journal of Criminal Law, 16,* 41–111.

Strader, J. K., Selvin, M., & Hay, L. (2015). Gay panic, gay victims, and the case for gay shield laws. *Cardozo Law Review, 36,* 1473–1531.

Taylor v. Louisiana, 419 U.S. 522 (1975).

U.S. Const. amend. VI.

U.S. Department of Justice (2017). *Hate crime statistics 2016: Uniform crime reports.* Washington, DC: Federal Bureau of Investigation, Criminal Justice Information Services Division. Retrieved from https://ucr.fbi.gov/hate-crime/2016/hate-crime

Wasarhaley, N. E., Lynch, K. R., Golding, J. M., & Renzetti, C. M. (2015). The impact of gender stereotypes on legal perceptions of lesbian intimate partner violence. *Journal of Interpersonal Violence, 32,* 635–658. doi:10.1177/0886260515586370

Wiley, T. R. A., & Bottoms, B. L. (2009). Effects of defendant sexual orientation on jurors' perceptions of child sexual assault. *Law and Human Behavior, 33,* 46–60. doi:10.1007/s10979-008-9131-2

Wiley, T. R. A., & Bottoms, B. L. (2013). Attitudinal and individual differences influence perceptions of mock child sexual assault cases involving gay defendants. *Journal of Homosexuality, 60,* 734–749. doi:10.1080/00918369.2013.773823

Wodda, A., & Panfil, V. R. (2015). "Don't talk to me about deception": The necessary erosion of the trans* panic defense. *Albany Law Review, 78,* 927–971.

Woods, J. B. (2008). Ensuring a right of access to the courts for bias crime victims: A section 5 defense of the Matthew Shepard Act. *Chapman Law Review, 12,* 389–431.

Woods, J. B. (2009). Don't tap, don't stare, and keep your hands to yourself! Critiquing the legality of gay sting operations. *Journal of Gender, Race, and Justice, 12,* 545–577.

Woods, J. B. (2017). LGBT identity and crime. *California Law Review, 105,* 667–734.

Woods, J. B., Sears, B., & Mallory, C. (2016). *Model legislation for eliminating the gay and trans panic defenses.* Los Angeles, CA: The Williams Institute.

Young, K. M. (2011). Outing *Batson*: How the case of gay jurors reveals the shortcomings of modern voir dire. *Willamette Law Review, 48,* 243–271.

# 5

## Implicit Jury Bias

### Are Informational Interventions Effective?

## Anna Roberts

In a 2016 presidential debate, Hillary Clinton (2016) voiced a belief that "Implicit bias is a problem for everyone." "Implicit bias" is an umbrella term for two mental processes. The first involves implicit attitudes, which are less than fully conscious evaluations, whether negative or positive, including evaluations of particular social groups (Greenwald & Krieger, 2006). The second involves implicit stereotypes, which are less than fully conscious beliefs that most members of particular social groups have particular characteristics, such as laziness or hostility (Greenwald & Banaji, 1995).

It is perfectly possible to harbor implicit biases without being aware that one does and, indeed, while actively disavowing prejudice. Thus one cannot hope to detect implicit bias by questioning alone. The most common and prominent tool for investigating implicit bias is the Implicit Association Test (IAT), which uses reaction times to assess the strength of one's automatic associations between categories (such as White people) and evaluations (such as evil or hurtful; Project Implicit, 2011). The IAT is available online, and it takes only 10 minutes to complete; researchers have also developed printed versions (Eisenberg & Johnson, 2004).

IATs have been developed in areas that include age, race, religion, disability, and weight, and millions of versions of the test have been taken by a diverse group of participants. Across social groups, research participants have "systematically preferred socially privileged groups: Young over Old, White over Black, Light Skinned over Dark Skinned, Other Peoples over Arab-Muslim, Abled over Disabled, Thin over Obese, and Straight over Gay" (for review, Kang & Lane, 2010, p. 474). The most prominent IAT results involve the extent to which test takers appear to harbor positive or negative associations with respect to African Americans. Almost 75% of all test-takers appear to have implicit bias in favor of Whites over Blacks (for review, Banaji & Greenwald, 2013). Over 90% of Whites appear to have an implicit preference for Whites over Blacks. Similar results exist regarding Whites' implicit bias against Latinos (Blair et al., 2013).

A crucial aspect of implicit bias research has involved efforts to assess the extent to which implicit bias has implications for real-life behaviors. Thus far, research has suggested concrete effects of implicit bias in contexts such as voting, employment, budget setting, and medical treatment (for review, see Jost et al., 2009). Implicit bias also appears to affect numerous players within, and to reach "all corners of," the criminal justice system (Ghandnoosh, 2014, p. 14). One area where it is a problem with potentially deadly consequences is in the criminal jury. In this chapter, I provide an overview of the implications of implicit bias for the criminal jury. I then investigate the attempts that have been made and proposed to mitigate implicit juror bias by educating jurors. Finally, I consider what obstacles might impede these kinds of initiatives.

## The Consequences of Implicit Bias for the Jury

There is evidence that potential jurors bring to the courthouse the same array of implicit biases as exist in other members of the populace (Kang et al., 2012) and that many potential jurors are unaware of their implicit biases (Lynch & Haney, 2011). Despite the constitutional guarantees of a fair trial and an impartial jury, and despite the Supreme Court's declaration that the jury is the criminal defendant's fundamental "protection of life and liberty against race or color prejudice" (*Pena-Rodriguez v. Colorado*, 2017), implicit biases have the ability to affect a variety of the key functions that jurors are called upon to perform, including the making of life-or-death decisions.

Certain implications of implicit jury bias are common to criminal and civil trials. Implicit bias can affect recall of facts, evaluation and interpretation of evidence, evaluation of witnesses, and the forming of decisions and judgments, including judgments of guilt (for review, see Roberts, 2016). In addition, implicit stereotypes can affect one's ability to imagine an individual (such as a defendant) engaging in certain behavior. Even if it is clear that a stereotyped individual did engage in a particular act, stereotypes can affect the perceived causes and meaning of that act (Kunda & Sherman-Williams, 1993). Thus when the behavior is consistent with a stereotype, jurors are more likely to view a defendant's behavior as caused by his or her internal disposition as opposed to external factors (Kunda & Thagard, 1996). This phenomenon may contribute to racially disparate probabilities that defendants will be found to be culpable. Tabak (2010) even hypothesizes that implicit bias can "affect assertions that there was excessive force by the police" (p. 257; for further reading on this topic, see Chapter 6 of this volume).

In the context of criminal trials, implicit bias threatens the fair evaluation of several additional key components of the case. For example, research suggests the existence of implicit stereotypes connecting Black individuals to violence, weaponry, hostility, and aggression (for review, see Roberts, 2016). Thus, in a case against a Black defendant that includes a weapons-related element, for example, the burden of proof may be greatly lessened when jurors harbor implicit associations between Blackness and weaponry. Tabak (2010) hypothesized that implicit bias can also affect assessments of self-defense claims and interpretations of the invocation of the right to remain silent: The race of the person invoking this right may affect the likelihood that the invocation is seen as an admission of guilt.

Implicit bias may indeed taint the overarching consideration in any criminal trial: whether the prosecution can overcome the presumption of innocence and meet the constitutionally guaranteed standard of proving the crime charged beyond a reasonable doubt. Tabak (2010) hypothesized that implicit bias may "affect whether there really is a presumption of innocence" (p. 257). Levinson, Cai, and Young (2010) detected implicit associations between African Americans and criminal guilt that "confirmed [their] hypothesis that there is an implicit racial bias in the presumption of innocence" (p. 204) and thus suggested that the standard of proof beyond a reasonable doubt may be diluted in the case of Black defendants. Consider also the Rashon Brown case, in which Juror 4 had expressed concern to two other jurors about the fact that she had seen two Black men in her neighborhood; she apparently feared that they were connected to the trial, in which both defendants were Black. After Juror 4 reported her concerns to the sheriff's officer, the trial judge asked her and the other two jurors whether their ability to continue as jurors would be affected. He retained all three jurors on the jury, which subsequently handed down a conviction. On appeal, however, the conviction was reversed. The appellate court judge said this about Juror 4: "Her initial instinctive, subliminal association of race with criminality or wrong-doing far trumped her subsequent assurances of impartiality" (*State v. Brown*, 2015, p. 881).

In sentencing, also, implicit bias raises profound questions about jury fairness. Jurors play a central role in capital sentencing (see Chapter 3 of this volume) and, in some states, in sentences for other types of crimes. Several of the key sentencing considerations are hotspots for implicit racial bias: dangerousness, culpability, empathy, and perception of pain, for example (for review, see Sommers & Marotta, 2014). Levinson, Smith, and Young (2014) report that mock jurors' implicit associations between Whiteness and worth and Blackness and worthlessness increased the probability that they would sentence a Black defendant to death.

While negative implicit bias is of great concern regarding guilt determinations and sentencing decisions, its impact in some cases may be paired with the effects of what Smith, Levinson, and Robinson (2015) call "implicit white favoritism." In a self-defense case, for example, in which the defendant is Black and the complainant White, there is a "doubly dangerous risk that race influences the decision of the jury" (Smith et al., 2015, p. 916):

Negative stereotyping could influence how jurors decide, for instance, which party was the aggressor: the fact that black Americans are stereotyped as violent and hostile, for instance, could influence whether the jury believes the black defendant when he testifies that the deceased white male started the altercation. Yet, even if the risk of negative stereotyping evaporated, white favoritism could still facilitate racialized decision making. First, white Americans are stereotyped as peaceful and law-abiding. When jurors filter the details of the altercation through a lens shaped by the association of these positive stereotypes with the deceased white person, it provides a boost to the prosecution's narrative that it was the black defendant—and not the dead white guy—that started the altercation. (p. 915)

Other courtroom phenomena can reinforce the biases that jurors bring to criminal trials. Attorneys may, wittingly or unwittingly, trigger certain stereotypes during trial. For example, Smith and Levinson (2012) hypothesize that the use of animal imagery in closing arguments may "perpetuate the negative effects of implicit race bias" (p. 820). Also, taking on the role of a juror may lead one to judge criminal defendants more harshly. In one study by Levinson (2006), participants who had been told that they were jurors in a criminal case (and thus were what Levinson calls "legally primed participants," p. 1075) judged mental states as more culpable than did participants who were not primed. As Levinson puts it, this research "indicates that Americans are harsher in the courtroom than in non-legal settings" (p. 1078). Levinson also notes that participants penalized people from other cultures more when they were legally primed than when they were not. The cognitive strain of resolving a case may also reinforce certain implicit biases (Levinson, 2007). Levinson hypothesizes that the complexity of factual and legal material with which jurors are faced may add to cognitive depletion and that, as a result, stereotypes are likely to have a significant influence on jurors' memories. Courtroom arrangements in which those in power are White and the person on trial is Black may also contribute to the risk of bias: Bryan Fair (1994) has asserted, for example, that "[i]t is misguided to believe that White folks can discard strongly held negative attitudes about Blacks when Whites act as police, jurors, lawyers, or judges in criminal cases with a Black criminal defendant" (p. 408). Finally, jury instructions on the presumption of innocence—thought of as one of a criminal defendant's key protections—have been shown to shift attention to Black faces as compared to White faces (Young, Levinson, & Sinnett, 2014). The study's authors suggest that this may result from the fact that such instructions rely heavily on the legal concept of guilt, and, as suggested by previous research, the "concepts of guilt and Black are implicitly associated" (p. 4). Young and colleagues note the need for further research into how such "racial primes" may affect "behavior, judgments, and decision-making" (p. 3).

In the death penalty context, the process of "qualifying" jurors for service skews demographics in a way that enhances the risk of implicit bias (Levinson et al., 2014; see also Chapters 2 and 3 of this volume). As Levinson and colleagues (2014) describe their findings, "death-qualified juries possess stronger implicit biases because the process results in the disproportionate elimination of non-White jurors" (p. 569). In addition, the contrasting demographics of criminal defendants (disproportionately people of color) and jurors (disproportionately White) lead to a frequent dynamic in which a social "ingroup" is judging a social "outgroup" (Levinson et al., 2014). In this dynamic, criminal defendants are vulnerable to two kinds of bias: that related to their being members of socially devalued groups and that related to their being members of different groups from that of the jurors, and thus being implicitly disfavored.

Given all of these opportunities for implicit biases to shape trial and sentencing outcomes, it is unsurprising that implicit bias has been linked to racial disparities in both verdicts and sentences, including death sentences (for review, see Elek & Hannaford-Agor, 2013). Judges have acknowledged their sense of the problems caused by implicit jury bias, including their sense that it can affect verdicts, and one has issued an explicit call for help (Arterton, 2008).

The fact that the vast majority of criminal convictions are imposed as a result of guilty pleas rather than trials does not erase the impact of implicit juror bias on case outcomes: Plea bargains are negotiated in the shadow of the trial, and the fear of implicit (as well as explicit) jury bias may form a significant part of that shadow. Using analogous coercion, in at least one documented instance, police interrogators have used the fear of a White jury as a tool to elicit a confession, successfully persuading the Black suspect that the jury's sympathies for him would be weaker than those of the police (Cohen, 2014).

One must then ask what can be done to address implicit jury bias. A variety of long-standing methods exist for shaping the group of people who show up at the courthouse into a jury that is willing and able to be fair and impartial. They include the orientation of jurors to their task, the process of voir dire (jury selection), and jury instructions. These tools have always been imperfect, but, at least as currently implemented, they are particularly unequal to the challenge of implicit juror bias.

While it may be impossible to eradicate implicit biases, researchers believe that under certain conditions it may be possible to find useful ways to address them. Jackson, Hillard, and Schneider (2014), who interpreted their recent study's results as indicating that "implicit associations can change as a result of participation in a brief diversity training" (p. 434), offered some suggestions about how to design educational interventions relating to implicit bias. The suggestions include the following: Presentations on this topic should "provide steps to address bias," "use non-confrontational language," and "explicitly acknowledge that everyone holds biases" (p. 434). The next section discusses how these and a variety of other techniques, existing and proposed, might address implicit jury bias.

## Informational Interventions to Address Implicit Jury Bias: Initiatives and Proposals

Implicit bias education has been attempted in a variety of other parts of our justice system. Training on this topic has been mandated for police departments, initiated for federal prosecutors and law enforcement agents, and introduced as part of education and training for court staff and judges. At this point, however, the concept of educating jurors or potential jurors about their implicit biases is relatively unexplored. Those initiatives that have been either attempted or proposed are discussed in the order in which they occur within trial-related procedure: They include jury orientation, jury selection, jury instructions, expert testimony, and other trial components.

### Jury Orientation

In most courthouses in the country, the bulk of jury orientation is done by videotaped instruction; with one exception, which will be discussed later, these videotapes say nothing about implicit bias, and some say nothing about bias at all (Roberts, 2012). Some of them instruct jurors to be fair and open-minded, but the expert take on these kinds of admonitions is that they have "zero impact" (Banaji, 2008, p. 567). This is a lost opportunity. Jury orientation represents the first educational opportunity for potential jurors when they reach the courthouse. It has significant potential as a site in which to address implicit bias, both because it comes first, and thus has the potential to prime the jurors for fairness and frame their task, and because it is universal: All potential jurors in the courthouse are exposed to it, and thus its content is not reliant on the preferences of individual judges or attorneys and cannot be blamed on the tactics of individual attorneys (Roberts, 2012). Sommers and Ellsworth (2001) have highlighted the risks related to attorneys' efforts to raise White jurors' consciousness about possible racial injustice, including the risks that the jurors resent attorneys for such efforts.

Several other factors make jury orientation a potential site of fruitful intervention. First, jury orientation videos invoke the kinds of egalitarian commitments that may be able to assist debiasing efforts (Dasgupta & Rivera, 2006). Second, jurors bring with them a desire to learn and to perform well (for review, see Roberts, 2012). And finally, at least some jurisdictions have not been averse to spending money on orientation material. The New York State video cost $150,000 to produce (O'Brien, 2003). Currently, however, it contains no mention of bias.

In the most detailed proposal for a possible intervention during juror orientation, Roberts (2012) suggested that jury orientation videos should

(a) maintain their invocation of egalitarian norms but be edited to include an introduction to implicit bias and (b) be followed by an invitation to take an IAT, in either electronic or paper form. The IAT should be offered only for educational purposes, and jurors should be reassured that the results would not be shared with anyone. Each juror interested in participating should take only one IAT (addressing race, for example, or gender), but the test should be contextualized for the jurors, so that it could serve as an example of one of the many types of bias to which jurors (and witnesses and government agents, among others) are vulnerable. The IAT has been proposed and used as an educational tool in a variety of settings, including classrooms and courtrooms. Research has supported the notion that it is a valuable means of providing education to doctors, for example (Green et al., 2007), and developers of the test have suggested that the IAT might be an appropriate teaching tool for jurors (Project Implicit, 2011). Because test-takers can feel the difference in their own reaction times, and because they receive a score that is specific to them, the IAT may be harder to dismiss than mere lecturing.

The one exception to the silence of orientation videos on the topic of implicit bias consists of a new initiative launched in 2017 in a federal district in Washington State (United States District Court, Western District of Washington, 2017b). This initiative, which involves both an orientation video and jury instructions (mentioned later), was the work of a committee of judges and attorneys, and has the aim of "highlighting and combating the problems presented by unconscious bias" (United States District Court, Western District of Washington, 2017b). The video, a little over 10 minutes long, features an introduction to implicit bias presented by a federal judge, an American Civil Liberties Union attorney, and a federal prosecutor and is available for public viewing on the district court's web page (United States District Court, Western District of Washington, 2017b).

## Jury Selection

Some have developed proposals designed to maximize the opportunities that jury selection offers for informational intervention. The process of voir dire serves multiple purposes in the hands of a skillful attorney, including not only elicitation of information about potential jurors but also imparting of information to potential jurors, including information "about the workings of implicit bias" (Lee, 2013, pp. 1592–1593). The American Bar Association (n.d.) thus proposes that "a goal of the jury selection process should be to discover, with the prospective juror, what life experiences and attitudes, if any, may implicitly affect how that juror might view the evidence and the law in the case" (p. 22).

Yet, with respect to jury selection, even experienced lawyers struggle in the face of implicit jury bias. First, the potential disconnect between explicit commitments and implicit bias means that jurors may not be aware of their implicit bias and thus will not mention it. Because of the prevalence of implicit bias, commentators have despaired that "even the most extensive and penetrating voir dire will not screen the vast majority of bigoted jurors" (Bell, 2008, p. 331). Second, even if potential jurors have some awareness of such bias, they may be chilled from admitting it, perhaps particularly if it is a judge who is questioning the jurors (Jones, 1987). Thus the standard questions, such as whether the jurors can be fair and impartial, are likely to receive uniformly positive responses. As a result, on the basis of typical juror responses, attorneys are unable to make informed efforts to reduce implicit bias by means of their two main jury selection tools: challenges for cause (in other words, challenges that assert that particular jurors cannot be fair) and peremptory challenges (which typically do not need a justification).

It may be that there are good questions that could help identify jurors who are particularly likely to bring an open mind to their task (see Chapter 4 of this volume for a discussion of questions designed to root out anti-LGBTQ bias during jury selection). The American Bar Association (n.d.), for example, has suggested some possible voir dire questions in its "Achieving an Impartial Jury Toolbox" (the "Toolbox"). In addition, Lee (2015) has identified voir dire as a forum for focusing on "race salience," or, in other words, "the process of making salient the potential for racial bias" (p. 861). This kind of proposal is motivated by the indications that those "who seek to be fair will endeavor to correct for potential bias when the threat of potential race bias is obvious" (Kang et al., 2012, p. 1146). Thus Lee (2013) advocates highlighting the significance of race in the case, so that "those who end up on the jury will be more cognizant of the ways in which race may have shaped the perceptions of the individuals involved in the case and the ways in which race may influence the jurors' own perceptions" (p. 1593). Lee (2015) argues as follows:

> For an attorney concerned that racial stereotypes about the
> defendant, the victim, or a witness might affect how the jury
> interprets the evidence, voir dire into racial bias can be extremely
> helpful. Calling attention to implicit racial bias can encourage jurors
> to view the evidence without the usual preconceptions and automatic
> associations involving race that most of us make . . . I believe that a
> series of open-ended questions educating jurors about implicit bias
> and encouraging them to reflect upon whether implicit racial bias
> might affect their ability to even-handedly consider the evidence . . . .
> calling attention to race can motivate jurors to treat Black and White
> defendants equally, whereas not highlighting race may result in
> jurors tending to be more punitive and less empathetic towards Black
> defendants than they might otherwise be without such attention.
> (pp. 846–847)

However, questioning prospective jurors as a method for addressing implicit bias is an approach whose efficacy has not been tested, and it remains uncertain how many lawyers will discover or use such questions. In addition, judges conduct or dominate voir dire in some jurisdictions and may engage only in brief "yes" or "no" group questioning (Page, 2005). Even if attorneys lead the questioning, they may be prohibited from asking questions about areas of potential bias (Forman, 1992). Only in limited circumstances do defendants have a federal constitutional right to such questions (Lee, 2015), and the cases in which courts permit this questioning may not line up well with those cases in which the threat from implicit bias is greatest.

Rapping (2013) suggests three informational interventions that might occur during voir dire. The first is that an attorney might request that the entire venire take an IAT, with the aim of starting to raise juror awareness. In support of this proposal, Rapping discusses the potential educational benefits mentioned earlier but concedes that such a request "might well be denied because of its perceived impact on efficiency, the logistical challenges associated with it, and judicial resistance to any significant change to the traditional way of doing things" (pp. 1029–1030). Rapping also suggests that attorneys could "inform the venire about [implicit racial bias] during voir dire" (p. 1030), though he does not offer a model for such an intervention. Finally, he suggests that attorneys might

> request that the court explain [implicit racial bias] to the jury and instruct the venire on the influence it has over all of us and the risk it poses to the jury's ability to reach a verdict based solely on appropriate considerations. (p. 1030)

**Jury Instructions**

Conventional jury instructions tell jurors that they should not let "bias, sympathy, prejudice, or public opinion influence [their] decision" (Elek & Hannaford-Agor, 2013, p. 197). Again, however, this kind of instruction has been described as useless (Banaji, 2008). Jury instructions generally say nothing about implicit bias (Roberts, 2012). There are, however, some exceptions. A pioneering federal judge in Iowa—Mark Bennett—was moved by his experience of taking the IAT and his subsequent research into implicit bias to address the issue as regards jurors (Bennett, 2010). He engages in a number of efforts in each jury trial, including a discussion with the jurors about implicit bias, a PowerPoint slide and video on the topic, an admission that even he—a federal judge—harbors his own implicit biases, and a pledge that all jurors must sign at the end of jury selection, which includes a "pledge . . . not [to] decide this case based on biases. This includes gut feelings, prejudices, stereotypes, personal likes or dislikes, sympathies or generalizations" (Kang et al., 2012, p. 1182). He also decided to craft a jury instruction that addresses implicit jury bias (Kang et al., 2012). He did so in consultation with the local United States Attorney and the local federal public defender, and a portion of the instruction reads as follows:

Do not decide the case based on "implicit biases." As we discussed in jury selection, everyone, including me, has feelings, assumptions, perceptions, fears, and stereotypes, that is, "implicit biases," that we may not be aware of. These hidden thoughts can impact what we see and hear, how we remember what we see and hear, and how we make important decisions. Because you are making very important decisions in this case, I strongly encourage you to evaluate the evidence carefully and to resist jumping to conclusions based on personal likes or dislikes, generalizations, gut feelings, prejudices, sympathies, stereotypes, or biases. (Kang et al., 2012, pp. 1182–1183)

Following Judge Bennett's lead, the Western District of Washington (United States District Court, 2017a) recently launched a set of implicit bias jury instructions, in coordination with the implicit bias jury orientation videotape mentioned earlier. The instructions are "intended to alert the jury to the concept of unconscious bias and then to instruct the jury in a straightforward way not to use bias, including unconscious bias, in its evaluation of information and credibility and in its decision-making" (p. 1). The preliminary instruction and closing instruction on the jury's duty note that

You must decide the case solely on the evidence and the law before you and must not be influenced by any personal likes or dislikes, opinions, prejudices, sympathy, or biases, including unconscious bias. Unconscious biases are stereotypes, attitudes, or preferences that people may consciously reject but may be expressed without conscious awareness, control, or intention. Like conscious bias, unconscious bias, too, can affect how we evaluate information and make decisions. (p. 2)

Turning to the state system, California has drafted a model jury instruction that includes a mention of implicit bias and that has been administered in trials:

Each one of us has biases about or certain perceptions or stereotypes of other people. We may be aware of some of our biases, though we may not share them with others. We may not be fully aware of some of our other biases.

Our biases often affect how we act, favorably or unfavorably, toward someone. Bias can affect our thoughts, how we remember, what we see and hear, whom we believe or disbelieve, and how we make important decisions.

As jurors you are being asked to make very important decisions in this case. You must not let bias, prejudice, or public opinion influence your decision. You must not be biased in favor of or against any party or witness because of his or her disability, gender, race, religion, ethnicity, sexual orientation, age, national origin, [or] socioeconomic status[, or [insert any other impermissible form of bias]].

Your verdict must be based solely on the evidence presented. You must carefully evaluate the evidence and resist any urge to reach a verdict that is influenced by bias for or against any party or witness. (Judicial Council of California: Advisory Committee on Civil Jury Instructions, 2012)

Lee (2013) proposed an instruction, to be used in certain self-defense cases, which pairs information about stereotypes with an invitation to the jury to consider "race-switching." Race-switching is a technique that requires someone who is contemplating a particular decision to stop first and ask him or herself whether, if the races of the relevant players were switched, he or she would reach a different conclusion.

Lee's (2013) work may have played an important role in a criminal case in Alaska. The attorney representing a Black teenager who was charged with hitting a White man in the head with a hammer, and who argued self-defense, asked that the jurors receive a race-switching instruction. The judge agreed to give the instruction, noting "that he personally engaged in a race-switching exercise whenever he was called upon to impose sentence on a member of a minority race, to insure that he was not being influenced by racial stereotypes" (McComas & Strout, 1999, p. 24). After hearing the instruction and deliberating, the jurors reached a not guilty verdict (McComas & Strout, 1999). According to Lee's proposed instruction,

> It is natural to make assumptions about the parties and witnesses
> based on stereotypes. Stereotypes constitute well-learned sets
> of associations or expectations correlating particular traits with
> members of a particular social group. You should try not to make
> assumptions about the parties and witnesses based on their
> membership in a particular racial group. If you are unsure about
> whether you have made any unfair assessments based on racial
> stereotypes, you may engage in a race-switching exercise to test
> whether stereotypes have colored your evaluation of the case
> before you.
>
> Race-switching involves imagining the same events, the same
> circumstances, the same people, but switching the races of the
> parties. For example, if the defendant is White and the victim is
> Latino, you would imagine a Latino defendant and a White victim.
> If your evaluation of the case before you is different after engaging in
> race-switching, this suggests a subconscious reliance on stereotypes.
> You may then wish to reevaluate the case from a neutral, unbiased
> perspective. (p. 1600)

Rapping (2013), whose proposals relating to jury selection were mentioned earlier, states that other methods such as jury instructions are also important, since "efforts must be made to continue to remind jurors of the tendency for subtle pressures to influence how they view the association between race and crime" (p. 1036). He recommends that even if the judge agrees to discuss implicit racial bias at the start of jury selection, lawyers should "also consider requesting an instruction at the beginning of trial and again when final instructions are read" (p. 1039).

Researchers suggest that any such jury instructions should be formulated by experts in bias and jury psychology (Herman, 1993); should be "couched in accurate, evidence-based, and scientific terms" (Kang et al., 2012, p.1183); should "detail a clear, specific, concrete strategy that individuals can use to debias judgment" (Casey, Warren, Cheesman, & Elek, 2012, p. G-8); and should be designed to avoid putting jurors on the defensive. Three possible models follow.

The American Bar Association (n.d.) group working on the Toolbox crafted a model instruction, using Judge Bennett's work as a starting point and incorporating input from social scientists:

> Scientists studying the way our brains work have shown that, for all of us, our first responses are often like reflexes. Just like our knee reflexes, our mental responses are quick and automatic. Even though these quick responses may not be what we consciously think, they could influence how we judge people or even how we remember or evaluate the evidence.
>
> Scientists have taught us some ways to be more careful in our thinking that I ask you to use as you consider the evidence in this case:
>
> Take the time you need to test what might be reflexive unconscious responses and to reflect carefully and consciously about the evidence.
>
> - Focus on individual facts, don't jump to conclusions that may have been influenced by unintended stereotypes or associations.
> - Try taking another perspective. Ask yourself if your opinion of the parties or witnesses or of the case would be different if the people participating looked different or if they belonged to a different group?
> - You must each reach your own conclusions about this case individually, but you should do so only after listening to and considering the opinions of the other jurors, who may have different backgrounds and perspectives from yours.
>
> Working together will help achieve a fair result. (American Bar Association, n.d.)

In addition, Lynch and Haney (2011) laid out a vision of an instruction for capital jurors deciding the fate of defendants of color:

> [It] is not difficult to envision the use of a "modern racism" judicial instruction that might be delivered in cases in which there are

capital defendants of Color. Given what is known about the persistence of racialized decision making in death penalty cases (i.e., ignoring race when it should matter, being influenced by it when it should not), explicitly voicing concerns about the potential for pernicious race-based processes to distort judgments— processes that we know are most problematic when they operate at an implicit level—might serve as an effective antidote. An instruction that acknowledged the kind of burdens and obstacles that many Black defendants face throughout their lives and sensitized jurors against allowing unconscious prejudices to play any role in their decision making may serve as a useful prophylactic against forces and factors that we know are likely to operate in this context. (p. 603)

Finally, Brown, Subrin, and Baumann (1997) propose the following instruction:

All of us, no matter how hard we try not to, tend to look at others and weigh what they have to say through the lens of our own experience and background. We each have a tendency to stereotype others and make assumptions about them. Often we see life and evaluate evidence through a clouded filter that tends to favor those like ourselves. I urge you to do the best you can to put aside such stereotypes, for all litigants and witnesses are entitled to a level playing field in which we do the best we can to put aside our stereotypes and prejudices. (p. 1531)

## Expert Testimony

In several civil cases, plaintiffs have sought permission to introduce expert testimony in order to help jurors understand the possible role of implicit bias in the alleged facts of the case. In some of those cases, the expert testimony has been excluded. For example, in a recent age discrimination case, *Karlo v. Pittsburgh Glass Works, LLC* (2015), the trial court excluded Anthony Greenwald's proposed testimony on implicit bias, finding that "Dr. Greenwald's opinion is more likely to confuse a jury rather than elucidate the issue(s) for the factfinder" (p. 8). The federal appeals court declined to overturn this decision, though the court rejected the notion that it was finding that implicit bias testimony could never be admissible (*Karlo v. Pittsburgh Glass Works, LLC*, 2017). Similarly, in a race discrimination case, *Jones v. National Council of Young Men's Christian Associations of the United States of America* (2014), the district court was "not persuaded that Dr. Greenwald's testimony and opinions [were] adequately tied to the facts of this case to be useful to a jury" (p. 900) and agreed with the magistrate judge that his testimony should be excluded.

In other cases, however, courts have denied defendants' requests that this kind of testimony be excluded. In a recent federal case alleging employment discrimination on the basis of race, *Samaha v. Washington State Department of Transportation* (2012), the plaintiff argued that information that Greenwald could offer would help the jury understand implicit bias, including its workings and prevalence in the employment context, and thus help the jury make its decision about whether illegal race discrimination had occurred. This time, the defendants' motion to exclude Greenwald's testimony was denied. Another expert, Phillip Goff, testified about implicit bias in a state case alleging race-based discrimination and harassment (*Salami v. Von Maur, Inc.*, 2013). Motions by the defendants to exclude Goff's implicit bias testimony were unsuccessful in both that case and a federal sexual orientation discrimination case that settled prior to trial (*Apilado v. North American Gay Amateur Athletic Alliance*, 2011).

Although experts such as Samuel Sommers and Mahzarin Banaji have testified about the potential for criminal case outcomes to be influenced by racial bias, expert testimony does not yet appear to have been offered to criminal jurors for the purpose of helping them understand their own implicit bias and how it might be addressed. Some scholars have suggested such an approach. Rapping (2013) goes into the most detail on this topic. He mentions expert testimony as one of several ways in which creative criminal defense lawyers could raise the issue of implicit racial bias and thus "remind jurors of the tendency for subtle pressures to influence how they view the association between race and crime" (p. 1036). Rapping outlines several opportunities that this kind of testimony could create: It could help jurors understand "the relationship between explicit and implicit bias" (p. 1036) and that implicit bias may not align with one's conscious commitments; it could explain to the jury that "by consciously working to make decisions consistent with their egalitarian ideals, they can help overcome the influence" (p. 1036) of implicit racial bias; it could encourage the jurors to be "patient and focused" (p. 1036) when evaluating the evidence, in an effort to avoid pressures of time or cognitive depletion; and it could help jurors to "understand the role of [implicit racial bias] in decision-making, and guard against its distorting effects" (p. 1037). Herman (1993) states her recommendation briefly: that judges be "requir[ed]" to allow "expert testimony on the impact of racism on jury verdicts," as one part of an effort to "begin to educate jurors to identify and neutralize their own unconscious biases" (pp. 1851–1852).

## Other Methods

Even if a judge refuses to instruct the jury on implicit bias or allow expert testimony on the topic, attorneys can raise awareness about bias in opening statements and suggest race-switching in closing arguments (see, e.g., Lee, 2013). Moreover, if part of the threat posed by implicit bias, particularly in a criminal courtroom with a defendant of color, is that the jurors may be blocked from appreciating the humanity of the defendant, more reform is needed in order to address that threat.

Defendant narrative has the potential to counter some of the implicit stereotypes that can mar the prospect of a fair trial. Defendant narrative can individuate—that is, paint a unique picture of—a defendant and thus potentially limit the influence of stereotypes that may associate the defendant with criminal guilt (Chan & Mendelsohn, 2010). Yet several impediments exist to defendant narrative, even where defendants may have narratives of innocence to share. Those impediments include the threat that defendants with criminal convictions will have their testimony destroyed by cross-examination about their past convictions (Roberts, 2016). In one recent study, fear of this kind of impeachment was named as the main reason why subsequently exonerated defendants refrained from testifying in their own defense (Blume, 2008). Thus one recent proposal focuses on the need for judges to consider the importance of defendant testimony as a potential debiasing tool when deciding whether to allow prosecutors to cross-examine defendants about their prior convictions (Roberts, 2016).

Other techniques exist for the purpose of conveying to the jury that the defendant is indeed a full human being. Caldwell and Hewitt (2014) offer techniques that are available during voir dire, opening statement, and the direct examination of defendants for the purpose of combating racial stereotypes. They provide a sample direct examination that aims "to identify individual aspects of the outgroup member's character beyond any potential racial identification" (p. 112) and, specifically, that "probes aspects of [the] client's life that help identify [him] as an individual rather than just as a black male" (p. 112). In other efforts to display the humanity of their clients, defense attorneys may take steps to ensure that they are displaying ease in their communications with them (Ross, 2004) and may look for witnesses who can introduce humanizing details about them. Finally, Judge Bennett shakes the hand of every criminal defendant on trial in his courtroom and does so in view of the jury (Bennett, 2015). He describes this as part of his effort to convey the full meaning of the presumption of innocence, but it may be that he achieves a humanizing effect also. Research into the effectiveness of this technique is currently underway.

Finally, each juror can offer useful informational interventions, whether to him or herself, fellow jurors, or court personnel. One recent example is the case *Pena-Rodriguez v. Colorado* (2017), whose path to the Supreme Court began with two jurors telling defense counsel, after a guilty verdict, that "another juror had expressed anti-Hispanic bias" (p. 861) toward the defendant and one of his witnesses. The Supreme Court resolved the case with a finding that in such cases the jury verdict may be "called into question" (p. 861).

Experts have proposed other ways in which jurors can mitigate the influence of implicit bias. One proposal would involve jurors taking notes during trial so that when it comes to deliberation they have something to rely on other than their memories, which are vulnerable to bias (Levinson, 2007). Other such proposals focus on the importance of diversifying juries. The failure to provide diverse juries is a widespread and ongoing problem (Sommers & Ellsworth, 2001), which results from a variety of factors that include failures to bring in a diverse jury pool, failure to make jury service economically and logistically feasible for all, purposeful discrimination in the exercise of jury strikes, and disparate effects of a variety of other filtering mechanisms (for review, see Sommers & Marotta, 2014; see also Chapter 2 in this volume). This lack of diversity matters in part because diverse juries may be able to assist in checking biases (Lee, 1996; Levinson, 2007), whether through individual jurors explicitly countering particular assumptions or adding additional perspectives and experiences (Sommers, 2006; "Developments—Race and the Criminal Process," 1988), through implicit messages that those in an outgroup need not be feared or distrusted (under this latter model, jurors would act as counterstereotypical exemplars; see Dasgupta & Greenwald, 2001), or simply by making race or other group identities salient (Sommers & Ellsworth, 2001). Thus efforts to diversify jury pools and juries, through methods such as reducing bars to jury service based on criminal records (Roberts, 2013) and limiting prosecutorial peremptory challenges (Roberts, 2015), have the potential to enhance the jury's ability to counter its own biases.

## Obstacles to Informational Interventions

Any initiative to enhance the provision of informational interventions to jurors needs to comprehend the level and types of obstacles that such efforts may inspire. This section reviews a range of obstacles: resource concerns; fear of making things worse, or not achieving anything worthwhile; an unwillingness of court actors to accept the relevant social science; and concerns about the potential ramifications for the broader criminal justice system of addressing this form of bias in this context.

A first obstacle is concern about resources, including money, technology, staffing, and time (Elek & Hannaford-Agor, 2013). Proposals that potential jurors be invited to take an IAT during orientation and that race-relevant questioning be added during voir dire have been described as "impractical in many courts" because of costs (Elek & Hannaford-Agor, 2013, p. 195). Judges are often said to spend surprisingly little time on voir dire—one source claims that the process of jury selection in felony trials takes an average of 3.6 to 3.8 hours (Wedel, 2011)—and they may be reluctant to change this. Rapping (2013) admits that his proposal that the jury venire should take an IAT might well be denied not only because of "judicial resistance to any significant change to the traditional way of doing things" but also because of its "perceived impact on efficiency" and "the logistical challenges associated with it" (p. 1030). In addition, expert witnesses can be costly (Vershuta, 2016). Nor is it advisable to seek ways of debiasing on the cheap: Elek and

Hannaford-Agor (2013), for example, recommend that "new jury instructions be carefully evaluated using rigorous empirical methods to determine their overall and differential effectiveness before they are broadly promoted for use in the courtroom" (p. 198).

At least one defense lawyer has cautioned that defense attorneys generally lack the time and training to attempt an effective debiasing strategy during voir dire and that to try to do so, unless one has "great skill and delicacy," would be to open a "Pandora's box," risking backlash from the jurors (Forman, 2015, p. 178). Forman makes the following recommendation:

> If lawyers are expected to educate juries about implicit bias, they
> should be provided with the tools to do this effectively. Law schools,
> bar organizations, and legal affinity groups should create programs
> for attorneys interested in mitigating the effects of hidden bias in
> their practice. (p. 177)

A second, and related, obstacle is the fear of making things worse. Judge Bennett (2010) reports that it is this fear that deters many of his colleagues from attempting implicit bias jury instructions. Jury instructions could, for example, lead to jurors feeling a false sense of confidence in the neutrality of their judgments if they believe themselves "properly immunized or educated about bias" (Kang et al., 2012, p. 1184). Instructions to suppress stereotypes may end up intensifying the risk posed by stereotypes, thanks to what researchers call rebound effects (Macrae, Bodenhausen, Milne, & Jetten, 1994). In addition, if disclosure of implicit bias creates anger and shame, the likelihood of stereotyping may increase (Bartlett, 2009). Finally, Elek and Hannaford-Agor (2014) have suggested that the traditional style in which jury instructions are phrased—what they describe as an "authoritarian legal style"—may "ultimately prove counterproductive by triggering a backlash effect" (p. 197).

Even if one is not afraid of making things worse, one may fear that little of value can be achieved through these reforms. First, it is possible that jury instructions have no useful effect on implicit juror bias. Even in less fraught areas, jury instructions are often thought to be overly long and insufficiently comprehended, and the only empirical study of instructions similar to Judge Bennett's failed to demonstrate any significant influence of the instructions on jurors' verdict preferences (Elek & Hannaford-Agor, 2014). Second, there may be skepticism about the extent to which any intervention during the relatively brief interaction between the court system and the jurors can do anything meaningful to combat biases that are grounded in our nation's history, internalized in early childhood, and reinforced in repeated fashion every day. The jury context is very different, for example, from Devine, Forscher, Austin, and Cox (2012)'s 12-week study of techniques designed to reduce implicit race bias. Moreover, Perry, Murphy, and Dovidio (2015) suggest that individual differences in bias awareness may have an effect on the extent to which people respond positively or negatively to anti-bias interventions. Specifically, they found that those higher in bias awareness were more likely than others to accept as credible IAT feedback relating to their personal bias. Third, one could see implicit bias in the jury context as a drop in a huge ocean and attempts at reform in this area as doing nothing to tackle explicit, institutional, or structural bias, or any of the other stages of the justice system (and other social systems) in which each of these forms of bias operates (Kang et al., 2012). Kang et al., for example, provide a helpful analysis of the numerous stages within both criminal and civil case trajectories at which biases can have an effect. Such stages within criminal case trajectories include the police encounter, the charge and the plea bargain, the trial, and sentencing.

An additional obstacle is that the relevant social science has not yet achieved broad understanding or support among the relevant decision-makers. Many people within the justice system are uninformed about implicit bias (Elek & Hannaford-Agor, 2013), and, as noted earlier, several judges have excluded expert testimony on this topic. While Rashon Brown's case provides an unusual example of judicial willingness to discuss—and act in response to—the risks of implicit bias (see *State v. Brown*, 2015), judges have generally been averse to this topic, whether the discussion relates to implicit bias in the courtroom (Larson, 2010) or elsewhere (Trenticosta & Collins, 2011). They might be particularly reluctant to acknowledge this phenomenon if such an acknowledgment would require them to alter the way in which they have always done things (Rapping, 2013). Nor are judges crazy to think that there is reason for caution. While there are indications that the kinds of proposals mentioned earlier could be beneficial, experts agree that more testing is needed before concrete changes are implemented (Levinson, 2007). As suggested earlier, this area is replete with hypotheses that require testing. Thus far, for example, the effects of the IAT when used as an educational device have not been tested in the juror context (Levinson, 2007).

A final obstacle may be a sense—conscious or unconscious—that it is better to avoid any recognition of implicit juror bias because of the potentially enormous consequences of taking it seriously. If we address implicit juror bias, one might wonder what else we have to address, and what would happen to the criminal justice system. If implicit bias cannot be effectively addressed in this context, what would happen? Would we continue to have jury trials even if they cannot be fair? If implicit bias *can* be effectively addressed in this context, what would have to change? Orientation, voir dire, instructions, appeals? These questions are relevant to implicit biases of all sorts but have the greatest urgency when it comes to race. As Sterling (2014) points out, race discrimination is largely missing from the courtroom conversation, which "manages to bypass race bias while being steeped in it" (p. 2265). It might be hard to imagine that one can allow race bias into the conversation just a little bit.

## Conclusion

Are informational interventions in this context effective? It is too early to say. Efforts to educate jurors about implicit bias are still being developed and tested, and their usefulness remains uncertain. This uncertainty may deter efforts, as may the fear of making things worse by trying or the sense that only limited steps can be taken in this context to contribute to the far larger project of addressing bias in all its many forms and in all its many settings. Finally, while much research has been done into implicit racial bias, one cannot forget the biases that exist in all other dimensions, or the need for further research on those fronts. None of these obstacles, however, should deter the work that is being done by many researchers and in many jurisdictions—urgent, careful, and multipronged efforts to tackle implicit juror bias and its ramifications for criminal trials as well as civil trials, to acknowledge the inability of the law as currently framed to provide sufficient protection, and to recognize the need to strengthen it with the tools and discoveries of social science. These obstacles cannot be allowed to deter such work, since it would be unacceptable if in our courthouses—the sites in which justice is supposed to be embodied, and in which constitutional guarantees of fairness are supposed to protect us—nothing was done to address the threats to justice and to constitutional guarantees posed by implicit juror bias.

## References

American Bar Association. (n.d.). *Achieving an impartial jury toolbox*. Retrieved from http://www.americanbar.org/content/dam/aba/publications/criminaljustice/voirdire_toolchest.authcheckdam.pdf

Apilado v. North American Gay Amateur Athletic Alliance, WL 13100729 (2011).

Arterton, J. B. (2008). Unconscious bias and the impartial jury. *Connecticut Law Review, 40*, 1025–1033.

Banaji, M. (2008, April 14). *Testimony from New Hampshire v. Addison, No. 07-S-0254*. [Transcript of Motion: Evidentiary Hearing].

Banaji, M. R., & Greenwald, A. G. (2013). *Blindspot: Hidden biases of good people*. New York: Bantam Books.

Bartlett, K. T. (2009). Making good on good intentions: The critical role of motivation in reducing implicit workplace discrimination. *Virginia Law Review, 95*, 1895–1972.

Bell, D. A. (2008). *Race, racism, and American law* (6th ed.). New York: Aspen.

Bennett, M. W. (2010). Unraveling the Gordian knot of implicit bias in jury selection: The problems of judge-dominated voir dire, the failed promise of Batson, and proposed solutions. *Harvard Law & Policy Review, 4*, 149–171.

Bennett, M. W. (2015). The presumption of innocence and trial court judges: Our greatest failing. *The Champion, 39*, 20–22.

Blair, I. V., Havranek, E. P., Price, D. W., Hanratty, R., Fairclough, D. L., Farley, T., . . . Steiner, J. F. (2013). Assessment of biases against Latinos and African Americans among primary care providers and community members. *American Journal of Public Health, 103*, 92–98. doi:10.2105/AJPH.2012.300812

Blume, J. (2008). The dilemma of the criminal defendant with a prior record: Lessons from the wrongly convicted. *Journal of Empirical Legal Studies, 5*, 477–505. doi:10.1111/j.1740-1461.2008.00131.x

Brown, J. O., Subrin, S., & Baumann, P. T. (1997). Some thoughts about social perception and employment discrimination law: A modest proposal for reopening the judicial dialogue. *Emory Law Journal, 46*, 1487–1531.

Caldwell, H. M., & Hewitt, A. M. (2014). Shades of guilt: Combating the continuing influence upon jury selection of racial stereotyping in post-Batson trials. *American Journal of Trial Advocacy, 38*, 67–120.

Casey, P. M., Warren, R. K., Cheesman II, F. L., & Elek, J. K. (2012). *Helping courts address implicit bias: Resources for education.* Retrieved from http://www.ncsc.org/~/media/Files/PDF/Topics/Gender%20and%20Racial%20Fairness/IB_report_033012.ashxis

Chan, W., & Mendelsohn, G.A. (2010). Disentangling stereotype and person effects: Do social stereotypes bias observer judgment of personality? *Journal of Research in Personality, 44*, 251–257. doi:10.1521/soco.1998.16.1.151

Clinton, H. R. (2016, September 26). Presidential debate. Hofstra University, Hempstead, NY.

Cohen, A. (2014). *Confessing while Black: When the threat of a White jury is an interrogation tool.* Retrieved from https://www.themarshallproject.org/2014/12/12/confessing-while-black#.x12lxD4Wc

Dasgupta, N., & Greenwald, A. G. (2001). On the malleability of automatic attitudes: Combating automatic prejudice with images of admired and disliked individuals. *Journal of Personality and Social Psychology, 81*, 800–814. doi:10.1037//0022-3514.81.5.800

Dasgupta, N., & Rivera, L. M. (2006). From automatic antigay prejudice to behavior: The moderating role of conscious beliefs and behavioral control. *Journal of Personality and Social Psychology, 91*, 268–280. doi:10.1037/0022-3514.91.2.268

Developments—race and the criminal process. (1988). *Harvard Law Review, 101*, 1472–1641.

Devine, P. G., Forscher, P. S., Austin, A. J., & Cox, W. T. L. (2012). Long-term reduction in implicit racial bias: A prejudice habit-breaking intervention. *Journal of Experimental Social Psychology, 48*, 1267–1278. doi:10.1016/j.jesp.2012.06.003

Eisenberg, T., & Johnson, S. L. (2004). Implicit racial attitudes of death penalty lawyers. *DePaul Law Review, 53*, 1539–1556.

Elek, J. K., & Hannaford-Agor, P. (2013). First, do no harm: On addressing the problem of implicit bias in juror decision making. *Court Review, 49*, 190–198.

Elek, J. K., & Hannaford-Agor, P. (2014). *Can explicit instructions reduce expressions of implicit bias? New questions following a test of a specialized jury instruction.* Retrieved from http://www.ncsc-jurystudies.org/~/media/Microsites/Files/CJS/What%20We%20Do/Can%20Explicit%20Instructions%20Reduce%20Expressions%20of%20Implicit%20Bias.ashx

Fair, B. K. (1994). Using parrots to kill mockingbirds: Yet another racial prosecution and wrongful conviction in Maycomb. *Alabama Law Review, 45*, 403–472.

Forman, D. L. (1992). What difference does it make? Gender and jury selection. *UCLA Women's Law Journal, 2,* 35–83.

Forman, S. J. (2015). The #Ferguson effect: Opening the Pandora's box of implicit racial bias in jury selection. *Northwestern University Law Review Colloquy, 109,* 171–179.

Ghandnoosh, N. (2014). *Race and punishment: Racial perceptions of crime and support for punitive policies.* Retrieved from http://sentencingproject.org/wp-content/uploads/2015/11/Race-and-Punishment.pdf

Green, A. R., Darney, D. R., Pallin, D. J., Ngo, L. H., Raymond, K. L., Iezzoni, L. I., & Banaji, M. R. (2007). Implicit bias among physicians and its prediction of thrombolysis decisions for Black and White patients. *Journal of General Internal Medicine, 22,* 1231–1238. doi:10.1007/s11606-007-0258-5

Greenwald, A. G., & Banaji, M. R. (1995). Implicit social cognition: Attitudes, self-esteem, and stereotypes. *Psychological Review, 102,* 4–27. doi:10.1037//0033-295X.102.1.4

Greenwald, A. G., & Krieger, L. H. (2006). Implicit bias: Scientific foundations. *California Law Review, 94,* 945–967.

Herman, S. N. (1993). Why the court loves Batson: Representation-reinforcement, colorblindness, and the jury. *Tulane Law Review, 67,* 1807–1853.

Jackson, S. M., Hillard, A. L., & Schneider, T. R. (2014). Using implicit bias training to improve attitudes toward women in STEM. *Social Psychology of Education, 17,* 419–438. doi:10.1007/s11218-014-9259-5

Jones, S. E. (1987). Judge- versus attorney-conducted voir dire: An empirical investigation of juror candor. *Law and Human Behavior, 11,* 131–146. doi:10.1007/BF01040446

Jones v. National Council of Young Men's Christian Associations of the United States of America, 34 F. Supp. 3d 896 (N.D. Ill. 2014).

Jost, J. T., Rudman, L. A., Blair, I. V., Carney, D. R., Dasgupta, N., Glaser, J., & Hardin, C. D. (2009). The existence of implicit bias is beyond reasonable doubt: A refutation of ideological and methodological objections and executive summary of ten studies that no manager should ignore. *Research in Organizational Behavior, 29,* 39–69. doi:10.1016/j.riob.2009.10.001

Judicial Council of California, Advisory Committee on Civil Jury Instructions. (2012). *Judicial council of California civil jury instructions: 113.* San Francisco, CA: LexisNexis Matthew Bender.

Karlo v. Pittsburgh Glass Works, LLC, 2015 W.L. 4232600 (2015).

Karlo v. Pittsburgh Glass Works, LLC, 849 F.3d 61, 3d Cir. (2017).

Kang, J., Bennett, M., Carbado, D., Casey, P., Dasgupta, N., Faigman, D., . . . Mnookin, J. (2012). Implicit bias in the courtroom. *UCLA Law Review, 59,* 1124–1186.

Kang, J., & Lane, K. (2010). Seeing through colorblindness: Implicit bias and the law. *UCLA Law Review, 58,* 465–520.

Kunda, Z., & Sherman-Williams, B. (1993). Stereotypes and the construal of individuating information. *Personality and Social Psychology Bulletin, 19,* 90–99. doi:10.1177/0146167293191010

Kunda, Z., & Thagard, P. (1996). Forming impressions from stereotypes, traits, and behaviors: A parallel-constraint-satisfaction theory. *Psychological Review, 103,* 284–308. doi:10.1037/0033-295X.103.2.284

Larson, D. (2010). A fair and implicitly impartial jury: An argument for administering the implicit association test during voir dire. *DePaul Journal of Social Justice, 3,* 139–171.

Lee, C. (1996). Race and self-defense: Toward a normative conception of reasonableness. *Minnesota Law Review, 81,* 367–500.

Lee, C. (2013). Making race salient: Trayvon Martin and implicit bias in a not yet post-racial society. *North Carolina Law Review, 91,* 1555–1612.

Lee, C. (2015). A new approach to voir dire on racial bias. *UC Irvine Law Review, 5,* 843–872.

Levinson, J. D. (2006). Suppressing the expression of community values in juries: How "legal priming" systematically alters the way people think. *University of Cincinnati Law Review, 73,* 1059–1079.

Levinson, J. D. (2007). Forgotten racial equality: Implicit bias, decisionmaking, and misremembering. *Duke Law Journal, 57,* 345–424.

Levinson, J. D., Cai, H., & Young, D. (2010). Guilty by implicit racial bias: The guilty/not guilty implicit association test. *Ohio State Journal of Criminal Law, 8,* 187–208.

Levinson, J. D., Smith, R. J., & Young, D. M. (2014). Devaluing death: An empirical study of implicit racial bias on jury-eligible citizens in six death penalty states. *New York University Law Review, 89,* 513–581.

Lynch, M., & Haney, C. (2011). Looking across the empathic divide: Racialized decision making on the capital jury. *Michigan State Law Review, 2011,* 573–607.

Macrae, C. N., Bodenhausen, G. V., Milne, A. B., & Jetten, J. (1994). Out of mind but back in sight: Stereotypes on the rebound. *Journal of Personality and Social Psychology, 67,* 808–817. doi:10.1037/0022-3514.67.5.808

McComas, J., & Strout, C. (1999). Combating the effects of stereotyping in criminal cases. *The Champion, 23*(22), 22–24.

O'Brien, R. (2003, August 31). Neighborhood report: Greenwich Village—CITYPEOPLE; For the Spielberg of civic duty, no jury prizes, just plenty of jurors. *The New York Times.* Retrieved from http://www.nytimes.com

Page, A. (2005). Batson's blind-spot: Unconscious stereotyping and the peremptory challenge. *Boston University Law Review, 85,* 155–262.

Pena-Rodriguez v. Colorado, 137 S.Ct 855 (2017).

Perry, S., Murphy, M. C., & Dovidio, J. F. (2015). Modern prejudice: Subtle, but unconscious? The role of bias awareness in Whites' perception of personal and others' biases. *Journal of Experimental Social Psychology, 61,* 64–78. doi:10.1016/j.jesp.2015.06.007

Project Implicit. (2011). Retrieved from https://implicit.harvard.edu/

Rapping, J. A. (2013). Implicitly unjust: How defenders can affect systemic racist assumptions. *New York University Journal of Legislation & Public Policy, 16,* 999–1048.

Roberts, A. (2012). (Re)forming the jury: Detection and disinfection of implicit juror bias. *Connecticut Law Review, 44,* 827–882.

Roberts, A. (2013). Casual ostracism: Jury exclusion on the basis of criminal convictions. *Minnesota Law Review, 98,* 592–647.

Roberts, A. (2015). Asymmetry as fairness: Reversing a preemptory trend. *Washington University Law Review, 92,* 1504–1550.

Roberts, A. (2016). Reclaiming the importance of the defendant's testimony: Prior conviction impeachment and the fight against implicit stereotyping. *University of Chicago Law Review, 83*, 835–891.

Ross, J. (2004). "He looks guilty": Reforming good character evidence to undercut the presumption of guilt. *University of Pittsburgh Law Review, 65*, 227–279.

Salami v. Von Maur, Inc, 838 N.W.2d 680 (2013).

Samaha v. Washington State Department of Transportation, 2012 W.L. 11091843 (2012).

Smith, R. J., & Levinson, J. D. (2012). The impact of implicit racial bias on the exercise of prosecutorial discretion. *Seattle University Law Review, 35*, 795–826.

Smith. R. J., Levinson, J. D., & Robinson, Z. (2015). Implicit White favoritism in the criminal justice system. *Alabama Law Review, 66*, 871–923.

Sommers, S. R. (2006). On racial diversity and group decision making: Identifying multiple effects of racial composition on jury deliberations. *Journal of Personality and Social Psychology, 90*, 597–612. doi:10.1037/0022-3514.90.4.597

Sommers, S. R., & Ellsworth, P. C. (2001). White juror bias: An investigation of prejudice against Black defendants in the American courtroom. *Psychology, Public Policy, and Law, 7*, 201–229. doi:10.1037/1076-8971.7.1.201

Sommers, S. R., & Marotta, S. A. (2014). Racial disparities in legal outcomes: On policing, charging decisions, and criminal trial proceedings. *Policy Insights from the Behavioral and Brain Sciences, 1*, 103–111. doi:10.1177/2372732214548431

State v. Brown, 121 A.3d 878, 442 N.J. Super. 154 (2015).

Sterling, R. W. (2014). Defense attorney resistance. *Iowa Law Review, 99*, 2245–2272.

Tabak, R. J. (2010). The continuing role of race in capital cases, notwithstanding President Obama's election. *Northern Kentucky Law Review, 37*, 243–271.

Trenticosta, C., & Collins, W. C. (2011). Death and Dixie: How the courthouse Confederate flag influences capital cases in Louisiana. *Harvard Journal on Racial and Ethnic Justice, 27*, 125–164.

United States District Court, Western District of Washington. (2017a). *Criminal jury instructions: Implicit bias*. Retrieved from http://www.wawd.uscourts.gov/sites/wawd/files/CriminalJuryInstructions-ImplicitBias.pdf

United States District Court, Western District of Washington (Prod.). (2017b). *Understanding the effects of unconscious bias* [Video File]. Retrieved from http://www.wawd.uscourts.gov/jury/unconscious-bias

Vershuta, N. A. (2016). New rules of war in the battle of experts: Amending the expert witness disqualification test for conflicts of interest. *Brooklyn Law Review, 81*, 733–777.

Wedel, C. P. (2011). Twelve angry (and stereotyped) jurors: How courts can use scientific jury selection to end discriminatory peremptory challenges. *Stanford Journal of Civil Rights & Civil Liberties, 7*, 293–328.

Young, D. M., Levinson, J. D., & Sinnett, S. (2014). Innocent until primed: Mock jurors' racially biased response to the presumption of innocence. *PLoS One, 9*, e92365. doi:10.1371/journal.pone.0092365

# 6

## In the Aftermath of Ferguson

### Jurors' Perceptions of the Police and Court Legitimacy Then and Now

### Lindsey M. Cole

The recent events surrounding police use of excessive force in the line of duty have rocked the nation, bringing issues of police disproportionate contact with and unfair treatment of racial and ethnic minorities into the spotlight and resulting in a call to action in protest of policing practices. Although these events and issues are troubling, raising concerns over the impartiality of our justice system, they are by no means new. Previous generations have experienced racial disproportionality in police use of excessive force, and the media has historically reported high-profile incidents (Capers, 2008). However, the recent events have spurred a whole new movement, which has the potential to change the culture of policing and the way individuals view the police in their communities in an unprecedented way. How have the knowledge and newfound awareness resulting from current widespread protests, activism, and media coverage of disproportionate police use of force on minorities translated into change? One important way this movement has impacted change is most certainly through individuals' perceptions of and trust in police and our legal institutions. The purpose of this chapter is to explore how incidents like the one in Ferguson, Missouri, and the rise of the Black Lives Matter movement have affected the courts and lay participation in the justice system through their effects on police and court legitimacy. That is, have recent events altered jurors' acceptance of the police as a valid authority for administering the law?

In the introductory chapter of this volume, Stevenson and Najdowski highlighted a *Time Magazine* article about one journalist's experience on a New York City jury as an example of the importance and far-reaching effects of police-community interactions in our justice system (Newton-Small, 2016). The journalist, Jay Newton-Small, noted that the perspectives of her fellow jurors diverged significantly and their interpretation of the case and evidence was highly influenced by their individual backgrounds. Where White jurors saw a clear-cut case with overwhelming evidence pointing to the defendant's guilt, African American jurors saw a very different picture, filled with reasonable doubt and distrust of evidence put forth by the police. From her experience over the course of several days of deliberation, Newton-Small described instances of intense debate, much of which centered on the believability of evidence and differing interpretations of the case. Where White jurors saw credible police witnesses, sound investigative work, and indisputable physical evidence, Black jurors saw police witnesses with motive to lie, incomplete or inadequate investigative work, and physical evidence that could only be verified from the testimony of a questionable witness at the scene.

The contrast between jurors in this case reflects the disparities different groups of individuals have in experiences with police and the justice system. Historically, people of color have experienced disproportionate contact with the justice system at all levels, including initial contact with police in their communities (Lofstrom & Raphael, 2016; Piquero, 2008; Roberts, 2015). Furthermore, racial and ethnic minority defendants tend to be convicted more often and receive harsher punishments than White defendants who are accused of similar offenses (Burch, 2015). One juror from this case put it aptly when she remarked, "a young White man would never have been on trial for [such a minor offense]" (Newton-Small, 2016, p. 3). This disproportionate minority contact and disparate treatment has given rise to a general distrust in police (Kahn & Martin, 2016) and cynicism about the fairness of the justice system in minority communities (Kirk & Matsuda, 2011; Sampson & Bartusch, 1998). To understand the potential impact these differing perceptions have on the courts, one must first examine the historical determinants and development of police and court legitimacy, the role police play in courts, and how jurors' perceptions of police and court legitimacy affect juror decision-making as revealed by research. It is also important to explore how the events in Ferguson and other cities across the United States and related media coverage and cultural movements have altered, exacerbated, and shaped perceptions on a national level and, in turn, potentially affected lay participation in the legal system.

## Jurors' Perceptions of Police and Court Legitimacy

Police play an integral role in the front end of our justice system, functioning as the "gatekeepers." In most cases, individuals' first contact with the justice system is police contact, which may consist of being stopped, arrested, interviewed, or approached for collection of evidence. However, police also play important roles in other subsequent areas of the legal system. In many ways, they serve as a bridge between what happens in the community and in the courtroom. Police have a role and perspective in court unlike any other legal entity: They appear as witnesses to convey information about the scene of the purported crime, impressions of the accused or others involved, discussion of evidence gathered, and technical interpretations (Lempert et al., 2013; Nemeth, 2010). However, police have also found themselves on the other side of the courtroom as defendants in cases of police misconduct, abuse of authority, brutality, or even unlawful killing of individuals in the community. Many of these cases have never made it past a grand jury, and historically very few have resulted in conviction (Fairfax, 2017). Yet, despite the frequency with which police appear in court either as witnesses or defendants, there remains a dearth of research focused on the complex role of police in the courts (Cole, 2015; Yarmey, 1986).

### Police as Witnesses in Court

Police truly qualify as a separate and distinct class of witness, neither serving strictly as eyewitnesses or expert witnesses, because of the types of information they can provide as witnesses as well as their status as legal authorities. In fact, there are likely few other witnesses besides police who can provide eyewitness testimony of a crime while simultaneously offering an expert opinion or exerting expert authority as frequently and consistently as police. The unique role of police witnesses in courts, however, has been largely understudied (Cole, 2015; Yarmey, 1986), with only a few studies that have examined police as witnesses, most of which focused on memory recall accuracy of police compared to lay individuals (Stanny & Johnson, 2000) or lay perceptions of police officer witness memory recall abilities (Schmechel, O'Toole, Easterly, & Loftus, 2005).

A considerable amount of attention has been directed toward the study of witness testimony and its effect on juror decision-making, especially eyewitness testimony (e.g., Bell & Loftus, 1988; Devine, Clayton, Dunford, Seying, & Pryce, 2001; Wells & Olson, 2003; Wrightsman, Willis, & Kassin, 1987). The majority of knowledge about witness testimony and its effect on juror decision-making has been drawn from the body of eyewitness research. Although there has been some, albeit less, research on expert witness testimony, a review of existing expert testimony literature revealed few studies focused on police and other legal professionals.

Eyewitnesses and expert witnesses serve different functions in the scope of the trial and, therefore, their testimony is interpreted differently by jurors (Kassin, Williams, & Saunders, 1990; Lempert et al., 2013; Nemeth, 2010). Eyewitnesses are generally lay individuals who have witnessed the crime or have some knowledge of the crime that is then shared with the court through presentation of their testimony. In the case of lay eyewitness accounts, no opinions or speculation are allowed to be rendered by the witness (Lampert et al., 2013; Nemeth, 2010). While eyewitnesses are generally lay individuals who testify about their own experience related to an event, expert witnesses are professionals with expertise in a particular field who testify about technical aspects of the crime in the range of their expertise that is not known or easily understood by the general public (Kassin et al., 1990; Nemeth, 2010). Moreover, unlike lay witnesses, expert witnesses are allowed to speculate on the case and include their own personal opinion and commentary. Police officer witnesses often serve in both capacities.

The general consensus among researchers is that jurors are willing to accept the accuracy of eyewitness testimony despite overwhelming empirical evidence that indicates myriad ways in which eyewitness accounts can be mistaken (Goodman & Loftus, 1992; Spellman & Tenney, 2010; Whitley, 1987). Additionally, jurors often passively accept testimony of expert witnesses as fact simply due to their expertise on the issue and their position as an authority on the subject (Kassin et al., 1990). From the scarce extant police-specific literature, researchers have found that lay individuals often perceive the police to have superior memory recall abilities compared to lay individuals (Cutler & Penrod, 1995; Deffenbacher & Loftus, 1982; Yarmey, 1986), and, therefore, jurors may more willingly accept the testimony of police officer eyewitnesses as accurate because they are viewed as more reliable. However, in reality, police are equally as prone to memory recall issues as lay individuals, producing only slightly better (Christianson, Karlsson, & Persson, 1998; Lindholm, Christianson, & Karlsson, 1997; Vredeveldt & van Koppen, 2016) or no more reliable and accurate testimony as everyday witnesses (Kaminski & Sporer, 2016; Stanny & Johnson, 2000; Tickner & Poulton, 1975).

Additionally, researchers find that police are no more knowledgeable about the factors known to influence eyewitness memory than lay individuals (Wise, Safer, & Maro, 2011), despite the relevance of such information to their jobs as interrogators of suspects and interviewers of victims and eyewitnesses. Kebbell and Milne (1998) even found that police perceive eyewitnesses to be highly accurate, often gauging eyewitnesses' accuracy by their level of confidence and response time. Accuracy and confidence are two measures used by jurors—as well as police—to determine witnesses' credibility (Spellman & Tenney, 2010). This is not particularly surprising, however, as police tend not to outperform lay individuals in assessing other factors related to credibility assessments, such as detecting deception. Many jurors (Zuckerman, Koestner, & Driver, 1981) and even legal professionals like police officers (Mann, Vrij, & Bull, 2004) rely on deception cues in order to make credibility judgments, often mistaking the veracious for the deceptive. In fact, most people, professionals included, perform no better than chance in detecting deception when using stereotypical cues (Vrij, 2000).

Despite the numerous credibility assessment pitfalls to which both police and jurors fall prey, whether jurors believe or disbelieve a witness's testimony largely hinges on the perceived credibility of the witness, making credibility assessments an important consideration in examining juror decision-making. To explore potential differences in juror credibility assessments of police officer witnesses compared to lay witnesses, an experimental study was conducted immediately following the events in Ferguson (Cole, 2015). The study utilized a video of court proceedings for a robbery case, specifically filmed for the purpose of creating two versions of the same case for the study: one in which the primary eyewitness was portrayed as an off-duty police officer and another in which the eyewitness was a lay individual. In both versions of the trial, the eyewitness testified on behalf of the prosecution and presented the same testimony, only altering information pertaining to his profession.

In this study, Cole (2015) found that a police officer eyewitness elicited greater perceptions of juror trust and credibility than a lay eyewitness when the testimony was held consistent and the same individual played both types of witnesses. Even so, the presentation of a police officer eyewitness rather than a lay eyewitness resulted in more acquittals, both for post-deliberation individual mock juror decisions and jury group decisions. A closer look at the data revealed that although mock jurors perceived the police officer to be more credible on average, jurors' ratings of the police witness were more variable than those of the lay witness. When mock jurors were questioned about their verdict decisions following deliberation, many commented that they had greater expectations of a police officer than a lay eyewitness because of the officer's training and experience, such as the ability to recall specific information and have confidence in his testimony (Cole, 2015). Indeed, because the officer could not definitively state the exact distance from which he saw the perpetrator, a minority of mock jurors thought the police officer testimony did not achieve the high standard they expected and deemed the officer to be unreliable. Although the lay eyewitness testimony was identical in almost every regard, including both witnesses' inability to identify their exact distance from the perpetrator, not a single mock juror in the lay condition stated that this factor affected their judgment of the witness's credibility (Cole, 2015). This finding further highlights the distinctions between juror perceptions of police and lay witnesses and the importance placed on credibility assessments.

Generally, when witnesses are perceived as credible, jurors trust their testimony is truthful and accurate (Friedland, 1989; Newcombe & Bransgrove, 2007) and feel obligated to consider the testimony when making verdict decisions. Police officer witnesses in particular may hold an added level of credibility (or lack thereof) based on jurors' perceptions of police legitimacy, as formed from their experiences with police in the community. These perceptions may ultimately affect verdict decisions if jurors discount witness testimony because they find a police officer witness to not be credible, assume policing procedures were unfair, or are skeptical about evidence gathered or presented by police. This precise situation is illustrated in the example described by Newton-Small (2016) at the beginning of this chapter and discussed further next.

## The Effect of Police and Court Legitimacy on the Juror Experience

In the legal system in the United States as well as in many other countries around the world, lay members of society are called upon to participate in deciding culpability of their peers who have been charged with a crime. As jurors, individuals must weigh the evidence presented to reach a verdict decision, including judging the veracity and accuracy of eyewitness testimony. However, as non-legally trained individuals, jurors may be susceptible to the influence of their own personal attitudes and biases, viewing evidence through the lens of their own experiences, and their decisions may be affected accordingly (Chapdelaine & Griffin, 1997; Cohn, Bucolo, Pride, & Sommers, 2009; Dane & Wrightsman, 1982).

Interactions that individuals have with various legal authority figures, such as police and judges, and how fair those experiences are perceived to be help to shape individuals' perceptions of the legitimacy of the law and legal system. These perceptions and experiences, in turn, affect behavior relevant to the legal institutions those actors represent (Hough, Jackson, Bradford, Myhill, & Quinton, 2010; Tyler & Huo, 2002; Tyler & Jackson, 2014). It is clear in the previously described example of Newton-Small's (2016) experience as a juror that the differences in opinions and perspectives between the jury members is driven primarily by differences in experiences with the law, whether directly through personal contact or indirectly through vicarious means. The Black jurors in the case displayed a greater sense of cynicism and distrust in the legitimacy of the system, and their dialogue also suggests an expectation of unfair treatment by legal actors for Black individuals. This idea of fairness, specifically fair treatment, is central to the formation of trust in and legitimacy of police and the courts and is conceptualized as the experience of procedural justice (Tyler, 2006).

Procedural justice researchers have long found distinct relations between treatment of individuals by the police and their perceptions of police legitimacy and law-related behaviors, including both complying with the law and violating it (Hough et al., 2010; Tyler & Huo, 2002; Tyler & Jackson, 2014). Lay participation in the legal system through juror service is a practice uniquely focused on the assessment of others' law-violating behavior and enables individuals to view police as partners in achieving justice. However, little is known about how perceptions of police legitimacy affect the way individuals view police in other settings within the legal system, such as when they appear as witnesses in court (but see Cole, 2015).

When jurors have strong attitudes, whether positive or negative, it can influence the way they view the defendant, victim, witnesses, and even the evidence presented (Devine et al., 2001; Hastie, 1993). Jurors can be skeptical of information from sources against whom they are negatively biased and may choose to ignore that information in their decision-making (Chapdelaine & Griffin, 1997). In contrast, jurors who have strong positive biases are more accepting of information from the sources toward whom they have a positive bias (Chapdelaine & Griffin, 1997; Dane & Wrightsman, 1982). The majority of research on juror attitudes and bias has focused primarily on bias against the defendant (Devine et al., 2001); however, these same principles hold true for legal authorities as well (Cole, 2015).

The limited research in this area has found that mock juror attitudes toward the police, specifically perceived police legitimacy, were positively related to mock juror credibility ratings of police officer witnesses (Cole, 2015; Cole & Cohn, 2017). In a study conducted prior to Ferguson, Cole and Cohn found that participants who reported viewing the police as legitimate prior to taking part in a mock trial experiment were more likely to find a police officer witness credible, while those who viewed the police as less legitimate were more likely to perceive the police officer witness as not credible.

Cole and Cohn (2017) demonstrated that mock jurors' perceptions of police legitimacy were also significantly related to their individual verdict decisions, both prior to and following group deliberation. In a case in which the police officer testified against the defendant for the prosecution, those who did not view the police as legitimate were more likely to acquit the defendant than those who viewed the police as legitimate. This effect was mediated by juror assessments of the police officer eyewitness' credibility. That is, those who perceived the police in general to be less rather than more legitimate perceived the specific police officer witness in the case to be less credible and, in turn, were less likely to render verdicts that were consistent with the police officer's testimony. These findings were later replicated in a separate study using a different case conducted shortly after Ferguson (Cole, 2015). Reminiscent of the Newton-Small (2016) case example, in these studies, jurors who ultimately moved to acquit often cited in their deliberation dialogue a distrust or elevated level of skepticism about the evidence gathered by police, the truthfulness and accuracy of the officer's testimony, or the fairness of the judicial process (Cole, 2015; Cole & Cohn, 2017).

### Juror Versus Jury Decisions in Cases Involving Police

Although jurors enter the court carrying their own experiences, biases, and skill sets, they are not solely responsible for the final verdict. Instead, to render a verdict for the defendant, jurors must engage in group deliberation and contribute to the decision-making process to reach a unanimous decision together (Diamond, Vidmar, Rose, Ellis, & Murphy, 2003; Salerno & Diamond, 2010). Yet not all members of a jury may share the same opinion or perspective, as in the case described by Newton-Small (2016), and these opinions and perspectives may change as a function of group deliberation, making the jury group as a whole an important consideration in the study of juror decision-making.

Juries are a valued method of legal decision-making and, in most instances, more impartial than any individual decision-maker (London &

Nuñez, 2000). For example, jury deliberation allows for jurors to share information and knowledge gained throughout the course of the trial that may have been missed or misinterpreted by any individual juror (Bornstein & Greene, 2011; Prichard & Keenan, 2002). Evidence and instructions can be consolidated, corrected, and directed into a thorough discussion toward a thoughtful verdict decision (McCoy, Nuñez, & Dammeyer, 1999). Furthermore, the importance of certain pieces of evidence and information relevant to the case and verdict decision become more salient during the deliberation process, often leading to a more considerate decision than at the individual level (Kerwin & Shaffer, 1994; London & Nuñez, 2000; Ruva, McEvoy, & Bryant, 2007).

Irrespective of the fact that individual jurors ultimately do not make final verdict decisions, the majority of research on jury decision-making has focused on decisions of individual juror participants (Bornstein & Greene, 2011). Some researchers who have focused on jury group decisions have found that the deliberation process and group interaction attenuate any extreme attitudes that might persuade individual jurors to make verdict decisions on the basis of peripheral information and not information pertinent to the case itself (Karpowitz & Mendelberg, 2007; Salerno & Diamond, 2010). Although there is support for an attenuation effect of group deliberation on some preexisting attitudes that jurors may hold, this may not be the case for juror attitudes toward the police. The two studies reviewed thus far examining the effect of mock juror perceptions of police legitimacy on verdict decisions have both found that group deliberation did not attenuate the relations, and, in fact, the effect became more pronounced following deliberation in most cases (Cole, 2015; Cole & Cohn, 2017). The precise reason for this persistence and exacerbation has yet to be definitively identified, but several explanations are plausible.

Unlike other types of pre-existing attitudes and biases, jurors may not view their attitudes toward and biases against the police as socially inappropriate the way one might find something such as racial bias to be. For example, in most instances it might not seem relevant to discuss or consider a defendant's race in deliberation, but a police officer witness's occupation as a legal authority and role in the case may seem more intuitively open for discussion. This may leave jurors open to their own attitudes toward and biases against the police when deliberating, affecting the narrative the group builds about the case in reaching a decision. This narrative or story building is the process by which jurors take evidence presented at trial and then build various stories around what is known about the case in order to understand what likely happened at the time of the crime (Pennington & Hastie, 1992).

Although often juries attempt to run through a variety of plausible scenarios until the most logical scenario is identified (Weinstock, 2011), some stories may premise reasoning based on analogical thinking (Pennington & Hastie, 1988; SunWolf, 2010), such as using one's own experience. For example, a juror might think, "If I were confronted with a potentially threatening situation, I would have called the police instead of doing what the defendant did." This personalization is problematic, because the jurors are not in fact the actor in the case and yet apply their own reasoning to the situation. The inability to recognize differences in perspectives and experiences may create tension among jurors during deliberations and hamper the decision-making process. In the case example, Newton-Small (2016) noted that the Black jurors were chastised by the other jurors for being too critical of the evidence and failing to accept what the White jurors viewed as straightforward, irrefutable facts. These different interpretations of the evidence painted disparate portraits of the case for different jurors and resulted in heated, if not hostile debate that ultimately ended in a verdict decision different from the preference of the group majority—an effect that would have been missed and result misjudged if only individual juror decisions prior to deliberation were examined. Taken together with the research findings in this area thus far, Newton-Small's case further illustrates the need to refocus empirical examination on the jury as a whole and the impact of deliberation on juror decisions.

## Juries in the Aftermath of Ferguson

In the first half of this chapter, I illustrated the degree to which police are both inextricably tied to the courts and the impact they have on jurors' decisions. Many of the ways police influence jurors' perceptions and decisions rely on beliefs that police are trained legal authorities who are trustworthy and credible. However, incidents such as the shooting of Michael Brown in Ferguson have brought issues of policing practices and disparate treatment of Black individuals to the forefront of the nation's attention, simultaneously raising awareness and generating social movements, both in support of and against police. The events in Ferguson and resulting social movements may be changing public perceptions of the police, particularly around the treatment of Black people. These changing attitudes may not only affect individuals' interactions with police in the community but may also impact the way jurors view police and their role in court, as well as the legitimacy of legal institutions in general.

Since the Ferguson case, there has been renewed focus in studying the impact of public perceptions of police on the legal system, yet research focused specifically on the courts and juries is only just starting to emerge. Therefore, I devote the remainder of this chapter to examining Ferguson's impact on policing and how these changes are likely to translate to the juror box, considering both the short- and long-term consequences of Ferguson on public perceptions toward the police and other legal institutions.

## Perceptions of Police Use of Force in the Digital Age

Concern over police use of force is not a new issue, particularly in the context of disproportionate minority contact. Cases of excessive police use of force against racial and ethnic minority individuals, particularly Black individuals, have been occurring for decades, including the case of *Graham v. Connor* (1989), which set forth the institution of "reasonable force" criteria and precipitated the Rodney King beating by the Los Angeles Police Department that resulted in riots locally and around the nation (Brown, 1990; Ross, 2002). Yet recently, unlike in previous eras, these cases are highlighted through mass and social media coverage, creating more public outcry than ever.

Over the past few years, cases of police use of excessive force have flooded news reports, social media, and YouTube, creating innumerable public exposures to police violence (Bonilla & Rosa, 2015). One of the most salient cases was the police officer shooting of Michael Brown in Ferguson, Missouri. In August 2014, Darren Wilson, a White Ferguson police officer, stopped 18-year-old Michael Brown, who was suspected of robbing a nearby convenience store (Buchanan et al., 2014). An altercation broke out between Officer Wilson and Brown, which resulted in Wilson firing two shots out of the window of his police vehicle at Brown. A foot pursuit ensued, ultimately ending in the fatal shooting of Michael Brown, who was unarmed at the time (Buchanan et al., 2014). News of the police shooting of an unarmed, young Black man by a White officer sent the city of Ferguson into a flurry of protests, catching national attention (Griffiths & Christian, 2015).

Reports and witness accounts of the incident leading up to the shooting of Brown varied widely, some of which ignited mass protests and demonstrations that persisted for weeks and prompted confrontations between protestors and police (Buchanan et al., 2014). In response to some of the more destructive protesting and rioting behavior, police employed riot gear and crowd-control procedures, such as the use of tear gas and rubber bullets (Moran & Waddington, 2016). Coverage of the events fanned national interest and support for the growing demonstrations against the police in Ferguson. Not long after Michael Brown's death, police shootings of other young Black men flooded the media and became a focal point of the nation's attention (Bonilla & Rosa, 2015).

The modern era has brought forth real-time sharing of public-generated media, including cellphone videos and pictures, in an unprecedented way. (For a discussion of the influence of such media evidence on jurors' decision-making, see Chapter 9 of this volume.) People post and tweet the everyday happenings of their lives, documenting their experiences openly on publically accessible platforms and creating a virtual world of interactions and relationships with others through technology. The rise of the public-generated media culture has produced a public need to capture important events as they occur, such as police use of excessive force, providing an unedited, first-person account that can be easily and immediately shared through social media. This ability to both document and share controversial police encounters with individuals in the community, as illustrated by the police-related deaths of Eric Garner and Tamir Rice, has fed and influenced national social movements like Black Lives Matter that call for justice system reform to address the disparate treatment of Black people by the police (Bonilla & Rosa, 2015).

Despite the heightened media attention and popular public belief, there is little evidence to suggest a "Ferguson effect" on actual police-related violence; the long-term trends in fatal shootings by police (Campbell, Nix, & Maguire, 2018) as well as police officers killed in the line of duty (Maguire, Nix, & Campbell, 2016) has neither increased nor decreased since Ferguson. Although the shooting in Ferguson has not significantly affected violent acts by or toward police, the explosion of media capturing police excessive use of force and the social movements that followed have affected perceptions of both the public and police surrounding the current policing climate.

### Ferguson's Impact on Perceived Police Legitimacy and Policing Practices

Since Ferguson, public attitudes toward the police as well as some policing practices have changed in several ways, although these changes are not seen across the board for all individuals or in all police departments. Prior to Ferguson and other incidents, media coverage of police violence was found to negatively impact public perceptions of the police; however, this effect was largely localized and national events had little impact on widespread public perceptions (Kaminski & Jefferis, 1998). In the post-Ferguson era, researchers suggest that the public attention toward and awareness of the shooting in Ferguson—and other highly publicized incidents involving police use of force—may have altered public perceptions of the justifiability of police shootings (Culhane, Boman, & Schweitzer, 2016). Before the police shooting in Ferguson, Culhane and colleagues found that the presentation of video documentation of a police shooting lowered participants' perceptions that the shooting was unjustified compared to reading a written transcript of the event. However, following the events in Ferguson, participants who viewed video documentation had greater perceptions that the shooting was unjustifiable compared to those exposed to either audio or written presentation, suggesting a sensitization to video media.

Other recent research supports this hypothesis, finding that viewing controversial police intervention videos can increase viewers' perceptions of the frequency of police use of force, even after a single viewing (Boivin, Gendron, Faubert, & Poulin, 2016). Such effects, however, may be stronger for racial and ethnic minority individuals, who are disproportionately more likely to be targets of police use of force (Goff, Lloyd, Geller, Raphael, & Glaser, 2016), than for Whites. For example, Kaminski and Jefferis (1998) found that local media coverage of police violence in Cincinnati increased

Black city residents' perceptions of police use of force in the community and decreased residents' perceptions of the ability of police to protect the community and police responsiveness to crime but did not significantly impact White residents' perceptions of police.

This finding is consistent with previous research in which media coverage consumption was found to be related to evaluations of police officers, but only for Black individuals. For Black but not White participants, exposure to police violence in the media has been found to relate to greater perceptions of officer guilt (Chermak, McGarrell, & Gruenewald, 2006) and disparate treatment of minorities by police (Dowler & Zawilski, 2007). Moreover, Kochel (2017) found that in St. Louis County, Missouri, following the unrest in Ferguson, Black residents' perceptions of procedural justice, trust, perceptions of police legitimacy, and willingness to cooperate with police decreased after the police shooting of Michael Brown; there was no impact on the perceptions of White residents, however. This pattern of research findings along with the case example discussed by Newton-Small (2016) suggests that recent events are likely primarily impacting Black community members, who have historically had lower trust and confidence in the police and justice system (Carr, Napolitano, & Keating, 2007), and highlights the division in perceptions toward the police and justice system between Black and White jurors.

### How Perceptions of Trials Involving Police Have Changed Post-Ferguson

In response to the rise of Black Lives Matter as a national movement against the disparate treatment of Black individuals by the justice system, a counter movement—Blue Lives Matter—has taken hold, particularly in law enforcement communities, exemplifying a polarization of attitudes toward police contacts and police-community relations. These movements have been fueled by more than just the highly publicized incidents of police use of force; they have been exacerbated in many ways by court decisions in the prosecution of officers involved in these incidents, particularly those of the grand jury.

**Grand juries and the indictment of police**. The grand jury process has long been criticized and a topic of debate in the legal community. The purpose of the grand jury is to determine whether there is sufficient evidence in a case to levy charges and bring it to trial (Fairfax, 2014). The grand jury does not function under the same rules and requirements as trial juries, however, often needing only a certain majority, not a unanimous vote, to indict a defendant. In the case of Michael Brown as well as several other cases of police excessive use of force, grand juries were summoned to determine if sufficient evidence was present to indict the involved police officers on criminal charges. The grand jury for Brown's case ultimately found that there was insufficient evidence and Officer Wilson was never indicted for the shooting (Fairfax, 2014). Unlike many grand jury proceedings, the Brown grand jury captured the attention of the growing national audience, and its decision not to indict Wilson felt, to some, like a miscarriage of justice.

In fact, very few of the highly publicized police excessive use of force cases in recent years have led to conviction or even indictment of the majority of officers involved. Although a failure to indict is not equivalent to finding a defendant innocent of a crime, the grand jury rulings have been viewed on social media and by the Black community as unfair, showing preferential treatment for law enforcement other the individuals who were injured (LeFebvre & Armstrong, 2016). In light of the number of high-profile grand juries that have failed to indict police officers accused of excessive use of force, renewed efforts have been waged to overturn use of grand juries in the United States (Henderson & Taslitz, 2014). The Michael Brown case, as well as similar cases across the nation, may have altered public perceptions of the grand jury system and, once again, brought the use of grand juries under public scrutiny.

Although Officer Wilson was not indicted for the shooting of Michael Brown, police officers do appear in court as defendants on occasion and changes in public perceptions of the police as well as of the courts may affect jurors' perceptions of cases against police. Daftary-Kapur, Penrod, O'Connor, and Wallace (2014) found that mock jurors who held extreme polarized beliefs about the police tended to render verdicts consistent with their beliefs when the defendant was a police officer: Those who held strong negative beliefs tended to convict more often while those with strong positive beliefs tended to acquit more often.

**The blue wall of silence.** Aside from direct implications of changes in juror attitudes for case outcomes, such changes may lead jurors to scrutinize more intensely police practices in court. Historically, police who are on trial have benefitted from hiding behind the Blue Wall (or Code) of Silence—a fraternal rule that police will not testify against other officers (Westmarland, 2005). In light of the recent events and increased scrutiny of police behavior by the public, jurors may be more attuned to these practices and the unwillingness of fellow officers to provide credible testimony could ultimately inflict greater damage on police officer defendants in the eyes of jurors. Therefore, jurors who are skeptical of police testimony or question the credibility of a police officer witness may actually have good reason to do so in some cases; however, these instances extend beyond the Blue Wall of Silence in protecting fellow officers from criminal convictions, as I discuss next.

**Testilying in court.** Unlike other types of expert witnesses, police officers tend to have a professional stake in their cases and their testimony can reflect their own assumptions about the defendant's guilt. When this is the case, police have been known to engage in a practice wittily coined *testilying* (Capers, 2008). Testilying, or telling blue lies, is a type of perjury by a police officer that involves either shading or failing to disclose facts of the case in an attempt to ensure that jurors or judges convict the "guilty" party (Cunningham, 1999). In fact, officers who testily often indicate feeling that it is their moral obligation to bring criminals to justice, even if it means engaging in manipulation of the facts. Jurors and judges then make decisions based on misinformation, leaving defendants exposed to miscarriages of justice. Testilying surely affects defendants' perceptions of the trustworthiness of police, but how does it affect jurors and the community?

Testilying is difficult to identify, and many instances go unchecked by prosecutors, even when they are aware that it is occurring. One survey found that prosecutors, defense attorneys, and judges believed police testilied in approximately 20% of their cases and 76% of police surveyed indicated that officers sometimes engage in testilying in order to establish probable cause (Capers, 2008). Testilying, from a jury perspective, is problematic for two primary reasons. First, if jurors do not know a police officer witness or defendant is being untruthful, then jurors are left to make decisions based on inaccurate information. Second, if jurors are aware providing false testimony is a practice in which police officer witnesses or defendants engage, then it will likely affect both their interpretation of testimony, even truthful testimony, and verdict decisions. Research examining the effect of police officer witness reputation on verdict decisions found that jurors who were presented with an officer with a history of dishonest behavior versus a history of exemplary service were less likely to find the officer to be a credible witness (Cole & Cohn, 2017). These findings suggest that widespread knowledge of what the public could view as intentional dishonest behavior could perpetuate or exacerbate distrust of police in the community and lower both credibility for police officer witnesses and defendants in court and legitimacy of courts overall.

### Policy Recommendations Following Ferguson

Although some courts may attempt to educate jurors on the effects of biased attitudes in decision-making, perhaps through the development of additional juror instructions or the inclusion of expert witnesses (see Chapter 5 of this volume for discussion), this represents only a reactive approach. Instead, to prevent juror biases from developing in the first place, efforts should be directed toward renewing and building public trust in our legal institutions and its actors to combat widespread dissent among jurors in appraising police and their work in court. It is clear in the case Newton-Small (2016) described that the differences in opinions and perspectives between the jury members is driven primarily by differences in experiences with the law, whether directly through personal contact or indirectly through vicarious means. The Black jurors in the case displayed a greater sense of cynicism and distrust in the legitimacy of the system, and their dialogue also suggested an expectation of unfair treatment by legal actors for Black individuals.

Fairness, specifically fair treatment, is central to the formation of trust in and legitimacy of police and the courts (Tyler & Huo, 2002; Tyler & Jackson, 2014). When individuals have interactions with authorities of an institution, such as the police, that are perceived to be unfair or procedurally unjust, it creates a sense of distrust of the police and erodes the legitimacy of law enforcement (Hough et al., 2010; Tyler & Huo, 2002). These interactions need not happen directly to influence perceptions of legitimacy; researchers have also found that the shared experience of others affects legitimacy as well (Augustyn, 2016; Tankebe, 2010). Therefore, one negative interaction may still have far reaching effects vicariously (Evans & Williams, 2017), an immensely important consideration in today's age of extensive media and social media outlets. Promoting more procedurally just policing practices, police transparency (e.g., through the use of body-camera technology), and police-community partnerships are important steps in repairing public perceptions and rebuilding jurors' trust in our legal institutions.

Additionally, to prevent further erosion of trust in our legal systems, policing practices of the Blue Wall of Silence and testilying need to be formally addressed. Purely sanctioning police who engage in these practices will likely be ineffective and may create rifts between police and the courts. Instead, efforts to change policing organizational culture to dismantle the practice from the inside may be most effective. Currently, the wall or code of silence exists to protect fellow members, but changes to the values of the policing organization could be redirected to protect the integrity of policing as an institution and normalize procedures for reporting and investigating cases of police misconduct (Miller, 2016). Similarly, the practice of testilying could be curtailed through changing the acceptance of these practices within the policing organization, as well as in the courts by promoting the investigation and reporting of officers known to use or suspected of using these practices by members of the court (e.g., prosecutors, defense attorneys, judges).

## Conclusion

Undoubtedly, the Ferguson shooting—along with other police-related deaths and injuries—and changes in policing practices have affected individuals' perceptions of and interactions with law enforcement in the community. Members of Black communities in particular have felt disproportionately targeted and treated more unfairly and harshly by police (Peck, 2015). In turn, Black individuals have greater distrust than White individuals of law enforcement overall (Tyler, 2005). However, the police are just one of many legal institutions representing the legal system as a whole. Although the police are the gatekeepers of the legal system and often withstand the worst of public sentiment toward the system, other areas of the legal system are also affected when people do not trust the police. What little is known about the transference of attitudes toward the police onto perceptions of the court and juror decision-making suggests that the current policing climate has likely impacted jurors, particularly those from the Black community.

Race, whether from the perspective of the defendant, victim, or juror—or some combination of the three—has been a known factor in and predictor of juror decision-making for decades (Devine et al., 2001). However, most researchers have focused on theories of defendant-jury similarities to explain differences in the past, with little consideration of the underlying mechanisms and factors that drive these differences in verdict decisions (Sommers, 2007). The experiences individuals have had with police in the community are brought with them into the courtroom when they serve as jurors, and their perceptions of the case reflect those experiences, whether in the form of skepticism of police officer witnesses or defendants or a general distrust of "the system." When individuals do not trust or have confidence in police, courts, or the institution of law, it directly impacts the ability of those institutions to function as intended. Individuals may fail to seek out or refuse involvement in matters of the law (Brunson, 2007; Carr et al., 2007), including an unwillingness to serve on a jury. They will refuse to adhere to the rules and laws set forth by those institutions (Tyler & Jackson, 2014), which may include engaging in practices such as juror nullification. Eventually, individuals may fail to accept decisions rendered through legal processes entirely, once the institution has lost all legitimacy (Mazerolle, Bennett, Davis, Sargeant, & Manning, 2013).

As noted, jurors' perceptions of police can exhibit a "spillover" effect into general perceptions of the legal system, including legitimacy and fairness of the courts (Baker et al., 2013). Jurors are sensitive to information about police officer witnesses' trustworthiness to a larger degree than lay witnesses (Cole, 2015)—an effect particularly relevant in a time when police are being charged for excessive use of force and subjected to heightened scrutiny in the national spotlight. Beyond consideration of juror decisions alone, differences in perceptions of and attitudes toward the police and courts can create a contentious environment during deliberation among jurors, as noted by the experience of several Black jurors with whom Newton-Small (2016) served, which precipitated their request for dismissal. Unfortunately, this facet of juror decision-making and the examination of police in court is largely absent in the literature, both in research conducted prior to Ferguson and thereafter, indicating a clear need for further study in this area. The current focus on police-community relations presents an opportunity to explore these issues and how, in addition to policing, they are impacting the courts. More research on the role of police in court and the impact of juror attitudes toward the police on juror decisions is needed to provide insight into this facet of juror decision-making and elucidate the long-term effect of Ferguson on the courts.

## References

Augustyn, M. B. (2016). Updating perceptions of (in) justice. *Journal of Research in Crime and Delinquency, 53*, 255–286. doi:10.1177/0022427815616991

Baker, T., Pelfrey, W. V., Bedard, L. E., Dhungana, K., Gertz, M., & Golden, K. (2013). Female inmates' procedural justice perceptions of the police and courts: Is there a spill-over of police effects? *Criminal Justice and Behavior, 41*, 144–162. doi:10.1177/0093854813497479

Bell, B. E., & Loftus, E. F. (1988). Degree of detail of eyewitness testimony and mock juror judgments. *Journal of Applied Social Psychology, 18*, 1171–1192. doi:10.1111/j.1559-1816.1988.tb01200.x

Boivin, R., Gendron, A., Faubert, C., & Poulin, B. (2016). The malleability of attitudes toward the police: Immediate effects of the viewing of police use of force videos. *Police Practice and Research, 18*, 1–10. doi:10.1080/15614263.2016.1230063

Bonilla, Y., & Rosa, J. (2015). #Ferguson: Digital protest, hashtag ethnography, and the racial politics of social media in the United States. *American Ethnologist, 42*, 4–17. doi:10.1111/amet.12112

Bornstein, B. H., & Greene, E. (2011). Jury decision making: Implications for and from psychology. *Current Directions in Psychological Science, 20*, 63–67. doi:10.1177/0963721410397282

Brown, J. I. (1990). Defining reasonable police conduct: *Graham v. Connor* and excessive force during arrest. *UCLA Law Review, 38*, 1257.

Brunson, R. K. (2007). "Police don't like Black people": African-American young men's accumulated police experiences. *Criminology & Public Policy, 6*, 71–101. doi:10.1111/j.1745-9133.2007.00423.x

Buchanan, L., Fessenden, F., Lai, R., Park, H., Parlapiano, A., Tse, A., . . . Yourish, K. (2014, November 25). What happened in Ferguson? *The New York Times.* Retrieved from https://www.nytimes.com

Burch, T. (2015). Skin color and the criminal justice system: Beyond Black-White disparities in sentencing. *Journal of Empirical Legal Studies, 12*, 395–420. doi:10.1111/jels.12077

Campbell, B. A., Nix, J., & Maguire, E. R. (2018). Is the number of citizens fatally shot by police increasing in the post-Ferguson era? *Crime & Delinquency, 64*(3), 398–420. doi:10.1177/0011128716686343

Capers, I. B. (2008). Crime, legitimacy, and testilying. *Indiana Law Journal, 83*, 835–880.

Carr, P. J., Napolitano, L., & Keating, J. (2007). We never call the cops and here is why: A qualitative examination of legal cynicism in three Philadelphia neighborhoods. *Criminology, 45*, 445–480. doi:10.1111/j.1745-9125.2007.00084.x

Chapdelaine, A., & Griffin, S. F. (1997). Beliefs of guilt and recommended sentence as a function of juror bias in the O.J. Simpson trial. *Journal of Social Issues, 53*, 477–485. doi:10.1111/j.1540-4560.1997.tb02123.x

Chermak, S., McGarrell, E., & Gruenewald, J. (2006). Media coverage of police misconduct and attitudes toward police. *Policing: An International Journal of Police Strategies & Management, 29*, 261–281. doi:10.1108/13639510610667664

Christianson, S. Å., Karlsson, I., & Persson, L. G. (1998). Police personnel as eyewitnesses to a violent crime. *Legal and Criminological Psychology, 3,* 59–72. doi:10.1111/j.2044-8333.1998.tb00351.x

Cohn, E. S., Bucolo, D., Pride, M., & Sommers, S. R. (2009). Reducing White juror bias: The role of race salience and racial attitudes. *Journal of Applied Social Psychology, 39,* 1953–1973. doi:10.1111/j.1559-1816.2009.00511.x

Cole, L. M. (2015). *Comparing police eyewitnesses and lay eyewitnesses: The effect of eyewitness reputation and procedural justice on juror verdict decisions* (Unpublished doctoral dissertation). University of New Hampshire, Durham.

Cole, L. M., & Cohn, E. S. (2017). *Too legit to acquit: The effect of police legitimacy on police witness credibility and juror verdict decisions.* Manuscript submitted for publication.

Culhane, S. E., Boman, IV, J. H., & Schweitzer, K. (2016). Public perceptions of the justifiability of police shootings: The role of body cameras in a pre- and post-Ferguson experiment. *Police Quarterly, 19,* 251–274. doi:10.1177/1098611116651403

Cunningham, L. (1999). Taking on testifying: The prosecutor's response to in-court police deception. *Criminal Justice Ethics, 18,* 26–40. doi:10.1080/0731129X.1999.9992064

Cutler, B. L., & Penrod, S. D. (1995). *Mistaken identification: The eyewitness, psychology and the law.* Cambridge, UK: Cambridge University Press.

Daftary-Kapur, T., Penrod, S. D., O'Connor, M., & Wallace, B. (2014). Examining pretrial publicity in a shadow jury paradigm: Issues of slant, quantity, persistence and generalizability. *Law and Human Behavior, 38,* 462–477. doi:10.1037/lhb0000081

Dane, F. C., & Wrightsman, L. W. (1982). Effects of defendants' and victims' characteristics on jurors' verdicts. In N. L. Kerr & R. M. Bray (Eds.), *The psychology of the courtroom* (pp. 83–115). New York: Academic Press.

Deffenbacher, K. A., & Loftus, E. F. (1982). Do jurors share a common understanding concerning eyewitness behavior? *Law and Human Behavior, 6,* 15–30. doi:10.1007/BF01049310

Devine, D. J., Clayton, L. D., Dunford, B. B., Seying, R., & Pryce, J. (2001). Jury decision making: 45 years of empirical research on deliberating groups. *Psychology, Public Policy, and Law, 7,* 622–727. doi:10.1037/1076-8971.7.3.622

Diamond, S. S., Vidmar, N., Rose, M. R., Ellis, L., & Murphy, B. (2003). Jury discussions during civil trials: Studying an Arizona innovation. *University of Arizona Law Review, 45,* 1–81.

Dowler, K., & Zawilski, V. (2007). Public perceptions of police misconduct and discrimination: Examining the impact of media consumption. *Journal of Criminal Justice, 35,* 193–203. doi:10.1016/j.jcrimjus.2007.01.006

Evans, D. N., & Williams, C. L. (2017). Stop, question, and frisk in New York City: A study of public opinions. *Criminal Justice Policy Review, 28*(7), 687–709. doi:10.1177/0887403415610166

Fairfax, Jr., R. A. (2014). Should the American grand jury survive Ferguson? *Howard Law Journal, 58,* 825–831.

Fairfax, Jr., R. A. (2017). The grand jury's role in the prosecution of unjustified police killings—Challenges and solutions. *Harvard Civil Rights-Civil Liberties Law Review, 52,* 397–537.

Friedland, S. I. (1989). On common sense and the evaluation of witness credibility. *Case Western Reserve Law Review, 40,* 165–225.

Goff, P. A., Lloyd, T., Geller, A., Raphael, S., & Glaser, J. (2016). *The science of justice: Race, arrests, and police use of force.* Retrieved from Center for Policing Equity website: http://policingequity.org/wp-content/uploads/2016/07/CPE_SoJ_Race-Arrests-UoF_2016-07-08-1130.pdf

Goodman, J., & Loftus, E. F. (1992). Judgment and memory: The role of expert psychological testimony on eyewitness accuracy. In P. Suedfeld & P. E. Tetlock (Eds.), *Psychology and social policy* (pp. 267–282). Washington, DC: Hemisphere.

Graham v. Connor, 490 U.S. 386 (1989)

Griffiths, E., & Christian, J. (2015). Considering focused deterrence in the age of Ferguson, Baltimore, North Charleston, and beyond. *Criminology & Public Policy, 14,* 573–581. doi:10.1111/1745-9133.12140

Hastie, R. (1993). *Inside the juror: The psychology of juror decision making.* Cambridge, UK: Cambridge University Press.

Henderson, S. E., & Taslitz, A. E. (2014). Reforming the grand jury to protect privacy in third party records. *American University Law Review, 64,* 195–229.

Hough, M., Jackson, J., Bradford, B., Myhill, A., & Quinton, P. (2010). Procedural justice, trust, and institutional legitimacy. *Policing, 4,* 203–210. doi:10.1093/police/paq027

Kahn, K. B., & Martin, K. D. (2016). Policing and race: Disparate treatment, perceptions, and policy responses. *Social Issues and Policy Review, 10,* 82–121. doi:10.1111/sipr.12019

Kaminski, R. J., & Jefferis, E. S. (1998). The effect of a violent televised arrest on public perceptions of the police: A partial test of Easton's theoretical framework. *Policing: An International Journal of Police Strategies & Management, 21,* 683–706. doi:10.1108/13639519810241692

Kaminski, K. S., & Sporer, S. L. (2016). Are police officers the better eyewitnesses? A comparison of police officers and laypersons regarding the accuracy of descriptions and identifications. *Recht & Psychiatrie, 34,* 18–26.

Karpowitz, C. F., & Mendelberg, T. (2007). Groups and deliberation. *Swiss Political Science Review, 13,* 645–662. doi:10.1002/j.1662-6370.2007.tb00092.x

Kassin, S. M., Williams, L. N., & Saunders, C. L. (1990). Dirty tricks of cross-examination: The influence of conjectural evidence on the jury. *Law and Human Behavior, 14,* 373–384. doi:10.1007/BF01068162

Kebbell, M. R., & Milne, R. (1998). Police officers' perceptions of eyewitness performance in forensic investigations. *The Journal of Social Psychology, 138,* 323–330. doi:10.1080/00224549809600384

Kerwin, J., & Shaffer, D. R. (1994). Mock jurors versus mock juries: The role of deliberations in reactions to inadmissible testimony. *Personality and Social Psychology Bulletin, 20,* 153–162. doi:10.1177/0146167294202002.

Kirk, D. S., & Matsuda, M. (2011). Legal cynicism, collective efficacy, and the ecology of arrest. *Criminology, 49,* 443–472. doi:10.1111/j.1745-9125.2011.00226.x

Kochel, T. R. (2017). Explaining racial differences in Ferguson's impact on local residents' trust and perceived legitimacy: Policy implications for police. *Criminal Justice Policy Review.* Advance online publication. doi:0887403416684923

LeFebvre, R. K., & Armstrong, C. (2016). Grievance-based social movement mobilization in the# Ferguson Twitter storm. *New Media & Society.* Advance online publication. doi:10.1177/1461444816644697

Lempert, R. O., Gross, S. R., Liebman, J. S., Blume, J. H., Landsman, S., & Lederer, F. I. (2013). *A modern approach to evidence: Text, problems, transcripts, and cases* (5th ed.). St. Paul, MN: West Academic.

Lindholm, T., Christianson, S. Å., & Karlsson, I. (1997). Police officers and civilians as witnesses: Intergroup biases and memory performance. *Applied Cognitive Psychology, 11,* 431–444. doi:10.1002/(SICI)1099-0720(199710)11:5<431::AID-ACP470>3.0.CO;2-9

Lofstrom, M., & Raphael, S. (2016). Crime, the criminal justice system, and socioeconomic inequality. *The Journal of Economic Perspectives, 30*(2), 103–126. doi:10.1257/jep.30.2.103

London, K. Y., & Nuñez, N. (2000). The effect of jury deliberation on jurors' propensity to disregard inadmissible evidence. *Journal of Applied Psychology, 85,* 932–939. doi:10.1037/0021- 9010.85.6.932

Maguire, E. R., Nix, J., & Campbell, B. A. (2016). A war on cops? The effects of Ferguson on the number of US police officers murdered in the line of duty. *Justice Quarterly, 34,* 739–758. doi:10.1080/07418825.2016.1236205

Mann, S., Vrij, A., & Bull, R. (2004). Detecting true lies: Police officers' ability to detect suspects' lies. *Journal of Applied Psychology, 89,* 137–149. doi:10.1037/00219010.89.1.137

Mazerolle, L., Bennett, S., Davis, J., Sargeant, E., & Manning, M. (2013). Procedural justice and police legitimacy: A systematic review of the research evidence. *Journal of Experimental Criminology, 9,* 245–274. doi:10.1007/s11292-013-9175-2

McCoy, M. L., Nuñez, N., & Dammeyer, M. D. (1999). The effect of jury deliberations on jurors' reasoning skills. *Law and Human Behavior, 23,* 557–575. doi:10.1023/A:1022348229558

Miller, S. (2016). Professional reporting and police culture. In *Corruption and anti-corruption in policing—Philosophical and ethical issues* (pp. 69–79). New York: Springer International.

Moran, M., & Waddington, D. (2016). *Riots: An international comparison.* London: Palgrave Macmillan.

Nemeth, C. P. (2010). *Law & evidence: A primer for criminal justice, criminology, law, and legal studies* (2nd ed.). Sudbury, MA: Jones & Bartlett.

Newcombe, P. A., & Bransgrove, J. (2007). Perceptions of witness credibility: Variations across age. *Journal of Applied Developmental Psychology, 28,* 318–331. doi:10.1016/j.appdev.2007.04.003

Newton-Small, J. (2016, August 18). What my week of jury duty taught me about race. *TIME.* Retrieved from http://time.com/4448516/jury-duty-race/

Peck, J. H. (2015). Minority perceptions of the police: A state-of-the-art review. *Policing: An International Journal of Police Strategies & Management, 38,* 173–203. doi:10.1108/PIJPSM-01-2015-0001

Pennington, N., & Hastie, R. (1988). Explanation-based decision making: Effects of memory structure on judgment. *Journal of Experimental Psychology: Learning, Memory, and Cognition, 14,* 521–533. doi:10.1037/0278-7393.14.3.521

Pennington, N., & Hastie, R. (1992). Explaining the evidence: Tests of the Story Model for juror decision making. *Journal of Personality and Social Psychology, 62,* 189–206. doi:10.1037/0022-3514.62.2.189

Piquero, A. R. (2008). Disproportionate minority contact. *The Future of Children, 18*(2), 59–79. doi:10.1353/foc.0.0013

Pritchard, M., & Keenan, J. (2002). Does jury deliberation really improve jurors' memories? *Applied Cognitive Psychology, 16,* 589–601. doi:10.1002/acp.816

Roberts, R. (2015). Racism and criminal justice. *Criminal Justice Matters, 101,* 18–20. doi:10.1080/09627251.2015.1080941

Ross, D. L. (2002). An assessment of *Graham v. Connor,* ten years later. *Policing: An International Journal of Police Strategies & Management, 25,* 294–318. doi:10.1108/13639510210429383

Ruva, C., McEvoy, C., & Bryant, J. B. (2007). Effects of pre-trial publicity and jury deliberation on juror bias and source memory errors. *Applied Cognitive Psychology, 21,* 45–67. doi:10.1002/acp.1254

Salerno, J. M., & Diamond, S. (2010). The promise of a cognitive perspective on jury deliberation. *Psychonomic Bulletin & Review, 17,* 174–179. doi:10.3758/PBR.17.2.174

Sampson, R. J., & Bartusch, D. J. (1998). Legal cynicism and (subcultural?) tolerance of deviance: The neighborhood context of racial differences. *Law & Society Review, 32,* 777–804. doi:10.2307/827739

Schmechel, R. S., O'Toole, T. P., Easterly, C., & Loftus, E. F. (2005). Beyond the ken: Testing jurors' understanding of eyewitness reliability evidence. *Jurimetrics, 46,* 177–214.

Sommers, S. R. (2007). Race and the decision making of juries. *Legal and Criminological Psychology, 12,* 171–187. doi:10.1348/135532507X189687

Spellman, B. A., & Tenney, E. R. (2010). Credible testimony in and out of court. *Psychonomic Bulletin & Review, 17,* 168–173. doi:10.3758/PBR.17.2.168

Stanny, C. J., & Johnson, T. C. (2000). Effects of stress induced by a simulated shooting on recall by police and citizen witnesses. *The American Journal of Psychology, 113,* 359–386. doi:10.2307/1423364

SunWolf. (2010). Counterfactual thinking in the jury room. *Small Group Research, 41,* 474–494. doi:10.1177/1046496410369562

Tankebe, J. (2010). Public confidence in the police: Testing the effects of public experiences of police corruption in Ghana. *British Journal of Criminology, 50,* 296–319. doi:10.1093/bjc/azq001

Tickner, A. H., & Poulton, E. C. (1975). Watching for people and actions. *Ergonomics, 18,* 35–51. doi:10.1080/00140137508931438

Tyler, T. R. (2005). Policing in black and white: Ethnic group differences in trust and confidence in the police. *Police Quarterly, 8,* 322–342. doi:10.1177/1098611104271105

Tyler, T. R. (2006). Restorative justice and procedural justice: Dealing with rule breaking. *Journal of Social Issues, 62,* 307–326. doi:10.1111/j.1540-4560.2006.00452.x

Tyler, T. R., & Huo, Y. (2002). *Trust in the law: Encouraging public cooperation with the police and courts through.* New York: Russell Sage Foundation.

Tyler, T. R., & Jackson, J. (2014). Popular legitimacy and the exercise of legal authority: Motivating compliance, cooperation, and engagement. *Psychology, Public Policy, and Law, 20,* 78–95. doi:10.1037/a0034514

Vredeveldt, A., & van Koppen, P. J. (2016). The thin blue line-up: Comparing eyewitness performance by police and civilians. *Journal of Applied Research in Memory and Cognition, 5*, 252–256. doi:10.1016/j.jarmac.2016.06.013

Vrij, A. (2000). *Detecting lies and deceit: The psychology of lying and the implications for professional practice*. Chichester, UK: Wiley.

Weinstock, M. (2011). Knowledge-telling and knowledge-transforming arguments in mock jurors' verdict justifications. *Thinking & Reasoning, 17*, 282–314. doi:10.1080/13546783.2011.575191

Westmarland, L. (2005). Police ethics and integrity: Breaking the blue code of silence. *Policing and Society, 15*, 145–165. doi:10.1080/10439460500071721

Wells, G. L., & Olson, E. (2003). Eyewitness identification. *Annual Review of Psychology, 54*, 277–295. doi:10.1146.54.101601.145028

Whitley, B. E. (1987). The effects of discredited eyewitness testimony: A meta-analysis. *The Journal of Social Psychology, 127*, 209–214. doi:10.1080/00224545.1987.9713681

Wise, R. A., Safer, M. A., & Maro, C. M. (2011). What U.S. law enforcement officers know and believe about eyewitness factors, eyewitness interviews and identification procedures. *Applied Cognitive Psychology, 25*, 488–500. doi:10.1002/acp.1717

Wrightsman, L., Willis, C., & Kassin, S. (Eds.). (1987). *On the witness stand*. Thousand Oaks, CA: SAGE.

Yarmey, A. D. (1986). Perceived expertness and credibility of police officers as eyewitnesses. *Canadian Police College Journal, 10*, 31–52.

Zuckerman, M., Koestner, R., & Driver, R. (1981). Beliefs about cues associated with deception. *Journal of Nonverbal Behavior, 6*, 105–114. doi:10.1007/BF00987286

# PART II

TECHNOLOGICAL CHANGES AND CHALLENGES

*New Sources of Influence on Jurors' Decisions*

# 7

## The Impact of Legally Relevant Media Exposure on Criminal Juror Decision-Making

*Jennifer L. Groscup*

Media in its various forms inundates our lives, and in the past few decades journalists have been guided by the popular phrase "if it bleeds, it leads" (Pooley, 1989, p. 37). This means that the most sensational and gory stories headline the news. An obvious and common source of blood and violence and sensational headlines in the media is the criminal justice system. From the nightly news to highly publicized cases of murder to the omnipresent fictional crime drama, American media is saturated with stories about crime.

One of the most highly publicized cases alleging a wrongful acquittal in recent years was Casey Anthony's trial for the murder of her two-year-old daughter Caylee (Battaglia, 2011; Hoffmeister, 2011). Cloud (2011) called this case the "social media trial of the century." The circumstantial and public opinion case against Anthony was strong (Battaglia, 2011; Hoffmeister, 2011). Caylee was missing for a month before the police were notified, during which time Anthony was seen out partying and enjoying life. When first questioned by the police, Anthony said Caylee was abducted by her babysitter, a person who did not exist. Later, she changed her story, claiming her daughter accidentally drowned in the family pool. Caylee's body was found near Anthony's residence, and it was alleged that her car smelled as though a dead body had been inside it. However, little forensic evidence existed to tie her to her daughter's death. First, the medical examiner could not determine a cause of death. The prosecution argued that Caylee was suffocated with duct tape, but there was no DNA evidence on the tape implicating Anthony. Also, no forensic evidence linked Anthony to the location where the body was found or Caylee's body to her car. At the end of the trial, Anthony was acquitted of murder, and the media speculated about whether and why this might have been a case of wrongful acquittal (Battaglia, 2011; Hoffmeister, 2011). Because of the publicity specifically linking perceptions of the verdict in this case to media influences, the Casey Anthony case is referred to as an example throughout this chapter.

What effect does the kind of media saturation observed in the Anthony case and related to the criminal justice system in general have on the "impartial jury," which must decide the fate of persons within the legal system? To answer this question in this chapter, I first explore research on the content of legally relevant news media, reality television, and scripted television dramas to better understand the messages the media might be delivering. Next, I review research suggesting how various media sources influence the development of legally relevant attitudes and, in turn, impact juror decision-making. I then investigate the media's direct influence on juror decision-making, focusing particularly on the CSI Effect. Finally, I discuss recommendations for jury system reform that might decrease media influence as well as future research directions.

## Sources of Media Effects in the Courtroom

Opinions about the legal system can come from multiple media sources, including news, reality television programming, and fictional media such as scripted television dramas. To understand how these various sources could be influencing potential jurors in real cases, it is important to understand the message delivered about the legal system via each of these sources. First, news media can serve as a source of information about the legal system, particularly about crimes and criminals in highly publicized cases. Research on the content of news media indicates several trends in how crime is portrayed, consistently indicating that crime reporting presents a racially biased vision of criminals. White people are portrayed as victims more than they are portrayed as perpetrators, are portrayed and overrepresented as victims and law defenders more than Black and Latino people, and are overrepresented as victims as compared to actual crime victim statistics (Dixon, Azocar, & Casas, 2003; Dixon & Linz, 2000a, 2000b). In contrast, Black and Latino people, including juveniles, are more likely to be portrayed as and overrepresented as perpetrators and law breakers than as victims and law defenders (Chiricos & Eschholz, 2002; Dixon et al., 2003; Dixon & Azocar, 2006; Dixon & Linz, 2000a, 2000b). Overall, the research on the portrayal of crime in the news indicates that it may be biased in terms of race. This biased portrayal could translate into implicit or explicit bias in jurors' attitudes and expectations for the trials on which they serve, as discussed later.

Highly publicized cases in the news also serve as a source of information about the legal system for potential jurors. The media is filled with news about cases as they are tried as well as commentary about the final verdicts in cases after they conclude. Popular podcasts like *Serial* and documentaries about real cases like *Making a Murderer* also provide information to the public about how cases are tried and about the legal system in general. Cases that receive some of the most critical post-verdict media attention are those in which the media reports a perceived wrongful acquittal, as in the cases of

O.J. Simpson, George Zimmerman, and Robert Blake (Podlas, 2006a). The Casey Anthony case described earlier is a prototypical example of a highly publicized case involving a perceived wrongful acquittal. Highly publicized cases provide the public with information about how the criminal justice system operates and might result in the cultivation of attitudes about the effectiveness of the system. Battaglia (2011) argued that the extensive coverage of the Anthony case in particular turned the public into an armchair jury that disagreed with the verdict found by the actual jury, and this disagreement resulted in the public questioning whether the criminal justice system is broken. This case, and others that similarly call into question the public's perception of the effectiveness of the legal system, can serve as a source for negative views about the system that could affect jurors in other cases.

"Reality" television also could provide potential jurors with a media-driven worldview about the legal system. Popular legal reality television programming includes shows about police practices (such as *Cops, America's Most Wanted,* and *48 Hours*) and courtroom practices (such as *Judge Judy* or *The People's Court*). These programs may appear to be similar in accuracy to news programming because they are about "real" cases or "real" courtrooms. Thus the content chosen for these shows may become an important part of developing potential jurors' views about the police and the legal system. However, they have the secondary purpose of providing entertainment, which does not exist in a real police situation or courtroom. Although police officer duties and activities may be accurately portrayed in police officer reality television shows (Soulliere, 2004), perpetrators and police officers are represented in a similarly biased manner to how they are represented in the news. In police reality television, Black people are underrepresented as police officers and White people are overrepresented as police officers. Additionally, violent crime and the percentage of crimes solved by the police tend to be overrepresented in police reality television (Oliver, 1994). Cases that are represented on courtroom reality shows tend to be sensationalized, and the courtroom players behave more aggressively and less professionally than in real courtrooms (Podlas, 2001, 2002). Overall, research indicates that the legal "reality" presented on television may be lacking in actual realism. Yet, as I point out later, jurors who are insensitive to the discrepancy between television and actual reality are likely to have inaccurate beliefs about the criminal justice system.

Scripted crime dramas are a particularly popular source of television media about the legal system. In 2000, *CSI: Crime Scene Investigation* premiered, providing a unique combination of crime fighting and science (Cole & Dioso-Villa, 2007). *CSI* and shows like it are wildly popular— recognized as the most-watched television shows in the world in 2006 through 2009 (Gorman, 2010). The content of information about the legal system presented during scripted crime dramas has been investigated and provides an essential context to understanding the messages that some jurors are receiving about the legal system. The types of forensic evidence that are most commonly presented in *CSI* include fingerprint analysis, blood analysis, and DNA testing (Podlas, 2006b; Smith, Stinson, & Patry, 2011). DNA evidence is presented as particularly common and infallible. For example, DNA evidence was found in 84% of the cases in *CSI*, analyzed in 77% of the episodes, used to solve the case in 39% of episodes, and was never the source of mistakes (Ley, Jankowski, & Brewer, 2012). In another study, 92% of cases in crime dramas that had DNA evidence were solved (Rhineberger-Dunn, Briggs, & Rader, 2016). Researchers also have found that the perpetrator was almost always caught and errors were rarely made by the forensic scientists (Smith et al., 2011). Overall, examinations of crime drama content indicate that forensic science is featured prominently, portrayed as infallible, and usually favorable to the prosecution.

However, other research indicates that the message portrayed in crime dramas does not accurately reflect reality. Forensic science practitioners have reported that crime dramas portray the field of forensic science inaccurately (Smith et al., 2011; Weaver, Salamonson, Koch, & Porter, 2012). For example, the fictional depiction of the role of DNA in criminal cases is starkly contrasted with research on the actual role of DNA in solving cases. One study of the actual use of DNA in almost a decade of New York City Police Department homicide investigations revealed that DNA was collected, analyzed, and used in only 7% of the investigations and led to clearance in only 28% of the cases in which it was used (Schroeder & White, 2009). Another issue is the inaccurate portrayal of the police and forensic scientists as infallible. The near-perfect crime clearance rate portrayed in crime dramas is in stark contrast to actual crime clearance rates—46% for violent crimes and 19% for property crimes in 2015 (Federal Bureau of Investigation, 2015). Police infallibility is also contrasted by the work of the Innocence Project, whose mission is to exonerate wrongfully convicted persons with DNA evidence and has successfully exonerated more than 350 people to date (Innocence Project, 2017). This small window into the realities of actual police investigations clearly contrasts with what is portrayed on television. Inaccurate television portrayals could impact jury decision-making by leading jurors to have inappropriate expectations about the presence and reliability of forensic evidence, police, and the legal system generally, which could lead to inappropriate expectations that affect jury verdicts in real trials (Tyler, 2006). I discuss these potential impacts in depth next.

## Research on Media Effects in the Courtroom

It is possible that the portrayal of crimes, criminals, criminal investigations, and courtrooms in both nonfictional and fictional media could cultivate a worldview of the legal system in potential venirepersons. This worldview could take the form of legally relevant attitudes or orientations toward trial players and evidence that could influence perceptions of a specific case and, in turn, influence verdicts. The influence of the media also could take the form of direct impacts on verdicts. That is, media viewership could affect jurors' verdicts in actual cases regardless of the case facts or trial evidence presented. The research I review next investigated the association between media viewership and the development of legally relevant attitudes and juror decision-making.

## Media Development of Legally Relevant Attitudes

How does the representation of crime in the media affect jurors' attitudes about and perceptions of crimes, criminals, the police, and the legal system generally? Much of the research on this issue examines the influence of news viewing. Overall, heavy news viewers are likely to assume that racially unspecified suspects are Black and that racially unspecified police officers are White, demonstrating that news viewing is associated with stereotypes that could influence jurors' trial expectations (Dixon, 2007, 2008; Dixon & Azocar, 2007). One series of studies revealed that exposure to typical newscasts increased participants' concern about crime, perceptions that Black people are violent, and perceived criminal culpability of Black but not White suspects (Dixon, 2006, 2008; Dixon & Azocar, 2007). Heavy as opposed to light news viewers also were more concerned about the crime, had more positive views of the victim, and found the suspect more memorable as the suspect's skin tone becomes darker (Dixon & Maddox, 2005). In contrast, heavy news viewers have more positive views of White police officers (Dixon, 2007). Together, this research indicates that racially biased news portrayals of crime may affect people's perceptions of alleged suspects and the trustworthiness of police witnesses (or defendants; see Chapter 6 of this volume by Cole), effects that may increase as typical news viewing increases. Although no research has explicitly examined the effect of general news viewership on juror verdicts, this research has clear implications for juror decision-making. Inaccurate media-cultivated beliefs that Black people are more often perpetrators of crimes could explicitly or implicitly influence perceptions of actual defendants based on their race. Previous research on defendant and victim race demonstrates that these characteristics can impact juror decisions by creating outgroup bias in verdicts (see, e.g., Sommers & Ellsworth, 2009).

Also potentially relevant to juror decision-making, research has found that exposure to various types of television programming can influence perceptions of legal issues, such as fear of crime (Callanan, 2012; Custers & Van den Bulck, 2011; Eschholz, Chiricos, & Gertz, 2003; Holbert, Shah, & Kwak, 2004; Kort-Butler & Hautshorn, 2011; Romer, Jamieson, & Aday, 2003). Results of this research are inconsistent. The majority of studies have found an association between increased fear of crime and crime-related news viewership (Callanan, 2012; Custers & Van den Bulck, 2011; Holbert et al., 2004; Romer et al., 2003), police reality television show viewership

(Callanan, 2012; Eschholz et al., 2003; Kort-Butler & Hautshorn, 2011), and crime drama viewership, which specifically has been found to increase perceived risk of sexual violence victimization (Custers & Van den Bulck, 2013). However, other research has found no effect of television news viewership (Grabe & Drew, 2007; Kort-Butler & Hautshorn, 2011; Lane & Meeker, 2003), police reality shows (Holbert et al., 2004), or crime dramas (Callanan, 2012; Grabe & Drew, 2007; Kort-Butler & Hautshorn, 2011) on fear of crime. Some research has even found that news viewing is associated with decreased fear of crime (Custers & Van den Bulck, 2013). Further, although there is clearly evidence that some forms of traditional television news viewership can influence fear of crime, research indicates that Internet news consumption may not influence fear of crime in parallel amounts (Roche, Pickett, & Gertz, 2015). None of this research examined the relations between increased fear of crime and juror decision-making, but it is possible that jurors could perceive defendants and evidence and render verdicts in ways that reduce their cultivated fear of becoming crime victims themselves.

News and police reality television viewing have also been associated with positive attitudes toward gun ownership (Holbert et al., 2004). News (Dixon, 2006; Holbert et al., 2004), police reality television (Holbert et al., 2004), and crime drama viewing (Holbert et al., 2004; Kort-Butler & Hautshorn, 2011; Slater, Rouner, & Long, 2006) can also potentially increase support for the death penalty, but some research indicates news (Dixon, 2006; Kort-Butler & Hautshorn, 2011) and crime drama viewing (Grabe & Drew, 2007) do not affect these attitudes. Similar to the research on media and the fear of crime, the research on media and gun ownership and death penalty attitudes did not test their relations to juror decision-making. However, previous research has demonstrated a strong link between attitudes like these and verdicts. For example, favorable attitudes toward the death penalty predicted increased conviction-proneness in a meta-analysis (Allen, Mabry, & McKelton, 1998), indicating that death penalty attitudes that are formed by the media could impact juror verdicts.

Research also has demonstrated a link between television viewing and other legally relevant attitudes that could impact juror decision-making. Increased news and police reality show viewing are related to general attitudes toward the criminal justice system, though the nature of this association is unclear. Some research demonstrates that this type of television viewing is associated with positive attitudes toward the legal system (Callanan & Rosenberger, 2011), and some shows a negative relationship between viewing and these attitudes (Kort-Butler & Hautshorn, 2011; Reith, 1999). Viewing courtroom reality programming also has the potential to impact jurors' perceptions of courtroom players and procedures. Podlas (2001, 2002) found that potential jurors who were frequent viewers of syndi-court programs were more likely than infrequent or nonviewers to think that judges should have an opinion, make that opinion obvious, argue with litigants, and express displeasure with the parties, all of which could influence how those jurors view actual judges during real trials.

To summarize, research on legally oriented television shows indicates that the news, reality television, and crime dramas present an unrealistic picture of crimes and criminals. This is particularly true with regard to portrayals of the race of perpetrators and victims and the infallibility of police investigation techniques. This research highlights some areas in which the content of information presented in the media influences the attitudes venirepersons hold about the legal system. These attitudes could, in turn, affect jurors' evidence processing and verdict decisions in actual cases. For example, the influence of death penalty attitudes was an issue in the Casey Anthony case because it was a capital case; however, the media publicity about the case was not specifically related to these attitudes (Gabriel, 2011). Fear of crime also could have been an issue in the Anthony case, particularly because the victim was a child. Although it is clear that exposure to legally oriented shows could impact juror decision-making, in this body of research, the link between news content and verdict decision-making has yet to be established.

## The CSI Effect and Juror Decision-Making

Beginning in 2002, the prevalence and popularity of shows like *CSI* resulted in media speculation of the impact *CSI* viewership could have on decision-making in real criminal cases, dubbed the "CSI Effect" (Cole & Dioso-Villa, 2007). The CSI Effect is perhaps the most highly discussed form of media effects in the courtroom. Broadly defined, it is the potential for crime dramas such as *CSI*, its progeny, and related shows to provide viewers with unrealistic expectations about criminal investigations and forensic science, which may, in turn, influence perceptions of the legal system and jury decision-making in real cases (Cole & Dioso-Villa, 2007; Tyler, 2006). According to popular media reports, the CSI Effect exists and is affecting jurors in actual cases (Cole & Dioso-Villa, 2009; Harvey & Derksen, 2009; Smith et al., 2011). Next, I review the various paths by which the CSI Effect has been proposed to influence juror decision-making as well as the research evidence substantiating or disproving the effect.

**Defining the CSI Effect.** The media and researchers have tended to use the general term "CSI Effect" to refer summarily to a variety of possible effects on a variety of possible participants in the legal system; however, the CSI Effect may manifest itself in several ways. Cole and Dioso-Villa (2007) articulated several potential but differing types of influence crime dramas could have on the criminal justice system that are relevant to jury decision-making. They called the most commonly discussed effect the *strong prosecutor effect*, or when a perceived wrongful acquittal occurs due to a perceived lack of forensic evidence. In other words, the burden on the prosecutors to prove their case is higher—and the prosecution case must be stronger—because jurors expect that copious forensic evidence will be presented. The jury will acquit if it is not, even if the case against the defense is otherwise strong. In contrast, Cole and Dioso-Villa define the *weak prosecutor effect* as prosecutors taking remedial steps to decrease the potential strong prosecutor effect, such as changes in how they voir dire the jury or present their cases to address jurors' expectations for forensic evidence.

Judges have expressed belief in the strong prosecutor effect and claimed the CSI Effect is making it more difficult to convict defendants—in fact, the vast majority of judges report they have observed an increase in jurors' expectations of forensic evidence (Hughes & Magers, 2007; Robbers, 2008). Most of the research on attorneys' beliefs about the CSI Effect has been conducted on prosecutors, and it indicates that prosecutors believe the strong prosecutor effect exists. Prosecutors believe that jurors have unrealistic expectations about forensic evidence, expect forensic evidence to be presented, and are disappointed when it is not presented (Maricopa County, 2005; Robbers, 2008). Consistent with judges' beliefs, prosecutors believe a lack of forensic evidence leads to more not guilty verdicts (Maricopa County, 2005). These beliefs tend to be more common among prosecutors than defense attorneys, but the majority of both types of attorneys believed conviction was easier if any kind of forensic evidence was presented (Robbers, 2008). Judges, prosecutors, and defense attorneys all observe that attorneys take remedial steps to decrease the strong prosecutor effect, supporting the existence of the weak prosecutor effect (Maricopa County, 2005; Robbers, 2008; Stevens, 2008).

Contrary to the media's argument that the CSI Effect makes prosecution more difficult, instead of increasing acquittals, the CSI Effect could potentially increase convictions. Cole and Dioso-Villa (2007) define the *defense effect* or the *reverse CSI Effect* as crime drama viewership resulting in an increase in perceptions of the credibility of prosecution witnesses, especially those presenting forensic science. This overreliance on forensic science witnesses could increase convictions, possibly even wrongful convictions. In line with the defense effect, Tyler (2006) argued that shows like *CSI* could make jurors favorably disposed to the prosecution prior to trial because the shows are prosecution oriented, just as pretrial publicity tends to be slanted in favor of the prosecution (for further discussion of pretrial publicity, see Chapter 8 of this volume). Some attorneys believe in the defense effect, reporting their belief that the CSI Effect led to more guilty verdicts in their cases (Maricopa County, 2005; Podlas, 2006b; Stevens, 2008).

In contrast to the media representations of the CSI Effect as negative and as likely resulting in wrongful acquittals or wrongful convictions, some commentators argue that shows like *CSI* could have positive effects on the legal system, such as creating a well-informed jury. Cole and Dioso-Villa (2007) defined this as the *producer's effect*: the potential for crime drama viewing to increase laypersons' knowledge about forensic science and, thus, result in a more forensic-evidence-savvy jury. This could result in a negative effect on the jury if this increased knowledge causes potential jurors to have unrealistic expectations about the type of information that can be provided by forensic science in a case. However, it also could result in a positive impact, in that jurors may become more sensitive to variations in the reliability and validity of forensic evidence (Hayes & Levett, 2013).

The CSI Effect, specifically the strong prosecutor effect, was a major point of media discussion about the Casey Anthony trial. After Anthony was acquitted of the charges relating to the murder of her child, the media started to speculate about whether television shows emphasizing the importance of forensic evidence could have influenced the verdict (Battaglia, 2011; Hoffmeister, 2011). Commentators believed there was a "strong possibility that the 'CSI' effect was a factor" (Hoffmeister, 2011, para. 6). In support of the CSI Effect influencing the verdict, Hoffmeister argued that the forensic evidence was potentially problematic for three reasons: The medical examiner was unable to determine a cause of death, there was no DNA evidence linking Anthony to the duct tape found on her daughter's mouth, and there was no physical evidence linking Anthony to the site where her daughter's body was found. The media argued that the jury's perceived lack of forensic science evidence was generated by *CSI* viewership and decried the CSI Effect as the reason for the acquittal, although the jurors themselves never stated anything like this (Battaglia, 2011; Hoffmeister, 2011). Next, I discuss whether the research supports this contention.

**Research on the CSI Effect and jurors.** The biggest question raised in the media about the CSI Effect is how it will influence juror decision-making in real trials, such as Casey Anthony's. One of the claims about the CSI Effect is that crime drama viewership will increase expectations about the presentation of forensic science evidence and about the quality of that forensic evidence (Cole & Dioso-Villa, 2007). In survey-style research in the area, researchers typically ask potential venirepersons about their television-viewing behavior and their opinions about forensic evidence in general. Consistent with the producer's effect, survey research has found that higher levels of crime drama viewership are associated with increased perceived understanding of forensic evidence like DNA (Brewer & Ley, 2010). Confirming the media's suspicions and consistent with the strong prosecutor effect, most survey research on the CSI Effect has found that higher levels of crime drama viewership are related to increased expectations that forensic evidence will be presented in trials (Baskin & Sommers, 2010). Crime-drama viewership also is associated with increased beliefs that scientific evidence (i.e., DNA and fingerprint evidence) is reliable (Brewer & Ley, 2010; Holmgren & Fordham, 2011) and is more reliable than nonscientific evidence (i.e., testimony by police, victims, and eyewitnesses; Baskin & Sommers, 2010). However, some research has found no link between crime drama viewership and perceptions that DNA evidence is reliable or accurate (Lieberman, Carrell, Miethe, & Krauss, 2008). Respondents who were heavy crime drama viewers also were more likely to believe that defendants would not be convicted without forensic evidence than lighter crime-drama viewers (Baskin & Sommers, 2010;

Holmgren & Fordham, 2011), would be less likely to be convicted without DNA evidence specifically (Baskin & Sommers, 2010; Holmgren & Fordham, 2011), and could be wrongly acquitted when no forensic evidence was available (Hayes & Levett, 2013), as has been argued for Casey Anthony. Overall, survey research on the CSI Effect indicates crime drama viewership is related to increased perceived knowledge about forensic evidence, supporting the producer's effect, and viewership is related to increased expectations about the reliability and presentation of forensic evidence at trials, supporting the strong prosecutor effect.

Research also has investigated the relationship between crime drama viewership and juror decision-making using the mock trial paradigm. In mock trial stimuli, typically some aspect of the case evidence is manipulated, such as the type of case (Podlas, 2006b), the type of evidence presented (Kim, Barak, & Shelton, 2009; Shelton, 2010; Shelton, Kim, & Barak, 2006, 2009), or the amount of forensic evidence presented (Hayes-Smith & Levett, 2011). First, how does crime drama viewership affect jurors' perceptions of case evidence in mock trial studies? Similar to the survey research showing a link between crime drama viewership and general expectations about forensic evidence (Baskin & Sommers, 2010; Hayes & Levett, 2013; Holmgren & Fordham, 2011), mock trial research has demonstrated that television viewership can affect perceptions of forensic evidence within a specific case. Consistent with the producer's effect, heavier viewers of crime dramas reported a perceived increase in their understanding of the scientific evidence in a mock trial (Schweitzer & Saks, 2007), were more critical of the forensic evidence in a mock trial (Mancini, 2011; Schweitzer & Saks, 2007), and found the forensic evidence presented in the mock trial to be less believable (Schweitzer & Saks, 2007) than nonviewers of crime dramas. However, crime drama viewership may not affect jurors' perceived familiarity with forensic evidence within a trial (Mancini, 2011, 2013). Consistent with the strong prosecutor effect, heavier crime drama viewers had increased expectations that forensic science evidence would be presented in mock trials than did nonviewers of crime dramas (Kim et al., 2009; Shelton, 2010; Shelton et al., 2006, 2009). Expectations that forensic science would be presented in mock trials were even higher for cases involving violent crimes than for nonviolent crimes (Shelton et al., 2006). Overall, mock juror research on the CSI Effect demonstrates that crime drama viewership can affect jurors' perceptions of their own abilities to process forensic evidence and can increase forensic evidence expectations in the context of actual trials, but these expectations do not necessarily result in different verdicts, as discussed next.

Second, how does crime drama viewership affect jurors' verdicts in mock trial studies? Within the studies using the mock trial paradigm, few have been able to establish a link between crime drama viewership and juror verdicts or between evidence expectations and verdicts. For example, the majority of mock juror studies have found no relationship between crime drama viewership and mock jurors' likelihood of conviction (Hayes-Smith

& Levett, 2011; Schwietzer & Saks, 2007; Shelton, 2010; Shelton et al., 2006, 2009), even in trials for different crimes (Podlas, 2006b) and with potentially tainted (Mancini, 2011) or absent forensic evidence (Podlas, 2006a, 2006b). Other research has found a direct effect of television viewership on mock juror verdicts. Supporting the strong prosecutor effect, some research has found that not-guilty verdicts increased as the amount of crime drama television viewing increased (Mancini, 2013). Also consistent with the strong prosecutor effect, research has found indirect effects of crime drama viewership on verdicts. Crime drama viewership has increased expectations for the presentation of forensic science evidence, which then resulted in decreased willingness to convict in a circumstantial case when no forensic evidence was presented (Kim et al., 2009). In contrast, some research has found that high viewing frequency was indirectly associated with increased guilty verdicts, consistent with the defense effect (Maeder & Corbett, 2015). Specifically, high viewing frequency and increased perceived realism of crime dramas led to increased weight given to eyewitness and DNA evidence, which then led to increased guilty verdicts. Overall, the results of the mock trial research that has measured both crime drama viewing and verdict has demonstrated inconsistent effects juror verdicts, but the majority indicates that viewing is unrelated to verdict.

**Evidence for the CSI Effect in real trials.** One of the most important questions about the CSI Effect is whether exposure to shows like *CSI* can influence jury verdicts in real court cases, such as evidence of increased acquittals due to *CSI* viewership. The limited research conducted on the influence of the CSI Effect on acquittal rates in actual cases does not provide evidence of a *CSI* impact on verdicts in real trials. Cole and Dioso-Villa (2007, 2009, 2011) investigated acquittal rates in federal and state courts prior to and following the creation and airing of *CSI*. Although they found a general decrease in federal acquittals over the entire time period from 1945 to 2005, they did not find any significant change in acquittals in the 10 years surrounding the premiere of *CSI* in 2000 (Cole & Dioso-Villa, 2007). They found no change in acquittal rates across all states, even after focusing specifically on the three-year period after the show's premiere (Cole & Dioso-Villa, 2011). They conclude that research on actual acquittal rates provides very little evidence of a strong prosecutor-type CSI Effect (Cole & Dioso-Villa, 2007, 2009).

**Summary of the CSI Effect and juror decision-making.** It is clear from the research that many people in the media and legal system believe that prosecution-oriented, science-heavy shows like *CSI* influence how jurors understand evidence and make decisions in real trials. The media portrays this effect mainly as an increased likelihood for wrongful acquittals, but various potential effects on juror decision-making have been identified, including the potential for increased wrongful convictions. Although the media is confident that crime drama viewership has some influence on the legal system (Cole & Dioso-Villa, 2007, 2009), research has found inconsistent effects of viewership on jurors. Crime drama viewership may increase expectations people have about the presentation of forensic evidence (Baskin & Sommers, 2010; Kim et al., 2009; Shelton, 2010; Shelton et al., 2009), especially in certain types of cases (Shelton et al., 2006), but these raised expectations do not necessarily affect case verdicts. The majority of the research investigating crime drama effects on juror verdicts has found no relationship between viewership and mock trial verdicts (e.g., Hayes-Smith & Levett, 2011; Mancini, 2011; Schweitzer & Saks, 2007; Shelton, 2010). Research that has found a link between crime drama viewership and mock trial verdicts has found contrasting effects, with viewership sometimes increasing acquittals (Kim et al., 2009; Mancini, 2013) and sometimes increasing convictions (Maeder & Corbett, 2015).

The methods used in the research on the CSI Effect must be considered, as they have been largely correlational and not experimental in regards to television exposure. None of the research reported here experimentally manipulated exposure to crime dramas. Thus the research in the area can only demonstrate correlations between crime drama viewership, evidence expectations, and verdicts. Although it would be reasonable for increased crime drama viewership to increase expectations regarding forensic evidence, as has been argued in the media about the CSI Effect, it is equally plausible that people who expect more from forensic evidence are drawn to crime drama shows (Schweitzer & Saks, 2007). The lack of an established causal relationship between television viewing and any effects relevant to juror decision-making is a major weakness of this body of research. Other weaknesses that could impact the scope of the legal implications of this research have been identified, including the use of undergraduate samples (Maeder & Corbett, 2015; Mancini, 2011), the lack of realism in written trial stimuli (Maeder & Corbett, 2015; Mancini, 2011), the lack of deliberations (Mancini, 2011), and the small effect sizes found (Hayes-Smith & Levett, 2011). The focus on specific shows also could be a limitation if the impact of crime dramas is actually a larger phenomenon not tied to any one show (Hayes-Smith & Levett, 2011). The research investigating the CSI Effect should be expanded to include a wider variety of methods.

## Applying the Research on the CSI Effect to the Casey Anthony Case

Despite its limitations, the research on the CSI Effect can shed light on cases in which wrongful acquittal is alleged due to media exposure, like in the Casey Anthony case. Mancini (2013) found that heavier crime drama viewers were more likely to render not guilty verdicts, which is consistent with the media's claim about Anthony's case. However, the bulk of the CSI Effect research found no effect of the media on verdict, or support for the opposite possibility—that heavy viewers of crime dramas were more likely to render guilty verdicts. More specifically, it was alleged that the lack of forensic evidence linking Anthony to the crime scene resulted in her acquittal. Although Hayes-Smith and Levett (2011) found no effect of the presence or strength of forensic evidence on verdict, contradicting this claim about Anthony's case, Kim et al. (2009) found that a lack of forensic evidence in circumstantial cases resulted in increased acquittals, supporting this claim about Anthony's case. Additionally, the media claimed the specific lack of DNA evidence linking Anthony to the crime resulted in her acquittal. Research indicates that jurors might find it more difficult to convict without DNA evidence (Brewer & Ley, 2010; Holmgren & Fordham, 2011), supporting the media's claim that the lack of DNA in the Anthony case was persuasive. However, this survey research did not connect a lack of DNA evidence to verdicts, leaving open the question of how the absence of DNA might affect juror decision-making. Although some of the research on the CSI Effect contradicts the media's claims about the Casey Anthony case, some of it indicates that it is possible media exposure influenced the verdict in the case.

## Legal Practice Issues Relevant to Media Effects in the Courtroom: Recommendations for Reform

Although there is little empirical research demonstrating that media representations of the legal system directly influence juror verdicts, there is some evidence suggesting that the media affects trial-relevant attitudes and perceptions. Regardless, players in the legal system *believe* that the media negatively affects juror decision-making. Therefore, legal practitioners have proposed and used safeguards against media effects, based on their (perhaps incorrect) beliefs that these negative effects exist in the context of the CSI Effect (Cole & Dioso-Villa, 2011; Holmgrem & Fordham, 2011; Maricopa County, 2005; Podlas, 2002). However, these proposed safeguards could be equally applicable to media effects from other news and media content. For example, Podlas (2002) suggested that the juror orientation videos shown to venirepersons at the start of jury service could include information intended to correct misconceptions that potential jurors have about crimes, the legal system, and forensic evidence. Although this is an interesting suggestion and one that courts could accomplish fairly easily, there is no research to date on whether courts use this strategy, or, if they do, how effective it is at managing any influence the media may have on jury decision-making.

Voir dire of jurors including questioning about their media consumption behavior, their beliefs about trials, their expectations for evidence, and any pre-existing biases they may have stemming from viewership also has been suggested as a means to reduce media influence on trials (Cole & Dioso-Villa, 2011; Holmgrem & Fordham, 2011; Podlas, 2002). Although commentary on the CSI Effect influencing the Casey Anthony case was common after the not-guilty verdict, fictional media consumption was not an explicit focus of the voir dire in the case (Gabriel, 2011). Judges have observed changes in the strategies used by attorneys during trials including changes in voir dire (Hughes & Magers, 2007; Robbers, 2008). Some attorneys are using voir dire as a technique to eliminate jurors who report high crime drama viewership (Maricopa County, 2005; Robbers, 2008). Although it has been used in real cases, the effectiveness of voir dire as a potential safeguard against media effects is unknown. Similar research on the effectiveness of voir dire for identifying biases resulting from pretrial publicity indicates that it may not be an effective way to identify jurors who are potentially biased by the media or effectively remove them from service (see Chapter 8). Jurors may not be aware of or honest about their media exposure during voir dire, and they may not be able to accurately assess their impartiality (Studebaker & Penrod, 1997).

Opening statements and closing arguments also provide opportunities for attorneys to address the inappropriateness of relying on television to form perceptions of a case (Cole & Dioso-Villa, 2011), and they are already being used by attorneys for this purpose (Maricopa County, 2005; Robbers, 2008). In the Casey Anthony trial, during opening statements (*Florida v. Anthony*, 2011b) and closing arguments (*Florida v. Anthony*, 2011c), the prosecution and defense both mentioned the forensic science involved in the case, but neither mentioned any media influence on interpreting this evidence. Research on opening statements and closing arguments in general indicate that they can be persuasive tools in the courtroom (McCullough, 2007; Spiecker & Worthington, 2003) so they have the potential to be effective safeguards against media influence. However, research has not been conducted specifically on curbing media effects with opening statements and closing arguments.

During the presentation of trial evidence, attorneys may engage in several strategies to combat media effects on their cases. Prosecutors have reported changing their case strategy in terms of deciding whether to present forensic science evidence post-*CSI*, for example deciding to present weak forensic evidence in a post-*CSI* world when they previously would have only presented strong evidence (Kim et al., 2009; Podlas, 2006a; Stevens, 2008). Attorneys also must consider whether to present *negative evidence* (Cole & Dioso-Villa, 2011). Negative evidence is testimony that is presented with the intent of explaining a lack of forensic evidence on a particular topic, such as an expert who is called to testify that a lack of forensic evidence is "normal" (Hoffmeister, 2011). In Robbers's (2008) study, 44% of judges observed the use of negative evidence in their courtrooms. Thirty-eight percent of prosecutors and 11% of defense attorneys reported using negative evidence to combat perceived media-driven expectations related to forensic evidence (Robbers, 2008). Although research indicates that a lack of forensic evidence can influence jurors (Kim et al., 2009), studies also suggest that negative evidence may decrease this influence (Jenkins & Schuller, 2007; Schuller, Ryan, Krauss, & Jenkins, 2013). For example, an expert that explains the potential for inconclusive results can bolster the impact of a forensic expert with weak or nonexistent findings in a rape trial (Jenkins & Schuller, 2007; Schuller et al., 2013). However, no research has been conducted directly linking the effectiveness of presenting negative evidence to minimize effects of media exposure.

Finally, courts could attempt to combat the influence of the media on trials with jury instructions (Cole & Dioso-Villa, 2011; Holmgrem & Fordham, 2011; Podlas, 2001, 2002). Pretrial instructions could be used to inform jurors of the unrealistic nature of television shows about the legal system (Podlas, 2002). During regular instructions, jurors could be given enhanced instructions on the burden of proof, duties of jurors, and charges to focus jurors' attention on legally relevant decision criteria (Podlas, 2002). Jury instructions also could specifically inform jurors not to use information from television shows in their decisions (Cole & Dioso-Villa, 2011; Holmgrem & Fordham, 2011; Podlas, 2001). Consistent with this suggestion, many jurisdictions now have pattern instructions that include reference to the CSI Effect, stating that television shows are fictional, portray an inaccurate view of the legal system, and should not be relied on in decision-making (Ohio State Bar Association, 2010). Although this was an option for the court in the Casey Anthony case, the jury instructions did not include any reference to the media or the CSI Effect (*Florida v. Anthony*, 2011a). Research has not examined the effectiveness of jury instructions as a safeguard against media influence, but instructions do not decrease jurors' reliance on media in the form of pretrial publicity when reaching their verdicts (for review, see Chapter 8 of this volume). Instructions may be similarly ineffective in reducing other types of media effects on juror decision-making.

Other reforms relating to the root of the problem have been suggested. Some researchers have suggested that the content of television could be changed to more accurately reflect the reality of the legal system (Podlas, 2001). Unfortunately, this suggestion requires writers, directors, producers, and studio executives to refrain from creating fictional shows that could potentially be the most entertaining (as is clear from the high ratings associated with these shows). It also would require news writers and producers to engage in similar editing of nonfictional media content. The alternative would require some other version of content policing that would likely raise First Amendment issues similar to those considered when discussing gag orders or other media restrictions as a solution to pretrial publicity issues. Censorship of creative media is uncommon (Schweitzer & Saks, 2007), as evidenced by recent Supreme Court decisions refusing to limit restrictions on television and other media (*Brown v. Entertainment Merchants Association*, 2011; *FCC v. Fox Television Stations, Inc.*, 2012). Therefore, it is likely that the legal system will have to determine how to guarantee trial fairness despite the burgeoning presence of crime-related fictional and nonfictional media.

## Future Research Directions

There are many possible directions for future research on the media and the jury. The presentation of perpetrators in the media has been a major area of research (Chiricos & Eschholz, 2002; Dixon et al., 2003; Dixon & Azocar, 2006; Dixon & Linz, 2000a, 2000b) and that presentation is related to the development of attitudes about the legal system that could, in turn, be related to juror decision-making (Callanan, 2012; Custers & Van den Bulck, 2011; Eschholz et al., 2003; Holbert et al., 2004; Kort-Butler & Hautshorn, 2011; Romer et al., 2003). However, research has yet to investigate any indirect effect of news and reality television portrayals of crimes on verdicts through their potential impact on attitudes. Thus, future research could examine the impact of various portrayals of crimes on juror decision-making.

Highly publicized cases can be a source of information about the legal system, but their impact on jurors' perceptions of evidence and verdicts in other cases has not been empirically examined outside the context of pretrial publicity. Most of the research on the impact of media in highly publicized cases has focused on the impact of pretrial publicity on the verdict in the specific case that has been publicized—that is, case-specific pretrial publicity (Steblay, Besirevic, Fulero, & Jimenez-Lorente, 1999). However, some research has found that publicity about similar cases, called general publicity, impacts jurors' decisions in other cases to a lesser degree than case-specific publicity (Steblay et al., 1999). Future research could expand on these investigations to examine how highly publicized cases could interact with other media effects, like the CSI Effect, using methods from the pretrial publicity area. This research would be particularly relevant to the Casey Anthony case, considering that both the CSI Effect and pretrial publicity were potentially an issue for that jury.

Another major area of research on the media and juror decision-making has been conducted on the CSI Effect. Most of this research has found a link between increased crime drama viewership and increased expectations that forensic evidence will be presented at trial and will be reliable (Baskin & Sommers, 2010; Kim et al., 2009; Shelton, 2010; Shelton et al., 2006, 2009). However, the link between crime drama viewership and verdict is not as clearly established (Mancini, 2011; Podlas, 2006a, 2006b; Schwietzer & Saks, 2007). The methods used in the extant research on the CSI Effect have largely relied upon associations between self-reported measurements of crime drama viewing and not on experimental exposure to crime dramas. This makes finding causal relations between the media and decision-making impossible, and it does not account for other confounding variables that could be influencing the relations between the media and decision-making. Future research could further investigate the CSI Effect by experimentally manipulating exposure to particular types of crime dramas and to other types of television shows for comparison to investigate, first, the differences between the influences of different types of shows and, second, a causal relationship between exposure and verdict. Some have suggested that future research on the CSI Effect should expand the content of the mock trials presented to jurors, use more representative samples and materials, and include deliberations (Hayes-Smith & Levett, 2011; Maeder & Corbett, 2015; Mancini, 2011; Schweitzer & Saks, 2007). Critiques (Hayes-Smith & Levett, 2011) have highlighted that the extant CSI Effect research might be too focused on the effects of watching specific crime dramas and not on the broader message being delivered by fictional crime media, potentially resulting in the research missing existing CSI Effects. Future research on the CSI Effect could expand how media is defined to solve this problem.

One of the most important future directions for research on media effects and juror decision-making is in the area where no research has been done: the effectiveness of suggested safeguards against media effects in the courtroom. No matter what the actual effect of the media is on jurors, players in the legal system believe the CSI Effect exists, and this belief is impacting their practice (Cole & Dioso-Villa, 2007; Maricopa County, 2005; Robbers, 2008; Stevens, 2008). Lawyers are clearly interested in minimizing any impact of media on their cases. Thus they are using strategies they believe will be effective but for which there is no empirical evidence. It is possible that the suggested strategies are totally ineffective, or worse, could cause a backfire effect that exacerbates the negative influence of the media on trials by focusing the jury's attention on it. Research could specifically test the effectiveness of potential safeguards against the CSI Effect, such as jury orientation videos, voir dire, opening statements, trial evidence tactics, closing arguments, and jury instructions. Future research also could examine the effectiveness of these safeguards against other media effects, such as exposure to highly publicized cases like the Casey Anthony case. This research could provide valuable information about whether changes in legal practice responding to perceived media effects are helping, hurting, or not impacting trial fairness.

## Conclusion

Media about crimes, criminals, and the legal system is plentiful in 21st-century life, as illustrated by highly publicized cases like the Casey Anthony trial. It is clear from the research on the content of this media that consistent messages about the legal system are being delivered in various media formats like the news, legal reality shows, and fictional crime dramas. It also is clear that the messages about the legal system that are presented in the media are not entirely representative of the reality of the criminal justice system. Research also has shown that this cultivation of potentially inaccurate beliefs about the legal system through the media can affect venirepersons' legally relevant attitudes and can influence juror verdicts. Because the legal system cannot control the content of the media, safeguards that can be used during trials to minimize media effects on jurors in actual cases must be considered. To this end, research should continue to examine how the media affects jurors' perceptions of evidence and decision-making and the ways in which the legal system can guarantee trial fairness.

## References

Allen, M., Mabry, E., & McKelton, D. (1998). Impact of juror attitudes about the death penalty on juror evaluations of guilt and punishment: A meta-analysis. *Law and Human Behavior, 22*, 715–731 doi:10.1023/A:1025763008533

Baskin, D. R., & Sommers, I. B. (2010). Crime-show-viewing habits and public attitudes toward forensic evidence: The "CSI effect" revisited. *The Justice System Journal, 31*, 97–113.

Battaglia, N. (2011). Comment: The Casey Anthony trial and wrongful exonerations: How "trial by media" cases diminish public confidence in the criminal justice system. *Albany Law Review, 75*, 1579–1611.

Brewer, P. R., & Ley, B. L. (2010). Media use and public perceptions of DNA evidence. *Science Communications, 32*, 93–117. doi:10.1177/1075547009340343

Brown v. Entertainment Merchants Association, 131 S.Ct. 2729 (2011).

Callanan, V. J. (2012). Media consumption, perceptions of crime risk and fear of crime: Examining race/ethnic differences. *Sociological Perspectives, 55*, 93–115. doi:10.1525/sop.2012.55.1.93

Callanan, V. J., & Rosenberger, J. S. (2011). Media and public perceptions of the police: Examining the impact of race and personal experience. *Policing & Society, 21*, 167–189. doi:10.1080/10439463.2010.540655

Chiricos, T., & Eschholz, S. (2002). The racial and ethnic typification of crime and the criminal typification of race and ethnicity in local television news. *Journal of Research in Crime and Delinquency, 39*, 400–420. doi:10.1177/002242702237286

Cloud, J. (2011, June 16). How the Casey Anthony murder case became the social-media trial of the century. *TIME*. Retrieved from http://www.time.com/time/nation/article/0,8599,2077969,00.html

Cole, S. A., & Dioso-Villa, R. (2007). *CSI* and its effects: Media, juries, and the burden of proof. *New England Law Review, 41*, 435–469.

Cole, S. A., & Dioso-Villa, R. (2009). Investigating the "CSI effect" effect: Media and litigation crisis in criminal law. *Stanford Law Review, 61*, 1335–1373.

Cole, S. A., & Dioso-Villa, R. (2011). Should judges worry about the CSI effect? *Court Review, 47*, 20–31.

Custers, K., & Van den Bulck, J. (2011). The relationship of dispositional and situational fear of crime with television viewing and direct experience with crime. *Mass Communication & Society, 14*, 600–619. doi:10.1080/15205436.2010.530382

Custers, K., & Van den Bulck, J. (2013). The cultivation of fear of sexual violence in women: Processes and moderators of the relationship between television and fear. *Communication Research, 40*, 96–124. doi:10.1177/0093650212440444

Dixon, T. L. (2006). Psychological reactions to crime news portrayals of Black criminals: Understanding the moderating roles of prior news viewing and stereotype endorsement. *Communication Monographs, 73*, 162–187. doi:10.1080/03637750600690643

Dixon, T. L. (2007). Black criminals and White officers: The effects of racially misrepresenting law breakers and law defenders on television news. *Media Psychology, 10*, 270–291. doi:10.1080/15213260701375660

Dixon, T. L. (2008). Crime news and racialized beliefs: Understanding the relationship between local news viewing and perceptions of African Americans and crime. *Journal of Communication, 58*, 106–125. doi:10.1111/j.1460-2466.2007.00376.x

Dixon, T. L., & Azocar, C. L. (2006). The representation of juvenile offenders by race on Los Angeles area television news. *Howard Journal of Communications, 17*, 143–161. doi:10.1080/10646170600656896

Dixon, T. L., & Azocar, C. L. (2007). Priming crime and activating blackness: Understanding the psychological impact of the overrepresentation of Blacks as lawbreakers on television news. *Journal of Communication, 57*, 229–253. doi:10.1111/j.1460-2466.2007.00341.x

Dixon, T. L., Azocar, C. L., & Casas, M. (2003). The portrayal of race and crime on television network news. *Journal of Broadcasting & Electronic Media, 47*, 498–523. doi:10.1207/s15506878jobem4704_2

Dixon, T. L., & Linz, D. (2000a). Race and the misrepresentation of victimization on local television news. *Communication Research, 27*, 547–573. doi:10.1177/009365000027005001

Dixon, T. L., & Linz, D. (2000b). Overrepresentation and underrepresentation of African Americans and Latinos as lawbreakers on television news. *Journal of Communication, 50*, 131–154. doi:10.1111/j.1460-2466.2000.tb02845.x

Dixon, T. L., & Maddox, K. B. (2005). Skin tone, crime news, and social reality judgments: Priming the stereotype of the dark and dangerous Black criminal. *Journal of Applied Social Psychology, 35*, 1555–1570. doi:10.1111/j.1559-1816.2005.tb02184.x

Eschholz, S., Chiricos, T., & Gertz, M. (2003). Television and fear of crime: Program types, audience traits, and the mediating effect of perceived neighborhood racial composition. *Social Problems, 50*, 395–415. doi:10.1525/sp.2003.50.3.395

FCC v. Fox Television Stations, Inc., 132 S.Ct. 2307 (2012).

Federal Bureau of Investigation. (2015). *Uniform Crime Report: 2015*. Retrieved from https://ucr.fbi.gov/crime-in-the-u.s/2015/crime-in-the-u.s.-2015

Florida v. Anthony (2011a). *Transcript of jury instructions*. Retrieved from https://myeclerk.myorangeclerk.com

Florida v. Anthony (2011b). *Transcript of opening statements*. Retrieved from https://myeclerk.myorangeclerk.com

Florida v. Anthony (2011c). *Transcript of rebuttal arguments*. Retrieved from https://myeclerk.myorangeclerk.com

Gabriel, R. (2011, July). American justice or *American Idol*? Two trials and two verdicts in the Casey Anthony case. *The Jury Expert, 23*(1), 1–7.

Grabe, M. E., & Drew, D. G. (2007). Crime cultivation: Comparisons across media genres and channels. *Journal of Broadcasting & Electronic Media, 51*, 147–171. doi:10.1080/08838150701308143

Gorman, B. (2010). *CSI: Crime Scene Investigation is the most watched show in the world!* Retrieved from http://tvbythenumbers.zap2it.com/2010/06/11/csi-crime-scene-investigation-is-the-most-watched-show-in-the-world/53833

Harvey, E., & Derksen, L. (2009). The CSI effect: Science fiction or social fact? In V. M. Johnson & M. Byers (Eds.), *Deconstructing the CSI effect: Producing narratives of justice and science, producing television drama* (pp. 25–26). Lanham, MD: Lexington Books.

Hayes, R. M., & Levett, L. M. (2013). Community members' perceptions of the CSI Effect. *American Journal of Criminal Justice, 38,* 216–235. doi:10.1007/s12103-012-9166-2

Hayes-Smith, R. M., & Levett, L. M. (2011). Jury's still out: How television and crime show viewing influences jurors' evaluations of evidence. *Applied Psychology in Criminal Justice, 7,* 29–46.

Hoffmeister, T. (2011, July 11). Did "CSI" effect sway Anthony jury? *CNN.* Retrieved from http://www.cnn.com

Holbert, R. L., Shah, D. V., & Kwak, N. (2004). Fear, authority, and justice: Crime-related viewing and endorsements of capital punishment and gun ownership. *Journalism and Mass Communication Quarterly, 81,* 343–363. doi:10.1177/107769900408100208

Holmgren, J., & Fordham, J. (2011). The CSI effect and the Canadian and the Australian jury. *Journal of Forensic Sciences, 56,* 63–71. doi:10.1111/j.1556-4029.2010.01621.x

Hughes, T., & Magers, M. (2007). The perceived impact of crime scene investigation shows on the administration of justice. *Journal of Criminal Justice and Popular Culture, 14,* 259–276.

Innocence Project. (2017). *Exonerate.* Retrieved from https://www.innocenceproject.org/exonerate/

Jenkins, G., & Schuller, R. A. (2007). The impact of negative forensic evidence on mock jurors' perceptions of a trial of drug-facilitated sexual assault. *Law and Human Behavior, 31,* 369–380. doi:10.1007/s10979-006-9068-2

Kim, Y. S., Barak, G., & Shelton, D. E. (2009). Examining the "CSI-effect" in the cases of circumstantial evidence and eyewitness testimony: Multivariate and path analyses. *Journal of Criminal Justice, 37,* 452–460. doi:10.1016/j.jcrimjus.2009.07.005

Kort-Butler, L., & Hartshorn, K. J. S. (2011). Watching the detectives: Crime programming, fear of crime, and attitudes about the criminal justice system. *The Sociological Quarterly, 52,* 36–55. doi:10.1111/j.1533-8525.2010.01191.x

Lane, J., & Meeker, J. W. (2003). Fear of gang crime: A look at three theoretical models. *Law and Society Review, 37,* 425–456. doi:10.1111/1540-5893.3702008

Ley, B. L., Jankowski, N., & Brewer, P. R. (2012). Investigating *CSI:* Portrayals of DNA testing on a forensic crime show and their potential effects. *Public Understanding of Science, 21,* 51–67. doi:10.1177/0963662510367571

Lieberman, J. D., Carrell, C. A., Miethe, T. D., & Krauss, D. A. (2008). Gold versus platinum: Do jurors recognize the superiority and limitations of DNA evidence comparted to other types of forensic evidence? *Psychology, Public Policy, and Law, 14,* 27–62. doi:10.10371/1076.8971.14.1.27

Maeder, E. M., & Corbett, R. (2015). Beyond frequency: Perceived realism and the CSI effect. *Canadian Journal of Criminology and Criminal Justice, 57,* 83–114. doi:10.3138/cjccj.2013.E4410.3138/cjccj.2013.E44

Mancini, D. E. (2011). The CSI effect reconsidered: Is it moderated by need for cognition? *North American Journal of Psychology, 13,* 155–174.

Mancini, D. E. (2013). The "CSI effect" in an actual juror sample: Why crime show genre may matter. *North American Journal of Psychology, 15,* 543–564.

Maricopa County Attorney's Office. (2005). *CSI: Maricopa County: The CSI effect and its real-life impact on justice: A study by the Maricopa County Attorney's Office.* Maricopa, AZ: Maricopa County Attorney's Office.

McCullough, G. W. (2007). Function of text structure in jurors' comprehension and decision making. *Psychological Reports, 101,* 723–730. doi:10.2466/PRO.101.3.723-730

Ohio State Bar Association. (2010). *OSBA Jury Instructions.* Retrieved from http://federalevidence.com/downloads/blog/2010/OSBA.Jury.Instructions.pdf

Oliver, M. B. (1994). Portrayals of crime, race, and aggression in "reality-based" police shows: A content analysis. *Journal of Broadcasting & Electronic Media, 38,* 179–192. doi:10.1080/08838159409364255

Podlas, K. (2001). Please adjust your signal: How television's syndicated courtrooms bias our juror citizenry. *American Business Law Journal, 39,* 1–24.

Podlas, K. (2002). Blame Judge Judy: The effects of syndicated television courtrooms on jurors. *American Journal of Trial Advocacy, 25,* 557–586.

Podlas, K. (2006a). The "CSI effect" and other forensic fictions. *Loyola of Los Angeles Entertainment Law Review, 27,* 87–124.

Podlas, K. (2006b). "The CSI effect": Exposing the media myth. *Fordham Intellectual Property, Media & Entertainment Law Journal, 16,* 429–465.

Pooley, E. (1989). Grins, guns, and videotape: The trouble with local TV news. *New York Magazine, 22*(40), 36–44.

Reith, M. (1999). Viewing of crime drama and authoritarian aggression: An investigation of the relationship between crime viewing, fear, and aggression. *Journal of Broadcasting & Electronic Media, 43,* 211–221. doi: 10.1080/08838159909364485

Rhineberger-Dunn, G., Briggs, S. J., & Rader, N. (2016). Clearing crime in prime-time: The disjuncture between fiction and reality. *American Journal of Criminal Justice, 41,* 255–278. doi:10.1007/s12103-015-9300-z

Robbers, M. (2008). Blinded by science: The social construction of reality in forensic television shows and its effect on criminal jury trials. *Criminal Justice Policy Review, 19,* 84–102. doi:10.1177/0887403407305982

Roche, S. P., Pickett, J. T., & Gertz, M. (2015). The scary world of online news? Internet news exposure and public attitudes toward crime and justice. *Journal of Quantitative Criminology, 32,* 215–236. doi:10.1007/s10940-015-9261-x

Romer, D., Jamieson, K. H., & Aday, S. (2003). Television news and the cultivation of fear of crime. *Journal of Communication, 53,* 88–104. doi:10.1111/j.1460-2466.2003.tb03007.x

Schroeder, D. A., & White, M. D. (2009). Exploring the use of DNA evidence in homicide investigations. *Police Quarterly, 12,* 319–342. doi:10.1177/1098611109339894

Schuller, R. A., Ryan, A., Krauss, D., & Jenkins, G. (2013). Mock juror sensitivity to forensic evidence in drug facilitated sexual assaults. *International Journal of Law and Psychiatry, 36,* 121–128. doi:10.1016/j.ijlp.2013.01.011

Schweitzer, N. J., & Saks, M. J. (2007). The CSI effect: Popular fiction about forensic science affects the public's expectations about real forensic science. *Jurimetrics Journal, 47,* 357–364.

Shelton, D. E. (2010). Juror expectations for scientific evidence in criminal cases: Perceptions and reality about the "CSI effect" myth. *Thomas M. Cooley Law Review, 27,* 1–35.

Shelton, D. E., Kim, Y. S., & Barak, G. (2006). A study of juror expectations and demands concerning scientific evidence: Does the "CSI effect" exist? *Vanderbilt Journal of Entertainment and Technology Law, 9,* 331–368.

Shelton, D. E., Kim, Y. S., & Barak, G. (2009). An indirect-effects model of mediated adjudication: The CSI myth, the tech effect, and metropolitan jurors' expectations for scientific evidence. *Vanderbilt Journal of Entertainment & Technology Law, 12,* 1–43.

Slater, M. D., Rouner, D., & Long, M. (2006). Television dramas and support for controversial public policies: Effects and mechanisms. *Journal of Communication, 56,* 235–252. doi:10.1111/j.1460-2466.2006.00017.x

Smith, S. M., Stinson, V., & Patry, M. W. (2011). Fact or fiction? The myth and reality of the CSI effect. *Court Review, 47,* 4–7.

Sommers, S. R., & Ellsworth, P. C. (2009). "Race salience" in juror decision-making: Misconceptions, clarifications, and unanswered questions. *Behavioral Sciences & the Law, 27,* 599–609. doi:dx.doi.org.ccl.idm.oclc.org/10.1002/bsl.877

Soulliere, D. M. (2004). Policing on prime-time: A comparison of television and real-world policing. *American Journal of Criminal Justice, 28,* 215–233. doi:10.1007/BF02885873

Spiecker, S. C., & Worthington, D. L. (2003). The influence of opening statement/closing argument organizational strategy on juror verdict and damage awards. *Law and Human Behavior, 27,* 437–456. doi:0147-7307/03/0800-0437/1

Steblay, N. M., Besirevic, J., Fulero, S. M., & Jimenez-Lorente, B. (1999). The effects of pretrial publicity on juror verdicts: A meta-analytic review. *Law and Human Behavior, 23,* 219–235. doi:10.1023/A:1022325019080

Stevens, D. J. (2008). Forensic science, wrongful convictions, and American prosecutor discretion. *Howard Journal of Criminal Justice, 47,* 31–51. doi:10.1111/j.1468-2311.2008.00495.x

Studebaker, C. A., & Penrod, S. D. (1997). Pretrial publicity: The media, the law and commonsense. *Psychology, Public Policy, and Law, 3,* 428–460. doi:10.1037/1076-8971.3.2-3.428

Tyler, T. R. (2006). Viewing *CSI* and the threshold of guilt: Managing truth and justice in reality and fiction. *The Yale Law Journal, 115,* 1050–1085. doi:10.2307/20455645

Weaver, R., Salamonson, Y., Koch, J., & Porter, G. (2012). The CSI effect at university: Forensic science students' television viewing and perceptions of ethical issues. *Australian Journal of Forensic Sciences, 44,* 381–391. doi:10.1080/00450618.2012.691547

# 8

## Pre- and Midtrial Publicity in the Age of Internet and Social Media

*Tarika Daftary-Kapur and Steven D. Penrod*

Well, I was curious.

—Juror caught Googling defendant's name during trial
(Schwartz, 2009)

In 2011 in Arkansas, despite having been admonished by the judge, a juror tweeted during both the trial and deliberations, leading to a mistrial in a capital murder case (Zand, 2011). In 2016, a juror was jailed for eight days for looking up the definition of words on the Internet during a murder trial ("PBC Juror Jailed," 2016). Another recent and particularly high-profile case involved defendant John Goodman—a famous multimillionaire tried for manslaughter for a hit-and-run while intoxicated that resulted in the death of 23-year-old Scott Smith (Shammas, 2015). Juror misconduct in the original trial resulted in a second trial of Goodman's case. Voir dire revealed that one prospective juror, 23-year-old Travis Van Vliet, had discovered it was a retrial after Googling the case and shared the information he uncovered with another potential juror. Van Vliet was charged with and convicted for contempt of court. The jurors who were selected were then sequestered for 19 days at a hotel. They were constantly monitored to prevent them from being exposed to details related to the original trial. One alternate juror was found to have been using his tablet computer in his room, but he claimed he was only checking sports scores and had done no research related to the case. The trial went on and Goodman was finally convicted of manslaughter in 2014.

As these cases demonstrate, the explosive growth of social networking and Internet use has placed enormous pressure on one of the most fundamental of American institutions—the impartial jury. A growing number of appellate cases address issues arising from allegations of improper juror use of social media and the Internet, including conducting independent research, contacting parties involved in the case, and posting about their experiences during the trial and deliberations. According to a Reuters Legal study (Grow, 2010), 90 verdicts were challenged on the basis of Internet-related juror misconduct between 1999 and 2010—more than half within a two-year period. Of the 90 challenges, 28 were overturned or had mistrials declared. In three-quarters of the cases in which judges declined to declare mistrials, Internet-related juror misconduct was deemed to have been present.

The Internet gives jurors the ability to instantly publish information about an ongoing trial to a large audience. Easy access to social media applications and Internet search engines via cellphones and other Internet-ready devices like iPads presents a concern for courts in deciding how to address and prevent jury misconduct. Although many courts have adopted jury instructions that specifically address the issue of social media use, others have taken more extreme prevention efforts, including banning all use of electronic devices within the courtroom or punishing jurors using fines and criminal contempt charges (Robinson, 2011). Jurors in the Goodman case mentioned previously were even sequestered and prohibited from using laptops, iPads, and so on in their hotel rooms. Judges and attorneys contend that jurors' use of the Internet increases the risk that the juror will form premature opinions of the case, be exposed to extraneous information, or improperly communicate with third parties (Aronson & Patterson, 2013).

Jurors have an intense need to know, and given that the Internet is now an integral part of everyday life, it is commonplace to do "research" through blogs and websites, such as Wikipedia; search engines, such as Google; or other social networking websites, such as Facebook, LinkedIn, and YouTube. This has led to an increase in criticism of jurors and commentary classifying this as juror misbehavior (Marder, 2014). But, as Morrison (2011) pointed out, this criticism might be too simplistic. She argues that jurors are trying to gain information about the defendant's background and the circumstances of the case, and understand the law and legal terms better, all in an effort to be fair and accurate in their decision-making. As such, as opposed to juror misbehavior, this juror behavior might represent a misplaced sense of responsibility to render the "right" decision.

All of this raises issues about jurors' rights, how use of the Internet is changing the nature of trials, and strategies to deal with modern jury-media relationships. Traditional pretrial publicity (PTP) research focused on the pre-Internet reality that jurors would mostly bring case knowledge with them to the courtroom and the issues were whether the knowledge produced bias and whether it could be detected in voir dire (i.e., juror questioning) or offset with traditional safeguards. Next, we present what we have learned from this literature and how these findings might apply to midtrial publicity or information gained during the trial outside of the courtroom. Additionally, we discuss how, given the ease with which jurors can engage in midtrial research, traditional safeguards may not fully apply. Finally, we provide recommendations for strategies to combat this problem as well as ideas for future research.

## The Impartial Jury in the Age of Twitter

Historically jurors have been thought to use the story model of decision-making when evaluating evidence and arriving at a decision (Pennington & Hastie, 1992). Jurors essentially construct narratives from the evidence presented at trial, filling gaps using common sense and their own worldview. These narratives are then subjected to the legal standard to help jurors make decisions of guilt. The trial, with the presentation of evidence in a slow methodical process, allows jurors to reflect on the evidence and adjust their narratives appropriately. This slow, deliberate process may change with access to the Internet and social media. We now live in the Internet age of "140 characters or less," and jurors are used to constant and immediate access to information in small sound bites that dominate their daily lives. Contemporary jurors may reflexively seek out information online, whether it be via social media, blogs, or news websites. Additionally, Aronson and Patterson (2013) point out the possibility that contemporary jurors might be cognitively less reliant on collective common sense and, instead, find it necessary to verify initial impressions about the evidence.

At the same time, it is unclear how often jurors turn to the Internet during the course of a trial, although it seems to be an increasing trend. A study by the National Center for State Courts (NCSC; Waters & Hannaford-Agor, 2014) found that a significant number of jurors had access to and reported interest in using the Internet to conduct research on case-related topics and to discuss their jury experience, but none of them admitted to actually engaging in any Internet research or social media activity. According to a recent survey administered by the Federal Judicial Center (Dunn, 2014), only 6% of district court judges said they have experienced jurors using social media to communicate during a trial or deliberations. But some have questioned the reliability of the survey. Grow (2010) pointed out that most Americans can access the Internet from their cellphones, which a judge is unlikely to witness, so these survey results likely underestimated the extent to which jurors engaged in Internet-related misconduct without getting caught. Given the increase in court opinions regarding the issue (see prior discussion) and news stories discussing the "Google mistrial" and "Googling jurors," the risk can be considered real.

This changing landscape has led to a dilemma for the courts on how to balance juror impartiality with the increasing reliance of jurors on the news media via the Internet to inform their decision-making. Also, the courts must determine how harmful this exposure might be. Improper use of the Internet and social media might be viewed as harmless as opposed to prejudicial error by the courts. Judges have vast discretion to determine whether juror misconduct is prejudicial enough to warrant removing a juror from the jury, declaring a mistrial, or reversing a conviction. To do this, courts have used the totality of circumstances standard to assess whether a juror's misconduct is prejudicial. This typically involves examining the type of information that resulted from an Internet search, the stage of the trial when the misconduct occurred, whether extralegal information obtained was shared with other jurors, and whether it is related to a critical aspect of the case (McGee, 2010).

Blackman and Brickman (2011) have classified the types of information jurors might access into five categories: (a) media accounts of the case; (b) virtual physical or other factual evidence; (c) expert opinions; (d) personal and professional information on the parties involved, including the judge, attorneys, and the defendant in criminal cases; and (e) the law (such as researching sentences associated with conviction for the particular crime charged). The courts have been attempting to distinguish which errors are harmless versus prejudicial. For example, Internet research to look up the meaning of a word might not be considered prejudicial, but research that leads to a juror discovering a prior conviction of a defendant will most likely result in some sort of judicial intervention. In the Goodman case highlighted earlier, although an alternate juror was found to have been using his iPad against the court's admonitions, the judge did not consider this egregious enough to call a mistrial. This issue of whether the trial court reasonably addressed juror misconduct came up before the Ohio Supreme Court in *State v. Gunnell* (2012). The misconduct involved a juror who researched "involuntary manslaughter" on the Internet and attempted to bring the printed material into the jury room during deliberations. The judge questioned her about the information she found but did not ask her "a single question about the prejudice or bias, if any, created by the improper information or her ability to disregard it" (p. 247). The Ohio Supreme Court ruled that the trial court had not used its discretion well in determining whether juror bias existed and could be reversed, concluding that "it was error for the judge to make no more than a limited inquiry of the juror—an inquiry that merely established the misconduct, not any prejudice from it" (p. 251). In *Wardlaw v. State* (2009), a juror's online research led the Maryland Court of Special Appeals to order a new trial for the defendant accused of raping his 17-year-old daughter. At trial, the defendant's daughter testified that she had sexual intercourse with the defendant on three different occasions and that she had been diagnosed with oppositional defiant disorder. A juror conducted online research on "oppositional defiant disorder" and reported to the other jurors her finding that lying was associated with the disorder. Because the daughter's credibility was a crucial issue and there was no other evidence to substantiate her allegations, the court found that the juror's research constituted egregious misconduct and that the trial court's failure to question the jurors about the influence of the individual juror's online research required a reversal.

Despite the increasing number of court cases grappling with this issue as well as speculations in the media about the impact of the Internet and use of social media, there is limited research on how harmful this information might be and how it may bias jurors. Hoffmeister (2012) pointed out that, despite the anecdotal discussions and catchy names such as "Twitter effect," "Google mistrials," and "Internet-tainted jurors," there is little academic research on the issue. Hoffmeister questioned whether juror use of social media is actually a pervasive and growing problem that is truly different from past concerns over juror impartiality. He explained this lack of research by noting that juror use of social media is an emerging issue and that juror misconduct is an underexamined area of the law. However, some inferences can be gained by considering earlier studies focused on understanding how jurors are influenced by information they learn prior to the beginning of trial, and researchers have begun to explore the impact of exposure to social media and the Internet while proceedings are ongoing. We review this work next.

## Impact of Pretrial Publicity on Juror Decision-Making

As news coverage became progressively more accessible via the Internet, the influence of PTP on jurors, too, became an increasing concern. Given the strong constitutional protections afforded to the press in the United States, the justice system must deal with the possibility that a citizen who has been called for jury duty has been exposed to information about the case on which he or she is being asked to sit in judgment (Posey & Wrightsman, 2005). As has been pointed out by the courts, not all publicity is problematic. The standard is not that jurors should be ignorant of the case and have no knowledge whatsoever regarding the defendant, but rather that they not have formed an opinion regarding guilt or innocence based on this knowledge (*Newcomb v. State of Alaska*, 1990). Exposure to basic facts about the indictment or an outline of the facts in the case might not be considered prejudicial, whereas publicity that is inherently false, incomplete, biased, or inflammatory, for example, inadmissible evidence, emotionally charged editorials, and so on, might be (see, e.g., *Newcomb v. State of Alaska*, 1990; Vidmar, 2002). In such cases, it has the potential to undermine the constitutional guarantees to trial by an impartial jury and to due process in both criminal and civil trials.

What have psychologists learned about the potential biasing effects of pretrial publicity and the implications of that bias for jurors' perceptions and performance that could inform judges' decisions about PTP? This issue has been of intense interest to legal professionals as well as to psychologists (see, e.g., Otto, Penrod, & Dexter, 1994; Ruva, McEvoy, & Bryant, 2007; Studebaker, Robbennolt, Pathak-Sharma, & Penrod, 2000). The first wave of research examining PTP effects centered on juror bias and juror awareness of this bias. These early studies were crucial in establishing the existence of PTP effects as a phenomenon. A comprehensive examination of PTP effects based on this first wave of research exists in a meta-analytic review of the literature conducted by Steblay, Besirevic, Fulero, and Jiminez-Lorente (1999). They examined 44 empirical tests of PTP effects from articles published between 1966 and 1997. Steblay and colleagues found that participants who had been exposed to negatively biasing accounts of PTP were significantly more likely to prejudge the defendant as guilty when compared to those not exposed to this type of information.

More recently, researchers have begun to explore the various cognitive mechanisms that underlie these effects. This second wave of research (Hope, Memon, & McGeorge, 2004; Kovera, 2002) attempts to explain how PTP imparts its biasing effect and is primarily driven by theory (Bruschke, Gonis, Hill, Fiber-Ostrow, & Loges, 2016; Butler, 2012; Capuozzo, 2013; Daftary-Kapur, Penrod, O'Connor, & Wallace, 2014; Fulero, 2002; Ruva & LeVasseur, 2012; Ruva & McEvoy, 2008; Ruva et al., 2007). While some experimental studies suggest that jurors are insensitive to PTP when making judgments about a defendant (Carroll et al., 1986), the majority of past studies indicate that PTP can bias jurors' perceptions of defendant guilt and criminality as well as juror sympathy for the defendant both pretrial and after evidentiary presentations (Studebaker & Penrod, 2005).

## Midtrial Publicity and Juror Decision-Making

In addition to the influence of PTP, another factor that may be potentially problematic for the courts is midtrial publicity. For our purposes, we define midtrial publicity as any external information empaneled jurors are exposed to following their appearance and selection for jury duty. Although it is possible that potential jurors are exposed to PTP before they are called to jury duty in a case, that information may not be salient for them. As noted in *United States v. Williams* (1978), "information reported during the trial seems far more likely to remain in the mind of a juror exposed to it, and he may be more inclined to seek out this information when he is personally involved in the case" (p. 38). Once people are empaneled on a jury, any extralegal information they are exposed to potentially becomes increasingly more salient as they are now invested in the proceedings, and that information may consciously or subconsciously influence their decision-making. Additionally, midtrial inquiry may be much more focused and motivated by desires to answer questions which have arisen during trial, versus a more vague, undirected, and perhaps even more balanced exposure to PTP. Midtrial publicity has been a concern in the courts, and jurors' exposure to it has been the basis for a number of successful appeals (Vidmar, 2002). Despite judicial admonitions to ignore the media, a LexisNexis search revealed over

5,300 cases in which midtrial publicity was brought up as a potential issue on appeal between 2004 and 2016.

At the same time, there has been substantial variance in the success of these appeals. An examination of a selection of successful appeals, and some unsuccessful ones, will illuminate the issues raised in the midtrial context. A number of circumstances have led to successful arguments that midtrial publicity has sufficiently tainted the jury and that legal remedies were warranted. In some instances, however, trial judges have not sufficiently attended to the potential danger of midtrial publicity. For example, in *Marshall v. United States* (1959), the 10th Circuit reversed a conviction because the jurors had been exposed to two newspaper accounts of the defendant's criminal record during the course of the trial. The trial court questioned jurors individually, and, even though the jurors admitted reading the articles, the judge concluded that they would not be prejudiced as they claimed they could be impartial in deciding the case. Despite this, the higher court overturned the conviction on the grounds that jurors' exposure to the two newspaper articles regarding the defendant's criminal record was potentially prejudicial.

Although there is no empirical research on the effects of midtrial publicity on juror decision-making per se, an extensive search of the literature revealed one survey conducted in Australia by Chesterman, Chan, and Hampton (2001). The researchers found that jurors did engage in out-of-the-courtroom investigations, including investigations on the Internet. Despite judicial instructions to ignore newspaper coverage of the trial, at least one juror in each of the 34 trials they examined followed the daily newspapers. In one of the cases, a juror placed a special order for a newspaper that was likely to cover the case. Additionally, in 32 of these trials, the coverage was discussed in the jury room. Of all the jurors interviewed, 77% reported being exposed to some sort of midtrial publicity. In other research, Cameron, Potter, and Young (1999) conducted extensive interviews with jurors from 48 cases in New Zealand. They found that jurors engaged in similar ex parte investigations, despite being instructed not to do so. Although jurors in both surveys had a high level of exposure to midtrial publicity, the majority of them claimed that it did not influence their verdicts. For example, 98% of Chesterman and colleagues' respondents claimed that they could put specific publicity out of their mind and that it did not influence their ability to assess the evidence in an impartial manner.

Traditional PTP research focused on the pre-Internet reality that jurors would mostly bring case knowledge with them to the courtroom and the issues were whether the knowledge produced bias and whether it could be detected in voir dire or offset with traditional safeguards such as sequestration, jury instructions, and so on (as discussed in more detail later). One question that can be raised is: If midtrial publicity is merely exposure to publicity during a trial, how and why would its effects be any different from those of PTP? The main focus of experimental and survey studies in the area of PTP research has been on establishing the relations between PTP and judgments of culpability. Although PTP research is relevant to midtrial publicity effects, it is unclear whether PTP research findings map perfectly onto midtrial publicity effects and whether they would produce identical or even similar results. Midtrial publicity can be distinguished from PTP in several ways. Next we present what we have learned from this literature and how these findings might apply to exposure to extralegal information midtrial.

### Timing of Exposure

PTP exposure can occur at any point in time before the start of the trial. The period between the PTP exposure and the commencement of the trial could be anywhere from years, months, or weeks to days. In contrast, midtrial exposure occurs during the actual course of the trial, after a person has been seated on a jury.

Timing of exposure to PTP stimuli has been shown to be an important factor in PTP research. For instance, continuance is a traditional safeguard employed by the legal system, whereby the trial is started after a forced delay so as to avoid any prejudicial effects of PTP. Davis (1986) used a mock jury paradigm to expose participants to negative PTP regarding the defendant's character either one week or immediately before the mock trial. He found that those in the immediate-exposure condition returned more guilty verdicts as compared to those in the delayed-exposure condition. In Kramer, Kerr, and Carroll's (1990) mock trial study, some jurors were exposed to publicity 12 days prior to the beginning of the trial and others were exposed right before the trial began. Jurors were more likely to render guilty verdicts if they had been exposed to publicity that was high versus low in bias just prior to the trial, regardless of whether the publicity contained factual or emotional content. Although experiencing a delay between exposure and trial onset did not affect the impact of exposure to highly biasing emotional publicity on juror verdicts, the delay reduced the likelihood of conviction among those exposed to highly biasing factual publicity. Thus the more proximal publicity exposure is to trial onset, the more influential it may be on juror decision-making. It follows that exposure to information midtrial might be highly influential on decision-making, as it occurs in the midst of the trial.

### Durability in Light of Trial Evidence

One might initially think that significant insights into midtrial publicity effects might be adduced from research which examines whether PTP effects endure through the presentation of trial evidence. In fact, such research is unlikely to help for several reasons. First, the exact mechanisms through which PTP influences juror and jury decision-making are not well understood, so it is difficult to make arguments on purely theoretical grounds about whether the effect of prejudicial midtrial publicity persists long enough to influence verdicts—maybe it does because it appears while decisions are being formulated; maybe it does not because jurors have already heard opening statements and a bit of trial evidence and their impressions are already solid enough to resist extraneous influences. Also, the effect may be attenuated as jurors may heed judicial admonitions to ignore publicity surrounding the case. One aspect of understanding publicity effects includes whether PTP effects are sustained through the presentation of trial evidence. Although a substantial body of research exists in the area of PTP, there are no authoritative answers to this question at present. Otto et al.'s (1994) mock trial study revealed that PTP regarding the defendant's criminal record negatively biased jurors' assessment of the defendant's culpability relative to when there was no PTP. However, trial evidence weakened bias created by PTP. Similar results were found by Freedman and Burke (1996). They showed that mock jurors who had been exposed to more versus less PTP were more likely to indicate that they thought the defendant was guilty before they read the script of the trial. However, after reading the trial script, the PTP effect disappeared. In a field study, Daftary-Kapur and colleagues (2014) demonstrated stronger effects of PTP (albeit fading ones, in that strength of the effect decreased through the course of the trial): the impact of PTP persisted throughout the course of eight weeks and was strongest for those who received pro-defense as opposed to pro-prosecution PTP. Thus although findings point to a diminishing effect of PTP in light of trial evidence, only a handful of studies have examined this issue, and no published studies have considered whether the effects of midtrial publicity persist through the trial process.

**Pretrial/Midtrial Publicity and Information Salience**

Another factor that potentially distinguishes midtrial from pretrial publicity is salience of the information. Jurors potentially pay more attention to publicity acquired during the trial process as compared to publicity they have been exposed to pretrial. That is, information that is acquired pretrial may be given scant attention and as a result may not be easily accessible. Yet information that is acquired during the trial process may be highly salient for jurors. This high level of salience is likely to lead to the activation of related schemas or thought patterns that have been formed during the trial. The midtrial information may then be incorporated into these schemas.

Midtrial information has the potential to become even more salient if it fits with the story that jurors have developed regarding the fact pattern during the course of the trial. Research indicates that "the extent to which information about a person influences a judgment is a function of the implicational relationship between the content of that information and the judgment being made" (Hamilton & Fallot, 1974, p. 444). Thus the more in line the midtrial information is with a juror's story, the more potential for influence.

Again, this is potentially more influential than PTP exposure which occurs before a juror has developed a story for the trial.

## Efforts to Limit Juror Use of Social Media and Exposure to Midtrial Publicity During Trials

Courts have implemented a variety of measures to educate jurors on the use of social media during trial and deliberations. They also have developed strategies to deal with jurors who have been discovered using social media or conducting Internet research during the trial process. Many of these are safeguards that have been employed in the past to counter PTP, and as such we discuss their potential effectiveness for midtrial publicity given what we know about how effective they are in curbing the impact of pretrial publicity effects.

### Jury Instructions

Most courts have adopted jury instructions that specifically address use of social media and the Internet to conduct research during trial and deliberations (Robinson, 2011). These instructions are given typically at the start of the trial and reiterated before deliberations. A survey of federal district court judges conducted by the Federal Judicial Center for the Committee on Court Administration and Case Management reported that 60% of the judges use model jury instructions to address use of social media (Dunn, 2014). A portion of the model instructions developed by the Judicial Conference Committee on Court Administration and Case Management (2012) reads as follows:

> I know that many of you use cell phones, Blackberries, the [I]nternet
> and other tools of technology. You also must not talk to anyone
> at any time about this case or use these tools to communicate
> electronically with anyone about the case. This includes your family
> and friends. You may not communicate with anyone about the
> case on your cell phone, through e-mail, Blackberry, iPhone, text
> messaging, or on Twitter, through any blog or website, including
> Facebook, or Google+. You may not use any similar technology
> of social media, even if I have not specifically mentioned it here.
> I expect you will inform me as soon as you become aware of another
> juror's violation of these instructions.

The effectiveness of these types of instructions has not received much scholarly attention (although we know from related research on jury instructions that they tend to be ineffective, Liberman & Sales, 1997; Tanford, 1990), but some survey research exists on judges' and jurors' perceptions of their effectiveness. Most judges believe that social media was not used by jurors after they gave their instructions but at the same time admitted that they had no way of knowing this (Robinson, 2012). Hannaford-Agor, Rottman, and Waters (2012) surveyed jurors and found that although they understood the instructions given, they wished they could make use of the Internet for additional research about the cases. A survey of jurors conducted for the NCSC (Waters & Hannaford-Agor, 2014) showed that a number of jurors wished they could use the Internet to obtain information about legal terms (44%), the case (26%), the parties involved (23%), the lawyers (20%), the judge (19%), and the witnesses (18%). At the same time, the percentage of those who wished to use the Internet to communicate with others about the case was substantially lower—few jurors said they would like to use the Internet to connect with other jurors (5%), connect with one of the trial participants (3%), tweet about the trial (3%), blog about the trial (3%), or post information about the trial on a social networking site (2%). Although these surveys give us a glimpse at how jurors might engage in using social media and the Internet, additional research is needed in this area related to the effectiveness of jury instructions at curbing such behavior.

## Online Investigations of Jurors

Attorneys may use jurors' digital presence to track them before, during, and after trials. The most basic kind of search done is a name search via an Internet search engine like Google. Additionally, many attorneys conduct more in-depth searches of jurors by collecting information from social networking sites and monitoring their online activities (Lundberg, 2012).

Online investigation of jurors has become increasingly common and is gaining acceptance within the legal profession (Comisky & Taylor, 2011). Courts and state bar associations have even approved and, in some cases, encouraged this type of research. Proponents assert that the online investigation of jurors during a trial can uncover juror misconduct (Hoffmeister, 2011). Further, proponents also assert that once jurors know their voir dire answers can be verified, they will either be more truthful or ask to be relieved from service. Finally, proponents argue jurors who know their online activities are being monitored will be more likely to adhere to jury instructions given throughout the duration of the trial (Comisky & Taylor, 2011).

## Sequestration

In cases in which potentially prejudicial midtrial publicity can be anticipated in advance, the presiding judge may choose to sequester the jury. Although given much attention when employed, judges rarely use this practice due to the high costs involved (McGee, 2010). Jurors were sequestered for 19 days during the Goodman retrial. Despite being sequestered, one juror reported being heckled, and an alternate juror was questioned because he had an iPad in his hotel room, which was in violation of a court order (Shammas, 2015).

When a judge does decide to sequester a jury, it is often because there is a critical piece of inadmissible material being discussed in the press (e.g., a suppressed confession) or, as in the Goodman case, widespread publicity regarding the case. The Internet has resulted in one potential twist on sequestration called "virtual sequestration" (Hoffmeister, 2011). This allows jurors to stay in their own homes but consent to having their Internet disconnected or monitored. Some see this as overly intrusive, and others have questioned whether it is effective given that jurors could access the Internet offsite or via other methods such as through their mobile devices.

## Voir Dire

Once the trial is set to begin, if the case has generated substantial publicity in the media, the courts may expand their normal voir dire process by including additional or specific questioning of potential jurors (also known as extended voir dire; Studebaker & Penrod, 2005). The goal is to uncover biases and prejudices against the parties that might have been generated from that publicity so as to ensure the impaneling of an impartial jury. Psycholegal research has called into question whether general voir dire processes can achieve this goal (Hastie, 1990). The inclusion of jurors with strong pre-existing attitudes and beliefs has the potential to create a biased jury and impede the defendant's right to a fair and impartial trial. The use of extended voir dire as a legal remedy has been suggested as a potential safeguard for identifying and educating jurors with particularly strong beliefs (i.e., authoritarianism; Narby, Cutler, & Moran, 1993). However, the empirical literature detailing the effectiveness of extended voir dire in identifying potentially biased jurors is limited. Dexter, Cutler, and Moran (1992) found that extended voir dire was more effective than minimal voir dire in decreasing perceptions of defendant culpability but failed to significantly reduce the impact of PTP. Extended voir dire also has been shown to reveal greater insights into jurors' attitudes, thus better explaining variation in juror verdicts than data gathered from minimal voir dire procedures (Moran, Cutler, & Loftus, 1990). Further, there is evidence to suggest that attorney-conducted voir dire procedures result in greater juror candor about exposure to PTP than procedures directed by the judge, which tend to be less elaborate (Jones, 1987). However, Dexter and colleagues (1992) found that mock jurors continued to be more punitive to the defendant after exposure to PTP in spite of an extended voir dire focused on raising awareness and educating jurors.

Freedman, Martin, and Mota (1998) found that the negative effects of PTP were increased as opposed to decreased when jurors were questioned about their pretrial exposure. Additionally, they found differences in post-trial guilty verdicts across conditions (negative or neutral publicity toward the defendant) only when jurors were asked to render pretrial verdicts. They interpreted this as participants being reluctant to change their opinions once they had committed to one position. Steblay et al.'s (1999) meta-analysis found greater PTP effects when participants were asked to render pretrial judgments as opposed to when judgments were rendered post-trial only. To the extent that voir dire encourages jurors to anticipate their verdicts, it seems to be a somewhat ineffective tool to control the effect of PTP and may have somewhat of a backfire effect. Ultimately, it is a self-report measure of attitudes and biases and is thus at risk of intentional as well as unintentional deception.

## Threat of Criminal Punishment

At least one state (California) has adopted a statute that specifically prohibits jurors from using social media and the Internet to research or disseminate information related to the trial. California passed the law in 2011, expanding the state's existing jury instructions. Under the law, a juror can be charged with contempt of court or a misdemeanor for willful disobedience of a court admonishment related to the prohibition of any form of communication or research about the case, including all forms of electronic or wireless communication or research. Currently, no known research exists examining whether these threats are effective in deterring jurors from engaging in Internet research or any sort of Internet-related misconduct.

## Recommendations for Addressing the Issue of Jurors and the Internet

Although limiting juror access to the Internet might seem like a daunting task, a number of actions can be taken to reduce the likelihood that jurors will utilize the Internet to search cases for which they are asked to serve. Next we discuss some strategies to reduce juror misconduct.

### Extended Voir Dire

A common suggestion is to instruct jurors to avoid the Internet, but as we know from previous research on juror instructions, this strategy is not very effective (Tanford, 1990). Although instructions are extremely important, research suggests that thorough and pointed voir dire could be a more effective method for preventing juror misconduct. Along with instructions, voir dire questions should address actual juror Internet use (e.g., how much they use the Internet, if they have accessed any information about the current case via the Internet, their ability to abstain from using social media during the course of the trial).

## Juror Declarations

Some courts have required jurors to sign declarations swearing that they will not engage in Internet research regarding the case they are seated on under penalty of perjury (e.g., *Strange v. Entercom Sacramento, LLC*, 2007). Typically, a juror who signs such a declaration and is then found to have conducted any research on the case could face fines and possibly probation or jail time. Sanctions such as these might prevent jurors from engaging in extralegal research. This is an area ripe for research as none exists to date in the published literature.

## Revised Jury Instructions

Jury instructions should be revised to add specific language to address the use of electronic devices and social networking sites in relation to accessing information about the case. These instructions should be repeated several times throughout the trial—at the start and end of each day and, if possible, before each recess.

## Juror Education

Beyond instructions and admonitions, judges should remind jurors of the importance of using only case facts presented in court in their decision-making and of not seeking out information elsewhere. At the same time, jurors are curious and intelligent and might not be content taking information presented at face value. As such, courts are encouraged to allow jurors to ask questions of the judge, attorneys, and experts to clarify any questions they might have. As we have seen in most cases of online misconduct, jurors searched cases because they had questions regarding the evidence presented. If jurors are allowed to ask questions of the parties involved, the need to Google information might be dissipated. To the extent that they have reasonable and proper questions for the trial parties, they are less likely to conduct research on their own if the parties address them more completely. Satisfying jurors' reasonable "need to know" may help to gain compliance with the rules.

## Conclusion

The current media landscape has changed the way individuals and, as a function, institutions operate. Major social media sites have memberships in the millions, and mobile technology has made these available at the tip of our fingers. Through the use of the Internet and social media, individuals can access and disseminate information relatively easily, which can lead to issues when it comes to jury service. Juror misconduct involving use of social media and the Internet has garnered national attention, and courts are now faced with how to best protect a defendant's right to a fair trial. There is a steady increase in the number of trials that are challenged on the basis of Internet-related juror misconduct. At the same time, limited research exists on the impact of this increased access to information and communication on trial outcomes. Yet, as we have reviewed, several suggestions have been proposed to address juror social media and Internet use. Social science researchers are well poised to examine these recommendations and their effectiveness in ensuring that defendants' constitutional rights are protected.

## References

Aronson, D., & Patterson, S. (2013). Modernizing jury instructions in the age of social media. *Criminal Justice, 27*(4), 2–11.

Blackman, J., & Brickman, E. (2011, March 30). Let's talk: Addressing the challenges of Internet-era jurors. *Jury Expert.* Retrieved from http://www.thejuryexpert.com/2011/03/lets-talk-addressing-the-challenges-of-internet-era-jurors/

Bruschke, J., Gonis, III, A., Hill, S. A., Fiber-Ostrow, P., & Loges, W. (2016). The influence of heterogeneous exposure and pre-deliberation queries on pretrial publicity effects. *Communication Monographs, 83*, 521–534. doi:10.1080/03637751.2016.1182639

Butler, B. (2012). Capital pretrial publicity as a symbolic public execution: A case report. *Journal of Forensic Psychology Practice, 12*, 259–269. doi:10.1080/15228932.2011.588522

Capuozzo, K. I. (2013). *Pretrial publicity and its biasing effects: Investigating the effectiveness of voir dire as a remedy* (Unpublished doctoral dissertation). University of Houston, Houston, TX.

Cameron, N., Potter, S., & Young, W. (1999). The New Zealand jury. *Law & Contemporary Problems, 62*, 103–139. doi:10.2307/1192254

Carroll, J. S., Kerr, N. L., Alfini, J. J., Weaver, F. M., MacCoun, R. J., & Feldman, V. (1986). Free press and fair trial: The role of behavioral research. *Law and Human Behavior, 10*, 187–201. doi:10.1007/BF01046209

Chesterman, M., Chan, J., & Hampton, S. (2001) *Managing prejudicial publicity: An empirical study of criminal jury trials in New South Wales.* New South Wales: Law and Justice Foundation of New South Wales.

Comisky, H. A., & Taylor, W. M. (2011). Don't be a twit: Avoiding the ethical pitfalls facing lawyers utilizing social media in three important arenas—Discovery, communications with judges and jurors, and marketing. *Temple Political & Civil Rights Law Review, 20*, 297–322.

Daftary-Kapur, T., Penrod, S., O'Connor, M., & Wallace, B. (2014). Examining pretrial publicity in a shadow jury paradigm: Issues of slant, quantity, persistence, and generalizability. *Law and Human Behavior, 38*, 462–477. doi:10.1037/lhb0000081

Davis, R. W. (1986). Pretrial publicity, the timing of the trial, and mock jurors' decision processes. *Journal of Applied Social Psychology, 16,* 590–607. doi:10.1111/j.1559-1816.1986.tb01161.x

Dexter, H. R., Cutler, B. L., & Moran, G. (1992). A test of voir dire as a remedy for the prejudicial effects of pretrial publicity. *Journal of Applied Social Psychology, 22,* 819–832. doi:10.1111/j.1559-1816.1992.tb00926.x

Dunn, M. A. (2014). *Juror's and attorneys' use of social media during voir dire, trials, and deliberations: A report to the Judicial Conference Committee on Court Administration and Case Management.* Washington, DC: Federal Judicial Center.

Freedman, J. L., & Burke, T. M. (1996). The effect of pretrial publicity: The Bernardo case. *Canadian Journal of Criminology, 38,* 253–270.

Freedman, J. L., Martin, C. K., & Mota, V. L. (1998). Pretrial publicity: Effects of admonition and expressing pretrial opinions. *Legal and Criminological Psychology, 3,* 255–270. doi:10.1111/j.2044-8333.1998.tb00365.x

Fulero, S. M. (2002). Afterword: The past, present, and future of applied pretrial publicity research. *Law and Human Behavior, 26,* 127–133. doi:10.1023/A:1013885309899

Grow, B. (2010, December 8). As jurors go online, U.S. trials go off track. *Reuters Legal.* Retrieved from http://www.reuters.com/article/us-internet-jurors-idUSTRE6B74Z820101208

Hamilton, D. L., & Fallot, R. D. (1974). Information salience as a weighting factor in impression formation. *Journal of Personality & Social Psychology, 30,* 444–448. doi:10.1037/h0037033

Hannaford-Agor, P., Rottman D., & Waters N. L. (2012). *Jurors & new media: An experiment.* Williamsburg, VA: National Center for State Courts.

Hastie, R. (1990). Is attorney-conducted voir dire an effective procedure for the selection of impartial juries? *American University Law Review, 40,* 703–726.

Hoffmeister, T. (2011). Investigating jurors in the digital age: One click at a time. *Kansas Law Review, 60,* 611–648.

Hoffmeister, T. (2012). Google, gadgets, and guilt: Juror misconduct in the digital age. *University of Colorado Law Review, 83,* 409–470.

Hope, L., Memon, A., & McGeorge, P. (2004). Understanding pretrial publicity: Predecisional distortion of evidence by mock jurors. *Journal of Experimental Psychology: Applied, 10,* 111–119. doi:10.1037/1076-898X.10.2.111

Jones, S. E. (1987). Judge- versus attorney-conducted voir dire: An empirical investigation of juror candor. *Law and Human Behavior, 11,* 131–146. doi:10.1007/BF01040446

Judicial Conference Committee on Court Administration and Case Management. (2012, June). *Proposed model jury instructions: The use of electronic technology to conduct research on or communicate about a case.* Retrieved from http://www.uscourts.gov/sites/default/files/jury-instructions.pdf

Kovera, M. B. (2002). The effects of general pretrial publicity on juror decisions: An examination of moderators and mediating mechanisms. *Law and Human Behavior, 26,* 43–72. doi:10.1023/A:1013829224920

Kramer, G., Kerr, N., & Carroll, J. (1990). Pretrial publicity, judicial remedies, and jury bias. *Law and Human Behavior, 14,* 409–438. doi:10.1007/BF01044220

Liberman, J. D., & Sales, B. D. (1997). What social science teaches us about the jury instruction process. *Psychology, Public Policy, and Law, 3*, 589–644. doi:10.1037/1076-8971.3.4.589

Lundberg, J. C. (2012). Googling jurors to conduct voir dire. *Washington Journal of Law, Technology, and Art, 2*, 123–587.

Marder, N. S. (2014). Jurors and social media: Is a fair trial still possible? *Southern Methodist University Law Review, 67*, 617–668.

Marshall v. United States, 360 U.S. 310, 79 S. Ct. 1171, 3 L. Ed. 2d 1250 (1959)

McGee, A. (2010). Juror misconduct in the twenty-first century: The prevalence of the Internet and its effect on American courtrooms. *Loyola of Los Angeles Entertainment Law Review, 30*, 300–325.

Moran, G., Cutler, B. L., & Loftus, E. F. (1990). Jury selection in major controlled substance trials: The need for extended voir dire. *Forensic Reports, 3*, 331–348.

Morrison, C. M. (2011). Jury 2.0. *Hastings Law Journal, 62*, 1579–1632.

Narby, D. J., Cutler, B. L., & Moran, G. (1993). A meta-analysis of the association between authoritarianism and jurors' perceptions of defendant culpability. *Journal of Applied Psychology, 78*, 34–42. doi:10.1037/0021-9010.78.1.34

Newcomb v. State, 800 P.2d 935, Alaska Ct. App. (1990).

Otto, A. L., Penrod, S. D., & Dexter, H. R. (1994). The biasing impact of pretrial publicity on juror judgments. *Law and Human Behavior, 18*, 453–469. doi:10.1007/BF01499050

PBC juror jailed for eight days for misconduct in Three Amigos trial [Blog Post]. (2016, May 26). Retrieved from http://postoncourts.blog.mypalmbeachpost.com/2016/05/26/pbc-juror-jailed-for-eight-days-for-misconduct-in-three-amigos-trial/

Pennington, N., & Hastie, R. (1992). Explaining the evidence: Tests of the Story Model for juror decision making. *Journal of Personality and Social Psychology, 62*, 189–206. doi:10.1037/0022-3514.62.2.189

Posey. A., & Wrightsman, L. S. (2005). *Trial consulting.* New York: Oxford University Press.

Robinson, E. (2011). Jury instructions for the modern age: A 50-state survey of jury instructions on Internet and social media. *Reynolds Courts & Media Law Journal, 1*, 307–415.

Robinson, P. M. (2012). Yes, jurors have a right to freedom of speech too . . . Well, maybe: Juror misconduct and social networks. *First Amendment Law Review, 11*, 593–609.

Ruva, C. L., & LeVasseur, M. (2012). Behind closed doors: The effect of pretrial publicity on jury deliberations. *Psychology, Crime & Law, 18*, 431–452. doi:10.1080/1068316X.2010.502120

Ruva, C. L., & McEvoy, C. (2008). Negative and positive pretrial publicity affect juror memory and decision making. *Journal of Experimental Psychology: Applied, 14*, 226–235. doi:10.1037/1076-898X.14.3.226

Ruva, C., McEvoy, C., & Bryant, J. B. (2007). Effects of pre-trial publicity and jury deliberation on juror bias and source memory errors. *Applied Cognitive Psychology, 21*, 45–67. doi:10.1002/acp.1254

Schwartz, J. (2009, March 17). As jurors turn to the web, mistrials are popping up. Retrieved from https://archive.nytimes.com/www.nytimes.com/2009/03/18/us/18juries.html

Shammas, B. (2015, June 9). Prospective juror arrested in Goodman case sentenced to community service. *The Sun Sentinel.* Retrieved from http://www.sun-sentinel.com/local/palm-beach/fl-juror-contempt-disposition-20150609-story.html

State v. Gunnell, 132 Ohio St. 3d 442, 2012 Ohio 3236, 973 N.E.2d 243 (2012).

Steblay, N. M., Besirevic, J., Fulero, S. M., & Jimenez-Lorente, B. (1999). The effects of pretrial publicity on juror verdicts: A meta-analytic review. *Law and Human Behavior, 23,* 219–235. doi:10.1023/A:1022325019080

William A. Strange, et al. v. Entercom Sacramento, LLC, et al., No. 07AS00377 (Cal. Super. filed Jan. 25, 2007).

Studebaker, C. A., & Penrod, S. D. (2005). Pretrial publicity and its influence on juror decision making. In N. Brewer & K. D. Williams, *Psychology and law: An empirical perspective* (pp. 254–275). New York: Guilford Press.

Studebaker, C. A., Robbennolt, J. K., Pathak-Sharma, M. K., & Penrod S. D. (2000). Assessing pretrial publicity effects: Integrating content analytic results. *Law and Human Behavior, 24,* 317–336. doi:10.1023/A:1005536204923

Tanford, A. (1990). The law and psychology of jury instructions. *Nebraska law Review, 69,* 72–111.

United States v. Williams, 583 F.2d 1194 (2d Cir. 1978).

Vidmar, N. (2002). Case studies of pre- and midtrial prejudice in criminal and civil litigation. *Law and Human Behavior, 26,* 73–105. doi:10.1023/A:1013881208990

Wardlaw v. State, 971 A.2d 331, 185 Md. App. 440, Ct. Spec. App. (2009).

Waters, N. L., & Hannaford-Agor, P. (2014). Jury impartiality in the modern era. In G. Bruinsma & D. Weisburd (Eds.), *Encyclopedia of criminology and criminal justice* (pp. 2735–2745). New York: Springer.

Zand, J. (2011, December 9). Juror's tweets during death penalty trial, sentencing deliberations, reverse conviction. [Blog Post]. Retrieved from https://lawblog.justia.com/2011/12/09/jurors-tweets-during-death-penalty-trial-reverses-conviction

# 9

## The Psychology of Surveillance and
## Sousveillance Video Evidence

*Neal R. Feigenson and Christina O. Spiesel*

Film and video evidence have been offered in American courts for nearly a century (Schwartz, 2009). In recent decades, however, the amount of video evidence in the courtroom has increased exponentially, due largely to the profusion of what Silbey (2004) calls *evidence vérité*: ostensibly unstaged and unedited footage of legally relevant events captured by the vast and growing number of government and private fixed surveillance cameras, police dashboard and body-worn cameras, and by cellphones and other recording devices wielded by ordinary citizens (e.g., Edmond & San Roque, 2013), sometimes referred to as *sousveillance* (Mann, 2004).[1] These videos have come to be expected elements of the evidentiary landscape, not only in notorious cases of police officers' use of arguably excessive and sometimes deadly force against members of the public but in criminal cases generally.

This chapter explores the psychology of jurors' responses to this evidence. We begin by reviewing the research, primarily from perceptual and cognitive psychology, that indicates why jurors are likely to find video evidence in general to be reliable, probative, and persuasive, as well as the research indicating why jurors' perceptions and interpretations of this evidence are prone to being biased by many factors of which they may be unaware. We then examine the technical and formal characteristics of surveillance and sousveillance video in more detail, showing how these can affect what jurors see and hear and how they construe it. We illustrate our observations with a brief analysis of the video evidence in a recent, highly publicized police shooting case. (For a general discussion of jurors' reactions to police defendants and witnesses, see Chapter 6 of this volume.)

We also argue that the existing research fails to illuminate what is likely an important feature of jurors' responses to video evidence: Their perceptions and interpretations of video are malleable not only in the sense of being prone to multiple contextual and other biasing influences, but also in being subject to change over the course of the trial, especially if the video is shown in different formats. The research on video evidence (e.g., Granot, Balcetis, Schneider, & Tyler, 2014; Kahan, Hoffman, & Braman, 2009; Sommers, 2016), while adding considerably to our knowledge of how jurors' attitudes may bias their construals of that evidence, tells us little about whether and how repeated watching and listening may affect their understandings of it. We wrap up the chapter by presenting ideas for researching this question.

## The Psychology of Visual and Video Evidence

In this section we explain why jurors are likely to regard surveillance and sousveillance video as highly reliable, probative, and persuasive. We then discuss why, at least initially, they are inclined to be overconfident in their perceptions and interpretations of this evidence, remaining largely unaware of the endogenous (e.g., their own prior beliefs and attitudes) and exogenous (e.g., features of the video itself and the context in which it is presented) influences on how they construe what they see and hear. We then survey some of those influences. We conclude the section with a brief discussion of the often-neglected audio component of evidentiary video.

### Video as Highly Reliable and Probative Evidence

Many features of people's perceptual and cognitive responses to video evidence incline them to regard that evidence as especially credible, probative, and persuasive. To begin, *processing fluency* (for a review, see Oppenheimer, 2008) would be expected to enhance jurors' belief in the truthfulness of video (and photographic) evidence. People can mentally process visual evidence more quickly and efficiently than they can a verbal description of the same events (e.g., Potter, Wyble, Hagmann, & McCourt, 2014). And the easier it is for people to understand incoming information, the more likely they are to believe it is true (Reber & Schwarz, 1999).

Videos (and ordinary photographs) also tend to be understood as highly probative evidence for several closely related reasons. Because videos and photos resemble what viewers think the depicted reality looks or should look like, viewers tend to believe that these images represent that reality accurately and truthfully (e.g., Kemp, 2014). In addition, videos and photos are believed to offer reliable proof of the existence or occurrence of what they depict because they are thought to be *indexically* related to it (Sebeok, 1994), in two ways. First, the recorded image is physically caused by what it depicts (in that light reflected off of objects is captured by the camera's film or sensors) and is thus naturally and materially bound to it. Second, the act of taking the video or photo deictically indicates the reality in front of the camera when the image was taken (Green & Lowry, 2003), thus providing independent evidence of that reality as of that moment. Videos and photos are also widely believed to offer highly probative evidence of reality because they are thought to be *objective* representations of that reality: produced mechanically (cf. Daston & Galison, 2007) and thus free from the subjective factors that necessarily influence drawings or, *a fortiori*, verbal testimony. Popular belief overstates the objectivity of video evidence (e.g., Kahan et al., 2009), yet it is undeniable that video often can, at a minimum, yield highly reliable proof of what video archivist Eileen Clancy (2006) has called "a thin layer of facts," for instance, placing (sometimes) identifiable persons at a particular location on a particular date and time.

In short, people are inclined to trust the evidence of their eyes and hence media that seem to offer an experience more or less like ordinary vision and to regard as reliable media that reproduce that external reality with mechanical objectivity. As a result, jurors are likely to believe that video evidence puts them more or less directly in touch with what really happened. They tend to "look through" the medium to the depicted reality (see Feigenson & Spiesel, 2009). This converts jurors into virtual witnesses of the crucial events and imbues their belief that the events happened as depicted with the sort of confidence they invest in knowledge derived from their own personal experience.

At the same time, the nature of evidentiary videos as representations at trial also tends to make them highly persuasive. First, like much visual evidence, video tends to be more vivid than verbal evidence and thus more likely to attract and hold viewers' attention, generate more related thoughts, and be better remembered (see, e.g., Bell & Loftus, 1985). The picture superiority effect (Stenberg, 2006) confirms that visual evidence tends to be remembered better than verbal evidence. And the simple fact that video moves makes it more likely than verbal or nonmoving visual evidence to attract and hold viewers' attention, because the visual system is particularly sensitive to perceiving movement (Palmer, 1999). Second, seeing video can give jurors an even more intense sense of being in the presence of the real than they would have had as live witnesses (see Battye, 2014). This feeling of presence would be predicted to enhance not only the perceived probative value of the evidence but also the intensity of jurors' emotional responses to it (Lombard & Ditton, 1997).

Finally, the legal system and the law of evidence itself encourage jurors' tendencies to invest video evidence with strong probative value. As Mnookin and West (2001) observe, "Our system of rules governing the admissibility of evidence rests upon a set of basic assumptions, and fundamental among them is that we prefer that proof which comes closest to direct sensory perception" (p. 384). A contemporaneous, reliable, unedited video recording of events as they unfolded approaches this ideal form of proof more closely than any other type of evidence.

## Biases in the Perception and Construal of Video Evidence

Despite its reliability and probative value, video evidence can pose considerable judgmental risks. In this section we explain why jurors are prone to overvalue video evidence and to be overconfident in their perceptions and construals of it, and we survey how those perceptions and construals may be biased by a host of factors, both endogenous (attributable to the perceiver) and exogenous (attributable to the formal characteristics and context of the video presentation itself). In any given case, the possibilities of fabrication and deceptive editing must also be addressed. Throughout this chapter, however, we proceed on the assumption that the video evidence to which jurors are exposed has been properly authenticated and not deceptively or otherwise improperly manipulated.

**Naïve realism, overconfidence, and overvaluing of visual evidence.** We begin with the cognitive biases most closely associated with people's tendency, explained previously, to believe that video provides thoroughly objective and reliable evidence of the events it depicts. Viewers of evidentiary video are prone to *naïve realism*, the belief that the video simply shows them reality as it was (Feigenson & Spiesel, 2009). Naïve realism about visual evidence (including videos and photos) is a special instance of naïve realism more generally, or, as Robinson, Keltner, Ward, and Ross (1995) describe, "the individual's unshakable conviction that he or she is somehow privy to an invariant, knowable, objective reality—a reality that others will also perceive faithfully, provided that they are reasonable and rational" (p. 405). Naïve realists tend to remain unaware of how their construals of reality are shaped by their own perceptual, cognitive, and emotional biases, as well as by features of the situation (see Gilovich & Griffin, 2010).

Viewers' tendency to think that video evidence simply portrays reality as it actually was can prompt or exacerbate overconfidence in the beliefs and judgments they derive from their viewing (see Feigenson, 2014). The combination of processing fluency and naïve realism makes viewers less likely to look for either disconfirming information or the ways in which their understanding of what they see has been shaped by their preconceptions, the medium, or other factors (see, e.g., Benforado, 2010). Experimental research indicates that people tend to be overconfident in the inferences and judgments they derive from video and other visual evidence (e.g., Davis & Valentine, 2009; Sommers, 2016).

Partly as a consequence of naïve realism and any resulting overconfidence, video evidence can also be overvalued, distracting decision-makers from other probative evidence. Indeed, videos and photos can be so powerful as not only to displace other sources of information about world events (e.g., Neisser & Harsch, 1992) but to supplant people's memories of their own recent personal experiences (Nash & Wade, 2009). Moreover, compared to listening to testimony, attending to visual evidence tends to be more entertaining and to occupy more cognitive resources, prompting more associated thoughts and memories (Stenberg, 2006). As a result, jurors may, at least initially, be both less able and less willing to examine visual evidence critically (Sherwin, Feigenson, & Spiesel, 2006), which further contributes to its overvaluing.

**Biases from endogenous sources: Attentional focus, prior beliefs and attitudes, and current motivations.** Jurors are prone to perceive and interpret video evidence in biased fashion due to their attentional focus; their prior knowledge, beliefs, expectations, and attitudes; and their current motivations. To begin, different people attend to the visual environment differently. Selective attention, which causes people to notice some things and ignore others, depends not only on the saliency of available visual information (i.e., "bottom-up" factors) but also on viewers' personal experiences, expectations, cultural background, and attitudes, as well their purposes in looking (i.e., "top-down" factors; see, e.g., Itti, 2005). Selective attention may have consequences for legal judgments. In one study by Granot et al. (2014) in which participants watched a video of a police-citizen altercation, participants who strongly identified with the police judged the officer less harshly than those who weakly identified with the police, but only when they frequently visually fixated on the officer. In a second study by the same researchers, participants who watched a video of an altercation between two members of arbitrarily defined groups judged the outgroup member (i.e., an individual who belonged to a different group than the participant) more harshly, but only when they fixated often on that outgroup member.

People's prior beliefs and attitudes are especially prone to biasing their perceptions and interpretations of visual evidence. For instance, in one study, participants who were subliminally exposed to images of Black male faces more quickly identified an ambiguous image as a handgun than did participants not so primed or primed with images of White male faces (Eberhardt, Purdie, Goff, & Davies, 2004). Viewers' attitudes can also affect how carefully they parse ongoing behavior. In other research, persons highly prejudiced against outgroup members (i.e., White participants prejudiced against Blacks, or straight participants prejudiced against gays) tended to parse videos of outgroup members' behavior into fewer units of meaningful action than did less prejudiced persons (Lassiter, Lindberg, Ratcliff, Ware, & Geers, 2010). The researchers concluded that "highly prejudiced individuals are not inclined to put in the effort to maximize their information intake about a person who belongs to a group that they view very negatively" (p. 245). An implication for the courtroom is that highly prejudiced jurors' construals of outgroup members' behavior captured on video may be guided more by their prior (negative) attitudes and less by the specific information that video evidence offers, compared to less prejudiced jurors' construals.

Jurors' prior attitudes can also bias the legally dispositive inferences they draw from video. In one study, participants who favored the death penalty were more likely than those opposed to the death penalty to think that the perpetrator of a convenience store robbery and homicide captured on store surveillance video intended to kill the victim (Goodman-Delahunty et al., 1998). In another study, participants were shown a video of an aggressive but not physically violent protest that was eventually halted by the police.

A majority of politically conservative participants believed that the police had violated the protesters' rights when told that the protest was at an abortion clinic but not when told it was at a military recruitment center; conversely, a majority of liberal participants believed that the police had violated the protesters' rights when told that the protest was at a recruitment center but not when told it was at an abortion clinic (Kahan et al., 2012; see also Kahan et al., 2009).

The prior beliefs and knowledge that can affect jurors' responses to video evidence may be shaped in part by their media consumption in everyday life, including both real and fictional narratives about crime or other case-relevant topics that jurors have seen on television, in movies, or online (e.g., Feigenson & Spiesel, 2009). For instance, viewers of *COPS* or similar reality television shows about policing may be inclined to see the citizens whom the police encounter in evidentiary videos as anonymous "others" whose seemingly irrational behavior poses a threat to social order, which the officer's intervention is needed to restore (Rapping, 2003). (See Chapter 7 of this volume for a discussion of other ways in which television shows and popular media can influence juror decision-making.)

People's current motivations can also bias their perceptions of visual evidence and the inferences they draw. According to the concept of motivated cognition, "when decision makers have a preference regarding the outcome of an evaluative task, they are more likely to arrive at that desired conclusion by engaging in inadvertently biased processes for accessing, constructing, and evaluating beliefs" (Sood, 2013, p. 309). Dunning and Balcetis (2013) have reported numerous studies of "wishful seeing": If people are incentivized (e.g., by the prospect of a monetary reward) to perceive an ambiguous figure as belonging to one category rather than another, they tend to do so (but cf. Firestone & Scholl, 2016). An implication is that jurors who are inclined to favor a given party, based on their prior attitudes and/or the lawyers' initial presentations of the case, may perceive ambiguous features of video evidence consistently with the case outcome they prefer.

**Biases from exogenous sources: Video display contexts and formal features.** What people think they see in or recall from an evidentiary video and the inferences they draw from their viewing can also be strongly influenced by the visual and verbal contexts of the viewing. For instance, the semantic content of the visual context in which an ambiguous image is presented can affect viewers' construals of what they see (Palmer, 1999). An example from film is the Kuleshov effect: People will interpret an actor's identical facial expression as happy or sad depending on the emotional valence (i.e., positive or negative) of the adjacent scene (e.g., Barratt, Rédei, Innes-Ker, & van de Weijer, 2016). A possible implication is that the emotional valence of earlier portions of an evidentiary video (e.g., the urgency implied by the rapidly changing view and sound of sirens from a police dashboard camera video as the cruiser rushes to the scene) may influence jurors' interpretation of a later scene (e.g., whether the citizen was acting in a threatening fashion when confronted by the police).

The verbal context of an image can also influence how people perceive, interpret, and remember the visual information they glean from the image. For instance, verbally framing people's viewing of a picture by giving them tasks—for instance, asking them to answer different questions based on what they see—affects the patterns of their eye movements (fixations and saccades) directed at the picture (for the classic study, see Yarbus, 1967; see also DeAngelus & Pelz, 2009; Spiesel, 2009). More recent studies have extended these findings to video (Smith & Mital, 2013) and shown that different instructions lead viewers to pick up different information from the video (Lassiter, Geers, Apple, & Beers, 2000). Accordingly, jurors may attend to and extract different information from evidentiary video depending on the goals for watching or listening that the lawyers and/or witnesses prompt them to adopt.

Just as captioning a photo differently can lead viewers to interpret it differently, so may the prosecuting and defense lawyers' respective verbal descriptions of the events and the case, or words heard on the audio track of the evidentiary video itself, affect how jurors construe what they see in the video. The words that lawyers and/or witnesses use to describe a visual display viewers have already seen, moreover, can bias their recollections and understanding of it (Loftus & Palmer, 1974).

Evidentiary videos may be especially prone to contextual effects because these videos are likely to be *semi-legible* (Mnookin, 2014)—readily interpretable with regard to some facts of interest, but (at least initially) ambiguous and hence inconclusive in other important ways. Moreover, these videos are always narratively incomplete; they never depict the entire relevant story. Both aspects of evidentiary videos invite counsel and their witnesses at trial to reframe those videos, visually and verbally. The most famous instance of this remains the defense treatment of George Holliday's video of the 1991 beating of Rodney King by Los Angeles police officers (Loftus & Rosenwald, 1993): By reducing the video to a series of still images, each explained by a police expert on the use of force, the defense argued that each baton blow and kick was a measured and justified response to some apparent movement by King rather than a relentless beating of a helpless man.

Formal characteristics of the video can also bias what viewers see and infer. For instance, video has been shown to trigger the perceptual bias of illusory causation, people's tendency to overattribute causality to an especially salient stimulus (McArthur, 1980; Ratcliff, Lassiter, Schmidt, & Snyder, 2006). An especially robust example of this is the camera perspective bias: In many studies, mock jurors who watched a criminal suspect's videotaped confession in which only the suspect appeared on screen were significantly more likely than those who also saw the interrogator to believe that the confession was voluntary and that the suspect was guilty (Lassiter, Geers, Munhall,

Handley, & Beers, 2001; Ratcliff et al., 2006; for further discussion, see Chapter 10 of this volume). Camera perspective bias is obviously relevant to jurors' interpretations of video evidence: All things being equal, the perspective of police body-worn camera video and (in some cases) dashboard camera video would be expected to increase jurors' attributions of responsibility for the tragic outcome to the more visually salient citizen rather than the police officer (e.g., Benforado, 2010; Morrison, 2017).

The speed at which video is played back may also create judgmental biases. Viewers' interpretations of video evidence are subject to a slow motion intentionality bias: The more slowly the action appears to unfold, the more likely viewers are to judge that the actor behaved intentionally because viewers get the (false) impression that the actor had more time than actually elapsed to deliberate before acting (Caruso, Burns, & Converse, 2016). Thus video from a fixed surveillance camera with a low frame rate, or video that has been slowed down for courtroom display, may make jurors more likely to conclude that the target actor (e.g., a police officer defending a prosecution for use of excessive force) acted deliberately. Slow motion also reduces the apparent effort the depicted persons are exercising and the apparent force of physical impacts, so that replaying evidentiary video in slow motion may make violent action—for instance, the repeated baton blows and kicks to which Los Angeles police officers subjected Rodney King—appear less violent (Rogers, 2013).

The size of the video display may also affect jurors' perceptions of and responses to the evidence. For instance, increasing the display size has been shown to intensify viewers' emotional arousal, especially in response to unpleasant (i.e., gruesome or violent) images (Codispoti & de Cesarei, 2007), as well as to enhance viewers' sense of presence in the depicted scenes (e.g., Lombard & Ditton, 1997; Troscianko, Meese, & Hinde, 2012).

### Emotional Biases Associated with Video

Video evidence, especially of violent and/or fatal events, can also prompt strong and complicated emotional responses, responses that may be exacerbated by either jurors' pre-existing biases or contextual features of the video. In two studies, when mock jurors in a criminal case saw gruesome autopsy or crime scene photos, they became more anxious, anguished, disturbed, and shocked (Douglas, Lyon, & Ogloff, 1997) or angrier (Bright & Goodman-Delahunty, 2006) than those who did not see any pictures, and these emotions made them more likely to convict the defendant. Videos of police violence may prompt similar emotions, with similar effects on judgment. (For a more general discussion of how emotion influences juror decision-making, see Chapter 12 of this volume.)

The effects of gruesome images of the sort that videos of police violence may contain are likely to be quite complicated. Some people may turn away from gruesome images with revulsion or disgust; others, or even the same person at a different time, may be fascinated by the same gruesome pictures, unable not to look (see Spiesel, 2017). Moreover, not every depiction of violence or its consequences is gruesome, yet even images that are not may disgust and horrify viewers who are conscious of witnessing the sudden death of a fellow human being. And disgust may be an even stronger predictor than anger of punitiveness toward a criminal defendant (Salerno & Peter-Hagene, 2013).

## The Role of Audio

Although people tend to think of video primarily in terms of its visible content, it is also important to consider its auditory dimension. What jurors can hear on an evidentiary video, like what they can see, may be either clear or relatively ambiguous, and interpreting it correctly may be challenging. For instance, hearing, like seeing, is subject to context effects (e.g., phonemic restoration; Warren & Warren, 1970) and cross-modal effects (MacDonald & McGurk, 1978; Wright & Wareham, 2005). One psychological effect that is especially important for the present discussion is that sounds captured on video "enhance the sense of presence" (Serafin & Serafin, 2004, p. 2). Synchronous sound, in combination with photorealistic video, increases the sensory richness of the recording and hence its immersiveness, one component of the sense of presence (Steuer, 1995). And when listening to recorded sound, people tend not to pay attention to the recording medium in the same way they often do when conscious of looking at a video or a photo, so they are freer to experience the sounds as a present event. Finally, the audio track on evidentiary video may contain statements that are themselves admissible evidence under exceptions to the bar against hearsay and that may influence jurors' perceptions and interpretations of the video's visible content.

## *Evidence Vérité*: Surveillance and Sousveillance

Evidentiary videos today originate from a plethora of devices—fixed cameras, dashboard cameras, body-worn cameras, and cellphone cameras, to name the most common. These are often sorted into the broad categories of surveillance and sousveillance video. Sousveillance means "to watch from below," in contrast to surveillance, or watching from above (Mann, 2004). The distinction between the two is not primarily technological. Some types of cameras are uniquely associated with surveillance (e.g., fixed camera) or sousveillance (e.g., cellphone), respectively; other sorts of devices, however, may be deployed in either capacity. Rather, the distinction is sociological, based on who takes the video and why and how the video is stored and disseminated. Police and other government surveillance videos are part of networks of largely top-down control and regulation, facilitated by routinized, systematic observation (e.g., Yesil, 2009), archiving, forensic enhancement (Gates, 2013), and centrally controlled (non)disclosure. In contrast, sousveillance videos, in their motivation, creation, formal characteristics, and dissemination, are bottom-up: occasional, personalized, participatory, and democratic.

### Surveillance Video

Surveillance video is produced by many sorts of devices located in many places. In major cities, thousands of fixed cameras are positioned on exterior walls of buildings, light posts, or dedicated supports; at tollbooths; at traffic intersections; in train and subway stations; inside banks, stores, and ATMs; and elsewhere. Routine surveillance video is also generated by means of cameras without fixed geographic locations: cameras installed on police cruiser dashboards, inside and outside of city buses, on helicopters and drones, on police officers' Tasers, and on patrol officers' uniforms.

The technical features of surveillance devices and their uses, and hence the formal features of the resulting video, vary considerably depending on the type of camera. All are digital devices, recording video at a standard rate of 29.9 frames per second and audio (if any) on a separate, continuous track. The resolution or clarity of detail in the video depends on the density of the pixels on the camera's sensor, which may be limited for reasons of cost or system storage capacity; lower resolution produces images that are fuzzier or even obscure in important respects. Camera lenses are also specialized for depth of field, which also can affect how clearly the video depicts critical information. The field of vision depends on focal length but in good cameras approaches 180 degrees. Surveillance cameras also vary in their capacity for movement: Some "fixed" cameras may track action via limited pans and tilts, whereas dashboard cameras, for instance, move only with the vehicle to which they are attached, otherwise maintaining a fixed angle.

Fixed surveillance cameras record automatically and continuously; helicopter and dashboard cameras do so as well, but only upon a trigger (e.g., when the lights and siren on a police cruiser are activated) does the equipment actually start to save the data. Thus surveillance videos typically include at least half a minute of material, and sometimes much more, before the events of legal interest begin and may run for several minutes or more thereafter.

Body-worn camera technology is worth treating separately, for two reasons. The widely publicized calls for its adoption by police departments across the United States (e.g., Fan, 2016; Kampfe, 2015) and its prominence in some recent high-profile cases have made it the surveillance technology du jour and the subject of considerable academic interest (e.g., Fan, 2016; Kampfe, 2015; Morrison, 2017), including some psychological research (e.g., Boivin, Gendron, Faubert, & Poulin, 2017; Culhane, Boman, & Schweitzer, 2016). In addition, some of the features of bodycam video—in particular, that the camera moves with the officer wearing it—contribute to produce a style of *evidence vérité* typically associated more with citizen sousveillance than government surveillance, somewhat blurring the distinction between the two categories.

Body-worn cameras start and stop recording when the officers wearing them turn them on and off, although these decisions are at least in theory constrained by departmental policies (e.g., Fan, 2016). Many bodycams have a limited horizontal field of view, comparable to that of a typical cellphone camera held vertically but much narrower than the typical in-car dashboard camera (National Institute of Justice, 2012), although they may use fish-eye lenses to record a wider view than a normal lens would. The camera's location and other technical features, including its weight and how it is fastened to the officer's clothing or other equipment, also affect the likelihood that the camera may be dislodged or disabled during the officer's sudden, strenuous physical effort, which may result in the absence of video precisely when a recording may be most valuable.

As noted, some features of police bodycams may make the resulting videos more like sousveillance cellphone videos than like other forms of surveillance video. Because they are located on the police officer's uniform, these bodycams are closely associated with the officer's person—unlike other forms of video surveillance, which are impersonal and decidedly institutional. Moreover, because the officer wearing the bodycam is often an active participant in the events being recorded, the view that the video affords of critical events is typically much closer to those events than that of traditional surveillance video (see Fan, 2016). For this reason, and because of the sometimes volatile camera movement during critical moments, bodycam video can give the viewer a strong sense of presence at the scene of the events, albeit sometimes at the expense of intelligibility.

Due to its technological and formal features and its wide dissemination in the broader culture, surveillance video is ordinarily taken to provide highly probative evidence of legally relevant facts. For instance, because it is or appears to be operated automatically, free from internal edits, surveillance video suggests objectivity (see Daston & Galison, 2007) and hence trustworthiness. It may be critical in revealing that the police lied or seriously misrepresented the facts in their initial reports (e.g., Morrison, 2017). In other circumstances or with regard to other factual questions, surveillance video, due to its camera angle, width of visual field, distance from the events of interest, or occlusion of those events by intervening objects or persons, remains only semi-legible and hence less probative.

## Sousveillance Video

The bottom-up nature of sousveillance—occasional, personalized, participatory, and democratic—is reflected in the two interwoven threads of its relatively brief history. The first is personal: Mann (2004) conceived of sousveillance as part of his decades-long wearable technology project. The second is political: Sousveillance, first with handheld video cameras and then by means of cellphones, has been undertaken as part of international human rights witnessing (Ristovska, 2016); to document anticipated police abuses at organized protests (e.g., Wilson & Serisier, 2010); and to document individual police-citizen interactions, sometimes referred to as cop watching (e.g., Bock, 2016; Brucato, 2015).

Several characteristics of sousveillance video (taking cellphone video as its prototypical form) differentiate it from most surveillance video. The first is who takes it: anyone with a cellphone camera. Second, in contrast to surveillance cameras, which are installed in their locations before any particular event of interest occurs, cellphones used to capture video are taken out or oriented by their owners in the moment and pointed at the event of interest. Third, people deploying cellphone cameras can turn them on and off whenever they choose. This means that sousveillance videos are often temporally framed quite differently from most surveillance video: They tend to begin soon before the events of interest occur or, often, after they have already begun and to end very shortly thereafter.

Because cellphones are light, handheld, and usually wielded by people who are not professional videographers and who may often be caught up by the events they have found worth recording, the resulting videos tend to display a number of distinctive formal qualities. The videos are often in portrait rather than landscape format, likely reflecting the orientation in which people hold their cellphones when they use them as phones; this reduces the spatial context of the depicted events. The camera angle in relation to the events of interest and (to a lesser extent) the camera's height are often unsteady, in marked contrast to video captured by installed surveillance devices other than bodycams. The cellphone camera typically moves inadvertently because it is so lightweight and held by hand with the arm at least partly raised and extended, a posture that is difficult to keep fixed, especially when emotionally compelling events are being recorded. The cellphone holder may also deliberately move the camera in the middle of the recording or even accidentally drop it, leaving crucial moments of the events off-screen. Finally, cellphone videos are also often accompanied by the videographer's (and sometimes others') commentary, thus interjecting contemporaneous responses to events that differ from the police commentary audible on some surveillance videos. All of these features tend to indicate the live presence of the videographer at the scene, signaling the personal and participatory nature of sousveillance video and differentiating it from most surveillance video.

Next, we present a brief case study to illustrate some of the likely psychological effects of evidentiary video on jurors, including the implications of presenting the video in different formats.

## Body-Worn Camera Video of a Police Shooting: The Samuel DuBose Case

On July 19, 2015, during a routine traffic stop, University of Cincinnati police officer Raymond Tensing shot and killed Samuel DuBose, a 43-year-old African American man and local resident. When Officer Tensing became dissatisfied with DuBose's responses to his questions, he started to open the driver's side door and commanded DuBose to remove his seat belt. As DuBose started the engine and put the car in drive, Tensing reached into the car with his left hand, grabbed DuBose's seat belt in front of DuBose's chest, and, having drawn his service revolver with his right hand, shot DuBose in the head at point-blank range. Tensing insisted that he had been dragged when his arm was caught inside the car and that he had fired his weapon at DuBose's head to protect himself from being dragged further and run over. Tensing was tried on charges of murder and voluntary manslaughter. On November 12, 2016, after the jury deadlocked, the trial judge declared a mistrial. Tensing was retried and, on June 23, 2017, the second jury also deadlocked and a mistrial was again declared. The county prosecutor decided not to retry the case a third time.

Officer Tensing's body-worn camera depicts the crucial moments of the shooting from his perspective, at the level of his chest where the camera was located. The view is therefore extremely close to the events, and the camera angle changes quickly and erratically as Tensing struggles, shifts position, draws his weapon and fires, and then falls back. The narrow field of view and the rapid movements of both the camera and the depicted action, resulting in motion blur—both *cinema vérité* features that bodycam video shares with much sousveillance video—may well enhance the perceived authenticity and reliability of the evidence. Yet they also render the video semi-legible: highly probative with regard to some facts of interest to jurors, yet ambiguous or barely interpretable with regard to others, including exactly when the car started to move forward and where Tensing was positioned just before and as it did, when he fired his weapon.

Seen and heard at normal speed, the bodycam video fosters both the camera perspective and illusory causation biases. When viewers see Officer Tensing's hands and arms entering the screen, the camera placement and angle very much gives them the impression of being part of Tensing himself. By putting jurors in Tensing's shoes, the video may therefore have induced some of them to identify with him to a greater extent than they might have had they seen only dashcam or helicopter camera video, had either existed in this case, or even no video at all and, in turn, to attribute more causal and hence legal responsibility for the tragic outcome to the more visible actor, DuBose. Moreover, by immersing jurors in the events, Tensing's bodycam video likely conveyed to them a stronger sense of being present at the scene, which may have heightened their level of emotional arousal (Lombard & Ditton, 1997).

The bodycam video may also have distorted jurors' perceptions of the threat that Officer Tensing faced (Williams, Thomas, Jacoby, & Cave, 2016). The video shows Tensing and DuBose contesting control of the driver's side door, but not violently, when suddenly the camera whips around and lurches, while the audio track devolves into distorted shouts and sounds. The fast-moving, unstable view suggests a sudden, direct threat to the officer, and hence to the viewers who share his perspective. As a consequence, the video may have misled jurors into thinking that the threat to Tensing was greater and more imminent than it actually was and thus have biased their judgments about whether his use of deadly force was justified. These features of the medium may also have amplified the effects on jurors' construal of the video of any racial or other relevant biases they brought to the viewing (see, e.g., Lassiter et al., 2010; Rapping, 2003).

At trial, the prosecution's forensic video expert presented the video in a very different way. He walked the jurors and the court through the video frame by frame, the images corrected for the distortion introduced by the bodycam's fish-eye lens, numbered, and captioned. This representation of the video enabled jurors to grasp critical facts that viewing the video at normal speed left obscure. For instance, from the position of DuBose's car relative to that of a vehicle parked in a driveway visible through the front passenger window, it could be seen that DuBose's car did not move forward (and then only slightly) until barely a sixth of a second before the shot, by which point Officer Tensing had already grabbed DuBose's seatbelt with his left hand and thrust his right hand into the car, pointing the gun at DuBose's head.

Presenting the video in this way may have engendered psychological effects quite different from the display at normal speed with synchronous audio. For example, the expert's testimony directed jurors' attention to particular features of the video stills (cf. Smith & Mital, 2013) and the captions and other annotations instructed them how to resolve otherwise ambiguous images. Slowing the video down to a frame-by-frame display may have inclined jurors to perceive that Officer Tensing acted more deliberately when he unholstered his weapon and shot DuBose (see Caruso et al., 2016).

One might think that the frame-by-frame presentation of the video, without the accompanying audio, would attenuate jurors' emotional responses to the killing by distancing jurors from the sense of presence conveyed by the real-time video and especially its sound track: DuBose's voice, making him more present as a person; Officer Tensing's shouts of "Stop!" communicating the escalating urgency; and then the fatal gunshot. Yet this representation may actually have intensified the emotional impact of the evidence. The annotated countdown to the gunshot, constantly visible at the top of the screen, could have both cued and prolonged the anguish and horror jurors may have experienced watching someone they knew was about to die (Zelizer, 2010).

## The Benefits of Repeated Viewing

The experimental research to date tells us a good deal about jurors' likely responses to evidentiary video when they watch it once. It has not, for the most part, addressed the effects of repeated viewing of the sort that occurs in most if not all trials—including multiple viewings accompanied by different verbal framings and/or in different presentation formats designed to enhance jurors' understanding, as at the trial of Officer Raymond Tensing. None of the studies of responses to videos of police violence referenced previously (Granot et al., 2014; Kahan et al., 2009; Kahan et al., 2012; Sommers, 2016) gave participants the opportunity to watch the videos more than once. Moreover, no studies have given participants the opportunity to deliberate about the evidence, which may also lead jurors to modify their initial interpretations.

We speculate that repeatedly watching evidentiary videos, especially in different presentation formats and/or verbal contexts, may affect jurors' perceptions and construals of those videos. As Granot (2016) states, "A second viewing is a chance to gain new information, and research suggests that people may indeed take the opportunity to attend to aspects of a scene that they originally missed" (p. 40).

We are aware of only two experiments in which participants watched an evidentiary-style video more than once (Granot, 2016, Study 3, and Caruso et al., 2016, Study 4); in neither did the second viewing dramatically affect important features of perception and judgment. Granot found that whichever of two actors participants attended to more when watching the video the first time, they paid more attention to the same actor when watching the second time. Caruso and colleagues found that participants who watched the video at both regular and slow speeds did not judge the actor to have behaved significantly more intentionally than those who watched only the regular speed video or significantly less intentionally than those who watched only the slow-motion video. Our speculation, nevertheless, is grounded in our own experience of not merely watching and listening to the videos in Officer Tensing's case and other instances of police shootings multiple times, but doing so in very different presentation formats (e.g., freeze-framing, zooming in, replaying portions of the video), sometimes with the benefit of expert commentary from law enforcement officers, and always engaging in critical discussion as we did so.[2] We found that our understanding of those videos was thereby changed and enhanced. This experience helps to inform our recommendations for revised trial practices and indicates the need for additional research.

## Recommendations for Trial Reform

Several steps might be taken to enhance the just use of evidentiary video in the legal system. Each should be empirically evaluated to ensure that any changes to trial practice are and remain evidence-based. First, many trial lawyers and judges may be as susceptible as jurors are to naïve realism about video and to the belief that a single viewing can tell them what they need to know. Lawyers need to be better educated about video's technical and psychological dimensions so that they can raise appropriate objections and (re-)present the evidence most effectively; judges need to be as well, so that they can rule wisely on evidentiary challenges and properly instruct jurors. Second, well-crafted judicial instructions can inform jurors about the most important biases that may affect their evaluations of these videos. Research indicates that giving instructions before jurors watch the videos may reduce the effects of some biases (e.g., Elek, Ware, & Ratcliff, 2012; Park & Pyo, 2012). Third, in lieu of such instructions, judges should consider appointing expert witnesses to teach jurors about these biases and/or be readier to admit experts proffered by the parties. Fourth, judges should encourage jurors to review evidentiary videos freely during deliberations, under court supervision as appropriate.

## Suggestions for Future Research

The effects of multiple viewings on jurors' perceptions and interpretations of video evidence are ripe for experimental study. Studies might include combinations of the following independent variables in within-subjects designs, counterbalanced for order: number of viewings and position in sequence (first, second, etc. viewing); video speed and other playback variables; presence or absence of verbal instructions or tasks, including providing instructions to consider alternative interpretations of the video or otherwise encouraging metacognition; presence or absence of expert commentary; and content of other verbal context (i.e., prosecution versus defense theories of the case). Dependent measures, ascertained after each viewing, should include participants' recall of visible and audible details from the video; their factual and interpretive judgments about the video (see, e.g., Sommers, 2016); their emotional responses; and their verdict preferences and confidence levels. Researchers should seek to identify potential mediators as well as moderators of important effects, including whether individual juror variables in addition to prior attitudes exacerbate or attenuate the effects of other factors on perceptions and judgments— for instance, whether need for cognition affects the impact of multiple viewings, different presentation formats, and/or expert commentary on participants' understandings of the video. Finally, researchers can study whether and how jurors' interpretations of what they have seen and heard may change as a result of deliberations. These and other studies can help provide the evidenced-based support for the reforms recommended here, as well as expand more basic knowledge of psychological processes in the context of legal decision-making.

## Conclusion

Video evidence, both surveillance and sousveillance, is playing an increasingly important role in criminal cases. It is widely believed to provide the most reliable and probative evidence of critical facts and thus the most trustworthy basis for jurors' ultimate judgments. Yet the psychological research we referenced in this chapter indicates that video evidence is more problematic than often assumed. An enhanced appreciation of that research and its implications for trial practice can lead to the better use of video evidence at trials and, potentially, to more just verdicts.

## Notes

1. The category of *evidence vérité*, thus defined, should probably also include videotaped confessions and deposition testimony, which are also ostensibly unedited and purely "observational" (Nichols, 1991). Blandón-Gitlin and Mindthoff focus on jurors' reactions to videotaped confession evidence in Chapter 10 of this volume; research using videotaped confessions as stimulus materials is referred to herein where relevant.
2. We would like to thank Placer County, California Police Officer Donald Nevins; Canton, Connecticut Police Officer Mark Penney; and former Marana, Arizona Police Officer Michael Rapiejko for watching the videos and sharing their expertise with us.

## References

Barratt, D., Rédei, A., Innes-Ker, Å, & van de Weijer, J. (2016). Does the Kuleshov effect really exist? Revisiting a classic film experiment on facial expressions and emotional contexts. *Perception, 45*, 847–874. doi:10.1177/0301006616638595

Battye, G. (2014). *Photography, narrative, time*. Bristol, UK: Intellect.

Bell, B., & Loftus, E. (1985). Vivid persuasion in the courtroom. *Journal of Personality Assessment, 49*, 659–665. doi:10.1207/s15327752jpa4906_16

Benforado, A. (2010). Frames of injustice: The bias we overlook. *Indiana Law Journal, 85*, 1333–1378.

Bock, M. (2016). Film the police! Cop-watching and its embodied narratives. *Journal of Communication, 66*, 13–34. doi:10.1111/jcom.12204

Boivin, R., Gendron, A., Faubert, C., & Poulin, B. (2017). The body-worn camera perspective bias. *Journal of Experimental Criminology, 13*, 125–142. doi:10.1007/s11292-016-9270-2

Bright, D., & Goodman-Delahunty, J. (2006). Gruesome evidence and emotion: Anger, blame, and jury decision-making. *Law and Human Behavior, 30*, 183–202. doi:10.1207/s15327752jpa4906_16

Brucato, B. (2015). The new transparency: Police violence in the context of ubiquitous surveillance. *Media and Communication, 3*(3), 39–55. doi:10.17645/mac.v3i3.292

Caruso, E., Burns, Z., & Converse, B. (2016). Slow motion increases perceived intent. *Proceedings of the National Academy of Sciences, 113,* 9250–9255. doi:10.1073/pnas.1603865113

Clancy, E. (2006, April 12). *Cameras in the streets: I-Witness video and the justice system* [DVD]. Lecture at Quinnipiac University Law School.

Codispoti, M., & de Cesarei, A. (2007). Arousal and attention: Picture size and emotional reactions. *Psychophysiology, 44,* 680–686. doi:10.1111/j.1469-8986.2007.00545.x

Culhane, S. E., Boman, IV, J. H., & Schweitzer, K. (2016). Public perceptions of the justifiability of police shootings: The role of body cameras in a pre- and post-Ferguson experiment. *Police Quarterly, 19,* 251–274. doi:10.1177/1098611116651403

Daston, L., & Galison, P. (2007). *Objectivity.* Cambridge, MA: Zone Books.

Davis, J., & Valentine, T. (2009). CCTV on trial: Matching video images with the defendant in the dock. *Applied Cognitive Psychology, 23,* 482–505. doi:10.1002/acp.1490

DeAngelus, M., & Pelz, J. (2009). Top-down control of eye movements: Yarbus revisited. *Visual Cognition, 17,* 790–811. doi:10.1080/13506280902793843

Douglas, K., Lyon, D., & Ogloff, J. (1997). The impact of graphic photographic evidence on mock jurors' decisions in a murder trial: Probative or prejudicial? *Law and Human Behavior, 21,* 485–501. doi:10.1023/A:1024823706560

Dunning, D., & Balcetis, E. (2013). Wishful seeing: How preferences shape visual perception. *Current Directions in Psychological Science, 22,* 33–37. doi:10.1177/0963721412463693

Eberhardt, J., Purdie, V., Goff, P., & Davies, P. (2004). Seeing black: Race, crime, and visual processing. *Journal of Personality and Social Psychology, 87,* 876–893. doi:10.1037/0022-3514.87.6.876

Edmond, G., & San Roque, M. (2013). Justicia's gaze: Surveillance, evidence and the criminal trial. *Surveillance and Society, 11,* 252–271.

Elek, J., Ware, L., & Ratcliff, J. (2012). Knowing when the camera lies: Judicial instructions mitigate the camera perspective bias. *Legal and Criminological Psychology, 17,* 123–135. doi:10.1111/j.2044-8333.2010.02000.x

Fan, M. (2016). Justice visualized: Courts and the body camera revolution. *University of California-Davis Law Review, 50,* 897–959.

Feigenson, N. (2014). Visual common sense. In A. Wagner & R. Sherwin (Eds.), *Law, culture and visual studies* (pp. 105–124). Dordrecht, The Netherlands: Springer.

Feigenson, N., & Spiesel, C. (2009). *Law on display.* New York: New York University Press.

Firestone, C., & Scholl, B. (2016). Cognition does not affect perception: Evaluating the evidence for "top-down" effects. *Behavioral and Brain Sciences, 39,* 1–77. doi:10.1017/S0140525X15000965

Gates, K. (2013). The cultural labor of surveillance: Video forensics, computational objectivity, and the production of visual evidence. *Social Semiotics, 23,* 242–260. doi:10.1080/10350330.2013.777593

Gilovich, T., & Griffin, D. (2010). Judgment and decision making. In S. Fiske, D. Gilbert, & G. Lindzey (Eds.), *Handbook of social psychology* (5th ed., Vol. 1, pp. 542–588). Hoboken, NJ: Wiley.

Goodman-Delahunty, J., Greene, E., & Hsiao, W. (1998). Construing motive in videotaped killings: The role of jurors' attitudes toward the death penalty. *Law and Human Behavior, 22,* 257–271. doi:10.1023/A:1025750321795

Granot, Y. (2016). *More than meets the eye: Building a visual attention-based model of intergroup legal punishment* (Unpublished doctoral dissertation). New York University, New York.

Granot, Y., Balcetis, E., Schneider, K., & Tyler, T. (2014). Justice is not blind: Visual attention exaggerates effects of group identification on legal punishment. *Journal of Experimental Psychology: General, 143,* 2196–2208. doi:10.1037/a0037893

Green, D., & Lowry, J. (2003). From presence to the performative: Rethinking photographic indexicality. In D. Green (Ed.), *Where is the photograph?* (pp. 47–60). Brighton, UK: Photoforum and Photoworks.

Itti, L. (2005). Quantifying the contribution of low-level saliency to human eye movement in dynamic scenes. *Visual Cognition, 12,* 1093–1123. doi:10.1080/13506280444000661

Kahan, D., Hoffman, D., & Braman, D. (2009). Whose eyes are you going to believe? *Scott v. Harris* and the perils of cognitive illiberalism. *Harvard Law Review, 122,* 837–906.

Kahan, D., Hoffman, D., Braman, D., Evans, D., & Rachlinski, J. (2012). "They saw a protest": Cognitive illiberalism and the speech-conduct distinction. *Stanford Law Review, 64,* 851–906.

Kampfe, K. (2015). Police-worn body cameras: Balancing privacy and accountability through state and police department action. *Ohio State Law Journal, 76,* 1153–1200.

Kemp, M. (2014). A question of trust: Old issues and new technologies. In C. Coopmans, J. Vertesi, M. Lynch, & S. Woolgar (Eds.), *Representation in scientific practice revisited* (pp. 343–346). Cambridge, MA: MIT Press.

Lassiter, G.D., Geers, A., Apple, K., & Beers, M. (2000). Observational goals and behavior unitization: A reexamination. *Journal of Experimental Social Psychology, 36,* 649–659. doi:10.1006/jesp.2000.1428

Lassiter, G.D., Geers, A., Munhall, P., Handley, I., & Beers, M. (2001). Videotaped confessions: Is guilt in the eye of the camera? In M. Zanna (Ed.), *Advances in experimental social psychology* (Vol. 33, pp. 189–254). New York: Academic Press.

Lassiter, G.D., Lindberg, M. Ratcliff, J., Ware, L., & Geers, A. (2010). Top-down influences on the perception of ongoing behavior. In E. Balcetis & D. Lassiter (Eds.), *Social psychology of visual perception* (pp. 225–251). New York: Psychology Press.

Loftus, E., & Palmer, J. (1974). Reconstruction of automobile destruction: An example of the interaction between language and memory. *Journal of Verbal Learning and Verbal Behavior, 13,* 585–589. doi:10.1016/S0022-5371(74)80011-3

Loftus, E., & Rosenwald, L. (1993). The Rodney King videotape: Why the case was not Black and White. *Southern California Law Review, 66,* 1637–1645.

Lombard, M., & Ditton, T. (1997). At the heart of it all: The concept of presence. *Journal of Computer-Mediated Communication, 3*(2). doi:10.1111/j.1083-6101.1997.tb00072.x

MacDonald, J., & McGurk, H. (1978). Visual influences on speech perception processes. *Perception and Psychophysics, 24*, 253–257. doi:10.3758/BF03206096

Mann, S. (2004). "Sousveillance": Inverse surveillance in multimedia imaging. In *Proceedings of the 12th Annual ACM International Conference on Multimedia* (pp. 620–627). Retrieved from http://www.ics.uci.edu/~djp3/classes/2012_01_INF241/papers/sousveillance.pdf.

McArthur, L. (1980). Illusory causation and illusory correlation: Two epistemological accounts. *Personality and Social Psychology Bulletin, 6*, 507–519. doi:10.1177/014616728064003

Mnookin, J. (2014). Semi-legibility and visual evidence: An initial exploration. *Journal of Law, Culture and the Humanities, 10*, 43–65. doi:10.1177/1743872111435998

Mnookin, J., & West, N. (2001). Theaters of proof: Visual evidence and the law in *Call Northside 777. Yale Journal of Law and the Humanities, 13*, 329–402.

Morrison, C. M. (2017). Body camera obscura: The semiotics of police video. *American Criminal Law Review, 54*, 791–841.

Nash, R., & Wade, K. (2009). Innocent but proven guilty: Eliciting internalized false confessions using doctored-video evidence. *Applied Cognitive Psychology, 23*, 624–637. doi:10.1002/acp.1500

National Institute of Justice. (2012). *A primer on body-worn cameras for law enforcement*. Fairmont, WV: ManTech Advanced Systems International.

Neisser, U., & Harsch, N. (1992). Phantom flashbulbs: False recollections of hearing the news about *Challenger*. In E. Winograd & U. Neisser (Eds.), *Affect and accuracy in recall: Studies of "flashbulb" memories* (pp. 9–31). New York: Cambridge University Press.

Nichols, B. (1991). *Representing reality*. Bloomington: University of Indiana Press.

Oppenheimer, D. (2008). The secret life of fluency. *Trends in Cognitive Sciences, 12*, 237–241. doi:10.1016/j.tics.2008.02.014

Palmer, S. (1999). *Vision science*. Cambridge, MA: MIT Press.

Park, K., & Pyo, J. (2012). An explanation for camera perspective bias in voluntariness judgment for video-recorded confession: Suggestion of cognitive frame. *Law and Human Behavior, 36*, 184–194. doi:10.1037/h0093967

Potter, M., Wyble, B., Hagmann, C.E., & McCourt, E. (2014). Detecting meaning in RSVP at 13 ms per picture. *Attention, Perception, and Psychophysics, 76*, 270–279. doi:10.3758/s13414-013-0605-z

Rapping, E. (2003). *Law and justice as seen on TV*. New York: New York University Press.

Ratcliff, J., Lassiter, G.D., Schmidt, H., & Snyder, C. (2006). Camera perspective bias in videotaped confessions: Experimental evidence of its perceptual basis. *Journal of Experimental Psychology: Applied, 12*, 197–206. doi:10.1037/1076-898X.12.4.197

Reber, R., & Schwarz, N. (1999). Effects of perceptual fluency on judgments of truth. *Consciousness and Cognition, 8*, 338–342. doi:10.1006/ccog.1999.0386

Ristovska, S. (2016). Strategic witnessing in an age of video activism. *Media, Culture and Society, 38*, 1034–1047. doi:10.1177/0163443716635866

Robinson, R., Keltner, D., Ward, A., & Ross, L. (1995). Actual versus assumed differences in construal: "Naïve realism" in intergroup perception and conflict. *Journal of Personality and Social Psychology, 68*, 404–417. doi:10.1037/0022-3514.68.3.404

Rogers, S. (2013). Truth, lies, and the meaning in slow motion images. In A. Shimamura (Ed.), *Psychocinematics* (pp. 149–164). New York: Oxford University Press.

Salerno, J., & Peter-Hagene, L. (2013). The interactive effect of anger and disgust on moral outrage and judgments. *Psychological Science, 24*, 2069–2078. doi:10.1177/0956797613486988

Schwartz, L.-G. (2009). *Mechanical witness: A history of motion picture evidence in U.S. courts.* New York: Oxford University Press.

Sebeok, T. (1994). *Signs: An introduction to semiotics.* Toronto: University of Toronto Press.

Serafin, S., & Serafin, G. (2004, July 6–9). *Sound design to enhance presence in photorealistic virtual reality.* Poster presented at the Tenth Meeting of the International Conference on Auditory Display, Sydney, Australia. Retrieved from http://www.icad.org/websiteV2.0/Conferences/ICAD2004/posters/serafin_serafin.pdf

Sherwin, R., Feigenson, N., & Spiesel, C. (2006). Law in the digital age: How visual communication technologies are transforming the practice, theory, and teaching of law. *Boston University Journal of Science and Technology Law, 12*, 227–270.

Silbey, J. (2004). Judges as film critics: New approaches to filmic evidence. *University of Michigan Journal of Law Reform, 37*, 493–571.

Smith, T., & Mital, P. (2013). Attentional synchrony and the influence of viewing task on gaze behavior in static and dynamic scenes. *Journal of Vision, 13*(8), 1–24. doi:10.1167/13.8.16

Sommers, R. (2016). Will putting cameras on police reduce polarization? *Yale Law Journal, 125*, 1304–1362.

Sood, A. (2013). Motivated judgments in legal cognition: An analytic review. *Annual Review of Law and Social Science, 9*, 307–325. doi:10.1146/annurev-lawsocsci-102612-134023

Spiesel, C. (2009). Reflections on reading: Words and pictures and law. In M. Freeman & O. Goodenough (Eds.), *Law, mind, and brain* (pp. 391–411). Surrey, UK: Ashgate.

Spiesel, C. (2017). Gruesome evidence: The use of beheading videos and other disturbing pictures in terrorism trials. In D. Tait & J. Goodman-Delahunty (Eds.), *Juries, science, and popular culture in the age of terror* (pp. 67–85). London: Palgrave Macmillan.

Stenberg, G. (2006). Conceptual and perceptual factors in the picture superiority effect. *European Journal of Cognitive Psychology, 18*, 813–847. doi:10.1080/09541440500412361

Steuer, J. (1995). Defining virtual reality: Dimensions determining telepresence. In F. Biocca & M. Levy (Eds.), *Communication in the age of virtual reality* (pp. 33–56). Hillsdale, NJ: Lawrence Erlbaum.

Troscianko, T., Meese, T., & Hinde, S. (2012). Perception while watching movies: Effects of physical screen size and scene type. *i-Perception, 3*, 414–425. doi:10.1068/i0475aap

Warren, R., & Warren, R. (1970). Auditory illusions and confusions. *Scientific American, 223*(6), 30–36.

Williams, T., Thomas, J., Jacoby, S., & Cave, D. (2016, April 1). Police body cameras: What do you see? *The New York Times*. Retrieved from http://www.nytimes.com/

Wilson, D., & Serisier, T. (2010). Video activism and the ambiguities of counter-surveillance. *Surveillance and Society, 8*, 166–180.

Wright, D., & Wareham, G. (2005). Mixing sound and vision: The interaction of auditory and visual information for earwitnesses of a crime scene. *Legal and Criminological Psychology, 10*, 103–108. doi:10.1348/135532504X15240

Yarbus, A. L. (1967). *Eye movements and vision* (B. Haigh, trans.). New York: Plenum Press.

Yesil, B. (2009). *Video surveillance: Power and privacy in everyday life*. El Paso, TX: LFB Scholarly Publishing.

Zelizer, B. (2010). *About to die: How news images move the public*. New York: Oxford University Press.

# 10

## Do Video Recordings Help Jurors Recognize Coercive Influences in Interrogations?

*Iris Blandón-Gitlin and Amelia Mindthoff*

On September 21, 2008, Adrian Thomas's four-month-old son Matthew was taken to the hospital after his parents found him unresponsive and having difficulty breathing. The admitting doctors believed Matthew had a life-threatening infection and recommended more tests. In the process of further testing, a doctor formed the opinion that the child had head trauma indicative of intentional abuse. Matthew died two days later. The police initially focused their investigation on Adrian Thomas, who appeared to show inappropriate emotion when interviewed. Police interrogated Thomas in two phases lasting almost 10 hours. After the first two hours, Thomas was taken to the hospital because he was upset and said he might commit suicide if his child died. When Thomas was released, he was immediately taken back to the interrogation room for the longer questioning session.

After detectives accused Thomas repeatedly, discounted his denials, and frequently used psychologically coercive tactics—including lying about medical evidence and suggesting that Thomas could save his child's life by telling them what he did—Thomas confessed. In a dramatic turn, Thomas, a large man, got up from the chair and demonstrated with a binder how he threw Matthew down, very hard, on a low-laying mattress. Jurors who watched the interrogation video at Thomas's first trial found him guilty of second-degree murder. He was sentenced to 25 years in prison. This verdict resulted despite the lack of corroborating evidence, as there were no broken bones, no bruises, and no head fractures on the child. This jury seemed convinced of Thomas's guilt, despite contradictory evidence demonstrating that the child died of a bacterial infection (Babcock & Hadaegh, 2011). Six years later, the New York Court of Appeals, on a 7 to 0 vote, excluded the confession, finding it coerced and involuntary (*People v. Thomas*, 2014). In a new trial, a jury hearing the same evidence minus the video-recorded confession, found Thomas not guilty. Adrian Thomas was released.

Among the many psycholegal issues highlighted by this case is the critical real-life test of the power of a confession on jurors. Scientific studies have shown that when one group of participants is exposed to a confession (even if involuntary and unreliable) and another group is not, the group shown the confession provides significantly more verdicts of guilt than the other (for a review, see Kassin et al., 2010). Similarly, in the Thomas case, one jury saw the confession evidence, and the other jury did not; both were presented the same circumstantial evidence, yet the outcomes were completely different. After the verdict at the second trial, a juror recalled, "There was a lot of emotion in the room, but also a lot of uncertainty . . . we all agreed in the end he was not guilty based on what we had in front of us" (Gardinier, 2014, para. 14).

Importantly for this chapter, the Thomas case highlights the issue of the available video-recorded interrogation for full evaluation. Many scientists, legal scholars, and practitioners would applaud law enforcement for videotaping the interrogation and making it available in its entirety to all fact finders, including the jury (Sullivan, 2005, 2010). Recorded interrogations may help reduce miscarriages of justice by inhibiting police from using coercive tactics known to promote false confessions (Kassin, Kukacka, Lawson, & DeCarlo, 2014). Moreover, full recordings can improve fact finders' ability to better assess what actually happened in the interrogation room rather than relying on people's memories or police reports that can be biased, distorted, or incomplete (Kassin, Kukucka, Lawson, & DeCarlo, 2017).

Yet in the Thomas case showing the jury the video-recorded interrogation did not fully serve a protective function against an erroneous conviction, as the jury did not seem to fully understand the factors that lead to unreliable confessions. Jurors were not influenced by the fact that detectives repeatedly fed details to Thomas, that he was told numerous times the child would die if Thomas did not talk, and that Thomas was repeatedly told he would not be arrested and could go home if he told detectives the "truth." The jury did not appear to have been influenced by the fact that only through guided imagery exercises and suggestive demonstrations by the detectives themselves that Thomas finally demonstrated the incriminating acts. The length of interrogation, Thomas's vulnerabilities, the lack of corroborating evidence to support the confession, and the medical evidence pointing to an infection as the cause of death were also seemly not as influential to the jury as the confession with visual "reenactments" was. Basically, what the jury *saw* Thomas do is what appeared to be the most salient and heavily weighted in the verdict.

Indeed, in a documentary on the case (Babcock & Hadaegh, 2011), the prosecuting attorney, Christa Book, intimated that having the binder being thrown by Thomas was "better than words." Clearly, that powerful imagery of an act—even if the product of coercion—was critically influential to fact finders. Thus, in cases like this, is the video-recorded interrogation helpful or detrimental to jury decision-making? How should that evidence be presented to the jury? What does the empirical evidence suggest? Do we need trial safeguards to ensure a probative value in video-recorded confessions? These are the questions guiding this chapter.

## Interrogations and Confessions: Scientific Findings

Certain dispositional factors, such as youth, mental impairments, and personality disorders, can place some suspects at high risk to falsely confess (Kassin et al., 2010). However, given a set of situational factors in the interrogation, suspects with no documented vulnerabilities can also be at risk to falsely confess. Costanzo, Blandón-Gitlin, and Davis (2016) suggested that accusatory interrogation approaches (i.e., the Reid Technique; Inbau, Reid, Buckley, & Jayne, 2013) are primarily about control—control of the setting (e.g., room, timing of events), control of the information suspects receive (e.g., evidence ploys such as real or fake DNA, polygraph, or eyewitness evidence), and control of suspects' choices (e.g., minimization versus maximization of culpability). Through a strategic process, police reverse the suspects' initial cost-benefit analysis of seeing denials as a benefit and confession as a cost to a change of perceiving denials as a cost and admitting to some version of committing the crime as a benefit. In their totality, these legal interrogation methods are powerful weapons of influence that often lead to confessions from the guilty (Davis & Leo, 2012). If misused, however, these tactics can also mislead innocent people to confess.

The resulting police-induced confession, whether true or false, is often enough to convict a person. The power of confessions has been demonstrated in numerous laboratory studies, as well as through empirical analyses of actual cases (see Kassin et al., 2010). For example, the Innocence Project's research on more than 300 convictions overturned by DNA evidence reveals that about 25% of these wrongful convictions involved false confessions or admissions (Innocence Project, 2017). In those, and many other real-world cases (e.g., Drizin & Leo, 2004), the confession was believed to be true by fact finders. Laboratory experiments also reveal the powerful impact of confessions compared to other evidence. When Kassin and Neumann (1997) systematically compared the effects of eyewitness, character, and confession evidence on mock juror verdicts, they found that confessions produced the highest conviction rate.

Returning to the Thomas case, we see that his interrogation was laden with numerous factors empirically shown to be indicative of unreliable confessions, thus prompting the American Psychological Association (APA) to submit an amicus brief to the New York Court of Appeals in the Thomas case (APA Brief, *People v. Thomas*, 2012). The brief summarized the literature on interrogations and confessions, and noted that false confession research is "grounded in and builds on a century of psychological research—and the resulting voluminous literature—that examines the cognitive, motivational, and behavioral foundations of authority and influence" (p. 3). The brief argued that this extensive empirical base demonstrates the reliability and relevance of false confession expert testimony in cases such as Thomas's, where corroborating evidence was lacking.

Indeed, social scientists know a great deal about the effect of interrogation tactics on suspects' behavior (Kassin et al., 2010), we know about the dispositional risk factors that make some people more vulnerable in interrogations (Gudjonsson, 2003), and we have a good empirically based understanding of jurors' perceptions of interrogation tactics and confession evidence (Costanzo et al., 2016). Scientists have also accumulated recent evidence on the effect of expert testimony on jurors' decisions about confession evidence (Costanzo et al., 2016). However, what can be said about the effect of mode of presenting confession evidence at trial? There is available research (albeit limited) on the effects of various types of visual evidence (e.g., photographs, videos, computer animations) on jurors' perceptions and judgments (see Chapter 9 of this volume; also Feigenson, 2010). In this chapter, we focus on research examining video confession evidence presented to juries because (a) videotaping of interrogations is now a widely recommended practice, if not required by certain United States law enforcement agencies (Mnooken, 2014), and (b) a video is the most likely mode of presentation in confession cases, as many recommend a full visual record of events to have access to verbal and nonverbal behaviors of the people involved (Buckley & Jayne, 2005).

## Video Evidence and Jury Decision-Making

Intuitively one can argue that video recording events provides a picture of the truth (see Chapter 9 in this volume). However, video-recorded interrogations that provide a great deal of detail and vividness can shape, distort, and unduly influence jurors' perceptions. Next we review factors that may powerfully mislead and bias jurors' judgments in confession cases.

### Video Recording: Focus Invokes Bias

Daniel Lassiter and colleagues have conducted a great deal of research examining the phenomenon of camera perspective bias in video-recorded interrogations (for comprehensive summaries, see Lassiter, 2010; Lassiter, Ware, Lindberg, & Ratcliff, 2010). The original experimental procedures investigated whether the typical interrogation video perspective, focusing on the suspect produces an implicit bias in observers' legal judgments, including the critical assessment of whether self-incriminating statements were given voluntarily. The state of voluntariness is one of the assessments used to decide if a confession was not coercively obtained and, therefore, legal (Leo, 2008). In Lassiter and colleagues' studies, mock jurors were shown the exact same video-recorded interrogation except for one change: Depending on condition, the target of the camera's focus varied. Some mock jurors saw the suspect most prominently in the video (suspect focus); others saw the interrogator most prominently in the video (interrogator focus); and yet another group saw both the suspect and interrogator in an "equal focus" view. Compared to interrogator-focus and equal-focus conditions, when the camera focus was on the suspect, mock jurors were significantly (a) less likely to find an interrogation coercive, (b) more likely to find the incriminating statements voluntary, (c) more likely to believe in the validity of confessions even when the interrogator explicitly (and illegally) threatened the defendant, and (d) more likely to find the suspect guilty and deserving of a longer sentence (Lassiter, 2010).

According to Lassiter and colleagues, the camera perspective bias can be explained by illusory causation, which is the tendency for people to judge visually salient or attended-to stimuli (e.g., objects, persons) as being the cause of the events they observe, whether that is objectively true or not (McArthur, 1980). For example, our attribution of responsibility for who instigated an argument between two strangers could depend largely on which angle of view we had at the time of the argument. Who we focus our attention on will influence responsibility judgments, regardless of the actual reality of the situation. Lassiter (2002) suggests that the visual prominence of the suspect in video-recorded interrogations may prompt observers to judge incriminating statements as being the result of the suspect's choice, or free will, or perhaps internal guilt, rather than the consequence of a high-pressured and coercive interrogation. This bias is resistant to interventions such as forewarning observers of the bias or increasing accountability for their judgments. Individual differences in motivation to engage in complex thinking or legal expertise do not seem to moderate the bias either (Lassiter et al., 2010).

In this line of research, an important question for real-world cases—such as the Thomas case—is whether experienced fact finders assessing the voluntariness of a confession are less biased and immune to this camera perspective effect. Unfortunately, there is empirical indication that even judges and police interrogators are subject to the camera perspective bias (Lassiter, Diamond, Schmidt, & Elek, 2007). Such findings are alarming because, by the very nature of what judges do, it is assumed that they are more experienced than anyone else on assessing the issue of voluntariness of a confession, an issue that judges examine before a trial to determine if the confession is admissible for the jury to see in the first place.

The camera perspective bias research increased in ecological validity over time. Prior work on the perspective bias had included realistic case topics (Lassiter et al., 2010) but were simply reenactments of interrogations and confessions to ensure internal validity. In real-world cases, there is more complexity and naturally occurring factors that may influence the effect of camera perspective. For this reason, Lassiter, Ware, Ratcliff, and Irvin (2009) used authentic videotaped interrogations of cases involving serious crimes (i.e., sexual assault and murder-by-arson). They compared the perceptions of participants who watched a suspect-focus video or equal-focus video to participants who received corresponding audio-only or transcript-only versions of the video (Experiment 1). Findings showed that participants watching the suspect-focus video thought the confession was offered more voluntarily compared to participants who received the audio- and transcript-only versions. In the equal-focus condition, the perception of confession voluntariness was the same regardless of being presented in a video, audio, or transcript format. As before, these results show that the visual bias is present in suspect-focus conditions even with authentic video-recorded interrogations. Encouragingly, the bias was eliminated with an equal-focus presentation, suggesting that this is a potential safeguard to reduce the camera perspective bias in real-world situations. These results also suggest that other forms of presentation (e.g., transcripts) can be helpful in some cases by directing focus to content rather than a visually salient but potentially prejudicial stimulus.

These latter results on presentation mode are congruent with work in the deception domain, which reveals that observers tend to be better in detecting deception when they have access to written- or audio-only versions of speakers' accounts compared to when they have full access with audiovisual versions. Observers tend to focus on speech content in written- or audio-only accounts and are less distracted by nonverbal behaviors (e.g., gaze aversion) that tend to be salient but not reliable in detecting deception in videotaped interviews (see Vrij, 2008). This extends to the confession context as well. For example, Kassin, Meissner, and Norwick (2005) showed that participants more accurately distinguished between true and false confessions when the veracity of confessions was evaluated based on audio-only than full audiovisual format. Similarly, Bradford, Goodman-Delahunty, and Brooks (2013) investigated the effect of presentation modality on observers' ability to identify true and false confessions. Interviewees were asked to provide true and false accounts of transgressions, which observers either saw in written-only, audio-only, or full audiovisual format. Observers detected true confessions with a high rate of accuracy but detected false confessions at a rate less than chance. Moreover, fewer false confessions in the audiovisual condition (28%) were detected, compared to written-only (41%) and audio-only (37%) conditions. These results suggest that the ability to identify false confessions may be impaired not only because of an inherent truth bias in people's judgments of statement veracity (Levine, 2014) but also because confession evidence unduly influences people's perceptions of guilt (Kassin & Neumann, 1997). The audiovisual presentation likely exacerbates these biasing effects.

### Video Recording: Additional Biasing Factors

**Image size.** According to a New Yorker online article paired with a portion of a video-recorded police interview, in 2001, Marshall Morgan Sr. confessed to killing his girlfriend (Schmidle, 2014). The article notes that "Morgan's account of the incident is harrowing: precise, clear, measured, and bereft of emotion" (para. 1). What is interesting about this police video is that it seems as though it was created using an investigative reporting style reminiscent of the news show *60 Minutes*. Like the popular show, the video image is first set to reveal both the interviewers and interviewee talking, but at the moments when Morgan describes the events, the camera zooms in to the upper part of his body and then even more on his face. In essence, this amplification of the image makes Morgan seem much larger, magnifying every aspect of his facial and body expressions. What does this magnified image do to observers' perceptions? It is possible that interviewees' behaviors do not seem consequential in zoomed-out images with a visual of the context but become very important when exaggerated in close-up shots (note that this is reminiscent of the zoomed-in, suspect-only camera perspective). Essentially, the intensity of information may be influenced by video image size, as suggested in a recent study by Heath and Grannemann (2014; see also Chapter 9 in this volume).

Heath and Grannemann (2014) investigated how video image size influences mock jurors' decisions. Citing findings that people experience larger images as more arousing and attention grabbing than smaller images, the authors hypothesized that larger images may intensify evaluations of various aspects of the trial and affect person perception. In their study, mock jurors read a murder case description and a trial summary and then watched a three-minute video clip of the defendant's testimony (portrayed by an actress). Video images were presented on a 27-inch television monitor or a nine-foot projection screen, in conjunction with either strong or weak evidence. Results showed that with strong evidence, slightly more guilty verdicts were rendered when the image was large (65%) than when the image was small (52%). When weak evidence was presented, there were fewer guilty verdicts in the large-image condition (13%) compared to the small-image condition (32%). In other words, compared to the small image, the large image amplified the strength of the evidence, whether it was strong or weak, to observers.

More research is needed to replicate and unpack the effects of image size on jurors' perceptions, as well as on the underlying mechanisms that explain the effect. But these results suggest that there is a potential interaction between image size and evidence strength when it comes to assessments of guilt. This leads to the question: Would the strength of a video-recorded confession be amplified on a larger screen? Given the powerful influence of confessions as perceived indicators of guilt (Kassin et al., 2010), would a larger video screen enhance the guilt-biasing effect of a confession in the same manner by which evidence strength is enhanced? Although in the real world the presentation mode of visuals is restricted to the technology available in the courtroom, the thought of artificially amplifying the strength of confession evidence on jurors' perceptions of guilt is disconcerting. Recall that previous work suggests false confessions presented in audiovisual format are misclassified significantly more often as true compared to those presented in other formats (Bradford et al., 2013). It is thus possible that the bias in believing confession evidence may be even more enhanced by image size. This question needs empirical assessment because it will not be long before we see manipulations of presentations of video-recorded confessions with the goal of influencing perceptions of guilt.

**Video time distortions.** In addition to image size, presentation speed appears to also influence jurors' perceptions of evidence in general (see also Chapter 9 in this volume). For example, a series of experiments showed that a suspect's actions were perceived as premeditated when the speed of the video-recorded event was slowed down for mock jurors, compared to when the same video was presented at a regular speed (Caruso, Burns & Converse, 2016). The speed at which a video-recorded interrogation is presented to the jury may not be a concern in confession cases as a general rule, but distortion of time may be an issue. Usually video-recorded interrogations are presented at regular speeds, unless something specific needs to be emphasized and slowed down (e.g., to assess the validity of *Miranda* warnings read at a fast speed). In some cases, however, it is possible that only portions of the interrogation are presented to the jury because one side or the other successfully argued to limit what is shown. For example, it is possible that polygraph examinations—which are used as a coercive tactic in many interrogations (Leo, 2008)—will not be shown to the jury, as its results are inadmissible in court. Additionally, it is likely that the time the suspect spends in the interrogation room alone will not be shown to the jury unless there is a reason for it (e.g., the suspect displays signs of being unfit for interrogation—sleep deprivation, drug withdrawal, etc.). Finally, sometimes only the confession itself might be shown, with the hours of previous psychologically coercive interrogation sessions omitted from what is presented to jurors.

All of these potential manipulations in presenting interrogation phases may lead to distortions of time perception and misinform jurors on the suspect's actual psychological state during interrogation. They may erroneously think that time elapsed faster even when specifically told the length of an interrogation. Indeed, survey research shows that jurors do not seem to make appropriate links between interrogation length and its effects on innocent suspects, believing that the police need about 10 hours to interrogate suspects (e.g., Blandón-Gitlin, Sperry, & Leo, 2011). In the Thomas case, one of the jurors who voted guilty acknowledged that Thomas confessed because he was "worn down" by the length of the interrogation (Babcock & Hadaegh, 2011). Even so, the length of time Thomas was interrogated was not perceived as a risk factor for a false confession. It is as though the juror believed that prolonged time could negatively influence the guilty but not the innocent.

**Salience of suspect's race.** Race is a salient factor that activates all kinds of biases in observers. For instance, from recent work by Najdowski and colleagues (Najdowski, 2011; Najdowski, Bottoms, & Goff, 2015) we know that minorities in police encounters often experience "stereotype threat," a phenomenon characterized as "being at risk of confirming, as self-characteristic, a negative stereotype about one's group" (Steele & Aronson, 1995, p. 797). This affects the behaviors of minority group members interacting with the police, which can potentially mislead jurors' judgments of suspiciousness, deception, and guilt (Najdowski, 2011). Other research suggests that race plays a role in directing perceivers' attention in ways similar to the camera perspective bias. Ratcliff et al., (2010) found that when the suspect was of a minority status (Black or Chinese) and the interrogator was White, the minority suspect's statements were perceived as more voluntary than a White suspect's even when the suspect and interrogator appeared in an equal-focus view—thus, race was a salient factor that drew attention, regardless of camera perspective. This interpretation was further supported by data showing that when both the suspect and interrogator were of minority status, the bias did not occur in the equal-focus condition, presumably because no one person was racially salient (Ratcliff et al., 2010). Similarly, Pickel, Warner, Miller, and Barnes (2013) showed that conceptualizing a suspect as a member of a minority group (Arab or gay), regardless of physical appearance, led to the salience bias (i.e., greater perceived voluntariness of the minority suspect's confession), even in the equal-focus condition. Together, these results further support the notion that, in some cases, an audio-only or transcript-only presentation may be less prejudicial than the video-recorded interrogation, as salient suspect features are less prominent in these modalities. However, care must be taken to ensure that information presented does not activate incorrect conceptualizations about the suspect.

## Presenting Confession Evidence: The Need for Safeguards

At Thomas's first trial, after watching the video-recorded interrogation and hearing expert testimony on the science of interrogations and false confessions, the presiding judge ruled that the expert testimony was not necessary at trial because the jury could see the video for itself and decide on the reliability of the confession evidence. This ruling assumes that jurors possess accurate knowledge about the effects of interrogation tactics on suspects and that they can sensibly determine by themselves when a confession is true or false. These intuitive assumptions, shared by lawyers and judges (Sullivan, 2010), are contradicted by empirical research (see Kassin et al., 2010). Thus trial-level safeguards (e.g., expert testimony, jury instructions) are necessary to sensitize jurors to the factors that make confessions reliable or unreliable. Such safeguards could reduce potential prejudicial effects that video-recorded interrogations may have on jurors.

## Jurors Believe Confessions

Jurors tend to believe confessions. Unless mentally impaired or tortured, it is difficult to imagine an innocent person confessing—against self-interest—to a crime that he or she did not commit (Leo, 2008). A large literature in social psychology suggests that observers make attributional errors by underestimating the power of the situation when evaluating people's behaviors (e.g., Ross & Nisbett, 1991). This suggests that jurors are likely to infer that a confession is valid because they underestimate the power of the interrogation forces acting on the suspect. In support, a number of studies have surveyed diverse samples (e.g., jurors at a courthouse, community members) to assess juror knowledge and beliefs about interrogations and confessions, revealing significant juror misconceptions.

Thus, even if jurors watch an entire video, they may not be able to properly weigh the multiple factors they see pressuring a suspect. They may see situational factors when blatantly obvious (e.g., threats), but they may not understand their power on suspects and therefore incorrectly attribute a suspect's confession simply to guilt. This is clearly suggested by Lassiter and colleagues' (2010) research showing that this misattributional tendency is exacerbated when the camera angle is focused on the suspect. When the camera focus is on both the interrogator and the suspect, the confession is seen as less voluntary and more coerced, suggesting that being able to perceive the complete context on the screen may prompt jurors to consider situational forces. We review other factors that may bias perceptions of confession evidence when jurors view video-recorded interrogations next.

**The story model of juror decision-making.** Prosecutors' theories of the crime and plausible motives for why a defendant committed the crime, accompanied by a confession, can create a sense of a complete and coherent story that is convincing to the jurors. Circumstantial evidence may be perceived as valid in the context of a confession, whether it is reliable or not (Kassin, Bogart, & Kerner, 2012). Even when there is strong exculpatory evidence such as DNA, if there is a confession, observers often believe in the suspect's guilt and are likely to convict (Appleby & Kassin, 2016). Moreover, prosecutors' theories explaining away evidence that contradicts a confession lends to a story that may seem reasonable to jurors (Appleby & Kassin, 2016). The fluency in processing a good story can be powerful in persuading jurors that the confession is true despite contradictory evidence, and elements derived from a video-recorded interrogation can lend perceived merit to such stories.

Indeed, research shows that jurors organize information in story form (Pennington & Hastie, 1993), and the ease with which information is processed is considered a cue to authenticity, whether the information is true or not (Newman, 2017). Detectives are trained to elicit details to make for a compelling story to fact finders. In fact, Reid & Associates—the company responsible for the controversial Reid approach to interrogation in the

United States—teaches interrogators how to obtain the critical details and components needed to construct a good story in the confession (Inbau et al., 2013). Thus not only is obtaining an admission a major goal of interrogation but so is the development of a good confession story to later sell to fact finders. The truth may be lost at some point in pursuing these goals, as evidenced in the many proven false confession cases (Garrett, 2015). In a book dedicated to the topic of interviewing and interrogating child abuse offenders, Reid & Associates recommend that the suspect should be induced to demonstrate his or her actions, concluding that "Having the offender demonstrate his abusive actions is particularly powerful when videotaping the confession. Sometimes actions speak louder than words and have a great impact on a judge or jury" (Buckley, 2006, p. 305). Indeed, demonstrations are powerful in this context. In the documentary on the Thomas case, a juror, despite being "bothered" by the police tactics and being "angry" because of the techniques detectives used to "misrepresent things," explained the coercive interrogation by saying the police "have been doing this for a long time and if that is what works, then . . . that is the way to do it" (Babcock & Hadaegh, 2011). This fit directly with the prosecutor's story. In the documentary, Assistant District Attorney Book said that despite her concerns about police tactics and how the inter-rogation would seem to the jury, she knew that Thomas throwing the binder needed to be shown to the jury and believed that jurors would understand that police sometimes have to use unsavory tactics to get at the "truth." Thus, as suggested in some of the media coverage (e.g., Franco, 2014), Book used that element in the first trial to create a riveting and emotion-inducing story that made use of visual backing from the video-recorded interrogation. This likely skewed the jurors' perceptions of all other evidence.

**Jurors' failure to fully recognize coercion.** Survey research shows that while potential jurors are aware that false confessions can occur (Chojnacki, Cicchini, & White, 2008; Henkel, Coffman, & Dailey, 2008), most believe they are unlikely to be elicited from themselves (Henkel et al., 2008) or from innocent suspects (Chojnacki et al., 2008; Leo & Liu, 2009). Additionally, people can correctly recognize coercion in some police tactics (e.g., implicit and explicit threats of physical harm) and the use of deception (e.g., lying about evidence) but are unable to recognize coercion in other tactics known by scientists to pose a high risk for false confessions (e.g., minimization tactics; Blandón-Gitlin et al., 2011; Leo & Liu, 2009). Importantly, while people believe that true confessions from guilty suspects can be elicited using co-ercive tactics, they do not believe those tactics can elicit false confessions from the innocent (Blandón-Gitlin et al., 2011; Leo & Liu, 2009). Lack of knowledge about the existence, frequency, and legality of popular police tactics was also revealed in surveys (e.g., cutting off denials, deception, downplaying seriousness of the crime; Chojnacki et al., 2008; Henkel et al., 2008). Interestingly, a significant number of survey respondents believe that police officers are better than others at lie detection (even from just body language; Chojnacki et al., 2008; Costanzo, Shaked-Schroer, & Vinson,

2010) and that they themselves can discriminate true and false confessions from videos (Costanzo et al., 2010), both of which are contradicted by existing research (e.g., Kassin et al., 2005).

Researchers have also investigated jurors' perceptions and sensitivity to specific interrogation tactics believed by scientists to be coercive and pose a risk for false confessions. Moffa and Platania (2007) showed that while jurors understand the pressure inherent in implicit messages of threat (maximization) and leniency (minimization), they were not influenced by these tactics in their assessment of the suspect's guilt. Moreover, jurors are able to perceive deception and coercion in some false evidence ploys (e.g., fabricated eyewitness evidence; Forrest et al., 2012) but are insensitive to differences between ploys suggesting evidence exists (a "bluff") versus those ploys that explicitly tell suspects the evidence exists (Woody, Forrest, & Yendra, 2014). It is possible that jurors may not fully understand that false evidence ploys unequivocally indicate there is no such evidence and that it is, in fact, all a "ruse."

**Insensitivity to factors that make suspects vulnerable.** Jurors may be reluctant to discount recanted confessions from suspects with specific enhanced vulnerabilities, even when the interrogation context is presented as coercive. For instance, Henkel (2008) found that mock jurors were more likely to convict when a confession was present than when it was not, even if the suspect reported giving a coerced confession due to his acute anxiety disorder (i.e., a psychological disorder). Interestingly, however, jurors were willing to discount a coerced confession when the suspect claimed to suffer from a serious heart problem (i.e., a medical condition). In another study by Najdowski and Bottoms (2012), jurors were also willing to discount a confession only when they *perceived* coercion in a juvenile's interrogation, which was not necessarily dependent on whether the interrogation was actually coercive. These results show that even in the presence of important suspect vulnerabilities, confession evidence is not likely to be fully discounted.

**Summary.** Findings like those reviewed herein lead to the question: How do these beliefs play out in jury trials? Laboratory studies of mock jurors' evaluations of confessions consistently show a high conviction rate when a confession is presented as evidence compared to when no confession is presented, even when the confession was obtained in a highly coercive manner or when jurors were told explicitly to discount the confession (Henkel, 2008; Kassin & Neumann, 1997; Kassin & Sukel, 1997). The available data on proven false confession cases suggest that jurors indeed believed confessions that were in fact false. For example, Drizin and Leo's (2004) study of 125 proven false confession cases showed that for those cases in which the defendants pled not guilty and decided to go to trial, the conviction rate was 81%.

Overall, it appears that jurors are not sufficiently able to recognize that certain tactics can render a confession coerced and/or unreliable. Therefore, merely seeing those tactics on video will not sensitize them to coercion, as the judge in the first Thomas case claimed (Babcock & Hadaegh, 2011). Thus methods to inform and sensitize jurors must be considered.

### Educating the Jury

**Expert testimony.** In recent years there has been an increase in research on how jurors respond to expert testimony on confessions (Costanzo, Krauss, & Pezdek, 2007). This research is encouraging because expert testimony on situational factors in interrogations seems to have a small but educational influence on jurors,[1] which can be highly beneficial for making jurors aware of biasing effects, including the camera perspective bias, on perceptions of confession evidence. For example, Woody and Forrest (2009) showed jurors a mock trial that included a confession elicited using or not using false evidence ploys. Then, expert testimony about confessions was presented or not presented. As in other studies, interrogations with false evidence ploys were recognized as more coercive and deceptive than those without, but the presence of false evidence ploys did not lead to fewer convictions (also see Moffa & Platania, 2007, 2009). However, the presence of expert testimony resulted in fewer convictions, though not significantly so. Similarly, Blandón-Gitlin et al. (2011, Study 2) showed a small but significant decrease in conviction rates after mock jurors were exposed to expert testimony in a disputed confession case. Participants who changed their verdicts from pre- to post-presentation of expert testimony rated tactics used in the interrogation as more coercive and rated all aspects of the expert testimony as more influential in their decision-making in comparison to participants who did not change their verdicts.

Not only should expert testimony influence verdicts, though; rather than simply increase juror skepticism, it should also sensitize jurors (Penrod & Cutler, 1989). That is, expert testimony should help jurors identify the factors that increase the risk of a false confession and use that information to make decisions about culpability. Thus conviction rates would be reduced if significant risk factors are present in the case. Recent studies have specifically investigated whether expert testimony serves to sensitize jurors of risk factors; however, the results are not yet clear on the issue. For example, Jones and Penrod (2016) found that confession evidence significantly increased guilty verdicts compared to when there was no confession, consistent with previous research, but they found no effect of expert testimony on jurors' ability to recognize various coercive tactics.

Interestingly, Woestehoff and Meissner (2016) found that, independent of expert testimony, jurors were more likely to convict when the risk of false confession was low (a low-pressure interrogation condition) than when the risk of false confession was high (moderate- or high-pressure interrogation conditions). The expert testimony had no effect on jurors' verdict decisions, but it did improve jurors' knowledge about confession risk factors. Moreover, participants who heard the expert testimony were no more likely to convict just because a confession was present than were those who did not hear the testimony. Instead, it was the type of interrogation (high versus low risk of false confession) that influenced conviction rates. The authors concluded that their results, which depart from other findings that indicate confessions are a strong predictor of guilty verdicts, might have to do with an increase in jurors' knowledge about false confessions, one that may be heavily influenced by exposure to media of various sorts (e.g., *Making a Murderer*, Ricciardi & Demos, 2015; for further discussion of the influence of media on juror decision-making, see Chapter 7 in this volume). This explanation about jurors' becoming more savvy with media exposure to interrogation and confession issues seems at odds with the findings of Jones and Penrod (2016) discussed previously, which were published in the same year. However, data collection in the two studies likely spanned different years, and perhaps their results were affected differently by participants' varying exposure to media accounts of false confessions cases. Clearly, the conflicting results need to be further assessed in future replication studies that take account of jurors' media exposure. Nonetheless, these two studies provide more insight into jurors' decisions in confession cases with and without expert testimony.

Taking a different approach to confession reliability, Henderson and Levett (2016) investigated the effect of content consistency. The main question was whether jurors could detect differences between confessions that are consistent (high-quality confession) versus inconsistent (low-quality confession) with crime details. The authors found that when no expert was presented, jurors' verdicts were similar whether the confession was consistent or not. When the expert was presented, however, juror convictions were lower if the confession was inconsistent with case facts than if it was consistent. The authors concluded that the expert sensitized jurors to the consistency factor and therefore improved their decision-making.

Although there is still a great deal of research to be done, overall it seems that expert testimony may be helpful to jurors under some conditions. The quality of jurors' decisions will improve to the extent that expert testimony can focus jurors' attention to the relevant research on factors associated with high versus low risk of false confessions, as well as to the issue of confession quality. This is especially important if jurors use knowledge acquired from the media, as there is always the risk that the media will misinform jurors.

Expert testimony should assist judges too. In theory, when making voluntariness judgments, judges should look for evidence (or lack thereof) of coercive tactics such as implicit or explicit promises of leniency in exchange for a confession (a situation that makes the confession involuntary and not admissible). Due to their expertise and experience, judges should be better than laypeople at focusing on that issue and not being influenced by video characteristics, such as camera perspective. However, it seems that judges are not as impervious as expected. For instance, in one study, judges correctly recognized that high-pressure confessions were coerced and were improperly admitted into evidence; however, compared to when there was no confession, the erroneously admitted coerced confession led judges to believe the suspect was guilty anyway (Wallace & Kassin, 2012). Confessions' biasing effect on judges extends to camera perspective as well, as expertise serves no protection against camera perspective bias (e.g., Lassiter et al., 2007). In the Thomas case, even though coercive tactics were used—which clearly points to involuntary incriminating statements—the lower court's judge did not see it this way while the New York Court of Appeals did. Why the difference?

There may be many reasons, but one possible explanation is that the judges at the high court of appeals had more information at their disposal, including the APA's brief highlighting the psychology of interrogations and confessions, and even the research on the camera perspective bias. Thus the issue of coerciveness of the tactics was prominently raised and repeated throughout the appeals process, likely making it the center of the high court's attention. This potentially prompted the high court judges to evaluate the confession evidence through the lens of a coercion schema (a "coercion cognitive frame"). Essentially, the court of appeals could have used a different lens to evaluate coercion in the Thomas interrogation. This frame of reference is hinted at in the language of the decision and the data the judges gathered to support their views, including enumerating each of the tactics used by detectives (see opinion in *People v. Thomas*, 2014). Of course, we do not know whether the court of appeals judges realized their use of this schema or cognitive frame of reference, but it is possible given some recent findings on cognitive frames and the camera perspective bias, a topic we return to later in this section.

**Alternative safeguards.** Expert testimony is only one of several methods to guard against wrongful convictions based on unreliable confessions. Relying on experts may not be always possible: Experts are too few in number, or they may be unavailable or too expensive for a particular trial. Importantly, as in the Thomas case, experts may not be allowed to testify. Thus some studies have investigated the influence of other methods to sensitize the jury to factors that increase risk of false confessions. In one study, Gomes, Stenstrom, and Calvillo (2016) examined the influence of jury instructions and expert testimony on various juror decisions, including conviction rates. The jury instructions, meant to replace expert testimony, encouraged jurors to consider confession credibility on different factors. The expert testimony focused on the science of situational and dispositional factors associated with false confessions, as well as the case-relevant tactics that increase the risk for false confession. Results showed that there were more guilty verdicts when jury instructions were presented than when expert testimony was presented. A no-safeguard condition was similar to jury instruction. Thus jury instructions may serve the same function as providing nothing at all to the jury. However, this may be due to the particular instructions used, and various versions of the instructions should be investigated further.

Expanding on trial safeguard research, Mindthoff and Blandón-Gitlin (2015), investigated the effects of various methods to inform jurors, including expert testimony, simple jury instructions, enhanced jury instructions, and defense attorney closing arguments. The simple version of jury instructions merely provided a list of factors to consider in evaluating confession evidence while the enhanced version emphasized how jurors should apply perceptions of voluntariness in their decision-making. The defense attorney arguments—based on a scientific understanding of interrogations—highlighted the factors that led to what he characterized as a false confession in the case at hand. Results showed that expert testimony and closing arguments resulted in the lowest rate of guilty verdicts compared to other conditions and were both reported to be highly influential by those voting not guilty. Similar to Gomes et al. (2016), neither the simple nor enhanced jury instructions significantly reduced guilty verdicts compared to having no safeguard. These findings suggest that similar to expert testimony, attorneys' closing arguments may be more effective than jury instructions in drawing attention to the relevant factors that pose a risk of false confession.

Expert testimony and attorneys' arguments may be additionally useful in reducing the camera perspective bias by priming particular modes of thinking about the video-recorded confession. This is suggested by the results of a study by Park and Pyo (2012). They examined whether camera perspective bias may occur because focusing on the suspect (suspect-focus condition) automatically invokes a schema of voluntariness that prompts the observers to search for evidence of voluntariness (a voluntariness cognitive frame). Conversely, focusing on the interrogator (interrogator-focus condition) may invoke a schema of coercion that prompts observers to search for evidence of coercion (a coercion cognitive frame). Thus a voluntariness or coercion cognitive frame in this context refers to the schema used to interpret incoming perceptual and social information from the interrogation. The results would be that, in each case, the cognitive frame would induce observers to look for clues (e.g., verbal and nonverbal behaviors) that fit this initial cognitive framing. Thus the mechanism behind the camera perspective effect may be a confirmation bias. In three experiments, the authors measured the likelihood that the confession in each case was voluntary and/or coerced in a Korean community sample.[2] The first finding revealed the typical camera perspective bias in another cultural context. The second main finding showed that when the audio-only part of the interrogation was presented to observers and was preceded by instructions designed to prime participants to assess either voluntariness or coerciveness, a bias occurred in the direction of the prompted cognitive frame. That is, the same audio-recorded confession was perceived differently depending on whether the instructions primed the use of a particular cognitive frame. Prompting a voluntariness cognitive frame led observers to perceive the confession as more voluntary and less coerced, compared to when a coerciveness cognitive frame was primed. This latter condition also led the confession to be perceived as more coerced and less voluntary. Thus, even with no visual stimulus, the perception of voluntariness or coercion can be manipulated simply by prompting a particular schema or cognitive frame.

Lastly, the bias was eliminated when Park and Pyo (2012) showed the video recording using instructions that primed an opposing cognitive schema or frame than the one automatically activated by the camera focus. That is, one group of observers was primed with a coerciveness frame in the suspect-focus condition. Another group was primed with a voluntariness frame before watching the interrogator-only video interrogation. This manipulation led to similar perceptions of confession voluntariness in both conditions, suggesting that the instructions priming a particular frame supplants the cognitive frame automatically evoked by the camera perspective. This hints at the possibility that different cognitive frames or schemata (ideally ones inducing more objectivity) in evaluating video-recorded confessions may reduce the camera perspective bias, even in a suspect-focused video, as was the case in Thomas's interrogation. Perhaps an alternative cognitive frame may explain why, given the same powerfully biasing video evidence in Thomas, the New York Court of Appeals reached a unanimous and wildly different opinion than the lower court. Informing the fact finders via expert analysis may have induced a more balanced approach in evaluating the video-recorded confession.

## Conclusion

Returning to the main questions guiding this chapter, in cases like Thomas's, was the video-recorded interrogation helpful or harmful to jury decision-making? How should such evidence be shown to the jury? What does the empirical evidence suggest?

There is a strong possibility that the video of Thomas demonstrating how he purportedly hurt his child was a salient misleading visual that clouded jurors' ability to fully understand the entire interrogation context. Not only do insights from jurors' interviews suggest this interpretation but so does the empirical evidence from psychological science. Based on the work by Lassiter and colleagues (2010), we believe that, in cases like Thomas's, if the confession is to be admitted at trial, it would be less prejudicial to the defendant if the transcripts of the interrogation are provided instead of the video.[3] We say this for two reasons. First, most video-recorded interrogations today are likely to be suspect focused. For example, Cleary (2014) found that in 51 of 57 (89%) juvenile interrogations she empirically analyzed, the camera was focused on the suspect. Although Lassiter (2010) has proposed empirically based best practices on how to video record interrogations, the science has yet to lead to policy change in the United States. In fact, policies in contradiction to the empirically based recommendations may occur. For example, the Reid manual recommends a suspect-focus perspective because it is "excellent with respect to evaluating the suspect's nonverbal behavior" (Buckley & Jayne, 2005, p. 32), while not discussing the negative effects of the camera perspective bias. Thus, without changes in policy or proper education, suspect-focused interrogations will continue to be presented. Second, in cases such as Thomas's, there are other bias-inducing aspects that likely influence suspects' behaviors and observers' judgments (e.g., the suspect's minority status, as previously discussed). Thomas, a Black man, was probably at risk of bias, not only in the interrogation room but also in the courtroom, as jurors were not likely aware of how the defendant's race might influence their judgments.

Together, this research suggests that there is a need for trial safeguards to ensure a probative value in video recorded confessions. As noted by the APA's amicus brief on the Thomas case (*People v. Thomas*, 2012), given the multiple factors that can negatively affect suspects in interrogations and the subsequent evaluations of confessions by fact finders, expert testimony is necessary. During the Thomas documentary (Babcock & Hadaegh, 2011), jurors commented that there was no need to have an expert to "refute" the confession, that it would have been "insulting" to have someone explain it because they saw the video for themselves, and that regardless of what an expert would have said "you can just tell he [Thomas] was guilty." Even leading legal experts believe that fact finders can objectively decode video-recorded interrogations for themselves. For example, Cassell (1996) has suggested that video-recorded interrogations decreased the need to use the *Miranda* warning to protect against coercion because fact finders can see for themselves in the video if coercion occurred or not. Together, these accounts reveal misconceptions about what people are able to see in front of them (see also Chapter 9 in this volume), and what the function of the expert testimony is (i.e., helping jurors effectively apply what they see to their decisions).

Indeed, a great deal of research in cognitive science shows that most people hold an "illusion of complete perception." It is difficult to understand that even when directly looking at things, we do not necessarily see what is in front of us (see Simons, 2010, 2014). As reviewed, research suggests that it is unlikely jurors, on their own, can easily and accurately determine the validity of a confession, or even articulate the effects of coercive tactics on suspects, especially innocent suspects. As demonstrated in multiple studies, when a confession is present, jurors are not able to objectively analyze the strength of other evidence, even contradictory evidence. Even playing a full coercive interrogation on video may not fully protect against the power of a confession on perceptions of guilt. Moreover, the details and actions elicited by scripted police interrogation methods—designed to make the video-recorded confession captivating—may increase the power of confession evidence. Given that jurors do not seem offended by coercion and are willing to allow police great latitude in their approaches, trial safeguards are necessary.

As suggested previously, experts on confessions do not "refute" the evidence; they teach the jury to understand the science explaining the influence of interrogation methods on eliciting true and false confessions (Costanzo et al., 2016). Experts can discuss the aspects of methods, especially those relevant in the case at hand. In this way, experts can help jurors to look closely at the context of interrogation and to decode the confession evidence and assess reliability based on facts in evidence and not salient features that are nondiagnostic of veracity. By doing this, expert testimony may encourage the jury to use different cognitive frames and perhaps move them away from attributional bias and, in the case of video-recorded interrogations, reduce potential bias induced by tricks of the camera (e.g., perspective, angle, size, speed).

However, an expert on confessions may not be sufficient to educate the jury and sensitize them to factors that risk false confessions. A knowledgeable defense attorney who understands the science of interrogations and confessions is also necessary. Among the multiple defense tools available, it seems that defense attorney closing arguments highlighting coercive factors may be helpful to jurors' understanding (Mindthoff & Blandón-Gitlin, 2015). This might work more effectively if the video-recorded interrogation is shown along with the defense's arguments. Lassiter (2010) noted that because the prosecution presents its case first, it is likely that jurors encode the information in video-recorded confessions in a manner that is consistent with the prosecution's argument. This may lead to a fixed judgment of guilt (i.e., judgment perseverance) that the jury could hold throughout the trial. The associative encoding of the video-recorded confession and compelling prosecutor story may remain, even if the defense has a valid argument that the confession is unreliable and the defendant is not guilty. Lassiter (2010) suggested that if the videotape is shown again with the defense's alternative arguments of events, the bias may be reduced.

Lassiter's (2010) conceptualization is supported by findings in which participants who, after watching a video-recorded confession, developed an assumption of guilt that still persisted even after discrediting information was presented. But those who were presented with the discrediting information and saw the video a second time were likely to "move significantly toward not guilty" verdicts (Lassiter et al., 2005 [as cited in Lassiter, 2010, p.773]). Thus in some cases it might be important to re-review the video-recorded events if the defense attorney has a valid and compelling argument and wants to reduce a persistent bias of guilt. We add that it may also be useful to highlight in the video the coercive approaches during cross-examination. Given that detectives typically testify as part of building foundation to introduce the validity of confession evidence at trial, it is possible that this validation enhances juries' perception of reliability. As such, it might be helpful to cross-examine detectives using the video-recorded interrogation and reconceptualize the tactics to reveal their coerciveness. This may give the jury a different perspective, one that includes a complete interrogation context.

In conclusion, video recording of interrogations can help reduce miscarriages of justice based on false confessions and increase the likelihood that true confessions will lead to correct convictions. However, video-recorded interrogations may not always speak the truth. They are not the full solution that will solve all problems from the misuse of coercive tactics. Safeguards to help fact finders better evaluate videotaped confessions are absolutely necessary.

## Notes

1. Currently, there is very little empirical research investigating the influence of clinical expert testimony on jurors' evaluation and decision-making in confession cases (but see Gudjonsson, 2003).
2. These authors used both voluntariness and coercion assessments, because "although different psychological processes may be involved, voluntariness and coerciveness of a video-recorded confession would not be judged separately in court" (p. 188).
3. Note that even if a video or audio interrogation is provided, accompanying transcripts are almost always given to the jury.

## References

Appleby, S. C., & Kassin, S. M. (2016). When self-report trumps science: Effects of confessions, DNA, and prosecutorial theories on perceptions of guilt. *Psychology, Public Policy & Law, 22*, 127–140. doi:10.1037/law0000080

Babcock, G., & Hadaegh, B. (Producers/Directors). (2011). *Scenes of a crime* [Documentary Film]. New York: Submarine Entertainment.

Blandón-Gitlin, I., Sperry, K., & Leo, R. (2011). Jurors believe interrogation tactics are not likely to elicit false confessions: Will expert witness testimony inform them otherwise? *Psychology, Crime & Law, 17*, 239–260. doi:10.1080/10683160903113699

Bradford, D., Goodman-Delahunty, J., & Brooks, K. (2013). The impact of presentation modality on perceptions of truthful and deceptive confessions. *Journal of Criminology, 13*, 1–10. doi:10.1155/2013/164546

Brief for American Psychological Association as Amicus Curiae Supporting Appellant, People v. Adrian P. Thomas, 93 A.D. 3rd 1019, 3d Dept. (2012). Retrieved from http://www.apa.org/about/offices/ogc/amicus/thomas.pdf

Buckley, D. M. (2006). *How to identify, interview & interrogate child abuse offenders*. Chicago: John E. Reid.

Buckley, D. M., & Jayne, B. M. (2005). *Electronic recording of interrogations*. Chicago: John E. Reid.

Cassell, P. G. (1996). Miranda's social costs: An empirical reassessment. *Northwestern University Law Review, 90*, 387–499.

Caruso, E. M., Burns, Z. C., & Converse, B. A. (2016). Slow motion increases perceived intent. *Proceedings of the National Academy of Sciences, 113*, 9250–9255. doi:10.1073/pnas.1603865113

Chojnacki, D., Cicchini, M., & White, L. T. (2008). An empirical basis for the admission of expert testimony on false confessions. *Arizona State Law Journal, 40*, 1–45.

Cleary, H. M. D. (2014). Police interviewing and interrogation of juvenile suspects: A descriptive examination of actual cases. *Law and Human Behavior, 38*, 271–282. doi:10.1037/lhb0000070

Costanzo, M., Blandón-Gitlin, I., & Davis, D. (2016). The purpose, content, and effects of expert testimony on interrogations and confessions. In M. Miller & B. Bornstein (Eds.), *Advances in psychology and law* (Vol. 2, pp. 141–178). Cham, Switzerland: Springer.

Costanzo, M., Krauss, D., & Pezdek, K. (Eds.). (2007). *Expert psychological testimony for the courts.* Mahwah, NJ: Lawrence Erlbaum.

Costanzo, M., Shaked-Schroer, N., & Vinson, K. (2010). Juror beliefs about police interrogations, false confessions, and expert testimony. *Journal of Empirical Legal Studies, 7*, 231–247. doi:10.1111/j.1740-1461.2010.01177.x

Davis, D., & Leo. R. A. (2012). Interrogation-related regulatory decline: Ego-depletion, failures of self-regulation and the decision to confess. *Psychology, Public Policy & Law, 18*, 673–704. doi:10.1037/a0027367

Drizin, S. A., & Leo, R. A. (2004). The problem of false confessions in the post-DNA world. *North Carolina Law Review, 82*, 891–1007.

Feigenson, N. (2010). Visual evidence. *Psychonomic Bulletin & Review, 17*, 149–154. doi:10.3758/PBR.17.2.149

Forrest, K. D., Woody, W. D., Brady, S. E., Batterman, K. C., Stastny, B. J., & Bruns, J. A. (2012). False-evidence ploys and interrogations: Mock jurors' perceptions of false evidence ploy type, deception, coercion, and justification. *Behavioral Sciences & the Law, 30*, 342–364. doi:10.1002/bsl.1999

Franco, J. (2014, February 20). Adrian Thomas case tossed. *T-Spin.* Retrieved from http://troyspin.blogspot.com/2014/02/adrian-thomas-case-tossed-video-audio.html

Gadinier, B. (2014, June 12). Stunning "not guilty": Adrian Thomas acquitted of killing infant son six years ago at second trial. *Times Union.* Retrieved from http://www.timesunion.com/local/article/Adrian-Thomas-found-not-guilty-in-son-s-death-5548244.php

Garrett, B. L. (2015). Contaminated confessions revisited. *Virginia Law Review, 101*, 395–454.

Gomes, D. M., Stenstrom, D. M., & Calvillo, D. P. (2016). Examining the judicial decision to substitute credibility instructions for expert testimony on confessions. *Legal & Criminological Psychology, 21*, 319–331. doi:10.1111/lcrp.12068

Gudjonsson, G. H. (2003). *The science of interrogations and confessions: A handbook.* Chichester, UK: Wiley.

Heath, W. P., & Grannemann, B. D. (2014). How video image size interacts with evidence strength, defendant emotion, and the defendant-victim relationship to alter perceptions of the defendant. *Behavioral Sciences & the Law, 32*, 496–507. doi:10.1002/bsl.2120

Henderson, K. S., & Levett, L. M. (2016). Can expert testimony sensitize jurors to variations in confession evidence? *Law and Human Behavior, 40*, 638–649. doi:10.1037/lhb0000204

Henkel, L. A. (2008). Jurors' reactions to recanted confessions: Do the defendant's personal and dispositional characteristics play a role? *Psychology, Crime & Law, 14*, 565–578. doi:10.1080/10683160801995247

Henkel, L. A., Coffman, K. A. J., & Dailey, E. M. (2008). A survey of people's attitudes and beliefs about false confessions. *Behavioral Sciences & the Law, 26*, 555–584. doi:10.1002/bsl.826

Inbau, F. E., Reid, J. E., Buckley, J. P., & Jayne, B. C. (2013). *Criminal interrogation and confessions* (5th ed.). Burlington, MA: Jones & Bartlett Learning.

Innocence Project. (2017). *False confessions or admissions.* Retrieved from https://www.innocenceproject.org/causes/false-confessions-admissions/

Jones, A. M., & Penrod, S. (2016). Can expert testimony sensitize jurors to coercive interrogation tactics? *Journal of Forensic Psychology Practice, 16*, 393–409. doi:10.1080/15228932.2016.1232029

Kassin, S. M., Bogart, D., & Kerner, J. (2012). Confessions that corrupt: Evidence from the DNA exoneration case files. *Psychological Science, 23*, 41–45. doi:10.1177/0956797611422918

Kassin, S. M., Drizin, S. A., Grisso, T., Gudjonsson, G. H., Leo, R. A., & Redlich, A. D. (2010). Police-induced confessions: Risk factors and recommendations. *Law and Human Behavior, 34*, 3–38. doi:10.1007/s10979-009-9188-6

Kassin, S. M., Kukucka, J., Lawson, V. Z., & DeCarlo, J. (2014). Does video recording alter the behavior of police during interrogation? A mock crime-and-investigation study. *Law and Human Behavior, 38*, 73–83. doi:10.1037/lhb0000047

Kassin, S. M., Kukucka, J., Lawson, V. Z., & DeCarlo, J. (2017). Police reports of mock suspect interrogations: A test of accuracy and perception. *Law and Human Behavior, 41*, 230–243. doi:10.1037/lhb0000225

Kassin, S. M., Meissner, C. A., & Norwick, R. J. (2005). "I'd know a false confession if I saw one": A comparative study of college students and police investigators. *Law and Human Behavior, 29*, 211–227. doi:10.1007/s10979-005-2416-9

Kassin, S. M., & Neumann, K. (1997). On the power of confession evidence: An experimental test of the fundamental difference hypothesis. *Law and Human Behavior, 21*, 469–484. doi:10.1023/a:1024871622490

Kassin, S. M., & Sukel, H. (1997). Coerced confessions and the jury: An experimental test of the "harmless error" rule. *Law and Human Behavior, 21*, 27–46. doi:10.1023/a:1024814009769

Lassiter, G. D. (2002). Illusory causation in the courtroom. *Current Directions in Psychological Science, 11*, 204–208. doi:10.1111/1467-8721.00201

Lassiter, G. D. (2010). Psychological science and sound public policy: Video recording custodial interrogations. *American Psychologist, 65*, 768–779. doi:10.1037/0003-066X.65.8.768

Lassiter, G. D., Diamond, S. S., Schmidt, H. C., & Elek, J. K. (2007). Evaluating videotaped confessions: Expertise provides no defense against the camera perspective effect. *Psychological Science, 18*, 224–226. doi:10.1111/j.1467-9280.2007.01879.x

Lassiter, G. D., Munhall, P. J., Berger, I. P., Weiland, P. E., Handley, I. M., & Geers, A. L. (2005). Attributional complexity and the camera perspective bias in videotaped confessions. *Basic and Applied Social Psychology, 27*, 27–35. doi:10.1207/s15324834basp2701_3

Lassiter, G. D., Ware, L. J., Lindberg, M. J., & Ratcliff, J. J. (2010). Videotaping custodial interrogations: Toward a scientifically based policy. In G. D. Lassiter & C. A. Meissner (Eds.), *Police interrogations and false confessions: Current research, practice, and policy recommendations* (pp. 143–160). Washington, DC: American Psychological Association.

Lassiter, G. D., Ware, L. J., Ratcliff, J. J., & Irvin, C. R. (2009). Evidence of the camera perspective bias in authentic videotaped interrogations: Implications for emerging reform in the criminal justice system. *Legal and Criminological Psychology, 14*, 157–170. doi:10.1348/135532508X284293

Leo, R. A. (2008). *Police interrogation and American justice*. Cambridge, MA: Harvard University Press.

Leo, R. A., & Liu, B. (2009). What do potential jurors know about police interrogation techniques and false confessions? *Behavioral Sciences & the Law, 27*, 381–399. doi:10.1002/bsl.872

Levine, T. R. (2014). Truth-default theory (TDT): A theory of human deception and deception detection. *Journal of Language and Social Psychology, 33*, 378–392. doi:10.1177/0261927X14535916

McArthur, L. Z. (1980). Illusory causation and illusory correlation: Two epistemological accounts. *Personality and Social Psychology Bulletin, 6*, 507–519. doi:10.1177/014616728064003

Mindthoff, A. & Blandón-Gitlin, I. (2015, March). *No confession expert? Closing statements are just as effective, not jury instructions.* Paper presented at the annual meeting of the American Psychology and Law Society, San Diego, CA.

Mnookin, J. L. (2014, July 13). Can jury believe what it sees? Videotaped confessions can be misleading. *The New York Times.* Retrieved from https://www.nytimes.com/2014/07/14/opinion/videotaped-confessions-can-be-misleading.html

Moffa, M. S., & Platania, J. (2007). Effects of expert testimony and interrogation tactics on perceptions of confessions. *Psychological Reports, 100*, 563–570. doi:10.2466/pr0.100.2.563-570

Moffa, M. S., & Platania, J. (2009). The differential importance of the evidence and the expert on perceptions of confessions. *Journal of Forensic Psychology Practice, 9*, 280–298. doi:10.1080/15228930902935719

Najdowski, C. J. (2011). Stereotype threat in criminal interrogations: Why innocent Black suspects are at risk for confessing falsely. *Psychology, Public Policy & Law, 17*, 562–591. doi:10.1037/a0023741

Najdowski, C. J., & Bottoms, B. L. (2012). Understanding jurors' judgments in cases involving juvenile defendants: Effects of confession evidence and intellectual disability. *Psychology, Public Policy & Law, 18*, 297–337. doi:10.1037/a0025786

Najdowski, C. J., Bottoms, B. L., & Goff, P. A. (2015). Stereotype threat and racial differences in citizens' experiences of police encounters. *Law and Human Behavior, 39*, 463–477. doi:10.1037/lhb0000140

Newman, E. J. (2017). Cognitive fluency and false memories. In R. Nash & J. Ost (Eds.), *False and distorted memories* (pp. 102–115). New York: Routledge.

Park, K., & Pyo, J. (2012). An explanation for camera perspective bias in voluntariness judgment for video-recorded confession: Suggestion of cognitive frame. *Law and Human Behavior, 36*, 184–194. doi:10.1037/H0093967

Pennington, N., & Hastie, R. (1993). The story model for juror decision-making. In R. Hastie (Ed.), *Inside the juror: The psychology of juror decision-making* (pp. 192–222). New York: Cambridge University Press.

People v. Thomas, 22 N.Y.3d 629, 8 N.E.3d 308, 985 N.Y.S.2d 193 (2014)

Penrod, S. D., & Cutler, B. L. (1989). Eyewitness expert testimony and jury decision making. *Law & Contemporary Problem, 52*, 43–83. doi:10.2307/1191907

Pickel, K. L., Warner, T. C., Miller, T. J., & Barnes, Z. T. (2013). Conceptualizing defendants as minorities leads mock jurors to make biased evaluations in retracted confession cases. *Psychology, Public Policy, and Law, 19*, 56–69. doi:10.1037/a0029308

Ratcliff, J.J., Lassiter, G. D., Jager, V. M., Lindberg, M. J., Elek, J. K., & Hasinski, A. E. (2010). The hidden consequences of racial salience in videotaped interrogations and confessions. *Psychology, Public Policy & Law, 16*, 200–218. doi:10.1037/a0018482

Ricciardi, L., & Demos, M. (Producers/Directors). (2015). *Making a murderer* [Motion Picture]. Scotts Valley, CA: Netflix.

Ross, L. D., & Nisbett, R. E. (1991). *The person and the situation: Perspectives of social psychology*. New York: McGraw-Hill.

Schmidle, N. (2014, July 28). Video: A confession of murder. *The New Yorker*. Retrieved from http://www.newyorker.com/news/news-desk/video-confession-murder

Simons, D. J. (2010). Monkeying around with the gorillas in our midst: Familiarity with an inattentional-blindness task does not improve the detection of unexpected events. *Perception, 1*, 3–6. doi:10.1068/i0386

Simons, D. J. (2014). Failures of awareness: The case of inattentional blindness. In R. Biswas-Diener & E. Diener (Eds.), *Noba textbook series: Psychology*. Champaign, IL: DEF Publishers. Retrieved from http://nobaproject.com/chapters/failures-of-awareness-the-case-of-inattentional-blindness

Steele, C. M., & Aronson, J. (1995). Stereotype threat and the intellectual test-performance of African-Americans. *Journal of Personality and Social Psychology, 69*, 797–811. doi:10.1037/0022-3514.69.5.797

Sullivan, T. P. (2005). Electronic recording of custodial interrogations: Everybody wins. *Journal of Criminal Law & Criminology, 95*, 1127–1144.

Sullivan, T. P. (2010). The wisdom of custodial recording. In G. D. Lassiter & C. A. Meissner (Eds.), *Police interrogations and false confessions: Current research, practice, and policy recommendations* (pp. 127–142). Washington, DC: American Psychological Association.

Vrij, A. (2008). *Detecting lies and deceit: Pitfalls and opportunities* (2nd ed.). New York: Wiley.

Wallace, D. B., & Kassin, S. M. (2012). Harmless error analysis: How do judges respond to confession errors? *Law and Human Behavior, 36,* 151–157. doi:10.1037/h0093975

Woestehoff, S. A., & Meissner, C. A. (2016). Juror sensitivity to false confession risk factors: Dispositional vs. situational attributions for a confession. *Law and Human Behavior, 40,* 564–579. doi:10.1037/lhb00000201

Woody, W. D., & Forrest, K. D. (2009). Effects of false-evidence ploys and expert testimony on jurors' verdicts, recommended sentences, and perceptions of confession evidence. *Behavioral Sciences & the Law, 27,* 333–360. doi:10.1002/bsl.865

Woody, W. D., Forrest, K. D., & Yendra, S. (2014). Comparing the effects of explicit and implicit false-evidence ploys on mock jurors' verdicts, sentencing recommendations, and perceptions of police interrogation. *Psychology, Crime & Law, 20,* 603–617. doi:10.1080/1068316X.2013.804922

# 11

## Neuroscience and Jury Decision-Making

*Shelby Hunter, N. J. Schweitzer,*
*and Jillian M. Ware*

In early 2000, a 40-year-old Virginia schoolteacher developed a new and un-controllable appetite for child pornography (see Gander, 2016). This man (un-named for privacy), pained and fully aware of the wrongness of his sudden desires, eventually succumbed to them. Following an arrest and conviction for child molestation, the man began complaining of various neurological symptoms. Shortly before his prison sentence was to start, the man was admitted to a hospital where magnetic resonance imaging (MRI) revealed a relatively large brain tumor in his orbitofrontal cortex (a full discussion of the medical aspects of this case can be found in Burns & Swerdlow, 2003). Upon removal of the tumor, most of the man's neurological symptoms, along with all inclinations toward young children, disappeared. Throughout subse-quent psychiatric supervision, psychological therapy, and group counseling, the man's pedophilia appeared to truly be "cured." Unfortunately, nearly a year after his surgery and treatment, it was discovered that the man's urges had returned, and he had begun secretly obtaining and hiding pornography. Fearing the man's pedophilia had never really subsided, his psychiatrists or-dered a new MRI of the man's brain. They discovered that the initial surgery had missed a small portion of the tumor which had then rapidly grown until again, influencing the man's sexual desires. A new surgery was performed excising the entirety of the tumor, and the man's desires again disappeared, never to return. This story captivated the public and hinted at exactly how much power the brain has to control our behavior. In the case of this teacher, the tumor was essentially faulted as the "true cause" of his behavior. But does the mere presence of a biological basis for wrongdoing absolve the wrongdoer?

At about the same time that the Virginia schoolteacher was having his tumor removed, Steven Northington was living on the streets of north Philadelphia (see Kelkar, 2016). He became involved with an extremely vi-olent drug ring and was eventually arrested and charged with numerous crimes, the most serious leading to a federal capital murder conviction. When the penalty phase of the trial began, Northington's lawyers presented something that is rapidly becoming commonplace: expert testimony arguing that Northington's brain was "defective"—that it did not function like a normal person's brain should. Accompanying this testimony was a set of brightly colored images of Northington's brain, showing what the expert witness described to the jury as brain damage. While none of the jurors specifically claimed to believe that Northington actually had brain damage, they unanimously spared his life.

So what is the actual impact of this kind of evidence on juries? In this chapter, we review the research on how this kind of neuroscientific evidence might be used by jurors when making their decisions about criminal defendants.[1] We begin with an overview of the issue and then look at how and when neuroscience enters the courtroom in the United States and other countries. Next, we review the broader work on how neuroscience-based information is used by the lay public, focusing on the sometimes contradictory findings about whether such information is overly and unduly persuasive. We then turn to the relatively young body of work on how jurors use (and potentially misuse) neuroscience evidence and again tackle a set of contradictory findings. Finally, we conclude with a discussion of the current limitations of neuroscience evidence and some suggestions for future research.

## Overview of the Issue

The use of neuroscientific evidence is gaining in popularity within criminal courts. The uses of such evidence vary across several contexts within criminal law, ranging from arguing competency, mental state, brain damage, and propensities for mental illness or violent behavior. Many scholars argue that the rapidly advancing technology that drives neuroscientific research can help to demonstrate the physical basis for certain impairments that until recently were classified as psychological in nature (Jones & Ginther, 2015). Yet, plenty of others caution against the use of such technology in criminal courts, claiming it may lack the relevant capabilities to address questions it claims to answer or have unfairly prejudicial effects on jurors (Brown & Murphy, 2010; Dumit, 1999; Jones, Buckholtz, Schall, & Marois, 2009; Weisberg, Keil, Goodstein, Rawson, & Gray, 2008).

One such technology—functional MRI (fMRI)—has been particularly controversial with respect to its use by the courts. fMRI allows for the measurement of brain activity using oxygenated blood flow changes in the brain when the subject is engaged in very specific tasks. As a general and very oversimplified explanation, fMRI can be described as indicating which regions of the brain are working, and for how long, during particular tasks (see Jones et al., 2009, for an overview). This type of imaging is seen as having more potential uses within criminal law than the classic structural brain scans such as MRI, computed axial tomography (CAT), or computed tomography (CT) scans because of its ability to look at short-term changes in brain activation. And, because fMRI is a fully noninvasive procedure (unlike positron-emission tomography [PET] or single photon emission computed tomography [SPECT], which involve injecting a radioactive tracer into the bloodstream), fMRI research can be conducted on a broader population, increasing its reliability and validity. Another advantage to fMRI is that it has better spatial and temporal resolution compared to other neuroimaging methods (Parry & Matthews, 2002), opening the possibility of identifying much subtler neurological patterns. As such, fMRI has been touted as being helpful in a wide variety of legal contexts, including detecting deception, determining mental status (e.g., competency, *mens rea*, legal insanity), declaring brain death, and diagnosing brain injuries—including the cause of a particular injury (Feigenson, 2006).

The promise of neuroscience to inform legal decisions has not gone unnoticed by legal scholars. A search of Lexis Nexis for law review articles containing the word *neuroscience* showed only 121 articles in the five-year period of 1996 through 2000, increasing to 317 from 2001 to 2005, then to 875 from 2006 to 2010, and finally 1,325 articles published between 2011 and 2015. This is over a 10-fold increase across the past 20 years. But is this massive attention warranted? How frequently are the courts actually using neuroscientific evidence?

## The Prevalence of Neuroscience Evidence in Criminal Trials

Despite anecdotal evidence that neuroscience/neuroimage-based evidence was increasing in popularity within legal proceedings, the precise frequency and nature of the use of these tools remained unknown until recently. Fortunately, a series of analyses detailed the systematic use of neuroscientific evidence in the United States (Denno, 2015; Farahany, 2016; Gaudet & Marchant, 2016), the Netherlands (de Kogel & Westgeest, 2015), Canada (Chandler, 2015), and England and Wales (Catley & Claydon, 2015), providing insight to how and when this type of evidence is used during criminal trials. The analyses were based on information from available criminal trial records. A case-coding method identified specific trials in which neuroscientific evidence was discussed by judges. The authors of four of these papers selected cases that included phrases such as *neuropsychological, neurological, brain, scan, fMRI, CAT, MRI, genetic*, or *DNA* and considered the inclusion of these phrases under the neuroscientific evidence umbrella (Catley & Claydon, 2015; Chandler, 2015; de Kogel & Westgeest, 2015; Farahany, 2016). Alternatively, Gaudet and Marchant limited their selection to cases specifically referring to neuroimaging (fMRI, PET, CAT, SPECT, etc.) that was actually presented as evidence during the trial, and Denno included cases that referred to both neuroimaging and nonimaging (i.e., psychological evaluations) evidence that parties either introduced or attempted to introduce at trial. The data from all of the analyses were gathered from primarily appellate court trial records in the United States and England and Wales, while the Netherlands and Canada had access to both first instance and appellate court cases. Because of the nature of the trial information available, the authors acknowledge that their samples may not be completely representative of the general use of neuroscientific evidence across all criminal trials—especially the analyses that cover the United States, England, and Wales. As Denno describes, the defense (as opposed to prosecution) introduces the vast majority of neurological evidence, and so neuroscience-involved cases that initially produced a successful result for the defendant would not be represented in a database of only appellate cases. Beyond this, Farahany and Catley and Claydon note that, even though a judicial opinion does not include a discussion of neuroscientific evidence, it is still possible that it was introduced in the trial. Taken together, this means that the estimates of the prevalence of neuroscientific evidence are likely to be conservative compared to the number of cases in which such evidence is actually used.

What was made clear across these analyses is a major upward trend in the use of neuroscientific evidence within the span of time the data was collected. Farahany (2016) noted that in the United States overall, 5% of all murder trials and 25% of all death penalty trials involved the use of some sort of neuroscientific evidence, and the amount of such evidence more than doubled from only 100 reported cases in 2005 to 250 in 2012. Catley and Claydon (2015) illustrated that neuroscientific evidence discussions also doubled in England and Wales from 2005 to 2012 and that 80% of appellate cases overall included discussion of such evidence. Similar trends were observed in the Netherlands and Canada (Chandler, 2015; de Kogel & Westgeest, 2015). Interestingly, Farahany reported that not only did the quantity of neuroscientific evidence discussion increase year by year in the United States, but the quality of the judge's reports of such evidence also improved, suggesting an augmented familiarity and knowledge of neuroscientific information in general. In this chapter we review these recent analyses, including an examination of the prevalence of specific types of neuroscientific evidence across samples drawn from the United States, the Netherlands, Canada, and England and Wales, common legal circumstances in which that evidence was presented, and case outcomes as a result of the inclusion of neuroscientific evidence.

## What Type of Evidence Is Being Used?

In the United States, Farahany (2016) reported the most frequently cited type of neuroscientific evidence was neuropsychological testing, appearing in 37% of cases, followed by brain scanning at 15%. Interestingly, in 40% of Farahany's US sample, there was no discussion of specific neuroscientific evidence found, even though in those cases the offender's defense was at least partially grounded in neuroscientific claims. Again, this may reflect instances in which judges did not discuss neuroscientific evidence despite the fact that it was presented during the trial. Findings from another US sample reveal an even greater prevalence of neuroimaging technology, noting that at least one type of imaging test was discussed in almost two-thirds of the sample (Denno, 2015). In contrast, in Canada the most common use of neuroscientific evidence was by far the diagnosis of impairments due to fetal alcohol syndrome disorder (40%), followed by neuropsychological testing and neuroimages only, constituting 24% and 5% of the sample, respectively (Chandler, 2015). Notably, despite the recent hype about the development of functional brain imaging technologies such as fMRI, there are almost no reports of such evidence being presented in the Canadian sample. In one US sample, only 15% of the neuroscientific evidence discussed included scanning, and only 2% of those cases involved fMRI, none of which were admitted as evidence because of issues of scientific credibility, reliability, or relevance (Farahany, 2016). The most common type of neuroimaging technology discussed in both the Farahany and Denno US samples was MRI (about 25% of both samples), followed by CAT scans (24%) and electroencephalogram (18% in Farahany, 2016, and 25% in Denno, 2015). Similar trends were observed in England and Wales, where while 24% of the sample included mention of neuroimaging, that discussion primarily involved structural scanning techniques, and none mentioned fMRI (Catley & Claydon, 2015).

## In What Type of Case Is the Evidence Used?

Of the entire US sample in Farahany's (2016) study, 40% represented capital punishment cases; the remainder represented other serious felonies, including murder (23%), drugs (13%), and assault charges (11%). Similarly, 66% of Denno's (2015) US cases involved capital punishment. Gaudet and Marchant (2016) note that the common occurrence of neuroscientific evidence in capital murder cases in the US samples can be attributed to the more lenient rules of admissibility in the sentencing phase of these trials—like that of Steven Northington—where the court is constitutionally obligated to hear any evidence that may be relevantly mitigating for the defendant. Similarly, in the Netherlands, England, and Wales, violent crimes (including murder and assault) were the most common circumstances in which this evidence was discussed (Catley & Claydon, 2015; de Kogel & Westgeest, 2015), while in Canada sexual assault was the most common (20%), followed by homicide (17%) and assault (15%; Chandler, 2015). The United States (Farahany, 2016), Canada (Chandler, 2015), and England and Wales (Catley & Claydon, 2015) all report sentencing as the most frequent phase in which neuroscientific data was used during the trials. Farahany reported that within her US sample of cases, nearly half included claims of ineffective assistance of counsel who failed to present the neuroevidence at the initial trial; Gaudet and Marchant reported 27% of their US sample cases involved ineffective assistance of counsel, while Denno reported this issue in 53% of their sample. Competency was among the lowest reported uses for neuroscience evidence in cases across the Netherlands, Canada, England, and Wales (Catley & Claydon, 2015; Chandler, 2015; de Kogel & Westgeest, 2015); however, 15% of the cases in the US sample involved challenging competency as the aim (Farahany, 2016).

## Case Outcomes

Across these analyses, appeals cases were somewhat more successful when they involved the use of neuroscientific evidence than when they did not. Focusing on the US sample, Farahany (2016) reported that for 23% of capital cases, there was an at least partially positive outcome, defined as a reversal, remand, or modification to some component of the trial court's decision in the defendant's favor. In general, the likelihood of such outcomes in capital appeals cases is about 19% overall, suggesting a slight improvement in the current sample. For noncapital cases, positive outcomes occurred in 20% of the sample, compared to an average success rate of about 10% in appeals cases overall. In regards to cases of ineffective assistance of counsel, Denno (2015) reported an outcome in the defendant's favor for about 30% of both capital and noncapital cases in which a claim was made about the counsel's misuse or non-use of neuroscience evidence. These comparisons suggest that the use of neuroscientific evidence may offer an improvement on the likelihood of a positive appeals outcome but even more so for noncapital than capital cases. Despite these indications of improved outcomes, it should be noted that it may not be the use of neuroscientific evidence that resulted in the cases' success; rather, the evidence might have provided insight to a biological issue possessed by the offender rendering him or her less legally culpable for the crime.

The evidence of a mitigating effect is weaker, however, when examining the specific use of neuroimagery: Gaudet and Marchant (2016) reported that for their US sample, in the majority of capital punishment appeals in which neuroimage evidence was presented, the defendant's death sentence was upheld. Further, challenging the exclusion of neuroimaging evidence during the initial trial yielded success only 10% of the time, and of the 97 cases challenging ineffective assistance of counsel because of a failure to pursue neurological testing, the defendant was successful in just two cases. Perhaps the discrepancy in the outcomes between the two US samples can be attributed to the use—or discussion—of more than one type of neuroscientific evidence in Farahany's (2016) sample. It is possible that, compared to neuroimaging alone, utilizing more than one type of neuroscientific evidence creates a more convincing argument for a mental or biological impairment and, hence, increases the likelihood of a positive outcome for offenders on appeal.

## Neuroscience Evidence and the Public

Given the marked rise in neuroscience-based evidence, legal scholars and practitioners were naturally concerned about how lay jurors might interpret such evidence, particularly when neuroimagery is involved. Given jurors' weaknesses when dealing with scientific evidence (Kovera, Russano, & McAuliff, 2002; Schweitzer & Saks, 2012), the host of issues that arise when jurors are presented with a powerful visual piece of evidence (Feigenson, 2010; see also Chapter 9 of this volume), and the fact that jurors assume the courts pre-vet scientific evidence (Schweitzer & Saks, 2009), scholars began to question whether the presentation of neuroscience and neuroimage evidence might be unduly persuasive and, therefore, potentially prejudicial. These questions brought about a flurry of empirical research on how both the lay public and jurors interact with and use neuroscience and neuroimage evidence in making judgments.

The first wave of research on the persuasive power of neuroscience stemmed from a concern that, at a basic science level, the results of neuroscience studies might be unduly persuasive and could mislead a public that is generally unfamiliar with the technology (Beck, 2010; Brown & Murphy, 2010; Dumit, 1999; Racine, Bar-Ilan, & Illes, 2005). Specifically, scholars warned that the press and the public may uncritically accept neuroscientific information as fact. For example, Racine et al. (2005) examined print media coverage of fMRI between 1991 and 2004 and found that articles about fMRI often did not provide any explanation of the capabilities of the technology, while only 23% of the articles discussed such challenges as the complexity of interpreting fMRI data and the limitations and validity of the technology. As a conveyor of new scientific knowledge to the public, flawed understanding and/or misrepresentations of the science in the media can contribute to a public that is misinformed about what neuroscience research can actually tell us about human cognition and behavior (for more on media misinformation effects on juror decision-making, see Chapter 7 of this volume).

But why the specific concern about neuroscience versus the myriad other scientific methods and technologies? There are several reasons why the public may find neuroscience information particularly persuasive. To begin, people are innately curious about and seek a greater understanding of human behavior, and neuroscience provides a means for achieving this understanding by seemingly providing a window into the cognitions and emotions that drive human behavior (Beck, 2010; Racine et al., 2005). Beck discussed several possible explanations for the appeal of fMRI research to the media and the public, one of which was that fMRI research provides a simple explanation that sounds both definitive and scientific, something that is often found only in the natural sciences and not the social sciences. Indeed, other authors have commented on the public's skepticism of psychological research (e.g., Brown & Murphy, 2010; Compton, 2010; Fernandez-Duque, Evans, Christian, & Hodges, 2015). Thus neuroscience information may be overly influential for nonexperts because it is a product of "hard science" and is seen as more "real" (and therefore more persuasive) than other methodologies used to study cognition and behavior, such as psychological testing (Brown & Murphy, 2010; Compton, 2010; Dumit, 2003). As people are often drawn to subjectively satisfying explanations without regard to their accuracy (Trout, 2002), explanations for behavior that are based on neuroscience may seem to intuitively make more sense than other types of explanations, promoting a potentially false sense of understanding.

The communication of neuroscience information to the public creates an opportunity for oversimplification and misinterpretation of neuroscientific findings. For example, Racine et al. (2005) often found "staggering leaps," or what the authors termed "neurofallacies," in their analysis of fMRI print media coverage (p. 161). Specifically, commentators have noted that laypeople assume that brain scans are akin to objective and definitive photographs of the brain (Brown & Murphy, 2010; Feigenson, 2006; Kulynych, 1997; Roskies, 2007, 2008). fMRI scans, for example, are presented as clear-cut, objective representations of neural activity, rather than the product of a series of subjective decisions and inferences made by the researcher(s) and the resulting extrapolation of statistical data that they are. A significant amount of background knowledge is required to interpret these images correctly, opening the door for misinterpretation and overestimation of how much explanatory value these images actually provide (Brown & Murphy, 2010; Dumit, 1999; McCabe & Castel, 2008; Pratt, 2005; Racine et al., 2005). fMRI images, for instance, do not reflect actual neural activity but rather the changes in blood flow that occur as a result of this activity, a correlation that is not yet precisely understood (Brown & Murphy, 2010; Dobbs, 2005; Feigenson, 2006; Roskies, 2007, 2008). Racine et al. dubbed this tendency to assume that brain research shows reality *neuro-realism*. Specifically, the authors stated that fMRI studies can make a phenomenon, like brain activity, seem uncritically real and objective despite the complexities associated with obtaining fMRI data.

Initial support for the idea that the public may be unduly persuaded by neuroscientific forms of information came from a widely cited study in which participants were asked to rate high- and low-quality explanations of psychological phenomena that either did or did not include neuroscience information (Weisberg et al., 2008). Importantly, the neuroscientific information did not add any explanatory value. The authors found that their lay participants—including a sample of students enrolled in a cognitive neuroscience course—rated the explanations that included neuroscience information as more satisfying than those without, even though the neuroscience information in question added no substantive value to the explanation. Further, this effect was strongest for the poor explanations, suggesting that the mere addition of scientific-sounding information can make explanations appear better than they would otherwise be judged to be.

Extending the work of Weisberg et al. (2008), McCabe and Castel (2008) also tested the persuasive influence of neuroscientific research, focusing specifically on neuroimages rather than neuroscience information in general. The authors found that participants rated both fictional and real summaries of cognitive neuroscience research as more convincing when the summaries included a brain image than if the summary included no image, a bar graph, or topographical map of brain activity, even though the bar graph and topographical map conveyed the same information as the brain scan. These results seemed to suggest that some property of a brain image leads people to overestimate the quality of the information the brain image is used to support, a result with direct implications for forms of legal evidence that rely on brain scans to support particular claims about a defendant.

The widespread publicity received by the studies of Weisberg et al. (2008) and McCabe and Castel (2008) led subsequent researchers to search for evidence corroborating the existence of a neuroimage bias. In one such study, Keehner, Mayberry, and Fischer (2011) presented participants with different types of brain images, finding that the more realistic, three-dimensional brain images resulted in the accompanying research description receiving higher credibility ratings. Additional support came from a study in which participants viewed neuroimaging findings as more credible when they were paired with a neuroimage compared to a bar graph or no image (Ikeda, Kitagami, Takahashi, Hattori, & Ito, 2013). Although participants rated their understanding of the findings as better when a neuroimage was present, the participants did not show any actual improvements in comprehension, supporting initial concerns in the literature that laypeople may overestimate the explanatory value of brain images.

Other scholars, however, called into question studies claiming to support a neuroimage bias. For example, Gruber and Dickerson (2012) did not find any special effect of fMRI images on readers' evaluations of a news article describing neuroscience research compared to other popular science visuals or no image. Several studies specifically designed to replicate McCabe and Castel's (2008) study were also largely unsuccessful. Michael, Newman, Vuorre, Cumming, and Garry (2013), for example, conducted a series of 10 experiments, including a meta-analysis of McCabe and Castel's original data, and concluded that the presence of a brain image had little influence on the extent to which participants agreed with the conclusion of a news article that summarized the results of a neuroimaging study. In a similar replication of McCabe and Castel's work, Hook and Farah (2013) tested whether different images influenced judgments of scientific research. Participants' ratings of both fictional research descriptions and real news articles were the same regardless of whether the information included an fMRI image, bar graph, or photograph (Hook & Farah, 2013). Schweitzer, Baker, and Risko (2013) also failed to replicate McCabe and Castel's results across a series of direct and conceptual replications of the original study, further finding that neuroimage effects could be elicited only in the second block of a mixed-factor design—when participants had seen all study conditions and therefore had a means of directly comparing a neuroimage to a non-neuroimage alternative (in this case, a bar graph depicting neural activity).

More recent research has been dedicated to resolving the debate between the early studies that found a neuroscience bias (e.g., McCabe & Castel, 2008; Weisberg et al., 2008) and the larger body of work that failed to replicate such a bias (Gruber & Dickerson, 2012; Hook & Farah, 2013; Michael et al., 2013; Schweitzer et al., 2013). For instance, Baker, Schweitzer, Risko, and Ware (2013) utilized eye-tracking technology to determine if people attend to neuroimages and other visual displays of neuroscience data (e.g., a bar graph conveying identical information) differently and, if so, whether these attentional patterns could explain the differential impact of neuroimages on judgments. Participants were presented with a case summary in which claims regarding the defendant's impaired brain activity were substantiated with either a brain image or a bar graph. After reading the case summary, participants were asked to render a verdict, as well as judgments of whether the defendant should be punished and his likelihood of recidivism. Although the authors found that participants attended to the neuroimages and bar graphs differently, these differences largely did not affect decisions. Participants who viewed the neuroimage did judge the defendant to be more likely to recidivate, but this effect was not explained by attentional differences between the neuroimages and bar graph. These results indicated that when the neuroimage bias is present, attentional factors are likely not the driving force.

Rhodes, Rodriguez, and Shah (2014) also sought to explain the process by which neuroscience information influences judgments of research findings. Similar to the Weisberg et al. (2008) study, participants read a news article that either did or did not contain irrelevant neuroscience information and then provided ratings of the quality of the article, the quality of the study, and how convincing they found the article to be. They found that the presence of neuroscience information influenced all of these judgments, even after controlling for prior beliefs as well as individual differences in scientific knowledge and thinking dispositions. Further, the news articles with neuroscience information tended to be longer than those without, but the influence of neuroscientific information persisted even after the authors controlled for the length of the news article, ruling out the alternative explanation that people simply prefer longer explanations (Fernandez-Duque et al., 2015; Kikas, 2003; Rhodes et al., 2014). The authors suggested a potential mechanism for the effect, finding that the presence of the neuroscience information made people believe that they had a better understanding of the phenomenon described in the news article, even though the information was irrelevant to the explanation. The authors concluded that the concrete nature of neuroscience explanations may provide an illusion of clarity and understanding, which in turn heightens the perceived value of neuroscience information and thereby interferes with people's ability to accurately evaluate scientific evidence.

In a subsequent replication and extension of the original Weisberg et al. (2008) study, Fernandez-Duque et al. (2015) also corroborated the notion that the presence of irrelevant neuroscience information made arguments more compelling and that this influence could not be attributed to the length of the explanation. Across four experiments, the authors found that participants rated good arguments as more compelling than bad ones but that the presence of neuroscience information increased the perceived quality of both types of explanations. Contrary to the results of McCabe and Castel (2008), Fernandez-Duque and colleagues found that the presence of a brain image did not add any value over and above the written neuroscience information. The authors also tested whether the observed effects would generalize to other types of scientific information but found that explanations were rated the most compelling when paired with neuroscience information rather than social science information or information from other "hard sciences." Fernandez-Duque et al. theorized that the allure of neuroscience information may thus be due not only to the perception that neuroscience is a "real" science but that neuroscience is the best field of "real" science for explaining psychological phenomena. In other words, "part of neuroscience's allure may be that it allows the neat, tidy attribution [of psychological phenomena] to one causal source: the brain" (p. 939), consistent with Weisberg et al.'s (2008) original theory that people find neuroscience information unduly persuasive because of a preference for simple, reductionist explanations.

In light of the evidence from Rhodes et al. (2014) and Fernandez-Duque et al. (2015), Weisberg, Taylor, and Hopkins (2015) extended Weisberg's original study (Weisberg et al., 2008) by investigating why people find explanations more satisfying when they contain irrelevant neuroscience information. Consistent with both Rhodes et al. and Fernandez-Duque et al. (2015), Weisberg et al. (2015) found that the length of the explanation was not responsible for the seductive effect of neuroscience information. The authors also found that the presence of neuroscience information interfered specifically with participants' abilities to identify bad explanations: Participants were better able to identify the good explanation when either both or neither the good and bad explanation contained neuroscience, but had more difficulty identifying the good explanation when only the bad explanation contained neuroscience information. Weisberg et al. (2015) also tested whether the appeal of neuroscience explanations can be attributed to the technical jargon included in the explanations. The authors compared participants' ratings of explanations that contained neuroscience jargon including technical terms for the brain scans used and specific areas of the brain, simple neuroscience language that referred to brain scans and neural processes, or no neuroscience information. Again, the authors found that explanations that contained neuroscience were rated as more satisfying than explanations without neuroscience information but that the type of neuroscience information (technical or simple) did not impact ratings. These results suggest that the addition of technical jargon is not necessary to produce the effect; any reference to neuroscience will do. The researchers thus concluded that the tendency of laypeople to uncritically accept neuroscience information manifests because neuroscience information "exerts a seductive effect on people's judgments" (Weisberg et al., 2015, p. 429), although the specific mechanism responsible for this property of neuroscience has yet to be isolated.

Finally, hoping to shed some light on the often contradictory findings on the persuasiveness of neuroscience, Scurich and Schniderman (2014) tested whether the influence of neuroscience information can be attributed to motivated reasoning, or the tendency to selectively credit or discredit information in accordance with pre-existing beliefs. The authors hypothesized that the influence of neuroscience information, rather than being a unidirectional persuasive force, depends on how the information corresponds to a person's beliefs about the issue for which it is offered as evidence. Participants read an article describing a fictitious experiment in which fMRI evidence was offered in support of a claim that the death penalty either is or is not an effective deterrent to crime and then answered a series of questions about the validity of the study. The authors found that participants who opposed the death penalty gave much higher credibility ratings to the neuroscience when the fictitious study found that the death penalty is not a deterrent than when it did not; the opposite pattern was true for participants who supported the death penalty. In other words, participants rated a study as sound and the neuroscience persuasive when the outcome of the study was consistent with their prior beliefs but rated the same neuroscience study negatively when the results were inconsistent with their beliefs. This finding was replicated in a second experiment that used a different social issue. Overall, these results supported the authors' hypothesis that the influence of neuroscience information is conditional rather than universal, suggesting that although neuroscience might be viewed as more "scientific" by laypeople, it does not play a different role than other forms of scientific evidence in shaping people's beliefs and informing issues of social policy.

## Neuroscience Evidence and Jurors

Much of the debate on neuroscience and jurors is founded on the broader body of work described earlier on neuroscience and the lay public. If neuroscientific information is found to be persuasive, prejudicial, confusing, or alluring to an ordinary citizen, then those same effects are likely to be found in the jury context. Nevertheless, a number of experiments over the past several years have sought to identify the impact of neuroscience evidence on various legal decision tasks. Gurley and Marcus (2008) conducted one of the early widely cited studies that examined the impact of neuroimage evidence on jurors. In their mock trial experiment involving an allegedly mentally ill defendant accused of murder, participants were significantly more likely to render a verdict of not guilty by reason of insanity (NGRI) when presented with both neuroimages and court-appointed expert testimony supporting a brain injury compared to either neuroimages or expert brain injury testimony alone. This study, along with those of McCabe and Castel (2008) and Weisberg et al. (2008), seemed to point to neuroimages being particularly and perhaps unduly persuasive to jurors, raising the possibility that they may be considered prejudicial and therefore inadmissible in certain contexts. This seemed to be confirmed by McCabe, Castel, and Rhodes (2011), who tested the effects of fMRI lie detection evidence on juror decision-making and found that, compared to the polygraph and thermal imaging evidence, guilty verdicts were significantly more likely when fMRI evidence was presented. However, when the scientific validity of the fMRI technique was questioned (as neuroimage-based lie detection is nowhere near reliable enough to admit as evidence), the effect of the neuroimage was nullified.

Despite these initial findings, as researchers began to explore the effects of neuroscience and neuroimagery further, a more complicated picture emerged. Schweitzer and colleagues (2011) conducted one of the first systematic examinations of the persuasive influence of neuroscience and neuroimagery on jurors. Across a series of four mock trial experiments, Schweitzer et al. examined how a progressively more "neuro" range of evidence—from a basic psychological assessment, to a neuropsychological assessment, to a neurological assessment, to a neuroimage-based assessment—influenced jurors to accept an argument that a defendant lacked the *mens rea* to be held fully accountable for his crime. Notably, these experiments were designed such that the specific influence of a neuroimage could be measured. Earlier researchers who found neuroimage effects also tended to include additional expert testimony that accompanied the image. Schweitzer et al. (2011), however, included a series of control conditions in which the entirety of the expert testimony was identical but for the image that accompanied it—either an actual fMRI (or in one case static MRI) image, or a graph depicting the results of that same scan. In all four experiments, Schweitzer et al. found that, while jurors were more heavily persuaded by neuroscientifically informed expert evidence over traditional psychological assessments, there was no added effect whatsoever associated with the inclusion of neuroimagery.

Building on those findings, Schweitzer and Saks (2011) used a similar paradigm to examine the influence of neuroimagery on jurors' willingness to render NGRI verdicts—a conceptual replication of Gurley and Marcus (2008). Across four different NGRI standards, Schweitzer and Saks again found that, while neuroscientifically informed evidence was more persuasive than traditional psychological assessments, there was no effect of neuroimagery on verdicts independent of the expert testimony that accompanied it. Interestingly, while no image effect was found, the mock jurors in the conditions that did not include a brain image rated brain scan images as the single most important piece of evidence that they would have liked to have seen.

Similarly, Greene and Cahill (2011) manipulated dangerousness ratings for a defendant diagnosed with psychosis and found no differences between neuropsychological and neuroimaging evidence on sentencing recommendations for defendants rated high in dangerousness, although mock jurors were less likely to hand down a death sentence if they received either type of neuroevidence as compared to when they did not. When the defendant was described as low in dangerousness, no differences were found across all types of evidence. Along with neuroimagery, Scurich and Appelbaum (2016) added genetic evidence as a means of inducing a biological explanation for wrongdoing. As with the earlier findings, the genetic and neuroimage evidence did not generally influence their participants' judgments.

In another study examining lie detection evidence, West, Lawson, and Grose-Fifer (2014) compared neuroscientific lie detection evidence either in the form of brain waves, a brain map, or no image to a behavioral lie detection method (i.e., the Reid technique) to explore any differences in participants' assigned verdicts. While the participants who were randomly assigned to be presented with neuroscientific evidence rated it more highly than participants who saw and rated behavioral evidence, there was no difference in the proportion of guilty verdicts rendered as a function of neuroscience evidence type, nor was there a difference in the ratings of confidence in the assigned verdicts.

Other researchers suggest that the specific type of brain abnormality drives the persuasive effects of neuroimaging, not the neuroimages themselves. Choe (2014) suggested that structural abnormalities are more causally determinative of deviant behavior than functional abnormalities and are more stable over time; therefore, the causal link is easier for jurors to determine. This leads to structural abnormalities revealed with neuroimages as being more persuasive to jurors and having a more mitigating effect on their punishment decisions. Deficits revealed by functional images, on the other hand, are viewed as more variable and less treatable and therefore their effects on punishment tend to be aggravating. In fact, in Choe's collection of US capital murder cases in which neuroimages were presented as evidence, all defendants who presented functional neuroimages received capital punishment.

## A Double-Edged Sword?

The initial concern over the potentially prejudicial impact of neuroimages waned as the published evidence seemed to point to a complete lack of neuroimage effects on jurors. It became clear that even if neuroimages held any sort of persuasive power, it was certainly not at the level that commentators had feared. At a purely applied level, it seemed that the question of a neuroimage bias on juror decision-making was settled. However, the way neuroimages are used in court is not the same way that, for example, a crime scene image or an x-ray of a broken arm is used. Neuroimages are not just a simple depiction of facts—there is considerable baggage attached. When Steven Northington's lawyers showed pictures of his brain to the jury, they argued that it "doesn't function like [a regular person's]" and that it was "broken" (Kelkar, 2016, para. 11). Implicit in this argument is the notion that all of human behavior—including the ability to know right from wrong and to control one's anger—is simply a product of neural activity (or lack thereof) in the brain. This is a profound notion, and one that has widely varying degrees of support from the public. After all, to some extent this argument would mean that humans lack truly free will. Over the past few years, researchers have continued to examine the implications of neuroscience evidence (and accompanying arguments) on judgments of criminals and wrongdoers with a focus on the impact of a biological understanding of mental disorders (and human nature in general) that is implicit to neuroscientific evidence.

A widely cited experiment created support for the idea that presentation of neuroscientific evidence is a double-edged sword in that the result of presenting neuroscientific evidence can be both mitigating and aggravating to responsibility attributions and punishment decisions. Aspinwall, Brown, and Tabery (2012) asked a sample of actual US trial judges to assign punishment for a hypothetical assault case involving a male offender who was diagnosed as psychopathic. In one condition, judges were presented with a biologically based explanation for the defendant's mental illness—a "biomechanism"—while another condition had no biological explanation. The study found that the number of judges who listed mitigating factors doubled when the biomechanism was present. Examples of commonly reported mitigating factors included mentioning that the defendant "was mentally ill and lacked control over his actions, and thus was less legally culpable" (p. 847) and the fact that just as some people are physically disabled, psychopaths may be morally disabled because of their neurological inability to feel empathy. The presence of the biomechanism also resulted in less punitive sentencing recommendations and reduced the extent to which psychopathy was rated by the judges as aggravating. However, although the number of mitigating factors listed increased, there was also a simultaneous increase in mentions of balancing or weighing aggravating and mitigating factors. For example, judges mentioned that although the defendant was severely mentally ill, the presence of a biological basis for his illness suggests that he is not likely to recover and is also likely to reoffend in the future. This balancing- or weighing-factors effect conveys the double-edged nature of presenting biologically based arguments for mentally ill offenders.

In a variation of the double-edged sword, other researchers have found that neuroimage and neuroscience evidence have conditional and sometimes paradoxical effects. For example, Saks, Schweitzer, Aharoni, and Kiehl (2014) examined the influence of neuroscientific and neuroimage evidence in the sentencing phase of a capital case and found that, for a hypothetical offender labeled as psychopathic, the addition of neuroimage evidence was seen as mitigating; however, that same evidence was seen by jurors as aggravating when the defendant was labeled as schizophrenic. And, as previously described, Scurich and Schniderman (2014) reported that participants found neuroscience credible and gave it favorable ratings only when it supported their pre-existing attitudes and were oppositional about neuroscience when it differed from their attitudes.

These perplexing research findings suggest that judgments of mentally ill wrongdoers vary depending on both the specific disorder afflicting the offender and the type of neuroscientific evidence presented as support for said affliction, leaving scholars admittedly unsure about how and when neuroscientific evidence conveys a double-edged nature. The presentation of a piece of evidence designed to reduce criminal intent by calling into question an offender's control over his or her actions also, by nature, challenges perceptions of *future* behavioral control. Although that argument may be immediately mitigating, jurors are also likely to question the likelihood of an individual to reoffend or pose a continuing risk to society. Therefore, jurors must simultaneously process and account for neuroscientific evidence that is both guilt reducing and imminently condemning, and, to reach a verdict decision, one must outweigh the other. The specific circumstances that allow one to weigh more heavily than the other may revolve around specific details about the crime or the jurors' own philosophical beliefs about free will and/ or punishment, but for now this distinction remains unclear. Unfortunately, this uncertainty means scholars cannot provide concrete recommendations for attorneys in regards to when presenting neuroscientific evidence as support for a client's mental illness is beneficial or detrimental in criminal law contexts. Because the unique components of each case vary to such a great extent, it is not possible to generalize the somewhat inconsistent results of the related research to general use of neuroscientific evidence.

Many are fearful that, based on previous research, evidence that may provide an opportunity to highlight an offender's future dangerousness is particularly salient to jurors and could result in harsher sentencing. However, in a study that analyzed trial information for over 500 US criminal cases that utilized neuroscientific information, Denno (2015) discussed the overhype of these concerns. Denno noted that in only 14 cases did the prosecution leverage the defense's neuroscientific evidence to allege future dangerousness. Furthermore, Denno pointed out that in 21% of the cases, juror instructions were provided to alleviate any concerns that the defendant would still pose a risk to society if not sentenced to death. In almost all capital punishment cases, the alternative to death is a sentence of life without parole, so sparing an offender's life because of a brain-based anomaly should not raise concerns about the safety of society. Denno also noted that rather than attorneys fearing for the potentially harmful consequences of presenting neuroscientific evidence, they should be more concerned about the consequences of omitting such evidence. In fact, by excluding neuroscientific evidence out of fear of raising concerns of future dangerousness, attorneys are likely subjecting themselves to a claim of ineffective assistance of counsel. In the sample analyzed by Denno, half were ineffective assistance of counsel claims based on misuse or non-use of neuroscience evidence (254 total), and those claims were granted in the defendant's favor about 30% of the time. Therefore, the legal duty of attorneys to present any possible mitigating evidence in their client's favor may outweigh the possibility of the double-edged effect of doing so. In sum, the analyses provided by Denno suggest that although mock juror research may sometimes portray the dark side of presenting neuroscientific evidence in criminal cases, actual trial information suggests the use of such evidence is generally mitigating and received by the courts as such.

## Critiques and Future Directions

Given the unclear effects of neuroimages on jurors, some scholars suggest that neuroimage evidence might simply be irrelevant. Vincent (2011) nicely explained several of the key limitations of neuroscientific evidence in criminal law contexts. Most centrally, no brain scan taken after an event can, with any degree of certainty, identify what a person's brain state was at some previous point in time (e.g., at the time a crime was committed). Vincent further described the very plastic nature of our brains and argued that just because a person lacks certain brain mechanisms, we should not injudiciously conclude that he lacks the related capacities for a specific behavior; those capacities may be implemented in the brain in a unique way that we might not expect. Vincent also noted that if a person caused his impairment or had knowledge of its existence, that impairment should not be an exculpating factor; rather that person may be more responsible for his wrongdoing because he should have avoided putting himself in that situation to begin with.

Similarly, Jones et al. (2009) implored practitioners and legal decision-makers to remember that "[t]here is no brain structure, or set of brain structures, that is specifically 'for' criminal or law-abiding behavior" and "[t]o say that brain features influence behavior relevant to crime does not mean that brain features can necessarily explain why certain individuals behaved criminally" (p. 5). The authors continued to note that fMRI images do not speak for themselves, despite their obvious looking, brightly colored display. They require careful and proper analysis from an expert, whose interpretation may or may not have any legal relevance to the crime or criminal behavior of the offender. Even if a certain neurological deficit is linked to criminal-type behaviors, such as a lack of empathy or aggression, that correlation does not imply a causal relationship between the impairment and the specific behavior elicited during a crime.

On the other hand, perhaps it is not the neurotechnology that is questionable but the guidelines that our legal system uses to attribute criminal responsibility. In many cases, legal responsibility is assumed if the alleged wrongdoer has rational capacity and is not acting under coercion. But Eggen and Laury (2012) questioned these conditions as our understanding of biological bases for disorders becomes clearer, and even posited that these conditions may need a slight revision. For example, the recently discovered MAOA gene may be a risk factor for psychopathy as it is linked to a lack of moral rationality and may diminish an individual's capacity for rational decision-making and, therefore, responsibility for a criminal act. This conversation is still far from being seriously considered because, although scientists are uncovering biological risk factors or correlates for certain behaviors, they currently lack the ability to apply this knowledge beyond group correlative data to determine casual relations that can be universally generalized to individuals (see, e.g., Faigman, Monahan, & Slobogin, 2014). Additionally, Morse (2016) argued that because of the heterogeneity of some neurological and psychological disorders, the behavioral rather than the neurological indications of such impairments should be relied upon as more clear indicators of whether an individual is capable of rational thought for legal purposes.

While there have been concerns about the capability of neuroscientific evidence to unduly persuade jurors in the offender's favor, the experimental data suggests its use does not result in dramatic conviction or sentencing changes. That is not to say that it has absolutely zero effect; rather the extant research shows a preference for neuroscience-based explanations of behavior on the part of jurors, but that preference does not seem to extend beyond that to neuro*imagery*. Further, the actual impact of the neuroscience information seems to be highly contextual, in some cases being perceived as mitigating while in other cases seen as aggravating. Unfortunately, at this time there is no clear theory or systematic explanation for these contradictory effects, leaving a gap that is waiting to be filled by future researchers. Complicating this, work on this topic needs to address multiple layers: the simple persuasive impact of the neuroscientific evidence, the philosophical and attributional consequence of framing behavior as biologically based, the conflicting attitudes that guide punishment decisions when a biological impairment is the underlying cause of criminal behavior (perhaps absolving some moral blame but also dehumanizing the wrongdoer), the ability of jurors to understand complex evidence, the ability to take an understanding of "typical" neurological function and make claims about individual defendants, and, at the broadest level, how laws and legal policy can better recognize the biological basis of behavior and deal with wrongdoers appropriately. There are many researchers tackling these issues and still others testing new ways that neuroscientific analyses can aid the legal system (e.g., predicting future dangerousness, deception detection, rehabilitation methods); yet the advance of medical or imaging technology is perhaps outpacing the ability of the legal system to keep up. This necessitates that psycholegal and legal scholars be aware of new neuroscience technologies and new applications of existing technologies, subject each to rigorous testing, and be skeptical of claims made by those pushing the technology to ensure that only quality science-based neuroevidence reaches jurors.

The analyses of actual cases in which neuroscientific evidence was presented showed that, while it may occasionally result in positive outcomes for the offender, the changes are largely minimal—meaning the mitigating effects they can produce may mean a small reduction in sentence length or incarceration at a mental health facility as opposed to a prison. And still these findings should be viewed with caution, as they are based on just a small fraction of the criminal trials that find their way to an appeal. While difficult to accomplish, a systematic analysis of trial court cases involving neuroscientific evidence would be a huge scholarly contribution and would help guide future empirical research.

Although the utility of neuroscience and neuroimaging might be overestimated in legal realms, the previously detailed analyses suggest that neuroscience's role in the courtroom is not likely to diminish anytime soon. Therefore, to properly incorporate its use within the legal system, collaboration of knowledge between scientists and law professionals is crucial. Attorneys should familiarize themselves with commonly utilized neuroscientific tests to understand their advantages and limitations as well as the appropriate circumstances in which they are used. This knowledge will not only aid in a better understanding of their clients but also an ability to more effectively convey neuroscientific findings to jurors.

## Note

1. It is worth noting that there is a more general body of work that could speak to the neuroscience *of* jury decision-making. While much of that work is still in its infancy and aimed at studying basic cognitive processes, there are several reviews that cover relevant portions of this literature (see, e.g., Rilling & Sanfey, 2011, on general social judgments; Greene, 2009, on moral judgment; and Buckholtz & Marois, 2012, for punishment and the enforcement of norms).

## References

Aspinwall, L. G., Brown, T. R., & Tabery, J. (2012). The double-edged sword: Does biomechanism increase or decrease judges' sentencing of psychopaths? *Science, 337*, 846–849. doi:10.1126/science.1219569

Baker, D. A., Schweitzer, N. J., Risko, E. F., & Ware, J. M. (2013). Visual attention and the neuroimage bias. *PLoS ONE, 8*, e74449. doi:10.1371/journal.pone.0074449

Beck, D. M. (2010). The appeal of the brain in the popular press. *Perspectives on Psychological Science, 5*, 762–766. doi:10.1177/1745691610388779

Brown, T., & Murphy, E. (2010). Through a scanner darkly: Functional neuroimaging as evidence of a criminal defendant's past mental states. *Stanford Law Review, 62*, 1119–1208. Retrieved from https://www.stanfordlawreview.org

Buckholtz, J. W., & Marois, R. (2012). The roots of modern justice: Cognitive and neural foundations of social norms and their enforcement. *Nature Neuroscience, 15*, 655–661. doi:10.1038/nn.3087

Burns, J. M., & Swerdlow, R. H. (2003). Right orbitofrontal tumor with pedophilia symptom and constructional apraxia sign. *Archives of Neurology, 60*, 437–440. Retrieved from http://jamanetwork.com/journals/jamaneurology

Catley, P., & Claydon, L. (2015). The use of neuroscientific evidence in the courtroom by those accused of criminal offenses in England and Wales. *Journal of Law and the Biosciences, 2*, 510–549. doi:10.1093/jlb/lsv025

Chandler, J. A. (2015). The use of neuroscientific evidence in Canadian criminal proceedings. *Journal of Law and the Biosciences, 2*, 550–579. doi:10.1093/jlb/lsv026

Choe, S. Y. (2014). Misdiagnosing the impact of neuroimages in the courtroom. *UCLA Law Review, 61*, 1502–1547. Retrieved from http://www.uclalawreview.org

Compton, E. S. (2010). Not guilty by reason of neuroimaging: The need for cautionary jury instructions for neuroscience evidence in criminal trials. *Vanderbilt Journal of Entertainment and Technology Law, 12*, 333–354.

de Kogel, C. H., & Westgeest, E. J. M. C. (2015). Neuroscientific and behavioral genetic information in criminal cases in the Netherlands. *Journal of Law and the Biosciences, 2*, 580–605. doi:10.1093/jlb/lsv024

Denno, D. W. (2015). The myth of the double-edged sword: An empirical study of neuroscience evidence in criminal cases. *Boston College Law Review, 56*, 493–551.

Dobbs, D. (2005). Fact or phrenology? *Scientific American Mind, 16*(1), 24–31. doi:10.1038/scientificamericanmind0405-24

Dumit, J. (1999). Objective brains, prejudicial images. *Science in Context, 12*, 173–201. doi:10.1017/S0269889700003355

Dumit, J. (2003). *Picturing personhood: Brain scans and biomedical identity.* Princeton, NJ: Princeton University Press.

Eggen, J. M., & Laury, E. J. (2012). Toward a neuroscience model of tort law: How functional neuroimaging will transform tort doctrine. *The Columbia Science & Technology Law Review, 13*, 235–306.

Faigman, D. L., Monahan, J., & Slobogin, C. (2014). Group to individual (G2i) inference in scientific expert testimony. *University of Chicago Law Review, 81*, 417–479.

Farahany, N. A. (2016). Neuroscience and behavioral genetics in US criminal law: An empirical analysis. *Journal of Law and the Biosciences, 2*, 485–509. doi:10.1093/jlb/lsv059

Feigenson, N. (2006). Brain imaging and courtroom evidence: On the admissibility and persuasiveness of fMRI. *International Journal of Law in Context, 2*, 233–255. doi:10.1017/S174455230600303X

Feigenson, N. (2010). Visual evidence. *Psychonomic Bulletin & Review, 17*, 149–154. doi:10.3758/PBR.17.2.149

Fernandez-Duque, D., Evans, J., Christian, C., & Hodges, S. D. (2015). Superfluous neuroscience information makes explanations of psychological phenomena more appealing. *Journal of Cognitive Neuroscience, 27*, 926–944. doi:10.1162/jocn_a_00750

Gander, K. (2016, February 24). The man whose brain tumour "turned him into a paedophile." *The Independent.* Retrieved from http://www.independent.co.uk/life-style/health-and-families/features/a-40-year-old-developed-an-obsession-with-child-pornography-then-doctors-discovered-why-a6893756.html

Gaudet, L. M., & Marchant, G. E. (2016). Under the radar: Neuroimaging evidence in the criminal courtroom. *Drake Law Review, 64*, 577–661.

Greene, E., & Cahill, B. S. (2011). Effects of neuroimaging evidence on mock juror decision- making. *Behavioral Sciences & the Law, 30*, 280–296. doi:10.1002/bsl

Greene, J. D. (2009). The cognitive neuroscience of moral judgment. In M. S. Gazzaniga (Ed.), *The cognitive neurosciences* (4th ed., pp. 987–999). New York: W. W. Norton.

Gruber, D., & Dickerson, J. A. (2012). Persuasive images in popular science: Testing judgments of scientific reasoning and credibility. *Public Understanding of Science, 21*, 938–948. doi:10.1177/0963662512454072

Gurley, J. R., & Marcus, D. K. (2008). The effects of neuroimaging and brain injury on insanity defenses. *Behavioral Sciences & the Law, 26*, 85–97. doi:10.1002/bsl.797

Hook, C. J., & Farah, M. J. (2013). Look again: Effects of brain images and mind-brain dualism on lay evaluations of research. *Journal of Cognitive Neuroscience, 25*, 1397–1405. doi:10.1162/jocn_a_00407

Ikeda, K., Kitagami, S., Takahashi, T., Hattori, Y., & Ito, Y. (2013). Neuroscientific information bias in metacomprehension: The effect of brain images on metacomprehension judgment of neuroscience research. *Psychonomic Bulletin & Review, 20*, 1357–1363. doi:10.3758/s13423-013-0457-5

Jones, O. D., & Ginther, M. (2015). Law and neuroscience. In *International encyclopedia of the social and behavioral sciences* (Vol. 13, pp. 489–496). Amsterdam, The Netherlands: Elsevier.

Jones, O. D., Buckholtz, J. W., Schall, J. D., & Marois, R. (2009). Brain imaging for legal thinkers: A guide for the perplexed. *Stanford Technology Law Review, 5*, 81–91.

Keehner, M., Mayberry, L., & Fischer, M. H. (2011). Different clues from different views: The role of image format in public perceptions of neuroimaging results. *Psychonomic Bulletin & Review, 18*, 422–428. doi:10.3758/s13423-010-0048-7

Kelkar, K. (2016, January 27). Can a brain scan uncover your morals? *The Guardian.* Retrieved from https://www.theguardian.com/science/2016/jan/17/can-a-brain-scan-uncover-your-morals

Kikas, E. (2003). University students' conceptions of different physical phenomena. *Journal of Adult Development, 10*, 139–150. doi:10.1023/A:1023410212892

Kovera, M. B., Russano, M. B., & McAuliff, B. D. (2002). Assessment of the commonsense psychology underlying Daubert: Legal decision makers' abilities to evaluate expert evidence in hostile work environment cases. *Psychology, Public Policy, and Law, 8*, 180–200. doi:10.1037/1076-8971.8.2.180

Kulynych, J. (1997). Psychiatric neuroimaging evidence: A high-tech crystal ball? *Stanford Law Review, 49*, 1249–1270. doi:10.2307/1229252

McCabe, D. P., & Castel, A. D. (2008). Seeing is believing: The effect of brain images on judgments of scientific reasoning. *Cognition, 107*, 343–352. doi:10.1016/j.cognition.2007.07.017

McCabe, D. P., Castel, A. D., & Rhodes, M. G. (2011). The influence of fMRI lie detection evidence on juror decision making. *Behavioral Sciences & the Law, 29*, 566–577. doi:10.1002/bsl.993

Michael, R. B., Newman, E. J., Vuorre, M., Cumming, G., & Garry, M. (2013). Of the (non)persuasive power of a brain image. *Psychonomic Bulletin & Review, 20*, 720–725. doi:10.3758/s13423-013-0391-6

Morse, S. J. (2016). Actions speak louder than images: The use of neuroscientific evidence in criminal cases. *Journal of Law and the Biosciences, 397*, 336–342. doi:10.1093/jlb/lsw025

Parry, A., & Matthews, P. M. (2002). Functional magnetic resonance imaging: A window into the brain. *Interdisciplinary Science Reviews, 27*, 50–60. doi:10.1179/030801802225002908

Pratt, B. (2005). "Soft" science in the courtroom?: The effects of admitting neuroimaging evidence into legal proceedings. *Penn Bioethics Journal, 1*(1), 1–3.

Racine, E., Bar-Ilan, O., & Illes, J. (2005). fMRI in the public eye. *Nature Reviews Neuroscience, 6*, 159–164. doi:10.1038/nrn1609

Rilling, J. K., & Sanfey, A. G. (2011). The neuroscience of social decision-making. *Annual Review of Psychology, 62*, 23–48. doi:10.1146/annurev.psych.121208.131647

Rhodes, R., Rodriguez, F., & Shah, P. (2014). Explaining the alluring influence of neuroscience information on scientific reasoning. *Journal of Experimental Psychology: Learning, Memory, and Cognition, 40*, 1432–1440. doi:10.1037/a0036844

Roskies, A. L. (2007). Are neuroimages like photographs of the brain? *Philosophy of Science, 74*, 860–872. doi:10.1086/525627

Roskies, A. L. (2008). Neuroimaging and inferential distance. *Neuroethics, 1*, 19–30. doi:10.1007/s12152-007-9003-3

Saks, M. J., Schweitzer, N. J., Aharoni, E., & Kiehl, K. A. (2014). The impact of neuroimages in the sentencing phase of capital trials. *Journal of Empirical Legal Studies, 11*, 105–131. doi:10.1111/jels.12036

Schweitzer, N. J., Baker, D. A., & Risko, E. F. (2013). Fooled by the brain: Re-examining the influence of neuroimages. *Cognition, 129*, 501–511. doi:10.1016/j.cognition.2013.08.009

Schweitzer, N. J., & Saks, M. J. (2009). The gatekeeper effect: The impact of judges' admissibility decisions on the persuasiveness of expert testimony. *Psychology, Public Policy, and Law, 15*, 1–18. doi:10.1037/a0015290

Schweitzer, N. J., & Saks, M. J. (2011). Neuroimage evidence and the insanity defense. *Behavioral Sciences & the Law, 29*, 592–607. doi:10.1002/bsl

Schweitzer, N. J., & Saks, M. J. (2012). Jurors and scientific causation: What don't they know, and what can be done about it? *Jurimetrics, 52*, 433–455.

Schweitzer, N. J., Saks, M. J., Murphy, E. R., Roskies, A. L., Sinnott-Armstrong, W., & Gaudet, L. M. (2011). Neuroimages as evidence in a mens rea defense: No impact. *Psychology, Public Policy, and Law, 17*, 357–393. doi:10.1037/a0023581

Scurich, N., & Appelbaum, P. (2016). The blunt-edged sword: Genetic explanations of misbehavior neither mitigate nor aggravate punishment. *Journal of Law and the Biosciences, 3*, 140–157. doi:10.1093/jlb/lsv053

Scurich, N., & Shniderman, A. (2014). The selective allure of neuroscientific explanations. *PLoS ONE, 9*, e107529. doi:10.1371/journal.pone.0107529

Trout, J. D. (2002). Scientific explanation and the sense of understanding. *Philosophy of Science, 69*, 212–233. doi:10.1086/341050

Vincent, N. A. (2011). Neuroimaging and responsibility assessments. *Neuroethics, 4*, 35–49. doi:10.1007/s12152-008-9030-8

Weisberg, D. S., Keil, F. C., Goodstein, J., Rawson, E., & Gray, J. R. (2008). The seductive allure of neuroscience explanations. *Journal of Cognitive Neuroscience, 20*, 470–477. doi:10.1162/jocn.2008.20040

Weisberg, D. S., Taylor, J. C. V., & Hopkins, E. (2015). Deconstructing the seductive allure of neuroscience explanations. *Judgment and Decision Making, 10*, 429–441.

West, M. L., Lawson, V. Z., & Grose-Fifer, J. (2014). The effect of electrophysiological neuroscientific deception detection evidence on juror judgments in a criminal trial. *Basic and Applied Social Psychology, 36*, 133–144. doi:10.1080/01973533.2014.881288

# PART III

EMOTION AND THE CONTEMPORARY JURY

# 12

## The Role of Emotion and Motivation in Jury Decision-Making

*Colin Holloway and Richard L. Wiener*

The adversarial system of US criminal trials gives rise to salient emotional experiences, which can have a profound, and unpredictable, impact on jurors' objectivity. Victim testimony, visceral images of crime scenes, desperate pleas by innocent defendants, and a battery of harangues, polemics, and orations from charismatic attorneys expose jurors to emotional experiences which can compromise their position as neutral fact finders. The history of American law celebrates great legal minds such as Clarence Darrow and Thurgood Marshall for their ability to craft groundbreaking arguments, but perhaps equally important to their success was the ability to make jurors feel emotions which generated empathy with the attorneys' positions and promoted agreement with their conclusions. Although attorneys and legal professionals intuitively understand the importance of eliciting feelings from jurors, the precise influence emotion has in a courtroom remains underappreciated. In this chapter, we discuss how the relations between emotion and judgment affect juror behavior by focusing on theory and empirical research which explain how emotional experiences direct the types of choices jurors make. We begin by arguing that the legal system's expectations of a rational juror are inconsistent with the reality of human decision-making and present years of research to support a nuanced understanding of the emotional juror. We then explore the mechanisms of emotion-guided decision-making—namely, affective forecasting, affect as feedback, affect as cognitive appraisal, immediate emotion, disgust-driven moral judgments, and emotion regulation—to show how each influences juror decisions.

During the course of our review, we outline the basic contours of each emotion mechanism, first considering the theory behind the approach, then reviewing relevant studies of juror or jury decision-making, and, finally, examining the way in which the emotional theory under consideration might have played out in the June 2017 high-profile sexual assault trial of comedian Bill Cosby, which ended in a mistrial due to juror deadlock. The first Cosby case serves as a useful summary because the circumstances gave opportunity for emotional reaction by jurors, and the facts were sufficiently ambiguous for jurors to justify voting for either conviction or acquittal. We will not discuss the April 2018 second trial, which featured more witness testimony against the defendant that made the facts less ambiguous and resulted in Cosby's conviction. Throughout the chapter, we apply the theories of emotion that we discuss to the June 2017 Cosby case in light of what we know about the functioning of human emotion as a motivational influence in judgment and decision-making.

## How Motivation Makes Jurors Susceptible to Emotion and Irrationality

In order to understand how juror decision-making is influenced by emotion and its close cousin motivation, we need to step back to the early 1990s when Kunda (1990) broke ranks from the social-cognitive revolution of the 1970s and 1980s by arguing that emotionally generated motivations drive all our efforts at problem-solving, judgment, and decision-making. After repeated attempts by social psychological researchers to reinterpret motivational effects and closely aligned emotional biases as a simple misfiring of our cognitive machinery, Kunda turned the world of social cognitive psychology on its ear when she maintained that even the unabashed efforts of lay people to test hypotheses objectively are directed toward a desired outcome by motivation and emotion.

Sometimes, motivations to arrive at specific outcomes involve emotional expectations, which cause decision-making to attain anticipated positive affect (i.e., to realize positive emotional forecasts) or avoid expected negative affect (i.e., to avoid negative emotional forecasts; Baumeister, Vohs, DeWall, & Zhang, 2007; Gilbert, Pinel, Wilson, Blumberg, & Wheatley, 1998; Wilson, Wheatley, Meyers, Gilbert, & Axsom, 2000). At other times, people use the emotion that they actually experience to direct their thought processes by alerting them to risks or providing feedback for the cognitive effort people apply when making decisions (Forgas, 1995; Forgas, Laham, & Vargas, 2005; Forgas & Tan, 2013; Huntsinger, Isbell, & Gore, 2014).

Emotional states may also affect unconscious processing and appraisal of new stimuli. While there are a number of different approaches to studying the relations between emotion and environmental appraisal (Lerner, Li, Valdesolo, & Kassam, 2015; Loewenstein Weber, Hsee, & Welch, 2001; Smith & Ellsworth, 1985; Tiedens & Linton, 2001), all appraisal theorists agree that specific emotions vary in attributes, such as certainty, control, and blameworthiness, which, as a result, activate different types of cognitive processing tendencies. The experience of emotions can be explicit (above awareness) or implicit (below awareness), both of which can influence, directly or indirectly, the way we view the world (Damasio, 1994; Huang, Chang, & Chen, 2011; Zajonc, 1980).

Perhaps the purest example of implicit emotions influencing social judgments is the way affective impulses serve as a guide to solve moral dilemmas. Haidt (2001, 2012) theorized that social judgments are immediate and driven by affect, notably disgust or anger, elicited in response to violations of recognized moral rules. Haidt (2001, 2012) argues that people first generate an emotion-directed social judgment and then consider external evidence to conduct a post hoc review through the lens of their initial impulse. The external evidence often justifies the intuitive judgment rather than triggering a critical analysis. Thus jurors faced with making decisions about violence, sexual abuse, and some forms of corruption might find that the conduct in question automatically activates feelings of disgust or anger, which, in turn, drive judgments of wrongdoing. This process could lead jurors to make verdict or sentencing decisions with a limited or biased review of the relevant facts (Georges, Wiener, & Keller, 2013; Haidt, 2001, 2012; Wiener, Georges, & Congas, 2014).

Finally, research on emotion regulation informs us of the need to manage affect by interrupting and redirecting the natural flow of distracting emotional reactions through deliberative or even unconscious thought (Koole, 2009). Although affect is a natural component of decision-making, people do not function optimally under conditions of extreme emotional excitement. As a result, decision-makers seek an emotional equilibrium in an effort to maintain, increase, or decrease the experience of emotions so they can effectively problem-solve and reach solutions to social conundrums (Gross, 1998; Koole, 2009). We argue that emotion regulation processes very likely influence juror decision-making. In fact, one of the indirect influences of judicial instructions is the activation of emotion regulation strategies.

As Kunda pointed out in 1990, all social judgments, including juror judgments, are the product of motivated thinking. Even in the purist form, the very act of attempting to gather objective information from memory and the environment to reach a decision results from a conscious or unconscious choice to pursue a goal. The central theme of this chapter is that the rational actor model—which posits that decision-makers (including jurors) objectively sample all relevant pieces of information, weigh the information according to its value for the outcome of the decision with the probability of each outcome occurring, and sum the pieces of information before selecting the best outcome—does not accurately reflect juror decision-making. We instead support the alternative proposition that jurors process information to reach goal-determined objectives. In the rest of this chapter, we explore the mechanisms of emotion-guided decision-making—namely, affective forecasting, affect as feedback, affect as cognitive appraisal, immediate emotion, disgust-driven moral judgments, and emotion regulation—to show how each influences juror decisions.

## The Mechanics of Emotion and Decision-Making

To develop the portrait of an emotional juror, in the following section we identify some basic mechanics of affective decision-making and then in the next section apply the theory developed here to a specific instance, the trial of Bill Cosby. Emotional responses to environmental stimuli can have differing effects on judgment and decision-making depending on the nature of the emotion-eliciting event and the type of emotion experienced. First, it is intuitively sensible that both specific emotional reactions and general mood states can impact decision-making, and emotion researchers have committed considerable energy to understanding how both types of experienced affect operate. Emotional states which arise from a specific instance or an eliciting event which is central to the decision at hand are *integral* emotions. They are immediate, visceral, and easy to trace. On the other hand, emotional feelings, or mood states which are more abstract and unrelated to the decision at hand, are *incidental* emotions (Loewenstein & Lerner, 2003). The effects of integral emotion on decisions show measurable influence in risk assessment decisions and social judgments (Gilbert et al., 1998; Haidt, 2001; Loewenstein et al., 2001). At the same time, a substantial body of research on incidental emotion has shown that lasting mood states or emotional residue from unrelated experiences can impact risk probability determinations, cognitive processing of future events, and economic decision choice (Forgas, 1995; Johnson & Tversky, 1983; Lerner & Keltner, 2000, 2001).

Some researchers have studied the effects of specific emotional experiences by looking at differences either between the valence (positive or negative) of the affect, while others have focused on the unique effect of specific emotions (Loewenstein & Lerner, 2003). That is, emotion and motivation research has examined the differential effects of opposite *valence* emotions (positive versus negative) with the tacit assumption that emotions of the same valence will have similar effects on decision-making. This approach garnered attention from researchers in early work studying the effect that positive or negative moods have on risk assessment (Forgas, 1995; Johnson & Tversky, 1983), and a number of researchers continue to focus on the effects of emotional valence, especially those who study anticipated or forecasted emotions (Gilbert et al., 1998; Wilson et al., 2000) and emotion as a cognitive feedback device (Clore & Huntsinger, 2009; Huntsinger & Clore, 2012). Perhaps ironically, jurors in a negatively valenced mood experiencing emotions such as dread, rage, sorrow, or frustration are more likely to process case facts deeply and follow the law than are those experiencing positive emotions such as joy, serenity, hope, or cheerfulness.

At the same time, a separate line of research suggests that unique emotional experiences differentially impact decision-making, even if they are of the same valence. Under this approach, two emotions of the same valence could have distinct influences on both immediate and future judgment and decision-making processes. For instance, angry and fearful decision-makers are expected to react differently to the same stimulus and subsequently appraise their environments differently and make different decisions (Lerner & Keltner, 2000, 2001; Smith & Ellsworth, 1985). The effect of a specific emotion depends upon where it falls on a map of appraisal patterns associated with six primary dimensions of cognitive thought: certainty, control, attentional activity, pleasantness, anticipated effort, and responsibility (Smith & Ellsworth, 1985). The cognitive dimension that an emotion activates will influence judgment and decision-making by determining the manner in which decision-makers appraise environmental stimuli, influencing which emotions arise from experienced events, and shaping how decision-makers process information (Smith & Ellsworth, 1985). For example, emotions high in either the certainty or control dimensions beget confident, heuristic decisions (i.e., those relying on mental shortcuts) while, conversely, ones low in certainty or control demand more careful processing before a choice is made (Lerner & Keltner, 2000; Smith & Ellsworth, 1985). Thus this appraisal is thought to ultimately direct choice behavior so that it aligns the unique emotional response generated by the event with the actor's motivational goals (Lerner & Keltner, 2000, 2001; Lerner et al., 2015; Smith & Ellsworth, 1985; Tiedens & Linton, 2001). Constitutional standards of the justice system require criminal jurors, who are called upon to make final decisions in high-stakes trials, to be certain in their verdicts and confident in the control they have over the outcome. Emotional responses which influence those two dimensions can have a significant influence on juror motivation and decision-making behavior, sometimes aiding jurors in their search for high confidence and sometimes hindering that search.

## The 2017 Trial of Bill Cosby

Understanding the differences between integral and incidental emotions and the specific manner in which an experienced emotion directs judgment can help shed light on the particular impact an emotional experience has on juror decision-making. Consider the high-profile sexual assault trial of comedian Bill Cosby. In June 2017, prosecutors brought 79-year-old Bill Cosby to trial for allegedly drugging and sexually assaulting now 44-year-old Andrea Constand during a 2004 encounter in the entertainer's Philadelphia-area home (Bowley, Perez-Pena, & Hurdle, 2017). During the course of the trial, attorneys introduced jurors to an array of police investigators and expert witnesses who discussed the available physical evidence but also presented highly emotional content. Some of the strongest emotional statements arose out of Constand's and her mother's testimony, as well as out of the attorney statements made during the opening and closing segments of the trial (Bowley et al., 2017). Following weeks of trial and more than four days of deliberations, jurors in the case notified the judge that they could not make a decision, and the proceedings ended in a mistrial due to a hung jury. Although the judge instructed jurors to avoid discussing their deliberations with the press, anonymous statements from members of the jury indicated that the impasse resulted because 2 of the 12 jurors refused to convict Cosby (Bowley & Wodzak, 2017). Although Cosby was convicted in a second trial in April 2018, this first trial presents an interesting opportunity to theorize about decision-making of deadlocked jurors.

There is no way to unpack the Cosby jurors' decision-making processes, but we can intelligently guess how emotional reactions to the evidence might have influenced juror decision-making based on research on emotion and decision-making. For example, the pretrial publicity surrounding the Cosby case was extensive and emotionally intense (for further discussion of the impact of pretrial publicity on juror decision-making, see Chapter 8 of this volume). Jurors likely felt both integral and incidental emotions, very likely negative in valence, before the trial began, which would have helped them attend deeply to the facts and arguments in the case. Adding to this affect was the disruption that the trial brought to the jurors' lives, likely resulting in incidental frustration and disappointment unrelated to the facts of the case (for a review of the impact of jury service on juror well-being, see Chapter 13 of this volume). Some of the jurors likely felt angry as the trial continued, perhaps increasingly angry as more and more facts came out, leading them to be both conviction prone and certain of their decision. Other jurors may have felt fearful, leading them to search more carefully and uncovering factors leading to more and more doubt. It is conceivable that the mistrial was at least in part the product of different jurors experiencing different integral and incidental emotions before and after deliberation.

## Cognitive-Emotional Experiences

Research on affective judgment and decision-making has demonstrated an interplay between emotional experiences and cognitive thought, suggesting low-level affective response and high-level cognitive experiences share a deeply intertwined relationship (Gilbert et al., 1998; Huntsinger & Clore, 2012; Loewenstein & Lerner, 2003). The reciprocal relations between feeling and thinking are most evident in theory and research on affective forecasting, affect as feedback, and appraisal tendency framework. All three of these theories suggest ways in which emotion influences highly cognitive tasks central to the function of jurors, including risk assessment, thinking style, and assessment of incoming information.

## Affective Forecasting

According to affective forecasting theory, which describes how anticipated emotions impact choice and decision-making, predictions about future emotional responses to outcomes guide behavior by encouraging decision-makers to approach outcomes associated with projected positive feelings while avoiding outcomes with projected negative feelings (Gilbert et al., 1998; Kermer, Driver-Linn, Wilson, & Gilbert, 2006; Wilson et al., 2000). In this sense, anticipating emotion is a highly cognitive enterprise, often involving conscious evaluation, which provides decision-makers with information about how they will feel when they experience outcomes in the future (Baumeister et al., 2007). Conscious emotional experiences influence future behavior by encouraging approach or avoid tendencies based on anticipated affective responses to potential outcomes of a decision. The premise that decision-makers rely on anticipated emotion in order to determine choice behavior is at the core of affective judgment and decision-making in economic, political, and legal scenarios (Baumeister et al., 2007; Gilbert et al., 1998; Wiener et al., 2014; Wilson et al., 2000).

Research on affective forecasting has demonstrated that people consistently make errors in overestimating their affective responses to future events (Gilbert et al., 1998; Kermer et al., 2006; Wilson & Gilbert, 2005; Wilson et al., 2000). Affective forecasting researchers have shown that decision-makers generally exaggerate emotional predictions by (a) overestimating both the duration and intensity of emotional experiences and (b) underestimating their own ability and others' ability to cope with and mitigate emotional reactions to outcomes (Gilbert et al., 1998; Kermer et al., 2006; Loewenstein & Lerner, 2003; Wilson et al., 2000).

Applying affective forecasting errors to risk-choice behavior, Kermer et al. (2006) found that asymmetrical evaluations of emotions associated with losses and gains distorts risk assessment because decision-makers exaggerate predicted negative feelings of potential losses, focus primarily on the risks of those losses, and subsequently engage in risk-averse behavior. Further, Kermer et al. found that despite predicting intense negative feelings when thinking about losses, decision-makers who actually suffer loss demonstrate a shift in cognitive focus after the outcome which inclines them to experience less intense emotion than anticipated. Thus decision-makers faced with uncertain choices which carry risk of loss fail to account for coping strategies and positive framing when they confront risky choice and consequently rely on distorted predictions of uncomfortable emotion to make risk-avoidant decisions. Research in affective forecasting and risk judgments carries important implications for criminal jurors because verdict and sentencing decisions are typically made under conditions of uncertainty about the facts of the case, the mindset of the defendant, and the ultimate questions of culpability and appropriate punishment.

Research on juror decision-making has made use of these errors in emotional forecasting by showing that capital jurors considering sentencing are prone to judgment errors that stem from exaggerating anticipated emotions (Wiener et al., 2014). Mock capital jurors reviewing the same fact pattern and charged with issuing a sentence to a convicted murderer recommended different punishments depending upon their anticipated affect. Those who anticipated feeling more positive emotions when they sentenced the defendant to death versus life were more likely to issue a death sentence, while those who anticipated feeling more positive about a life sentence issued the lighter punishment (Wiener et al., 2014). Perhaps most importantly, regardless of what sentence jurors issued, anticipated feelings of positive emotion fell short of actual experiences recorded after the sentence was handed out, which suggests that capital murder sentences—the highest penalty available in law—are vulnerable to affective forecasting errors, allowing inaccurate predictions of emotion to drive legal decision-making (Wiener et al., 2014). Given that a death sentence once carried out is beyond the possibility of appeal, research suggesting that emotion can influence death penalty judgments reflects disturbing deviations from the model of rational juror decision-making.

## Affect as Cognitive Feedback

Psychologists have also distinguished between two types of processing systems: one in which immediate affect and heuristic-level processes direct judgment and decision-making (System I processing) and the other in which reason and careful evaluation drives rational thinking (System II processing; Epstein, 1994; Finucane, Alhakami, Slovic, & Johnson, 2000; Kahneman, 2011; Slovic, Finucane, Peters, & MacGregor, 2004). The cognitive processing style determines how people review information (i.e., quickly and heuristically in System I versus slowly and deliberately in System II). Importantly, research evidence suggests that affect can direct which type of cognitive style decision-makers adopt. Clore and colleagues (Clore & Huntsinger, 2009; Huntsinger & Clore, 2012) argued that mood does more than provide simple information about the benign versus malevolent nature of the problem; it also acts as a feedback mechanism letting the decision-maker know whether he or she has adopted the right type of thought. Huntsinger, Isbell, and Clore (2014) refer to this process as affect as cognitive feedback. They have shown that positive mood serves as a green light indicating that the evaluator should maintain the current processing style, while negative mood serves as a red light signaling a switch in thought type is in order.

More generally, Huntsinger et al. (2014) assume that, in most situations, social judgment begins with the default System I thinking (i.e., top-down processing, stereotypical thinking) that relies heavily on pre-existing thought structures or stereotypes and as a result requires less cognitive effort. Decision-makers (including jurors) who use a System I judgment process will maintain that approach if the initial results yield a positive mood. As a result, these decision-makers will be most susceptible to the influence of their own stereotypes and prejudices when reviewing evidence or making verdict and sentencing decisions. However, if the initial results yield a negative mood (i.e., the red light), decision-makers will switch to a System II approach (i.e., bottom-up processing, deliberate and analytical thinking); that is, they will turn to piecemeal processing of individual facts to reach a conclusion, rely less on their own stereotypes, and ultimately show less prejudice in their evaluations. At the same time, those who use System II judgment to reach a conclusion will maintain that approach after positive mood inducement (i.e., a red light) and will show less prejudice against litigants but will switch to a System I approach if the initial results yield a negative mood, again showing more stereotypical prejudice. Application of the affect as cognitive feedback theory may explain why jurors in criminal trials show changes in evidence evaluation as the trial unfolds. For example, Georges et al. (2013) demonstrate that emotions are highly labile across the guilt and penalty phases of a capital murder trial. Research in this area of emotion and decision-making is in its infancy and has not yet connected a change from System I to System II processing to juror decisions; however, the results of the Georges et al. study suggest a possible connection between information processing, emotion, and, ultimately, juror choice.

## Appraisal Tendency Framework

Another effort to understand the manner in which emotions impact cognitive processing comes from Lerner and Keltner's (2000, 2001) appraisal tendency framework, a subcategory of cognitive appraisal theory which posits that the unique appraisals associated with each specific emotion lead to distinct judgment and decision-making processes. The unique cognitive appraisals elicited by each emotion in turn direct decision-makers to process current and future information in a manner consistent with the cognitive dimensions that align with the experienced affect (Lerner & Keltner, 2000, 2001). For example, the oppositely valenced emotions of anger and happiness, both high in certainty and control dimensions, trigger confident and swift judgments by invoking a heuristic evaluation of events that undervalues situational or external information. Thus decision-makers under these emotion conditions are more likely to take risks and express optimism for positive outcomes (Lerner & Keltner, 2000, 2001).

Relevant to a trial setting, on the one hand, anger may encourage heuristic processing rather than deliberate or analytical reasoning, which could lead to more severe appropriations of blame or fault because angry jurors perceive events to be under human control and are more likely to disregard or minimize situational factors which would mitigate culpability (Lerner et al., 2015; Tiedens & Linton, 2001). On the other hand, compared to anger, fear and sadness emotions are on opposite ends of the certainty and control spectrum and therefore typically result in more deliberate and cautious judgment, which leads jurors to be more likely to avoid risk and instead rationally evaluate relevant situational or external factors (Lerner & Keltner, 2000, 2001). Fearful and sad decision-makers tend to be less susceptible to heuristic cues and more likely to process information in systematic detail during a legal case (Lerner & Keltner, 2001; Semmler & Brewer, 2002; Tiedens & Linton, 2001).

As evidence that cognitive appraisal occurs in legal settings, research shows that discrete emotions uniquely impact juror decision-making. Semmler and Brewer (2002) demonstrated that sad mock jurors evaluating a criminal trial scenario were able to identify inconsistencies in witness statements with higher accuracy than were emotionally neutral jurors, suggesting the sad jurors engaged in a more thoughtful analytical evaluation process. Along similar lines, Ask and Pina (2011) had sad, angry, and emotionally neutral participants read a case vignette describing ambiguous evidence about a defendant's intent to commit embezzlement. Results showed that angry jurors stood out from others by perceiving a greater degree of intent, assigning more control in the situation to the defendant, and behaving more punitively toward him as a result. Most recently, Georges et al. (2013) found support for cognitive appraisal theory and the appraisal tendency framework by demonstrating that angry jurors are more likely than fearful or emotionally neutral jurors to engage in heuristic-level processing, downplay the value of situational or external information, and rely instead on intuitive judgments to make capital sentencing decisions in death penalty cases.

Given the available research evidence, it is not hard to imagine that specific emotions such as anger could play a critical role in criminal trials by directing immediate perceptions of evidence and altering the manner in which a juror processes information. Angry decision-makers are less likely than are sad, fearful, or emotionally neutral ones to engage in deliberate and systematic cognitive evaluation of relevant facts (Georges et al., 2013; Lerner & Keltner, 2001). Therefore, during a criminal trial, angry emotions could expose defendants facing serious charges to critical decision-making flaws that jurors may make by issuing guilty verdicts, or, indeed, invoking death sentences.

## Considering the Cognitive-Emotional Experiences of the Cosby Jurors

Next, to contextualize the three theories—affective forecasting, affect as feedback, and appraisal tendency framework—and research, we return to Bill Cosby's sexual assault trial. Research on anticipated affect suggests that the Cosby jurors likely developed emotional expectations of the consequence of their case decision. On the one hand, anticipated emotions could have directed them toward acquittal if they anticipated feeling badly about convicting a venerated American performer absent a clear "smoking gun" piece of physical evidence. On the other hand, anticipated emotion could have directed them toward conviction if they anticipated feeling badly about the alleged victim, who was clearly harmed by the incident, if they voted not guilty. These potential anticipated emotional experiences, which are integral to the ultimate decision, could have directly influenced jurors to support a verdict consistent with their motivation to either achieve or avoid an expected mood state. Further, we theorize that individual differences in emotional expectations among jurors could have led to distinct emotional expectations, which could explain how a group of 12 people who saw the same evidence and trial presentation produced two conflicting results, both so deeply entrenched in their verdict determinations that the judge was forced to declare a hung jury.

Turning to the affect as cognitive feedback model, the existing research suggests that most decision-makers default to the System I style of cognitive processing, relying on heuristics, biases, and other decision-making shortcuts to process information and assess its value (Huntsinger et al., 2014). However, it is also possible that when the judge instructs jurors to act rationally and objectively assess the facts, they actually begin the trial in the more deliberate System II processing style. This is a testable hypothesis that has not yet received experimental scrutiny. Whether starting in a System I or II headset, the jurors in the Cosby case began the proceedings processing information consistent with one style or the other, which the jurors' emotional responses to testimony would have either reinforced or refuted throughout the trial. For example, jurors who began the trial in a System II processing style due to the seriousness of the proceedings may have experienced negative emotions (sadness, fear, or even anger), which could theoretically have led them to abandon their deliberate processing in favor of heuristic shortcuts, which devalue the facts and information presented. Given the range of emotional experiences, it is likely the jurors altered their processing style more than one time in predictable directions producing the labile affect that Georges et al. (2013) found in their research. This roller coaster of emotion and processing style could not only have impacted evaluation of evidence or testimony, but also could have altered the way jurors processed information they received subsequently or how they coalesced their thoughts in preparation for the deliberations. The application of affect as feedback offers a promising model for future jury studies.

Finally, appraisal tendency research suggests that unique emotions may have had distinct influences on jurors throughout the Cosby case. Jurors who experienced angry reactions could have turned against either the prosecutors for unfairly attacking Cosby or the defendant for using his position to commit an act of sexual assault, and the resulting emotional experience could have led to biased evaluation of subsequent evidence and increased likelihood to be more or less punitive depending upon the focus of the anger. Conversely, jurors who experienced a low-certainty emotion such as sadness—a perfectly reasonable response to the Cosby case—could have been less inclined to express punitive judgment, and more inclined to deliberately and rationally process all the information in order to better understand a situation that triggers emotional uncertainty. Jurors who appraised case information differently likely formed opposing perspectives, leading to the failure for the jury as a whole to agree on a verdict.

## Emotion Independent of Cognition

Affective forecasting and to some extent cognitive appraisal relies on the conscious and deliberative role that emotion plays in judgment and decision-making. However, there is a substantial body of evidence which suggests that affect also can direct the way in which people make attributions of causality below awareness, outside of conscious thought (Epstein, 1994; Loewenstein et al., 2001; Schwarz & Clore, 1983; Zajonc, 1980). Early research on affect as information appeared in the 1980s when Zajonc (1980) deviated from traditional emotion theory by demonstrating that emotional responses to environmental stimuli can be immediate, subconscious, and independent of deliberation. Experimental studies showed that effortless affective reactions are unavoidable and not only direct behavior but also influence higher level thinking (Schwarz & Clore, 1983; Zajonc, 1980). For example, Schwarz and Clore showed that, unbeknownst to themselves, people reported higher life satisfaction on sunny days than on rainy days because they misattributed their good moods to their own lifestyles rather than to the weather that they experienced. However, when the researchers made people consciously aware of the weather, this effect diminished. Here people made judgments based upon information that they processed below the level of awareness. Seminal work on affect as information has demonstrated that decision-makers are clearly influenced by subconscious emotional experiences which operate independent of deliberative cognition and likely influence the types of risk assessment and moral judgment jurors make during criminal trials.

## Affect as Information in Risk Assessment

Theories which argue that affect can provide a direct source of information to decision-makers emphasize the importance of top-down System I thought (Epstein, 1994). The System I experiential mechanism directs decision-making without substantive review of environmental information and, instead, leads to judgment by activating emotional memory of past events, life experiences, cultural and moral schema, and deeply held stereotypes (Epstein, 1994). Consequently, the database informing System I thinking is slow to change, usually doing so only with repeated exposure to information which runs counter to established structure, or after an intense experience which calls long-standing belief into question (Epstein, 1994).

Relevant to our understanding of juror choice, judgments that manifest through the experiential route (System I processing) provide automatic emotional determinants on two separate but overlapping aspects of decision-making: risk assessment and moral social judgment (Epstein, 1994; Finucane et al., 2000; Haidt, 2001, 2012; Slovic et al., 2004). Finucane et al. highlighted the role of affective heuristics in risk choice by showing that emotion alters the manner by which decision-makers perceive the relations between risks and benefits. People in a positive mood may see few risks and great benefits as the likely outcome of their choices, while those in a negative mood perceive the opposite, both high risks and few benefits (Bateman, Dent, Peters, Slovic, & Starmer, 2007; Finucane et al., 2000; Keller, Siegrist, & Gutscher, 2006; Townsend, Spence, & Knowles, 2014). This is, of course, the opposite of ecological reality in which risks and benefits are positively related—high benefits usually come at the cost of high risks. Loewenstein et al. (2001) demonstrated that these feelings about risk can exist independent of cognition and influence risk behavior either without deliberative thought or through altering effortful cognitive assessment of choice options. Research on emotion and risk choice has shown that the System I mechanism, which relies heavily on affect heuristics and emotional responses, can act independent of deliberative cognition.

Although there is a gap in research connecting System I risk assessment models to legal decision-making, there are relevant parallels in research connecting affect to prejudicial discrimination which may ultimately influence juror decision-making. For instance, White Americans who experienced immediate angry or fearful responses to Black, Hispanic, or Arab targets demonstrated enhancement of implicitly held beliefs about threat to safety or property associated with these groups (Dasgupta, DeSteno, Williams, & Hunsinger, 2009). Other research has shown disgust responses to gay men exaggerate biased beliefs that the target is a threat to social or cultural institutions (Cottrell & Neuberg, 2005; Dasgupta et al., 2009). It is a small step from these findings to the expectation that criminal jurors who process information under a System I heuristic system could rely on pre-existing social and cultural stereotypes to unfairly evaluate minority defendants. While researchers have yet to show that immediate affect mediates or moderates these effects in jury decisions, a line of work that explores how such affect motivates decisions during trial could explain some of the racial and ethnic biases in punishment and sentencing that appear both in the jury making literature (Devine & Caughlin, 2014) and actual case outcomes (e.g., Daudistel, Hosch, Holmes, & Graves, 1999).

## Social and Moral Judgment

Immediate emotional responses impact social evaluation by manifesting as moral judgments arising from intuitively perceived violations of social and cultural norms (Haidt, 2001, 2003). Haidt (2001) challenged conventional

belief that moral judgments emerge out of reasoned and rational evaluation of circumstances by arguing that fast and nearly effortless detection of
cultural violations elicit emotions, especially anger and disgust, that direct
moral judgments with little or no conscious effort. Moral emotions contribute
to attributions of blame for perceived violations, increase perceived culpability for offender behavior, and increase assigned punishment as directly
related to the level of emotional intensity the decision-maker experiences in
response to the potential violation (Haidt, 2001, 2003; Hutcherson & Gross,
2011). Thus compliance with social norms elicits affective signals of approval,
while violations elicit disapproval that influences judgment and decision-
making without the benefit of deliberative cognitive processes (Haidt, 2001).
Relevant to legal decisions, in response to perceived violations of social and
legal norms, experiences of anger give rise to inclinations of retributive punishment while feelings of disgust lead to social ostracism of offenders (Haidt,
2003). Nuñez, Schweitzer, Chai, and Myers (2015) applied the intuitionist
concepts in a study of mock jurors in a capital murder trial and found that
emotional reactions to the case arising out of violations of intuitive moral
rules, most notably anger, strongly influenced jurors' conviction proneness
and predicted increased willingness to sentence offenders to death.

Moral anger and disgust jointly experienced can create feelings of
moral outrage, which have strong implications for attributions of blame and
assignments of punishment (Bastian, Denson, & Haslam, 2013; Salerno &
Peter-Hagene, 2013). For example, when mock jurors judged a variety of
crimes—white collar, violent, and child molestation—their reports of elevated levels of both anger and disgust were highly correlated (Bastian et al.,
2013). Furthermore, these combined emotions, in turn, predicted mock
jurors' feelings of moral outrage, offender dehumanization, and, ultimately,
perceptions that offenders were beyond rehabilitation so that they assigned
severe sentences (Bastian et al., 2013). Disgust and anger are both high in
certainty of blame attribution, and this research suggests that when they
combine, the resulting expression of moral outrage predicts certainty of guilt
(Bastian et al., 2013; Salerno & Peter-Hagene, 2013).

Given the effect that intuitive emotions have on moral judgments, the
use of graphic photographs and victim impact statements, two staples of
the American legal system, create opportunity for potentially flawed juror
decision-making. Subconscious affect emerging from perceived violations of
moral norms may bias jurors, triggering social judgments that deviate from
the facts at hand. Bright and Goodman-Delahunty (2006) showed that jurors
viewing gruesome photos, as compared to those who did not observe these
images, distorted the factual value of the evidence, expressed more feelings
of anger toward the defendant, and, consequently, were more likely to support guilty verdicts and harsher punishments. Salerno (2017) contributed
to this line of research by demonstrating that mock jurors who are exposed
to gruesome color photographs of crime scenes reported a greater likelihood of criminal conviction and less sensitivity to defense evidence than

jurors who saw either gruesome black and white or non-gruesome crime scene photographs. Importantly, the increased conviction rate was directly influenced by higher measures of disgust experienced by the mock juror participants (Salerno, 2017). Taken together these mock juror studies demonstrate that gruesome crime scene photographs elicit emotional responses that can influence how a juror perceives evidence, processes defense testimony, and, ultimately, renders a verdict.

Similarly, mock jurors exposed to victim impact statements in laboratory research are more punitive toward defendants, particularly when highly emotional statements elaborate the harm the victim experienced (Bandes & Salerno, 2014; Myers, Godwin, Latter, & Winstanley, 2004; Nadler & Rose, 2003). Mock jurors in death penalty cases exposed to an angry victim impact statement report less attention to mitigating evidence and are more likely to support death penalty sentences than those who witness a sad impact statement or no statement at all (Nuñez, Myers, Wilkowski, & Schweitzer, 2017). This line of research highlights the manner in which these particularly salient pieces of evidence serve as norm violation markers to influence juror emotions and decision-making. These groundbreaking studies underscore the importance of future work applying Haidt's (2001) social intuitionist model to empirically test the link between visceral testimony and moral norm violation. (See Bandes & Salerno, 2014, for a review of the existing literature in this area.)

## Considering the Noncognitive-Emotional Experiences of the Cosby Jurors

Based on affect as information and moral judgment research, we believe that, to the extent that ubiquitous use of emotion-laden evidence alters risk perceptions and triggers thoughtless moral judgments, the introduction of such evidence at trial violates constitutional principles of fairness at the core of criminal law. Consider again jurors in the Cosby case and how subconscious affect could alter perceptions about risks and benefits associated with a verdict choice. Jurors voting for acquittal risked the experience of negative affect post judgment and negative public scrutiny for their role in allowing a serious norm violation. On the other hand, a risk of conviction might have been that rich or famous personalities would become future targets of spurious assault claims. Emotional responses to norm violation images and testimony could have influenced verdicts without jurors deliberatively and objectively weighing the evidentiary value of the case facts. For example, a juror who heard graphic victim testimony might have visualized Cosby violating a sexual norm and, as a result, may have experienced intense feelings of anger toward the defendant. The experienced anger could have caused the juror to perceive inflated risks of acquittal (real or imagined), which could have affected his or her verdict decision either directly or indirectly by altering the perception of evidence yet to come.

Intuitive social judgment resulting from emotional responses to perceived violations of social and cultural norms likely played a significant role among the Cosby jurors too. Although courts vet jurors for conflicting personal beliefs which could influence verdicts, particularly in high-profile criminal trials, it is unlikely that every juror was able to set aside the emotional triggers of moral judgment during the trial. While the extensive voir dire process in the Cosby case may have eliminated jurors who would always either acquit a beloved celebrity or always convict a suspected sexual assault defendant, unavoidable nuances of moral judgment likely came into play. For example, a juror who believed he or she could objectively evaluate a sexual assault trial may not have been able to control the feelings that the alleged victim, Andrea Constand, triggered when she described her experiences in highly emotional tones. Such a juror might have been able to say that sexual assault allegations in general would not trigger a moral violation, but the emotional strength of Constand's testimony combined with other unforeseen situations (e.g., Cosby's reaction to the testimony, attorney arguments, or even the weather) could have resulted in allegations involving drugging and abuse of power initiating a perceived violation of a moral code. It is not unreasonable to speculate that a juror could have arrived at a guilty verdict upon emotionally reacting to a possible sexual norm violation and evaluating every subsequent piece of evidence with the goal of justifying a predetermined conclusion (i.e., guilt). Conversely, a juror might have experienced an emotional response to a prosecutor or other testifying witness which offended a moral code that strongly opposed perceived false accusation or celebrity witch hunts, compelling a provisional not-guilty verdict. That juror might have similarly distorted new information to support post hoc justification of a not-guilty verdict. Perhaps differential activation of moral code emotions contributed to the hung jury verdict. Moral emotions can play a substantial but potentially dangerous role in jury decision-making by depriving parties of the carefully reasoned and thoughtful decisions that justice warrants. Further research should specify the conditions which lead to violations of constitutional, moral, or normative expectations and, most importantly, identify tools that the courts can use to minimize the impact of immediate and biased moral judgments.

## Emotion Regulation and Social Judgments

It is clear that emotion, whether anticipated or experienced, can either directly or indirectly influence the risk assessment, social judgment, and evidentiary analysis decisions that jurors face. However, research in emotion regulation offers promising strategies for mitigating flaws introduced by affective processing. Emotion regulation refers to the processes by which people manage their own emotions and redirect the experience of affect (Koole, 2009). In general, people act to increase, maintain, or decrease the experience of positive and negative emotions; alter the type of emotions they feel; change the time at which the emotions peak; adjust the intensity of their experienced emotions; and modify how they express their emotions after they have experienced the affect (Gross, 1998). The ability to regulate both the type and intensity of experienced emotions carries important implications for social judgments, including those involving ethical and political considerations, criminal culpability, and sentencing decisions (Feinberg, Willer, Antonenko, & John, 2012; Gross, 1998; Halperin, Porat, Tamir, & Gross, 2013; Kligyte, Connelly, Thiel, & Devenport, 2013).

In general, the emotion regulation literature documents successful and unsuccessful approaches to regulate overwhelming (often negative) emotions to return the decision-maker to a state of homeostatic balance so that people can carefully decide on the best course of action and make objective social judgments (Gross, 1998). For example, cognitive reappraisal reflects the regulation of experienced emotion by reinterpreting the emotional meaning of a situation and altering the goals associated with the emotional response (Brockman, Ciarrochi, Parker, & Kashdan, 2016; Gross, 1998; Gross & John, 2003). It involves thinking about and redefining the nature of an emotion-invoking situation before the impact of the situation has fully affected the judgment of the experiencer, sometimes before reaching the point at which the emotion has its strongest impact. Cognitive reappraisal reduces the intensity of negative affect with few if any negative side effects, as opposed to suppression strategies, which increase stress and other forms of maladaptive behavior (Gross, 2002; Mauss, Cook, Cheng, & Gross, 2007). Suppression strategies are active attempts to inhibit the expression of experienced emotional behavior, which tend to be less effective than cognitive reappraisal in offsetting the influence of negative emotions (Gross & Levenson, 1993).

While the earlier work in emotion regulation focused on the adaptive and maladaptive influence of cognitive reappraisal and suppression, more recent work has examined the influence of emotion regulation techniques on social judgments. Indeed, Feinberg et al. (2012) found that cognitive reappraisal moderates the impact of emotionally driven intuition and increases the reliance on deliberation to reach moral judgments. Furthermore, Kligyte et al. (2013) showed that cognitive reappraisal, as compared to processing as usual, could limit the punitive influence of anger on ethical judgments by helping emotional decision-makers better consider the circumstances of wrongdoing and focus more systematic attention on case details. Cognitive reappraisal can support the use of System II, bottom-up thinking instead of System I, top-down thinking for the purpose of making social judgments. Cognitive reappraisal training minimizes the intensity of emotional experiences, causing decision-makers to be less influenced by affect and, consequently, less likely to impose negative social judgments for alleged violations of moral norms (Feinberg et al., 2012).

264 Emotion and the Contemporary Jury

Together, these studies implicate emotional regulation as a possible ameliorative tool to lessen the motivating impact of affect in jury decision-making. Consider again the hypothetical angry juror in the Cosby trial, who would have been likely to process information from the top down, finding evidence to support either a verdict driven by feelings of anger against the defendant or similar feelings arising out of perceptions of an unjustifiable "witch hunt" targeting people with celebrity status. Compare that to a juror who might have begun the trial with determination to follow the judge's instructions to carefully process all evidence using a System II, bottom-up approach only to become saddened or fearful after hearing the testimony of Andrea Constand, and then switched to a top-down approach and activated tenaciously held stereotypes that those who are accused of sexual assault are most likely guilty. Finally, consider a juror who might have become overwhelmed with feelings of disgust after the prosecutor's opening arguments emphasizing the importance of moral code violations in the actions of men of power who manipulate others to achieve their own desires. Could we expect any of these jurors to withhold a final decision until they have carefully weighed all the facts and applied the law of the case?

In this chapter, we offer many reasons to doubt an affirmative answer to that question. However, the psychology of emotion regulation suggests that there might be ways to rehabilitate jurors so overwhelmed by their emotions that they are incapable of objectively weighing the evidence. Perhaps training jurors to more effectively regulate their emotions before the trial begins with techniques such as cognitive reappraisal might offer such an approach. We believe that studying emotion regulation in conjunction with legal decision-making will open an exciting and promising area of research in law and psychology that could teach us a great deal about how emotions impact jury decision-making and, perhaps more importantly, lead to the development of techniques that help jurors overcome some of the more negative influences of anticipated and experienced affect in court. Perhaps if the Cosby jurors had been trained in the techniques of emotion regulation, their deliberations would not have resulted in a hung trial.

## Conclusion

The law expects jurors to be neutral fact finders who assess evidence, weigh attorney arguments, evaluate witness credibility, and, ultimately, render final verdicts and sentence decisions that are consistent with the evidence and law. Although it is presumed that this process will proceed rationally, research in social psychology demonstrates that all information processing is motivated (Kunda, 1990) and that emotion plays a significant role in directing that motivation when it comes into contact with legal judgments (Wiener, Borstein,

& Voss, 2006). To be sure, the law and courts try to constrain the discretion of jurors as they review evidence and make decisions, but, despite the law's best efforts, it is certain that the emotional lives of jurors influence, sometimes more and sometimes less, their ability to reach objective decisions. As we have discussed throughout this chapter, even jurors in the high-profile Cosby case, who were under a microscope with intense surveillance from judges, attorneys, and the public, may have departed from the highly rational decision-making expectations of the legal system and acted instead under the influence of their own emotional reactions.

We have made some progress in understanding how emotions guide and direct juror decision-making; however, there is much more unknown than known in this burgeoning area of social science research. Here we catalogue two stand-out issues that we think should become priorities for new generations of jury researchers. First, almost all of the studies of emotion have been at the level of juror research and not jury research. What happens when jurors come together to deliberate and reach verdicts? There are almost a limitless set of possible ways that emotion can influence jury rather than juror decision-making. To highlight just a few important possibilities to investigate, jurors may share the same emotion or they may experience different emotions, they may all forecast positive or negative emotional outcomes, or some may experience intense moral emotions such as anger or disgust. All of these outcomes and many more have important implications for group interactions and the outcomes of trials. For example, recent work on jury group dynamics by Salerno, Peter-Hagene, and Jay (2017) suggests that expressed anger can have a persuasive impact for White men who disagree with the group but an opposite effect when holdouts are Black or women. The interaction of experienced and anticipated emotions during jury deliberation across multiple jurors is an exciting area for research, complete with its own theoretical and methodological challenges.

Second, psychologists have devoted a great deal of time to studying incidental emotions but not integral emotions, largely because it is much easier to manipulate incidental emotions independent of case content than it is to manipulate integral emotion. However, our work has picked through much of the low-hanging fruit in this area already, so it is now time to develop theoretically interesting and methodologically rigorous techniques to study how the ebb and flow of emotion during trial can and likely does influence outcomes. Work by Bright and Goodman-Delahunty (2006) and Nuñez et al. (2017) on the emotional effect of victim impact statements and gruesome evidence along with the capital jury decision research by Georges et al. (2013) offer a promising start to developing paradigms and procedures for manipulating integral emotions in mock jury research. The approach of introducing emotion-eliciting events throughout the study which are directly connected to the decision participants are asked to make shows promise for securing research outcomes of integral emotion investigations, which truly may be the current plums in this area of work. Theoretical models including affective forecasting, affect as information, appraisal tendency, and emotion regulation are promising avenues to explore with this type of methodology. We think the study of integral emotion in jury decision-making is both an exciting and challenging arena to test our improved theoretical and methodological approaches to the science of jury decision-making, and we anticipate seeing a lot of new work in this important area.

We have come a long way from the 1970s when social psychologists seldom ventured outside their laboratories and accepted the challenge of showing how it was possible to explain all motivational nuisance effects as cognitive errors. The jury decision-making research literature has both contributed to the change in the general field of motivated social judgment and been the recipient of the successes of the "new" model of motivated cognition. It is no longer a radical idea to study emotion and motivation in social judgment; rather it is the accepted approach. We are excited to apply what we have learned in the study of emotion and motivation in social judgment to psychology and law in the 21st century, and we are especially excited to learn more about how emotion and motivation shape justice stemming from jurors' decisions in criminal cases.

## References

Ask, K., & Pina, A. (2011). On being angry and punitive: How anger alters perception of criminal intent. *Social Psychological and Personality Science, 2*, 494–499. doi:10.1177/1948550611398415

Bandes, S. A., & Salerno, J. M. (2014). Emotion, proof and prejudice: The cognitive science of gruesome photos and victim impact statements. *Arizona State Law Journal, 46*, 1003–1056.

Bastian, B., Denson, T. F., & Haslam, N. (2013). The roles of dehumanization and moral outrage in retributive justice. *PLoS One, 8*, 1–10. doi:10.1371/journal.pone.0061842

Bateman, I., Dent, S., Peters, E., Slovic, P., & Starmer, C. (2007). The affect heuristic and the attractiveness of simple gambles. *Journal of Behavioral Decision Making, 20*, 365–380. doi:10.1002/bdm.558

Baumeister, R. F., Vohs, K. D., Nathan DeWall, C., & Zhang, L. (2007). How emotion shapes behavior: Feedback, anticipation, and reflection, rather than direct causation. *Personality and Social Psychology Review, 11*, 167–203. doi:10.1177/1088868307301033

Bowley, G., Perez-Pena, R., & Hurdle, J (2017, June 17). Bill Cosby's sexual assault case ends in a mistrial. *The New York Times*. Retrieved from https://www.nytimes.com

Bowley, G., & Wodzak, S. (2017, June 30). What divided the Cosby jurors? Words, for one thing. *The New York Times*. Retrieved from https://www.nytimes.com

Bright, D. A., & Goodman-Delahunty, J. (2006). Gruesome evidence and emotion: Anger, blame, and jury decision-making. *Law and Human Behavior, 30*, 183–202. doi:10.1007/s10979-006-9027-y

Brockman, R., Ciarrochi, J., Parker, P., & Kashdan, T. (2016). Emotion regulation strategies in daily life: Mindfulness, cognitive reappraisal and emotion suppression. *Cognitive Behavior Therapy, 46,* 91–113. doi:10.1080/16506073.2016.1218926

Clore, G. L., & Huntsinger, J. R. (2009). How the object of affect guides its impact. *Emotion Review, 1,* 39–54. doi:10.1177/1754073908097185

Cottrell, C. A., & Neuberg, S. L. (2005). Different emotional reactions to different groups: A sociofunctional threat-based approach to "prejudice." *Journal of Personality and Social Psychology, 88,* 770–789. doi:10.1037/0022-3514.88.5.770

Damasio, A. R. (1994). *Descartes' error: Emotion, reason, and the human brain.* New York: Putnam.

Dasgupta, N., DeSteno, D., Williams, L. A., & Hunsinger, M. (2009). Fanning the flames of prejudice: The influence of specific incidental emotions on implicit prejudice. *Emotion, 9,* 585–591. doi:10.1037/a0015961

Daudistel, H. C., Hosch, H. M., Holmes, M. D., & Graves, J. B. (1999). Effects of defendant ethnicity on juries' dispositions of felony cases. *Journal of Applied Social Psychology, 29,* 317–336. doi:10.1111/j.1559-1816.1999.tb01389.x

Devine, D. J., & Caughlin, D. E. (2014). Do they matter? A meta-analytic investigation of individual characteristics and guilt judgments. *Psychology, Public Policy, and Law, 20,* 109–134. doi:10.1037/law0000006

Epstein, S. (1994). Integration of the cognitive and the psychodynamic unconscious. *American Psychologist, 49,* 709–724. doi:10.1037//0003-066X.49.8.709

Feinberg, M., Willer, R., Antonenko, O., & John, O. P. (2012). Liberating reason from the passions: Overriding intuitionist moral judgments through emotion reappraisal. *Psychological Science, 23,* 788–795. doi:10.1177/0956797611434747

Finucane, M. L., Alhakami, A., Slovic, P., & Johnson, S. M. (2000). The affect heuristic in judgments of risks and benefits. *Journal of Behavioral Decision Making, 13,* 1–17. doi:10.1002/(SICI)1099-0771(200001/03)13:1<1::AID-BDM333>3.0.CO;2-S

Forgas, J. P. (1995). Mood and judgment: The affect infusion model (AIM). *Psychological Bulletin, 117,* 39–66. doi:10.1037/0033-2909.117.1.39

Forgas, J. P., Laham, S.M., & Vargas, P.T. (2005). Mood effects on eyewitness memory: Affective influences on susceptibility to misinformation. *Journal of Experimental Social Psychology, 41,* 574–588. doi:10.1016/j.jesp.2004.11.005

Forgas, J. P., & Tan, H. B. (2013). Mood effects on selfishness versus fairness: Affective influences on social decisions in the ultimatum game. *Social Cognition, 31,* 504–517. doi:10.1521/soco_2012_1006

Georges, L. C., Wiener, R. L., & Keller, S. R. (2013). The angry juror: Sentencing decisions in first-degree murder. *Applied Cognitive Psychology, 27,* 156–166. doi:10.1002/acp.2880

Gilbert, D. T., Pinel, E. C., Wilson, T. D., Blumberg, S. J., & Wheatley, T. P. (1998). Immune neglect: A source of durability bias in affective forecasting. *Journal of Personality and Social Psychology, 75,* 617–638. doi:10.1037/0022-3514.75.3.617

Gross, J. J. (1998). Antecedent-and response-focused emotion regulation: Divergent consequences for experience, expression, and physiology. *Journal of Personality and Social Psychology, 74*, 224–237. doi:10.1037//0022-3514.74.1.224

Gross, J. J. (2002). Emotion regulation: Affective, cognitive, and social consequences. *Psychophysiology, 39*, 281–291. doi:10.1017/S0048577201393198

Gross, J. J., & John, O. P. (2003). Individual differences in two emotion regulation processes: Implications for affect, relationships, and well-being. *Journal of Personality and Social Psychology, 85*, 348–362. doi:10.1037/0022-3514.85.2.348

Gross, J. J., & Levenson, R. W. (1993). Emotional suppression: physiology, self-report, and expressive behavior. *Journal of Personality and Social Psychology, 64*, 970–986. doi:10.1037/0022-3514.64.6.970

Haidt, J. (2001). The emotional dog and its rational tail: A social intuitionist approach to moral judgment. *Psychological Review, 108*, 814–834. doi:10.1037/0033-295X.108.4.814

Haidt, J. (2003). The moral emotions. In R. J. Davidson, K. R. Scherer, & H. H. Goldsmith (Eds.), *Handbook of affective sciences* (pp. 852–870). Oxford: Oxford University Press.

Haidt, J. (2012). *The righteous mind: Why good people are divided by politics and religion.* New York: Pantheon.

Halperin, E., Porat, R., Tamir, M., & Gross, J. J. (2013). Can emotion regulation change political attitudes in intractable conflicts? From the laboratory to the field. *Psychological Science, 24*, 106–111. doi:10.1177/0956797612452572

Huang, S. L., Chang, Y. C., & Chen, Y. J. (2011). Task-irrelevant angry faces capture attention in visual search while modulated by resources. *Emotion, 11*, 544–552. doi:10.1037/a0022763

Huntsinger, J. R., & Clore, G. L. (2012). Emotion and social metacognition. In P. Briñol & K. DeMarree (Eds.), *Frontiers of social psychology: Social metacognition* (pp. 199–217). New York: Psychology Press.

Huntsinger, J. R., Isbell, L. M., & Clore, G. L. (2014). The affective control of thought: Malleable, not fixed. *Psychological Review, 121*, 600–618. doi:10.1037/a0037669

Hutcherson, C. A., & Gross, J. J. (2011). The moral emotions: A social-functionalist account of anger, disgust, and contempt. *Journal of Personality and Social Psychology, 100*, 719–737. doi:10.1037/a0022408

Johnson, E., & Tversky, A. (1983). Affect, generalization, and the perception of risk. *Journal of Personality and Social Psychology, 45*, 20–31. doi:10.1037/0022-3514.45.1.20

Kahneman, D. (2011). *Thinking, fast and slow.* New York: Farrar, Straus, and Giroux.

Keller, C., Siegrist, M., & Gutscher, H. (2006). The role of the affect and availability heuristics in risk communication. *Risk Analysis, 26*, 631–639. doi:10.1111/j.1539-6924.2006.00773.x

Kermer, D. A., Driver-Linn, E., Wilson, T. D., & Gilbert, D. T. (2006). Loss aversion is an affective forecasting error. *Psychological Science, 17*, 649–653. doi:10.1111/j.1467-9280.2006.01760.x

Kligyte, V., Connelly, S., Thiel, C., & Devenport, L. (2013). The influence of anger, fear, and emotion regulation on ethical decision making. *Human Performance, 26,* 297–326. doi:10.1080/08959285.2013.814655

Koole, S. L. (2009). The psychology of emotion regulation: An integrative review. *Cognition and Emotion, 23,* 4–41. doi:10.1080/02699930802619031

Kunda, Z. (1990). The case for motivated reasoning. *Psychology Bulletin, 108,* 480–498. doi:10.1037/0033-2909.108.3.480

Lerner, J. S., & Keltner, D. (2000). Beyond valence: Toward a model of emotion-specific influences on judgement and choice. *Cognition & Emotion, 14,* 473–493. doi:10.1080/026999300402763

Lerner, J. S., & Keltner, D. (2001). Fear, anger, and risk. *Journal of Personality and Social Psychology, 81,* 146–159. doi:10.1037/0022-3514.81.1.146

Lerner, J. S., Li, Y., Valdesolo, P., & Kassam, K. S. (2015). Emotion and decision making. *Annual Review of Psychology, 66,* 799–823. doi:10.1146/annurev-psych-010213-115043

Loewenstein, G., & Lerner, J. S. (2003). The role of affect in decision making. In R. J. Davidson, K. R. Scherer, & H. H. Goldsmith (Eds.), *Handbook of affective sciences* (pp. 619–642). New York: Oxford University Press.

Loewenstein, G., Weber, E., Hsee, C., & Welch, N. (2001). Risk as feelings. *Psychological Bulletin, 127,* 267–286. doi:10.1037/0033-2909.127.2.267

Mauss, I. B., Cook, C. L., Cheng, J. Y., & Gross, J. J. (2007). Individual differences in cognitive reappraisal: Experiential and physiological responses to an anger provocation. *International Journal of Psychophysiology, 66,* 116–124. doi:10.1016/j.ijpsycho.2007.03.017

Myers, B., Godwin, D., Latter, R., & Winstanley, S. (2004). Victim impact statements and mock juror sentencing. *American Journal of Forensic Psychology, 22,* 39–55.

Nadler, J., & Rose, M. R. (2003). Victim impact testimony and the psychology of punishment. *Cornell Law Review, 88,* 419–456. doi:10.2139/ssrn.377521

Nuñez, N., Myers, B., Wilkowski, B. M., & Schweitzer K. (2017). The impact of angry versus sad victim impact statements on mock jurors' sentencing decisions in a capital trial. *Criminal Justice and Behavior, 44,* 862–886. doi:10.1177/0093854816689809

Nuñez, N., Schweitzer, K., Chai, C. A., & Myers, B. (2015). Negative emotions felt during trial: The effect of fear, anger, and sadness on juror decision making. *Applied Cognitive Psychology, 29,* 200–209. doi:10.1002/acp.3094

Salerno, J. M. (2017). Seeing red: Disgust reactions to gruesome photographs in color (but not in black and white) increase convictions. *Psychology, Public Policy, and Law, 23,* 336–350. doi:10.1037/law0000122

Salerno, J. M., & Peter-Hagene, L. C. (2013). The interactive effect of anger and disgust on moral outrage and judgments. *Psychological Science, 24,* 2069–2078. doi:10.1177/0956797613486988

Salerno, J. M., Peter-Hagene, L. C., & Jay, A. C. (2017). Women and African Americans are less influential when they express anger during group decision making. *Group Processes & Intergroup Relations.* Advance online publication. doi:abs/10.1177/1368430217702967

Schwarz, N., & Clore, G. L. (1983). Mood, misattribution, and judgments of well-being: Informative and directive functions of affective states. *Journal of Personality and Social Psychology, 45,* 513–523. doi:10.1037/0022-3514.45.3.513

Semmler, C., & Brewer, N. (2002). Effects of mood and emotion on juror processing and judgments. *Behavioral Sciences & the Law, 20*, 423–436. doi:10.1002/bsl.502

Slovic, P., Finucane, M., Peters, E., & MacGregor, D. (2004). Risk as analysis and risk as feelings: Some thoughts about affect, reason, risk, and rationality. *Risk Analysis, 24*, 311–322. doi:10.1111/j.0272-4332.2004.00433.x

Smith, C. A., & Ellsworth, P. C. (1985). Patterns of cognitive appraisal in emotion. *Journal of Personality and Social Psychology, 48*, 813–838. doi:10.1037/0022-3514.48.4.813

Tiedens, L. Z., & Linton, S. (2001). Judgment under emotional certainty and uncertainty: The effects of specific emotions on information processing. *Journal of Personality and Social Psychology, 81*, 973–988. doi:10.1037/0022-3514.81.6.973

Townsend, E., Spence, A., & Knowles, S. (2014). Investigating the operation of the affect heuristic: Is it an associative construct? *Journal of Risk Research, 17*, 299–315. doi:10.1080/13669877.2013.808687

Wiener, R. L., Bornstein, B. H., & Voss, A. (2006). Emotion and the law: A framework for inquiry. *Law and Human Behavior, 30*, 231–248. doi:10.1007/s10979-006-9025-0

Wiener, R. L., Georges, L. C., & Cangas, J. (2014). Anticipated affect and sentencing decisions in capital murder. *Psychology, Public Policy, and Law, 20*, 263–280. doi:10.1037/law0000014

Wilson, T. D., & Gilbert, D. T. (2005). Affective forecasting: Knowing what to want. *Current Directions in Psychological Science, 14*, 131–134. doi:10.1111/j.0963-7214.2005.00355.x

Wilson, T. D., Wheatley, T., Meyers, J. M., Gilbert, D. T., & Axsom, D. (2000). Focalism: A source of durability bias in affective forecasting. *Journal of Personality and Social Psychology, 78*, 821–836. doi:10.1037/0022-3514.78.5.821

Zajonc, R. B. (1980). Feeling and thinking: Preferences need no inferences. *American Psychologist, 35*, 151–175. doi:10.1037/0003-066X.35.2.151

# 13

## How Does Jury Service Affect 21st-Century Jurors?

### A Call to Action for Researchers

*Sarah A. Trescher, Monica K. Miller, and Brian H. Bornstein*

Jurors play a critical role in the criminal justice system, as the Sixth Amendment guarantees the right of a jury trial in criminal matters. There is substantial research on factors that affect juror and jury decision-making, as these decisions have important consequences for those involved in the legal system (e.g., Devine, 2012). However, there is less research on how jury duty affects jurors' well-being (e.g., Miller & Bornstein, 2013).

The 21st century has ushered in unique challenges for the jury system which largely stem from advances in technology that include a surge in social media use (see Chapter 8 in this volume), cellphone cameras (see Chapter 9 in this volume), and advances in scientific evidence (see Chapter 11 in this volume). Technology can have positive effects on jurors; for instance, on-line check-in and Wi-Fi in the waiting room might make jury duty easier. However, technology can have negative effects on jurors as well. For instance, jurors in the 14-week trial of James Holmes viewed a 45-minute video and graphic photos of the 12 dead and 70 injured victims of the Aurora, Colorado, movie theater shooting (Wirthman, 2015). Such technology was not available in past decades; thus modern jurors' well-being is at greater risk now than ever.

As society experiences technological advances, the jury system needs to make adjustments to meet the needs of 21st-century jurors. Our purpose in this chapter is to review research on juror stress and well-being, with a focus on the influence of modern technology. A recent chapter on juror stress and well-being focused on general stressors of jury duty and ways to address such stress (Miller & Bornstein, 2013). Therefore, in this chapter, we focus more specifically on the stressors in heinous or high-profile criminal trials and how modern technology can both enhance and mitigate juror stress and well-being. Last, we issue a call for research on juror stress and well-being as it relates to technology.

## Juror Stress and Satisfaction: A Brief Review

Jurors face a number of stressors that affect their well-being. Research has indicated there are a number of causes of stress, a variety of symptoms resulting from stress, and a number of factors that affect jurors' general satisfaction with jury duty. Such research provides a foundation for understanding how 21st-century technology can cause or mitigate juror stress.

### Causes of Juror Stress

Most jurors report a positive experience after serving on a jury (Bornstein, Miller, Nemeth, Page, & Musil, 2005; Gastil, Deess, Weiser, & Simmons, 2010). However, many experience some level of stress related to jury duty, ranging from minor frustrations to symptoms that are associated with posttraumatic stress disorder (PTSD; for review, see Miller & Bornstein, 2013). These stressors can be categorized as relating to inconvenience, the trial process itself, and factors outside of trial and the legal process.

**Inconvenience.** One of the most commonly reported causes of stress is the ways in which jury duty is an inconvenient disruption of daily life (Gilg, 2014; National Center for State Courts [NCSC], 1998). Jury duty interrupts both personal and work schedules, for instance, requiring jurors to find alternate daycare for children or make adjustments to their work schedule (NCSC, 1998). Employers cannot penalize employees for missing work due to jury duty, but that does not help individuals who are self-employed or whose income is tied directly to their work activity. Even employees who are granted leave to serve on a jury might experience anxiety from unattended work and tasks piling up in their absence.

Other inconvenience factors include finding transportation, parking difficulties and expenses, navigating a strange neighborhood (Miller, 2008; Reed, 2009), long days in court (Gilg, 2014), and inadequate conditions in the courtroom (Miller, 2008). In rare cases involving sequestration, jurors must also endure being isolated from friends and family. For example, jurors in the 1995 O.J. Simpson murder trial were sequestered for 8.5 months. This isolation can be a significant source of stress (Antonio, 2008; Gilg, 2014).

**Trial factors.** Jury trials formally begin with the questioning process of voir dire, which, depending on the case, judge, and jurisdiction, can cover a highly variable array of topics. Jurors might experience discomfort or embarrassment when answering personal questions during voir dire (Miller, 2008; NCSC, 1998; see also Chapter 4 of this volume for a discussion of this issue with regard to sexual and gender identities). Not only can questioning prospective jurors about sensitive topics in open court be a source of anxiety, but insofar as some jurors might not be forthcoming in their responses, it can also compromise the effectiveness of jury selection and, ultimately, the fairness of the trial (Bornstein & Greene, 2017).

Once a person is selected as a juror, new stressors emerge, as the juror faces a difficult task that comes with much responsibility yet is given little training and sometimes confusing instructions (McGrath & Ryan, 2004). Not surprisingly, the length of the trial might exacerbate stress, as 96% report stress in trials lasting three weeks or more (Reed, 2009). During virtually any trial, jurors experience minor stressors associated with unpredictability, delays (McGrath & Ryan, 2004), and boredom (NCSC, 1998). The trial evidence and procedures themselves can also cause stress. For instance, stress or confusion might result from trying to understand complex or conflicting testimony and elaborate, complicated, or even arcane legal language (Gilg, 2014). Jurors might also experience stress related to disturbing physical evidence and graphic testimony from victims (Antonio, 2008). Not knowing the applicable law until the end of the case can also prompt stress (Cutler & Hughes, 2001).

Deliberations are often stressful for a variety of reasons (Miller & Bornstein, 2004). First, simply rendering a definitive verdict that carries real consequences—and knowing what that means for the defendant—is stressful for jurors (Bornstein et al., 2005). Second, jurors are typically given very little, if any, guidance on how to deliberate. They are sent to a room and told to come to an agreement, typically with no instructions on procedural matters like how to select a foreperson or structure their discussions (Devine, 2012). Deliberations also can be stressful when some members perceive that their fellow jurors are misremembering facts from the trial or deciding on emotions rather than facts (Bienen, 1993).

The decision rule (unanimity versus some sort of majority rule) is a third source of deliberation-related stress. Depending on the jurisdiction and severity of the crime, juries apply different decision rules, but both unanimous and nonunanimous decision rules can create stress. The process of coming to a unanimous verdict is stressful in that jurors holding a minority position often feel pressured to change their preferred verdict (NCSC, 1998); when unanimity is not required, those same jurors are often taken less seriously and, as a result, feel frustrated (Bornstein & Greene, 2017).

Fourth, regardless of decision rule, many jurors experience conflicts with other jurors during deliberation, which can become quite heated. For example, in the first sexual assault trial of Bill Cosby which ended in a mistrial, one juror told reporters that in the deliberation room jurors were raising their voices when speaking to each other, some were crying, and some were becoming increasingly stressed and frustrated as they could not come to an agreement (Allyn, 2017; for discussion of the role of emotion in jury decision-making in the Cosby trial, see Chapter 12 of this volume).

**Outside factors.** Finally, sources outside the trial can cause juror stress. Jurors tend to take their duties seriously, as they want to do right by their community, family, and coworkers (McGrath & Ryan, 2004). Thus they might experience regret or fear that they came to the wrong verdict (Miller, 2008). In high-profile cases, media presence can be a source of stress, as well as a risk to jurors' anonymity (Gilg, 2014). In some cases (e.g., mob- or gang-related trials), threats to anonymity could lead jurors to be concerned about their safety. For example, jurors occasionally report fear of reprisal from the defendant or the defendant's friends or family (Antonio, 2008). In the 1992 criminal trial disputing whether Rodney King had been the victim of police brutality, jurors feared being targeted by protesters; one even reported receiving a bomb threat from someone who disagreed with the verdict (Miller, 2008). These concerns can persist even after the trial is over (Murphy, Hannaford, Loveland, & Munsterman, 1998). For example, several jurors from the James Holmes case have reported experiencing a lot of the public's anger over their verdict (life imprisonment rather than the death penalty) through social media. The jurors' names in the Holmes case were never made public, but one juror said she cut her hair because she was still afraid a victim from the trial might recognize her in public (Associated Press, 2016).

In high-profile trials, reporters might show up at a juror's home at any time of day or night; neighbors might threaten or shun jurors; and businesses might retaliate for an objectionable verdict (Johnson, 2015). In a recent case in England, jurors experienced many stressful incidents during the trial: People tried to bribe jurors with money to render a not-guilty verdict, jurors were filmed with a recording device by a person in a passing car, and someone pulled the fire alarm to evacuate the building (Sabur, 2017). As a result, the judge dismissed the jury and announced that he would decide the case himself. Although still uncommon, the use of anonymous criminal juries has increased (Liptak, 2002), such that the names of jurors are withheld, even sometimes from the defendant, to protect jurors' identities (Johnson, 2015). This suggests that protecting jurors is a concern among courts (Liptak, 2002).

## Symptoms of Juror Stress

Symptoms of stress vary among jurors (Miller & Bornstein, 2013), but, in the majority of cases, they are relatively minor. Even so, longer and more stressful trials can bring about substantial symptoms similar to PTSD or clinical depression (Graveland, 2017). Jurors can sometimes experience secondary traumatic stress, which refers to symptoms that arise out of exposure to another person's stress (Robertson, Davies, & Nettleingham, 2009). Hearing about a victim's experience can lead jurors to experience similar stress symptoms as the victims themselves.

"Stress" is difficult to define, as it could refer to mere annoyances and frustrations or serious depression or anxiety (Miller & Bornstein, 2013). Symptoms differ from one juror to the next, as what bothers one person might not bother another. Jurors report general anxiety, anger, guilt (McGrath & Ryan, 2004), nervousness, irritability, and a tendency to continue thinking about the trial after it is concluded (Miller & Bornstein, 2013). Jurors also report experiencing mood changes (especially mild depressive symptoms), loneliness, and detachment from family, friends, and colleagues (Miller &

Bornstein, 2013). Physical symptoms include nausea and headaches (McGrath & Ryan, 2004); flashbacks related to the trial (McGrath & Ryan, 2004); weight loss; and insomnia or other sleep disturbances, such as nightmares (Miller, 2008). Jurors also occasionally use alcohol, tobacco, or prescription drugs to cope with stress related to trial (Antonio, 2008).

Whereas some jurors experience symptoms of stress immediately, many have a delayed onset and only begin to experience stress months later (McGrath & Ryan, 2004). Each juror's experience is different, and although most jurors experience only temporary and mild stress, there is potential for more serious effects. In addition, severe symptoms during trial could interfere with jurors' ability to carry out their assigned duties, leading to unjust outcomes. As such, many courts have adopted procedures to help reduce these symptoms (for reviews, see Bornstein et al., 2005; Miller & Bornstein, 2004).

### Juror Satisfaction

Because jurors are an important part of the justice system—and participating because they were "summoned" and not by choice—judges are understandably, and rightfully, concerned about making jury duty as satisfying an experience as possible. Generally, jurors report being pleased with their service: they are proud of having served, consider it a good use of their time, and indicate a willingness to serve again (Bornstein & Greene, 2017; Bornstein et al., 2005; Chomos et al., 2011). Strategies to help jurors cope with stress and feel more satisfied with their experience can occur before, during, and after the trial, as we review next.

**Pretrial strategies.** Pretrial contacts from the court can begin to acclimate jurors to the court and trial process. Jurors can receive information by mail or email prior to their reporting date. Such programs inform jurors as to where to park, what to wear, where to report for duty, and where to go for lunch (Chomos et al., 2011). Such steps potentially relieve some of the inconvenience and more mundane stressors jurors experience related to jury duty. Juror orientation programs that begin once jurors arrive at court can provide some of the same information, while also familiarizing jurors with the various personnel and their roles (e.g., what the bailiff does), the structure of the trial and nature of their task, their rights and responsibilities, expectations about their conduct, and so on (Miller & Bornstein, 2004, 2013).

**Strategies during trial.** As noted previously, jurors often report being uncomfortable answering personal questions in front of others, sometimes giving incorrect answers or not answering at all, which can be detrimental to the trial process. Some judges have incorporated pretrial juror questionnaires or individual voir dire as a way of circumventing problems associated with jurors' reluctance to disclose sensitive information in open court (Chomos et al., 2011). Although relatively few judges employ these practices (Mize & Hannaford-Agor, 2008), they have considerable potential to both make jurors feel more comfortable and improve the quality of information elicited from jurors (e.g., Hans & Jehle, 2003).

Also, jurors can answer questions better if they know more about the case, which can be accomplished by having attorneys give mini-opening statements during voir dire (Bornstein & Greene, 2017). In addition to helping with the selection process, these case summaries can be used to inoculate jurors against upcoming features of the trial likely to create stress (e.g., graphic evidence). Judges can likewise warn jurors of any disturbing evidence or imagery that might come up during the trial (Antonio, 2008; Gilg, 2014).

Once the jury has been seated and jurors are faced with oral arguments, evidence, and judge's instructions, additional stressors can arise. Jurors might have difficulty understanding complex and competing testimony, especially from expert witnesses who often use difficult scientific terminology or jargon specific to their area of expertise. For this reason, allowing jurors both to take notes and submit questions to these witnesses has proven effective in increasing jurors' subjective sense of clarity and satisfaction (Bornstein & Greene, 2017; Chomos et al., 2011). Allowing jurors to take notes can also help jurors retain the great amount of information presented, particularly during a trial lasting many weeks or months.

Legal language also can be very difficult for jurors to understand because it often contains double negatives, esoteric terms, and complicated grammatical structure. Thus presenting instructions in simpler English can improve understanding in many cases (Alvarez, Miller, & Bornstein, 2016). Instructions on how to deliberate can also help jurors (Dann, Hans, & Kaye, 2004). Finally, jurors sometimes want to discuss the case facts during the trial instead of having to wait until the end of the trial. Jurors perceive predeliberation discussion—which many of them engage in whether they are supposed to or not—as helpful, especially in terms of improving their understanding of the evidence (Diamond, Vidmar, Rose, Ellis, & Murphy, 2003). Jurors who are not allowed to discuss the evidence prior to deliberation wish that they could (Hans, Hannaford, & Munsterman, 1999).

**Posttrial strategies.** After the trial, debriefing sessions led by either a judge or mental health professional can help jurors cope with stress (NCSC, 1998). Judges can ask jurors if they have questions; this simple act can improve jurors' satisfaction and reduce frustration (Chomos et al., 2011). Although Bornstein et al. (2005) found no significant difference in actual stress symptoms (on clinical dimensions such as anxiety and depression) between jurors who received a debriefing and those who did not, debriefed jurors reported a subjective reduction in stress.

Unfortunately, however, posttrial debriefing is not without costs. Many jurors are reluctant to devote additional time to the trial (Bornstein et al., 2005), and judges might not have the time. If mental health professionals are involved, it is unclear who would pay them for their services. Thus this strategy, like any of the others, must be carefully assessed on a cost-benefit basis (Miller & Bornstein, 2013). The Ontario government has decided that the benefits of debriefing outweigh the costs: In January 2017, it launched a free counseling service for jurors (Graveland, 2017). In the United States, if services are offered at all, it is on a jurisdiction-by-jurisdiction basis.

## Importance of Considering Juror Dissatisfaction

Overall, juror satisfaction tends to lead people to become more involved in the political process and their community (Gastil et al., 2010). The deliberative process of being on a jury leads people to be more likely to vote in the future. Both jury deliberations and voting involve private citizens having a voice in what happens in their community. Therefore, when jurors have a positive experience in the deliberation process and recognize that it is a process for citizens to participate in, that positive experience can carry over to other civic engagement behaviors such as voting (Gastil et al., 2010). However, if jurors have an unsatisfactory experience, they might be less likely to engage in such behaviors.

Individuals called for jury duty who do not serve on a panel generally report dissatisfaction with jury duty and view it as a waste of time (Gastil et al., 2010). Many people who appear for jury duty sit for hours without being called for a panel, which can be frustrating. Not surprisingly, jurors who are not called for a panel report being less satisfied with their experience compared to those who are called. People who have bad experiences serving as jurors are likely to go through great efforts to avoid jury service in the future and tell their friends and family about the negative experience (Diamond, 1993). This discourages others from wanting to serve on a jury. It is therefore important not only for jurors' well-being but also for the integrity of the jury system to understand and address juror dissatisfaction.

This general review of the causes and symptoms of juror stress and, more broadly, factors related to juror satisfaction helps lay the groundwork for understanding the unique stressors experienced by jurors in the 21st century. Juror stress and dissatisfaction have serious consequences for the legal system, as negative experiences (one's own experiences or the experiences of others) might lead people to fail to comply with a juror summons and, more broadly, could weaken public trust in the legal system (Gastil et al., 2010). Many stressors relate to modern technology, as we discuss next.

## Juror Stress and Advances in Technology

The legal system has seen significant advances in technology, ranging from the way evidence is displayed in the courtroom to the use of cellphone videos as evidence (Feigenson & Spiesel, 2009; see also Chapter 9 of this volume). Understanding these advances, discussed next, is the first step in understanding how they might affect jurors' experiences, stress, and well-being.

### Visual Evidence: Photographs, Video, and Neuroimaging

Jurors are now exposed to more complex and sophisticated visual evidence. Cellphone cameras and other small, inexpensive, digital cameras, as well as more widespread surveillance technology, have greatly increased the frequency and availability of static or moving images that could be relevant to legal disputes. (See generally, Chapter 9 in this volume.) The increasing sophistication of technology has also made it easier for attorneys to display evidence in the courtroom. In complex trials in which the sequence of events in a crime is unclear, attorneys sometimes use computer-generated exhibits to aid juror comprehension (Norris, 2015). These computer-generated videos or drawings, which are produced by forensic scientists and technicians, allow jurors to imagine what happened at a crime scene in a way that was not possible in previous generations.

Technology also has made it easier to alter evidence through image-editing software. For instance, Photoshop can enlarge or enhance an image (e.g., making a blurry image clearer). This too makes it easier for jurors to understand evidence (Feigenson & Spiesel, 2009). Finally, with the rise in popularity of cellphones and video technology, it has become easier and cheaper for the average person to take a video at any place and time. There has also been an increase in the use of law enforcement officer body cameras and dashboard cameras that capture footage of officers' encounters with civilians. Such videos and photographs often allow jurors to see the crime and its aftermath first hand (see Chapter 9 in this volume). All of these examples illustrate how technology has changed the experience of the modern juror.

Jurors are also becoming increasingly exposed to neuroimaging evidence (see Chapter 11 of this volume). For example, attorneys can use neuroimages such as functional magnetic resonance imaging (fMRI) to argue that the defendant did not have the moral capacity to understand the difference between right and wrong when committing the crime, or the images can be used as mitigating evidence in the sentencing phase of a death penalty trial (e.g., Knabb, Welsh, Ziebell, & Reimer, 2009). Viewing such neuroimaging evidence could be confusing for jurors, as it is one more complex feature that can be included in trials that jurors are likely to be unfamiliar with, thus making their experience more stressful.

### Television and Movies

Crime television shows, such as the *CSI*, *NCIS*, and *Law and Order* franchises, are popular in American culture and can now be watched in a number of ways (e.g., on handheld computers and devices, through different streaming services such as Netflix). For some viewers, their only exposure to the legal field is through television. As a result, jurors might have unrealistic expectations about how trials are conducted and what kind of evidence they will have to help them render a verdict (Durnal, 2010; for a review, see Chapter 7 in this volume). This has been termed the *CSI Effect* (Dowler, Fleming, & Muzzatti, 2006). The CSI Effect could be especially salient for jurors serving on horrific or high-profile criminal trials, as crime television shows generally keep their viewership and ratings up by depicting terrible crimes or crimes especially relevant to today's society.

Expectations about trials that stem from the CSI Effect seldom match the reality of an actual trial (Durnal, 2010). Mancini (2011) found that participants who watched television shows regularly were more frustrated with and skeptical of the scientific evidence presented compared to those who did not watch such shows. In Shelton, Kim, and Barak's (2007) study of actual jurors, jurors who watched these shows regularly did have higher expectations of scientific evidence compared to those who did not watch the shows, but those expectations did not affect their ultimate decision. Even so, the CSI Effect is important to consider because unmet expectations could lead jurors to be dissatisfied with their experiences. If jurors do not receive the concrete and indisputable scientific evidence they expect, they might experience anxiety or, at the very least, frustration. In one study, a mock juror indicated he had a difficult time understanding the forensic evidence that was presented because of multiple interpretations (Stevens, 2008). He even expressed his belief that evidence would have never been presented that way in a television show.

### The Internet and Social Media

One of the most significant advances in the 21st century has been the use of the Internet and social media. Nearly two-thirds of adults reported using social networking sites in 2015, compared to just 7% in 2005 (Perrin, 2015). People use social media as a source of news about crimes or even the trial they are experiencing as jurors (Duggan, 2013). Social media have made publicity during trials more prevalent than in the past (for review, see Chapter 8 of this volume). With access to news and information available at just the touch of a button, jurors are easily able to look up information online and on social media. People also use social media to communicate their experiences of jury duty. In an Arkansas case, it was discovered that a juror had posted updates about the trial on social media, which the defense argued was grounds for a mistrial (Schwartz, 2009).

Publicity around high-profile trials is stressful for jurors (NCSC, 1998). Jurors might be afraid of being photographed or seen at the courthouse, or afraid that someone could use the Internet to discover their identity. For instance, jurors in the James Holmes case were afraid of being recognized, in fear that someone would be upset that the jury sentenced Holmes to life in prison instead of death (Wirthman, 2015). One juror in the Casey Anthony trial (in which a mother was acquitted of the death of her child, as discussed in Chapter 7) moved out of state after experiencing backlash from the community (Johnson, 2015). Even with significant efforts to protect jurors' privacy and increasing use of anonymous juries (Liptak, 2002), 21st-century technology has made it much easier than before to take pictures of jurors, record who they are, and find them on social media or in their daily lives.

These increases in the use of and exposure to various forms of technology raise a question: How does technology affect stress and well-being for the 21st-century juror? We address this question next.

## The Impact of Technology on Juror Stress and Well-Being

Technology might increase juror stress in some respects, but it also has the potential to mitigate it in other ways and enhance juror well-being. For example, some of the jurors from the James Holmes case have reported that they text each other periodically to help one another deal with the lingering stressors from the trial (Associated Press, 2016). In this case, technology allowed them to form a support group to help each other cope with ongoing difficulties. Technology has and will continue to have a significant role in the jury system, and it is therefore crucial to understand how it will affect jurors.

### How Technology Can Increase Juror Stress

There are many ways technology can increase jurors' stress, including through exposure to gruesome evidence, confusion associated with complex trials, and the inconvenience of not being able to access technology. The effects of these stressors can range from relatively mundane stress to mild psychological symptoms, as we review next.

**Wi-Fi and Internet usage.** Some juror stress and frustration stems from boredom (Bornstein et al., 2005). Jurors are often required to sit and wait for hours at a time with little to do. Having Wi-Fi in the jury waiting room would allow jurors to use their computers, tablets, or cellphones while they wait to be called. In other words, a lack of technology (i.e., Wi-Fi) can be a stressor. If courts do offer Wi-Fi, it is important to inform jurors that they do. One juror reported that if she had known that Wi-Fi would be available, she would have brought her computer to jury duty (NCSC, 2015). People often can still connect to the Internet without a Wi-Fi connection on their cellphones, but they are less likely to be able to do so on other mobile devices such as laptops or tablets. It is therefore important for courts to be very explicit about what jurors should expect from jury duty, and, if Wi-Fi is available, courts should inform them in the initial jury summons.

Although often jurors are allowed to use Wi-Fi, they are typically forbidden from posting anything about the trial to social media (in addition to prohibitions on talking about the trial with other people in general). According to a recent Nielsen Company report, the average American spends more than 10.5 hours a day looking at some sort of a screen (Howard, 2016). And although Internet addiction is not considered a disorder in the American Psychiatric Association's (2013) latest *Diagnostic and Statistical Model of Mental Disorders*, problematic Internet use does satisfy a number of diagnostic criteria for addictive behavior and affects a large number of people (e.g., Block, 2008). The relations between abstaining from social media use and stress have yet to be studied systematically. However, some evidence suggests that it can be stressful for some people when they are not allowed to use their devices (e.g., to post to social media; Wallop, 2009). Thus forbidding jurors from using the Internet or social media might be an added source of stress and dissatisfaction for some jurors.

**Gruesome evidence.** Exposure to gruesome evidence is a substantial source of juror stress (Bornstein et al., 2005) and is especially an issue in criminal trials for serious felonies. Jurors in criminal trials are often exposed to graphic images of the crime (see Chapter 9 in this volume), which can cause substantial symptoms of stress (Kaplan & Winget, 1992). This stress can be an issue especially for jurors who serve in murder trials or trials for other violent crimes (Antonio, 2006), such as the James Holmes trial. In the previously mentioned Holmes case, jurors viewed 150 pieces of evidence, including a poster-sized photo of a six-year-old's bullet-riddled body and a 45-minute crime scene video; they handled the gun; and they listened to countless survivors recount their horror stories (Associated Press, 2016; Wirthman, 2015). Many of these stressful experiences, especially the visual aids, were made possible by 21st-century technology.

Modern trial evidence is sometimes quite gruesome, which can, in some cases, bias a jury's decision-making (Bright & Goodman-Delahunty, 2011). Jurors who see gruesome images of a crime have more negative emotional responses toward a defendant and are more likely to convict a defendant compared to jurors who did not see the gruesome images (for further discussion, see Chapter 12). However, this bias does not always occur (Bornstein & Greene, 2017); the effect might be more pronounced when the evidence against a defendant is weak rather than strong (Bright & Goodman-Delahunty, 2004). However, even if jurors are less likely to let their emotions bias their decisions when the evidence is strong, they could experience stress associated with being exposed to that evidence. Furthermore, jurors seem to be more emotionally influenced when visual gruesome evidence—increasingly common due to modern technology—is displayed rather than just hearing verbal testimony (Bright & Goodman-Delahunty, 2006).

In general, reactions to disturbing evidence are a significant source of juror stress (Bornstein et al., 2005). Thanks to modern technology, attorneys are now able to enhance photos, show them with better resolution, and be creative in displaying evidence using technology (see Chapter 9). These advancements could place jurors at even greater risk of stress if the evidence is especially gruesome or horrific.

**Trial complexity and ambiguity.** Another source of juror stress is the complexity of the trial (Bornstein et al., 2005). Jurors are often exposed to unfamiliar legal jargon and confusing evidence. To complicate matters, jurors are prohibited from searching for outside information. In this age of technology, it is now easy for jurors to use their cellphones to research something about a case they do not understand (for further discussion, see Chapter 8). This could also possibly be linked to the rise in juror misconduct (McGee, 2010). In one case in Florida that resulted in a mistrial, nine jurors used the Internet to research information about the case and definitions of terms they had heard during the trial (Schwartz, 2009). This included information the judge had excluded from evidence in the trial (Funcheon, 2009). It is common practice for judges to instruct jurors not to conduct any outside research during the trial, but this could have the unintended consequence of increasing jurors' stress. One Pennsylvania judge suggests that allowing jurors to ask questions could help curb juror misconduct in this age of technology (Turgeon, 2017).

In addition to being complex, trial evidence might also be ambiguous, which could promote juror stress. Whereas jurors of past centuries could only imagine how criminal events happened, modern jurors might view video footage from cellphones taken by civilians or video footage from body cameras worn by police officers (for a review of the issues related to video evidence and juror decision-making, see Chapter 9). On one hand, videos could reduce some of the ambiguities of evidence in criminal cases (Feigenson & Spiesel, 2009). However, both videos recorded by civilians and videos recorded by police body cameras are often chaotic and do not necessarily capture an entire encounter. Sometimes all that can be perceived from the video is the audio, which can be open to multiple interpretations. This has been evident in civilian recordings of police shootings in which part or all of the shooting is blocked from view. In general, complexity, ambiguity, and uncertainty of trial evidence can be stressful for jurors (NCSC, 1998).

## How Technology Can Be Used to Enhance Juror Well-Being

While advances in technology can increase jurors' stress, technology also has the potential to have a positive impact on jurors' experiences. Several of the NCSC's (2015) recommendations to improve jurors' experiences involve using technological resources. For example, it recommends that courts implement an online check-in system when jurors report for jury duty. This could help decrease the amount of time jurors spend waiting and subsequently increase satisfaction with jury duty. We discuss these positive aspects of technology next.

**Pretrial stressors.** Technology can promote juror satisfaction in the time prior to the jury duty date. Gwinnett County, Georgia, recently implemented a system to inform and remind prospective jurors about their upcoming jury duty (Estep, 2016). Jurors now receive text message updates about their upcoming jury duty, including information on when to report. Jurors in this county have reacted favorably to the new system; likely this has contributed to the increase in the juror reporting rate observed since the system was implemented (Estep, 2016). Jefferson County, Texas, recently implemented a system known as I-Jury, which allows jurors to go online after they are called for jury duty and select days for service that best fit their schedule (Kless, 2017). This allows jurors to register for jury duty when it is convenient for them and reduce wait time that jurors experience once they arrive at the courthouse; it hopefully increases satisfaction throughout the whole process as well.

Once prospective jurors report for jury duty, online or texting systems could reduce juror wait time (NCSC, 2015). Text messages inform jurors of their estimated wait time so jurors do not have to sit in the jury waiting room all day wondering if or when they will be called for a jury. Because jurors experience stress related to boredom and waiting (Bornstein et al., 2005), such systems would almost certainly promote jurors' well-being.

Because answering questions in front of a courtroom of people can be stressful, especially when the questions are of a sensitive nature (Seltzer, Venuti, & Lopez, 1991), online jury selection procedures could be utilized (e.g., responding to an online prospective juror survey). Such procedures, used either before or during jury selection, could reduce the stress related to answering sensitive questions publicly (NCSC, 2015). This procedure also could save time and provide attorneys with a quicker way to get information about potential jurors.

Juror orientation videos can be another effective tool to reduce juror stress and increase satisfaction. Orientation videos can educate jurors on what to expect during jury duty as well as help them navigate the courthouse (Chomos et al., 2011). Experimental research has shown that watching an orientation video increases juror satisfaction (Bradshaw, Ross, Bradshaw, Headrick, & Thomas, 2005). With 21st-century advances in technology, creating orientation videos for jurors is cost effective and relatively easy for courts to do. For example, the Wisconsin state courts developed a short orientation video that uses brief clips to explain specific aspects of jury service (see Wisconsin Court System, 2017). The video, produced by the director of the Wisconsin state courts in cooperation with the Office of Court Operations, features opening and closing remarks by Wisconsin Supreme Court Chief Justice Patience Roggensack and commentary from several trial court judges.

These examples illustrate ways in which technology can improve *prospective* jurors' experiences. Other examples we discuss next illustrate ways technology can improve experiences during the trial process itself.

**Trial stressors.** As mentioned earlier, one way to reduce jurors' stress is to allow them to take notes (see Chomos et al., 2011, for review). Notetaking increases satisfaction for both mock jurors (Horowitz & ForsterLee, 2001) and actual jurors (Bornstein & Greene, 2017). Traditionally, courts have provided jurors with pens and notepads to take notes. Now that many people routinely use digital technology, jurors might feel more comfortable having the option to take notes using a laptop or tablet.

Allowing jurors to ask questions also can benefit jurors' well-being. In one study, jurors who were allowed to ask questions reported feeling more satisfied with their juror experience than jurors who were not allowed to ask questions (Heuer & Penrod, 1988). Typically, when jurors ask questions they submit a written note to the bailiff, who then gives the note to the judge. One possibility to simplify this exchange of questions and answers between the jury and the judge would be to allow jurors to use a texting or Internet messaging service to ask the judge questions directly. During testimony, if jurors were given tablets to take notes, jurors also could use those tablets to submit questions for the witnesses to the judge. This would make it easier and faster for jurors to ask questions, though it might be more distracting for the judge.

To reduce juror stress associated with the complexity of the trial, attorneys and experts can and have used technology to help explain the case to jurors in a way that eases the burden of understanding complex issues. For example, attorneys have used technology to create visual displays of evidence to coincide with testimony (Feigenson & Spiesel, 2009). With significant advances in technology, attorneys (often with the help of graphics consultants) have used a variety of computer-based methods, ranging from PowerPoint to advanced computer animation technologies, to help explain complex topics to jurors. One company is even developing a virtual reality technology to allow jurors to view a crime scene (Lindstrom, 2017). Not only can these visual aids improve juror comprehension (and perhaps thus reduce juror stress), they also present jurors with something most of them are very familiar with—technology—which could mitigate juror stress.

**Posttrial stressors.** Technology also can be used to help jurors deal with stress after the trial. Although some courts offer posttrial debriefings in which a judge or a court-appointed counselor discusses the case with jurors and talks about the stressors of the trial (e.g., Miller & Bornstein, 2004), the research is unclear as to whether debriefing actually reduces jurors' stress (Miller & Bornstein, 2013). It is possible that jurors could benefit from some sort of online debriefing, especially because people already spend so much time using screens and online (Howard, 2016). An online platform for debriefing might also make jurors more comfortable, as they would not have to talk face-to-face with the judge or a counselor. Furthermore, because jurors seem to like to post updates about the trial online (e.g., Schwartz, 2009), it could be beneficial to give jurors the option to participate in a moderated chatroom following the trial. Jurors could discuss the stressors of the case with other jurors they served with, as well as jurors on other cases.

## Call for Research: Juror Well-Being and Technology

Although there is a moderate amount of research regarding juror stress and well-being in general (e.g., Miller & Bornstein, 2013, for review), there is little research specifically about the relations between juror well-being and trial-related modern technology. There are several areas in which research is needed, including the study of how stress relates to evidence presentation, use of social media, exposure to television, use of technology to take notes or as an aid during deliberation, possible benefits of pretrial orientation materials, and the effects on stress of security measures and safety concerns. An important consideration for researchers is to use real jurors and people recruited from jury duty as participants. Laboratory studies will be a good start to investigating how technology affects juror stress, of course, but to truly capture the juror experience and the stressors associated with it (e.g., making real, consequential decisions), using real juror samples will be the best way to answer some of these questions.

### Technology and Pretrial Orientation

Research on juror stress should focus on what happens before jury selection or the trial begins. Researchers have an interesting opportunity to investigate the effects of juror well-being as technology is implemented to reduce the pretrial burden of jury duty. As described earlier, several counties plan to or have introduced online and/or texting systems to help prospective jurors learn more about jury duty before they arrive (e.g., Estep, 2016; Kless, 2017). Other jurisdictions have recorded clear and juror-friendly orientation videos for jurors to view upon their arrival (Wisconsin Court System, 2017). Researchers can take advantage of such new programs to compare the experiences of jurors in these counties to jurors in other jurisdictions to determine if these programs have a significant positive effect on juror well-being. This could lead to more courts implementing such programs, which would benefit both jurors and the courts.

### Stress and Social Media

A second area of needed research concerns possible relations between juror stress and juror misconduct regarding social media. In general, many people want to talk about stressful aspects of their lives with others, and, as such, jurors could use social media as a way to vent or share their stressful experiences with others. Perhaps it is no surprise, then, that courts have seen a rise in juror misconduct due to jurors posting on social media (St. Eve & Zuckerman, 2012; see also Chapter 8 in this volume). When looking for ways to decrease juror misconduct, courts and researchers should consider that there might be a link between juror stress and use of the Internet and social media during trial. People who use social media heavily are more likely to be high in trait anxiety (Steers et al., 2016), and such jurors might experience anxiety if they are prohibited from using social media (Wallop, 2009). However, there is no empirical research as to how the court rules regarding technology and social media use affect jurors' well-being.

Research in this area should focus on both determining if there is a link between juror stress and misconduct and also ways in which juror stress can be reduced, even if jurors are forbidden from posting on social media during a trial. Researchers and courts should consider alternative ways for jurors to post about or discuss their emotions during the trial without violating a defendant's right to a fair trial. Perhaps if jurors were permitted to discuss their emotional reactions to a trial on a private forum designed just for the use of jurors, this could lead them to be less likely to post publicly on social media. One means of accomplishing this would be to allow jurors to discuss the case with one another prior to deliberation (Bornstein & Greene, 2017). Although the practice has only modest effects on juror satisfaction, jurors who are permitted to engage in predeliberation discussion generally find it helpful (Diamond et al., 2003; Hannaford, Hans, & Munsterman, 2000).

Not only do jurors post on social media during a trial, but they also use social media and other Internet sources to research information about the trial in the media or to search for definitions of terms they do not understand (e.g., St. Eve & Zuckerman, 2012). In the 1990s, before the explosion of handheld devices for accessing the Internet, jurors expressed the desire to find definitions of unfamiliar terms in a dictionary (NCSC, 1998). Part of this desire could be linked to the relations between trial complexity and juror stress (Bornstein et al., 2005). If jurors had more opportunities to ask questions and acquire information they needed, they might be less inclined to do their own Internet research.

If there is a link between juror stress and misconduct, then addressing juror stress could help curb juror misconduct. Some authors suggest that jury instructions regarding social media are not effective at reducing juror social media use (e.g., Aglialoro, 2015). Aglialoro argues that it might be best to criminalize juror use of social media to deter jurors' social media use and misconduct during trial. In California, jurors can be fined up to $1,500 if caught using social media to post case-related information during a trial (Thanawala, 2016). It is unclear if this approach reduces juror misconduct. More broadly, constant reminders of the ban and threats of fines might actually exacerbate stress in jurors, even if they are told that the prohibition is for a good reason.

Despite the concerns of some commentators (e.g., Aglialoro, 2015), jury instructions that address jurors' social media and Internet use could, under some circumstances, be effective in reducing juror stress and misconduct. St. Eve and Zuckerman (2012) discuss the importance of providing respectful, consistent, and regular jury instructions regarding social media and Internet use during a trial. In a pilot assessment, they found that if jury instructions, given on a regular basis, were specifically tailored to Internet use and why it is important for jurors not to do their own outside research during a trial, jurors did in fact decide not to do an Internet search, even if they were tempted to do so.

**Stress and Evidence Presentation**

A third area of research is needed with regard to how evidence is presented in the courtroom. As stated previously, computer-generated exhibits are tools that can be used to help jurors better understand the case (Norris, 2015). Forensic experts use the evidence from a crime scene or accident to create a computerized depiction of what happened. This can help jurors make sense of complex cases and reduce stress associated with lack of comprehension of trial material. However, there is little empirical research on how such exhibits affect juror stress and juror decision-making. In one study, they were helpful in assisting mock jurors in a civil case understand the evidence that was presented verbally by making it easier for them to visualize a sequence of events (Kassin & Dunn, 1997). However, when the physical evidence (i.e., non-computer-generated evidence) was weak or contradicted the evidence presented in computer-generated exhibits, mock jurors tended to give verdicts suggested by the exhibits but not other evidence. In other words, jurors relied too heavily on the computer-generated exhibits, which biased their verdicts. Research is needed to better understand how this technology could assist with criminal juror decision making without biasing the jury.

Virtual reality for jurors is also an area for future research. As mentioned earlier, one company is developing a virtual reality tool for jurors (Lindstrom, 2017); however, it is not clear how this type of technology will affect juror well-being. On one hand, it could help jurors better understand and visualize a crime scene, which could increase juror satisfaction. On the other hand, if a crime scene is particularly horrific, virtual reality might exacerbate juror stress associated with viewing gruesome evidence or a tragic crime scene by increasing jurors' sense of involvement and empathy. Experimental research using mock juror participants could test these assertions before introducing virtual reality technology in real trials. Researchers could compare participant experiences and reactions to a case presented with virtual reality evidence to the same case using more traditional ways of presenting evidence (e.g., still photographs of crime scenes). Such research will be an essential next step in understanding how technological advances affect jurors' well-being.

## Stress and Television Exposure

A fourth area in need of research involves an examination of how law-related television shows affect jurors' decisions and well-being. The research on viewing shows such as *CSI* has yielded mixed results in terms of its effect on juror decision-making (Devine, 2012; see also Chapter 7 in this volume), but, overall, regular viewership of crime-related television shows (especially those with an emphasis on forensic science) does not predict ultimate verdicts. However, it likely affects jurors' expectations of evidence presented at trial (e.g., Shelton, Barak, & Kim, 2011). What is less clear is whether these juror expectations regarding scientific evidence negatively affect the juror experience.

Whereas some studies (e.g., Kim, Barak, & Shelton, 2009) suggest that television exposure affects jury decision-making in some circumstances, there is less research on how crime-related television exposure affects jurors' well-being. Experimental research in this area is difficult, as researchers generally cannot randomly assign some people to watch crime-related television shows and other people to refrain from watching such shows. Quasi-experimental studies could be useful, however; researchers could recruit community members to serve as mock jurors and compare stress and satisfaction levels in response to a trial among participants who watch such television shows compared to those who do not. Furthermore, interviews and surveys given to actual jurors after a trial could allow researchers and courts to gain some insight into how these television shows relate to jurors' experiences.

## Stress and Jurors' Use of Technology

Last, research is needed that involves jurors' use of tablets or other technology during trial. Allowing jurors to take notes on a notepad tends to increase juror satisfaction (Heuer & Penrod, 1988), but there is no research that could determine if electronic note-taking would likewise increase jurors' satisfaction. Experimental studies in the laboratory would be a good start to test this. Researchers could explore whether allowing participants to use tablets or similar technology to take notes leads to increased satisfaction with a mock trial experience compared to a group allowed to write notes by hand on a notepad and a control group that did not take notes.

Tablets also could be used in the deliberation room. Jurors are given the physical and demonstrative evidence that was presented at trial to help them in their deliberations. However, when there is a lot of evidence, it can take time and effort to sort through all of the materials. If all the evidence presented at trial were organized and listed on a tablet, this could aid decision-making. It would also be more efficient if jurors could pull up a digital image of demonstrative evidence on a tablet or laptop rather than having to summon the bailiff and pass the exhibit around the room. Preliminary research suggests that the use of tablets during deliberations could help jurors locate evidence quickly without affecting the quality of deliberations (McDonald, Tait, Gelb,

Rossner, & McKimmie, 2015). Having the ability to access information presented at trial easily might increase satisfaction or reduce stress by reducing frustration and overall deliberation time—two known stressors for jurors (Bornstein et al., 2005; NCSC, 1998). With the cooperation of courts, these notions are testable, for instance, by interviewing jurors who used technology in deliberations and comparing their stress and satisfaction levels to jurors who did not use technology.

Another important question for researchers to answer is how the use of tablets or other technology affects jurors who are not technologically savvy or who would prefer not to use technology. It might be that the use of technology could increase satisfaction for some jurors, while increasing stress for others. Courts could allow jurors to choose if they want to take notes with a pen and paper or the modern way by using a tablet. However, it is unknown if this would affect jurors differently. For example, would seeing other jurors taking notes using a tablet be distracting to jurors who are taking notes using a pen and paper, or vice versa? Would jurors who use different note-taking methods (i.e., tablet versus pen and paper) process information differently? Research on college campuses suggests that students who take notes in lecture using a laptop process information less systematically, perform worse on tests, and do not understand the material at the same conceptual level compared to students who take notes with pen and paper (Mueller & Oppenheimer, 2014). Reduced performance could also result for jurors. And, of course, providing jurors with electronic devices would be expensive. These are all important questions to consider before investing a significant amount of money in these resources.

## Conclusion

The experience of the 21st-century juror is vastly different from the experience of jurors in the past. Jurors' essential roles and duties have changed little, but new technology offers unique experiences for the modern juror. Jury duty can be stressful, especially in cases that involve horrific or high-profile crimes, and advances in technology can either exacerbate or ameliorate stress. Research on jurors' well-being in general is important, and researchers should pay specific attention to how technology relates to jurors' well-being. Researchers can thereby inform courts as to how to minimize the negative effects and maximize the benefits of technology. Doing so has the potential to promote justice while protecting jurors' well-being and satisfaction.

## Acknowledgments

Sarah A. Trescher, Monica K. Miller, and Brian H. Bornstein would like to thank Nathan Prager for his assistance with parts of this Chapter.

## References

Aglialoro, M. (2015). Criminalization of juror misconduct arising from social media use. *Notre Dame Journal of Law, Ethics & Public Policy, 28*, 101–119.

Allyn, B. (2017, June 27). Pacing, crying, frustration: Cosby juror on the 52 hours that ended in mistrial. *National Public Radio.* Retrieved from http://www. npr.org/2017/06/27/534534765/pacing-crying-frustration-cosby-juror-on-the-52-hours-that-ended-in-mistrial

Alvarez, M. A., Miller, M. K., & Bornstein, B. H. (2016). "It will be your duty . . ." The psychology of criminal jury instructions. In M. K. Miller & B. H. Bornstein (Eds.), *Advances in psychology and law* (Vol. 1., pp. 119–158). New York: Springer.

Antonio, M. E. (2006). "I didn't know it'd be so hard": Jurors' emotional reactions to serving on a capital trial. *Judicature, 89*, 282–288.

Antonio, M. E. (2008). Stress and the capital jury: How male and female jurors react to serving on a murder trial. *Justice System Journal, 29*, 396–408.

Associated Press. (2016, January 11). The haunted lives of the jurors who convicted James Holmes. *New York Post.* Retrieved from http://nypost.com

Bienen, L. B. (1993). Helping jurors out: Post-verdict debriefing for jurors in emotionally disturbing trials. *Indiana Law Journal, 68*, 1333–1355.

Block, J. J. (2008). Issues for DSM-V: Internet addiction. *American Journal of Psychiatry, 16*, 306–307. doi:10.1176/appi.ajp.2007.07101556

Bornstein, B. H., & Greene, E. (2017). *The jury under fire: Myth, controversy, and reform.* New York: Oxford University Press.

Bornstein, B. H., Miller, M. K., Nemeth, R. J., Page, G. L., & Musil, S. M. (2005). Juror reactions to jury duty: Perceptions of the system and potential stressors. *Behavior Sciences & the Law, 23*, 321–346. doi:10.1002/bsl.635

Bradshaw, G. S., Ross, D. F., Bradshaw, E. E. Headrick, B., & Thomas, W. N. (2005). Fostering juror comfort: Effects of an orientation videotape. *Law and Human Behavior, 29*, 457–467. doi:10.1007/s10979-005-5524-7

Bright, D. A., & Goodman-Delahunty, J. (2004). The influence of gruesome verbal evidence on mock juror verdicts. *Psychiatry, Psychology, and Law, 11*, 154–166. doi:10.1375/1321871041335984

Bright, D. A., & Goodman-Delahunty, J. (2006). Gruesome evidence and emotion: Anger, blame, and jury decision-making. *Law and Human Behavior, 30*, 183–202. doi:10.1007/s10979-006-9027-y

Bright, D. A., & Goodman-Delahunty, J. (2011). Mock juror decision making in a civil negligence trial: The impact of gruesome evidence, injury severity, and information processing route. *Psychiatry, Psychology, and Law, 18*, 439–459. doi:10.1080/13218719.2010.492095

Chomos, J. C., Miller, M. K., Sicafuse, L. L., Richardson, J. T., Peoples, C. D., & Bremer, C. F. (2011). Increasing juror satisfaction: A call to action for judges and researchers. *Drake Law Review, 59*, 707–731.

Cutler, B., & Hughes, D. (2001). Judging jury service: Results of the North Carolina Administrative Office of the Courts juror survey. *Behavioral Sciences & the Law, 19*, 305–320. doi:10.1002/bsl.439

Dann, B. M., Hans, V. P., & Kaye, D. H. (2004). *Testing the effects of selected jury trial innovations on juror comprehension of contested DNA evidence.* Retrieved from https://www.ncjrs.gov/pdffiles1/nij/grants/211000.pdf

Devine, D. J. (2012). *Jury decision making: The state of the science.* New York: New York University Press.

Diamond, S. S. (1993). What jurors think: Expectations and reactions of citizens who serve as jurors. In R. E. Litan (Ed.), *Verdict: Assess the civil jury system* (pp. 282–305). Washington, DC: Brookings Institution.

Diamond, S. S., Vidmar, N., Rose, M., Ellis, L., & Murphy, B. (2003). Juror discussions during civil trials: Studying an Arizona innovation. *Arizona Law Review, 45,* 1–81.

Dowler, K., Fleming, T., & Muzzatti, S. (2006). Constructing crime: Media, crime, and popular culture. *Canadian Journal of Criminology and Criminal Justice, 48,* 837–850.

Duggan, M. (2013, September 19). *Cell phone activities 2013.* Pew Research Center. Retrieved from http://www.pewinternet.org

Durnal, E. W. (2010). Crime scene investigation (as seen on TV). *Forensic Science International, 199,* 1–5. doi:10.1016/j.forsciint.2010.02.015

Estep, T. (2016, November 4). Gwinnet launches text notifications for jurors. *The Atlanta Journal-Constitution.* Retrieved from http://www.ajc.com/news/local-govt--politics/gwinnett-launches-text-notifications-for-jurors/IbuyRMF9LjyLuiO9zIGmnN/

Feigenson, N., & Spiesel, C. (2009). *Law on display: The digital transformation of legal persuasion and judgment.* New York: New York University Press.

Funcheon, D. (2009, April 23). Jurors gone wild. *Miami New Times.* Retrieved from http://www.miaminewtimes.com

Gastil, J., Deess, E. Pl, Weiser, P. J., & Simmons, C. (2010). *The jury and democracy: How jury deliberation promotes civic engagement and political participation.* Oxford: Oxford University Press.

Gilg, D. R. (2014). Juror stress in high profile or violent crime trials. *Nebraska Lawyer Magazine, 17*(3), 35–38.

Graveland, B. (2017, February 26). "One of the burdens of being a juror is the isolation you have": Juror with PTSD urges others to get help. *National Post.* Retrieved from http://news.nationalpost.com/toronto/one-of-the-burdens-of-being-a-juror-is-the-isolation-you-have-juror-with-ptsd-urges-others-to-get-help

Hannaford, P., Hans, V., & Munsterman, G. (2000). Permitting jury discussions during trial: Impact of the Arizona reform. *Law and Human Behavior, 24,* 359–382. doi:10.1023/A:1005540305832

Hans, V. P., Hannaford, P. L., & Munsterman, G. T. (1999). The Arizona jury reform permitting civil jury trial discussions: The views of trial participants, judges, and jurors. *University of Michigan Journal of Law Reform, 32,* 349–377.

Hans, V. P., & Jehle, A. (2003). Avoid bald men and people with green socks? Other ways to improve the voir dire process in jury selection. *Chicago-Kent Law Review, 78,* 1179–1201.

Heuer, L., & Penrod, S. (1988). Increasing jurors' participation in trials: A field experiment with jury notetaking and question asking. *Law and Human Behavior, 12,* 231–261. doi:10.1007/BF01044383

Horowitz, I. A., & ForsterLee, L. (2001). The effects of note-taking and trial transcript access on mock jury decisions in a complex civil trial. *Law and Human Behavior, 25,* 373–391. doi:10.1023/A:1010655602400

Howard, J. (2016, July 29). Americans devote more than 10 hours a day to screen time, and growing. *CNN*. Retrieved from http://www.cnn.com/2016/06/30/health/americans-screen-time-nielsen/

Johnson, C. (2015). Why courts use anonymous juries, like in Freddie Gray Case. *National Public Radio*. Retrieved from http://www.npr.org/sections/thetwo-way/2015/11/30/457905697/why-courts-use-anonymous-juries-like-in-freddie-gray-case

Kaplan, S. M., & Winget, C. (1992). The occupational hazards of jury duty. *Bulletin of the American Academy of Psychiatry and the Law, 20*, 325–333.

Kassin, S. M., & Dunn, M. A. (1997). Computer-animated displays and the jury: Facilitative and prejudicial effects. *Law and Human Behavior, 21*, 269–281. doi:10.1023/A:1024838715221

Kim, Y. S., Barak, G., & Shelton, D. E. (2009). Examining the "CSI-effect" in the cases of circumstantial evidence and eyewitness testimony: Multivariate and path analyses. *Journal of Criminal Justice, 37*, 452–460. doi:10.1016/j.jcrimjus.2009.07.005

Kless, T. (2017, January 17). I-Jury system will soon take effect in Jefferson County. *12 News*. Retrieved from http://www.12newsnow.com/news/local/i-jury-system-will-soon-take-effect-in-jefferson-county/386852967

Knabb, J. J., Welsh, R. K., Ziebell, J. G., & Reimer, K. S. (2009). Neuroscience, moral reasoning, and the law. *Behavior Sciences & the Law, 27*, 219–236. doi:10.1002/bsl.854

Lindstrom, R. (2017, January 23). Decatur company hopes to take jurors inside crime with virtual reality. *11 Alive*. Retrieved from http://www.11alive.com/news/local/investigations/decatur-company-hopes-to-bring-virtual-reality-to-the-jury-box/379870833

Liptak, A. (2002, November 18). Nameless juries are on the rise in crime cases. *The New York Times*. Retrieved from http://www.nytimes.com

Mancini, D. E. (2011). The CSI effect reconsidered: Is it moderated by need for cognition? *North American Journal of Psychology, 13*, 155–174. doi:10.1037/t04601-000

McDonald, L. W., Tait, D. T., Gelb, K., Rossner, M., & McKimmie, B. M. (2015). Digital evidence in the jury room: The impact of mobile technology on the jury. *Current Issues in Criminal Justice, 27*, 179–194.

McGee, A. (2010). Juror misconduct in the twenty-first century: The prevalence of the Internet and its effect on American courtrooms. *Loyola of Los Angeles Entertainment Law Review, 30*, 263–300.

McGrath, T., & Ryan S. (2004, June 29). *Social and psychological issues: What are the main issues/causes and manifestations of stress amongst jurors, including the prevalence?* Paper presented at Criminology Research Council Sub-Group on Juror Stress and Debriefing, Sydney, Australia.

Miller, L. (2008). Juror stress: Symptoms, syndromes, and solutions. *International Journal of Emergency Mental Health, 10*, 203–218.

Miller, M. K., & Bornstein, B. H. (2004). Juror stress: Causes and interventions. *Thurgood Marshall Law Review, 30*, 237–269.

Miller, M. K., & Bornstein, B. H. (2013). The experience of jurors: Reducing stress and enhancing satisfaction. In M. K. Miller & B. H. Bornstein (Eds.), S*tress, trauma, and well-being in the legal system* (pp. 247–267). New York: Oxford University Press.

Mize, G. A., & Hannaford-Agor, P. (2008). Building a better voir dire process. *The Judges' Journal, 47*, 4–9.

Mueller, P. A., & Oppenheimer, D. M. (2014). The pen is mightier than the keyboard. Advantages of longhand over laptop note taking. *Psychological Science, 25*, 1159–1168. doi:10.1177/0956797614524581

Murphy, T. R., Hannaford, P. D., Loveland, G. K., & Munsterman, G. T. (1998). *Managing notorious trials*. Williamsburg, VA: National Center for State Courts. Retrieved from http://ncsc.contentdm.oclc.org/cdm/singleitem/ collection/juries/id/272/rec/17#img_view_container

National Center for State Courts. (1998). *Through the eyes of the juror: A manual for addressing juror stress*. Williamsburg, VA: Author.

National Center for State Courts. (2015). *Jury service revisited: Upgrades for the 21st century*. Williamsburg, VA: Author.

Norris, G. (2015). Judgment heuristics and bias in evidence interpretation: The effects of computer generated exhibits. *International Journal of Law and Psychiatry, 42–43*, 121–127. doi:10.1016/j.ijlp.2015.08.016

Perrin, A. (2015, October 8). *Social media usage: 2005–2015*. Pew Research Center. Retrieved from http://www.pewinternet.org

Reed, A. (2009). Juror stress: The hidden influence of the jury experience. *The Jury Expert, 21*(2), 70–75.

Robertson, N., Davies, G., & Nettleingham, A., (2009). Vicarious traumatization as a consequence of jury service. *Howard Journal, 48*, 1–12.

Sabur, R. (2017, February 22). Judge in "crash for cash case" dismisses jury and takes case on himself after jurors were offered bribes outside the courtroom. *The Telegraph*. Retrieved from http://www.telegraph.co.uk/news/2017/02/22/ judge-uses-rare-legal-power-dismiss-jury-take-case-jurors-offered/

Schwartz, J. (2009, 17 March). As jurors turn to web, mistrials are popping up. *The New York Times*. Retrieved from http://www.nytimes.com

Seltzer, R., Venuti, M. A., & Lopez, G. M. (1991). Juror honesty during the voir dire. *Criminal Justice, 19*, 451–462. doi:10.1016/0047-2352(91)90019-R

Shelton, D. E., Kim, Y. S., & Barak, G. (2007). A study of juror expectations and demands concerning scientific evidence: Does the "CSI effect" exist? *Vanderbilt Journal of Entertainment and Technology Law, 9*, 330–368.

Shelton, D. E., Kim, Y. S., & Barak, G. (2011). Studying juror expectations for scientific evidence: A new model for looking at the *CSI* myth. *Court Review: The Journal of American Judges Association, 47*, 8–18.

Steers, M. N., Quist, M. C., Bryan, J. L., Foster, D. W., Young, C. M., & Neighbors, C. (2016). I want you to like me: Extraversion, need for approval, and time on Facebook as predictors of anxiety. *Translational Issues in Psychological Science, 2*, 283–293. doi:10.1037/tps0000082

St. Eve, A. J., & Zuckerman, M. A. (2012). Ensuring an impartial jury in the age of social media. *Duke Law & Technology Review, 11*, 1–29.

Stevens, D. J. (2008). Forensic science, wrongful convictions, and American prosecutor discretion. *The Howard Journal of Criminal Justice, 47*, 31–51. doi:10.1111/j.1468-2311.2008.00495.x

Thanawala, S. (2016, April 24). California jurors misusing the Internet could face fines up to $1,500. *Los Angeles Daily News*. Retrieved from http://www.dailynews.com/general-news/20160424/ california-jurors-misusing-the-internet-could-face-fines-up-to-1500

Turgeon, J. (2017). Permitting jurors to ask questions during trials: Is it a solution to the problem of curious jurors conducting electronic and social-medial research? *The Pennsylvania Lawyer. 1*, 27–31.

Wallop, H. (2009, October 13). People "anxious" when cut off from internet. *The Telegraph*. Retrieved from http://www.telegraph.co.uk/technology/news/6307460/People-anxious-when-cut-off-from-internet.html

Wirthman, L. (2015, April 24). The personal cost of civic duty for jurors in high-profile cases. *The Denver Post*. Retrieved from http://www.denverpost.com/2015/04/24/wirthman-the-personal-cost-of-civic-duty-for-jurors-in-high-profile-cases/

Wisconsin Court System. (2017). *General information; Handbooks and orientation video*. Retrieved from https://www.wicourts.gov/services/juror/handbooks.htm

# PART IV

## CONCLUSION

# 14

## Coping with Modern Challenges and Anticipating the Future of Criminal Jury Trials

*Shari Seidman Diamond*

This remarkable volume presents in vivid and thoughtful detail how research on juror behavior in criminal trials informs our understanding of this crucial player in the criminal justice system. The volume also reveals many of the omissions and incomplete understandings that future researchers need to address in order to provide a full picture of this important human institution. Lurking in the background: Suppose we had a receptive legal system, ready and willing to implement the best advice social science has to offer in order to maximize the fairness of criminal jury trials. What would we say based on the research described here? This will be a continuing theme as I discuss the research findings revealed in these chapters.

The contributions to this volume are not traditional stuff. They introduce topics that were not on the radar of the legal system or the agenda of researchers just a few years ago, including, for example, jurors' use of the Internet and social media, videos taken by police body-worn cameras and citizen cellphones, and the entire field of neuroscience. Two related and challenging questions characterize all of the chapters.

First, what can research tell us about the behavior of juries in the actual cases that are and are not the subject of our daily diet of media reports on jury trials? Most of the chapters include descriptions of several high-profile cases with an analysis of what the research literature adds to our understanding of them. It is telling that the complex mixture of facts and potential explanations for how jurors might have reacted or did react in these high-profile cases reveals how difficult it is to extrapolate to probable behavior in response to these real events. Moreover, to what extent do these analyses apply to the ordinary mix of cases that juries regularly decide?

Second, what does the systematic controlled research that social scientists produce tell us about jury trials *in context*? The carefully controlled studies that make up the relevant research literature described in this volume are typically limited in complexity and duration, and they offer no comparisons with other potential methods of case resolution. Actual jury trials, in contrast, are embedded in the larger criminal justice system as alternatives to guilty pleas, bench trials, and dismissals. They present a variety of types of evidence and occur over days or weeks rather than hours. This pair of questions forms the framework for my discussion in this chapter and guides my suggestions for what researchers might consider in future research.

Two important issues run through the contributions to this volume that call for special attention. The first is race and ethnicity. The race issue permeates American social and political thought and societal conflict, on topics ranging from inequality and affirmative action to voting rights. Juries and the criminal justice system, too, reflect the unrepaired damage that racial bias has inflicted on the social fabric since the founding of the United States. Today we see its reflection in jury selection, death penalty sentencing, and judgments about police-citizen encounters.

The second pervasive issue is the proliferation of technological changes that the editors explicitly highlight in the chapters in Part II. We have come a long way from the purely verbal courtroom testimony of early jury trials. Jurors inside and outside the courtroom are exposed to, and produce, a wide array of media and other technological input. Courts and attorneys have been struggling with how to make appropriate use of these new technologies and how to respond to the expectations and behavior of jurors in this new environment. Researchers, too, have turned their attention to what these developments mean for the conduct of trials and the behavior of the jury. As the authors in Part II demonstrate, we still have much to learn about the impact of these new technologies on the jury.

## Who Is on the Jury and Does It Matter?

The evidence presented at trial is crucial, but research on the jury shows that it is not the only determinant of jury verdicts. Indeed, if it were, we could have single-member juries rather than the multimember juries we screen for in selecting our juries. The authors of the chapters in this volume palpably demonstrate that the composition of the jury matters for taking advantage of group decision-making strengths and, specifically, that it is ostrich-like to ignore the challenge of addressing potential racism on the jury.

As we consider how the American jury has changed over time, we can see some modifications that represent crucial improvements in the representativeness of the jury and thus improvement in the jury as a mini deliberative-democratic institution. No longer is jury eligibility confined to White male property owners: All citizens, including racial and ethnic minorities, are jury-eligible, and women need not volunteer in order to be eligible for jury service as some jurisdictions required before *Taylor v. Louisiana* (1975). For many years, most federal jurisdictions used a "key man" system, selecting prospective jurors identified by a (White male) political official as "esteemed in his community as a person of good character, approved integrity, sound judgment and fair education" (van Dyke, 1977, p. 86). Then, in 1968, Congress eliminated the federal "key man" selection system in favor of random selection of prospective jurors by passing the United States Jury Selection and Service Act. And as research on the jury has shown, this greater diversity of background and experience brings benefits not only of greater legitimacy of the jury system (Ellis & Diamond, 2003) but of more robust fact finding and deliberation (e.g., Cowan, Thompson, & Ellsworth, 1984; Sommers, 2007). This key feature of the jury—the ability to pool different perspectives—is one of its primary advantages when compared to its chief alternative, the single trial judge.

But if this expansion of jury eligibility is a positive indicator of an evolving system, we can see from these chapters that the jury system is not yet all that it should be. The most dramatic deficiency documented by the chapter authors is the evidence of racial bias that infiltrates jury selection, distorts jury composition, and threatens jury decision-making and the legitimacy of jury verdicts.

Perhaps we should not be surprised. We are hardly living in a post-racial society. There are daily reminders (e.g., the 2017 Charlottesville fiasco with the Neo-Nazi march and the failure of the president to condemn it; Cillizza, 2017). Employment discrimination, while illegal, is a well-documented reality. Studies of racial bias outside the justice system reveal both explicit and implicit bias. But we do—and should—expect more of our legal system. We have mastered the rhetoric of that demand by prohibiting racial discrimination in jury selection (e.g., *Batson v. Kentucky*, 1986), but we have failed to implement race-neutral jury selection in a meaningful way.

As Barbara O'Brien and Catherine Grosso show in Chapter 2 of this volume, *Batson v. Kentucky* (1986) and its progeny have not had the promised effect of eliminating race as a basis for the exercise of peremptory challenges. Only the most blatant and explicitly documented use of race, revealed recently in *Foster v. Chatman* (2016) when an odd procedural turn of events brought the 30-year-old case to the Supreme Court, is likely to produce a successful rejection of a racially biased challenge. Because a challenge need not be reasonable or even plausible but must be pretextual to warrant a successful rejection of the challenge, the judge must essentially call the attorney who wishes to exercise the challenge a liar (Charlow, 1997). It is no wonder the procedures created in *Batson* have not succeeded in removing race from jury selection.

In the wake of research on both the impact of *Batson* and the pervasiveness of implicit bias (outside and inside the courtroom; see Chapter 5 of this volume), we (or an enlightened court system) might consider several choices to reduce racism in jury selection. The easy option proposed by some (starting with Justice Marshall in *Batson*) is simply to eliminate the peremptory challenge: no challenges would mean no race-based exclusions (see also Hoffman, 1997; Marder, 1995; Melilli, 1996 and many others). But would that be the classic version of "throwing the baby out with the bathwater"? If per-emptory challenges do operate to remove potential jurors who claim they can be fair (and thus discourage judicial removal for cause) even though they have backgrounds, experiences, or attitudes that undermine the credibility of those claims (e.g., "Yes, my father and two brothers are police officers," in a case in which the defendant is a police officer), the peremptory challenge can act as a safety valve in jury selection. Two other choices, I would argue, are more appropriate and in combination could significantly reduce the effect of racial and ethnic bias in jury selection. One would be to reduce the number of peremptory challenges to, for instance, three or four per side for a 12-member jury. The majority of states and the federal courts currently allow six or more challenges per side and some allow 10 or more in noncapital felony cases. A reduction to three or four per side would treat the peremptory chal-lenge as a safety valve to control bias rather than an invitation to attorneys that they can use the peremptory challenge to try to mold the composition of the jury.

The other, more radical reform would require a change in legal doctrine. We have seen that, under the *Batson* standard, a challenge is only rejected if the court determines that the reason offered for the challenge is pretextual. A remedy for this cramped interpretation of bias is to recognize implicit bias as a basis for rejecting a peremptory challenge. Such a recognition would allow a judge (as in a disparate impact discrimination case) to find discrim-ination in the exercise of a challenge without requiring proof of pretext, that is, without needing to find that the attorney exercising the challenge inten-tionally took race or ethnicity into account in exercising the challenge. As Anna Roberts discusses in Chapter 5, implicit bias can be found in jurors and judges—in all of us—so we should not expect trial attorneys to be immune. Indeed, the experiments of Sommers and Norton (2007) show precisely that bias. Of course, the diagnosis of implicit bias can be challenging, but where attorneys justify their challenges on implausible grounds (e.g., a Black man's long hair in *Purkett v. Elem*, 1995), judges should have the tools to protect jurors from removals that are reasonably likely to be based on racial bias.

As Roberts acknowledges in Chapter 5, there is a difference between di-agnosis and correction of implicit bias in the individual who harbors that bias. Although many informational interventions have been proposed to re-duce implicit bias in the legal system (e.g., the American Bar Association's "Achieving an Impartial Jury" Toolbox, n.d.), their effect is uncertain at this point. Some diagnostic evidence is promising (e.g., the Implicit Association Test [IAT] as a diagnostic tool for assessing implicit bias in physicians; Green et al., 2007), but tools like the IAT would be difficult to use systematically in the courtroom and diagnosis is only the first step. Would we be willing to require prospective jurors to take the IAT as Judge Mark Bennett (2010) suggests in order to increase jurors' self-awareness and provide attorneys with information to assist in exercising their challenges? Even if we required attorneys to take the IAT, what would we do if they exhibited bias? The best we can do is monitor their challenge behavior, because it is hard to imagine purging prosecutorial (and public defender?) offices of racial and ethnic bias. And what about the effect of prophylactic measures like increased self-awareness generated by learning one's results on the IAT or specialized jury instructions? At this point, what little evidence we have from the use of these measures in the courtroom does not inspire confidence that implicit bias is easily countered (e.g., specialized jury instruction has no effect; Elek & Hannaford-Agor, 2014). There is clearly more research to be done to determine both the extent of the bias in all trial participants—jurors, attorneys, and judges—and measures that can reduce it.

Race infects death penalty trials not merely through failures in the vetting of peremptory challenges or due to implicit bias in decision-making but also as a result of the death-qualification process. As Amelia Hritz, Caisa Royer, and Valerie Hans show in Chapter 3 of this volume, because jurors in capital cases must be willing to sentence a convicted defendant to death, the composition of capital juries systematically underrepresents Black and women jurors. In light of the positive correlation between death penalty support and willingness to convict (Cowan et al., 1984), the loss of these excluded jurors is likely to increase conviction rates in capital cases. And, as Hritz and colleagues review, recent increases in opposition to the death penalty (Oliphant, 2016) mean that the death-qualified jury pool has been shrinking. A court responsive to the empirical evidence, unlike the Supreme Court in *Lockhart v. McCree* (1986), would mandate a more representative jury venire, not subject to death qualification, for a capital defendant's trial on guilt, with a second jury, a death-qualified one, to be empaneled for the sentencing phrase if the defendant is convicted.

A similar compositional distortion occurs in both capital and noncapital cases arising from other requirements for jury service. English-language proficiency, citizenship, and lack of a felony record are standard prerequisites for jury service. All three requirements have a disproportionate effect on the racial and ethnic composition of the eligible jury pool. The state of New Mexico permits non-English-speaking citizens to serve as jurors, and its constitution explicitly prohibits the exclusion of citizens who are unable to speak, read, or write English (N.M. Constit. Art. VII, §3, 1911). This provision has been interpreted to require reasonable efforts to accommodate the non-English-speaking juror by providing an interpreter (*State v. Rico*, 2002). Justice Edward Chávez (2008) reports that including non-English-speaking jurors in New Mexico has not caused difficulties for the system, and that 11 trials in the Third Judicial District Court in Las Cruces went to verdict with non-English-speaking jurors in the first three months of 2008. Thus far, no other state has followed New Mexico's lead, and research is needed to assess whether the presence of a non-English-speaking juror (and interpreter) in the deliberation room negatively affects the deliberations.

Although citizenship is a standard requirement for jury service, the State Assembly in California, where 3.4 million noncitizens are legal permanent residents, passed a bill that would have allowed those noncitizens to serve as jurors (Skelton, 2013). Governor Brown vetoed the bill, however, characterizing jury service as "quintessentially a prerogative and responsibility of citizenship" (Brown, 2013). The result of the citizenry requirement is that a substantial portion of legal permanent residents in the United States are not included in the population from which jury pools are drawn, a limitation that is likely to have differential effects across ethnic groups.

The qualification for jury service that may have the largest effect on racial and ethnic representation is the exclusion of individuals with felony convictions. A majority of states exclude convicted felons for life from serving on a jury, an exclusion that disproportionally affects Black men. According to Uggen, Manza, and Thompson (2006), the more than 16 million felons and ex-felons who constitute nearly 8% of the adult population represent approximately 33% of the population of Black men. Wheelock (2011) estimates that felony jury exclusion reduces the pool of eligible Black citizens in Georgia by nearly one-third, reducing the expected number of Black men on a jury from 1.61 to 1.17 per jury. To the extent that felon exclusion is justified by presumed antiprosecution bias among felons, that presumption may not be justified. Binnall (2014) found that convicted felons did not differ from law students on a measure of pretrial bias, suggesting that wholescale exclusion of felons is likely to be an overbroad correction for potential bias. Although more research is needed, a legislature or court persuaded that unreasonable blanket exclusions are not justified ought to revisit this bar to jury eligibility.

Although this volume gives substantial attention to jury composition, a valuable addition would have been an essay on race and jury decision-making. The evidence is mixed on the extent of the problem of racism in jury decision-making, although few scholars would doubt that it does occur. We need a better understanding, for example, of whether it interacts with racial stereotypes and is most prevalent in violent offenses or simply pervades decision-making across offenses, whether it interacts with criminal record, and how deliberations affect the influence of individual jurors' racial bias.

Even the US Supreme Court has intermittently acknowledged that racism can infect jury decision-making. In *Peña-Rodriguez v. Colorado* (2017), the Court was faced with affidavits from two jurors reporting evidence of ethnic bias during jury deliberations. A majority of the Court was persuaded that the Sixth Amendment required them to revisit the traditional no-impeachment rule (the so-called Mansfield Rule, codified in Fed.R.Evid. 606) that maintains the secrecy of jury deliberations with the goals of promoting free and full debate and protecting jurors from potential harassment. The majority was willing to overturn the conviction based on evidence provided by the jurors that bias had affected the verdict. Setting forth a new rule, the Court found that an inquiry was appropriate, albeit in extremely limited circumstances:

> For the inquiry to proceed, there must be a showing that one or more jurors made statements exhibiting overt racial bias that cast serious doubt on the fairness and impartiality of the jury's deliberations and resulting verdict. To qualify, the statement must tend to show that racial animus was a significant motivating factor in the juror's vote to convict. (p. 859)

Thus the Sixth Amendment protection would prevail only on evidence of explicit—not implicit—bias and only when there was evidence that the bias had a significant effect on the verdict, leaving ample room for a finding of harmless error. It is not unreasonable to predict that *Peña-Rodriguez* will, like *Batson*, lack the teeth to affect many trial or appellate responses to claims of bias during deliberations. We know that racial bias frequently affects jury selection. We should know more about how frequently it affects jury (and judicial) decisions.

Race is also a dominant factor in Chapter 6 of this volume, in which Lindsey Cole discusses juror perceptions of the police after Ferguson. The string of well-publicized police killings of Black victims since a police officer killed 18-year-old Michael Brown in Ferguson (some of them captured on videos and police bodycams) and the reports that jurors may divide along racial lines in the jury room recall the racial divisions that emerged in response to the acquittal of O. J. Simpson in 1995. But the current crop of killings now implicates the police themselves as sources of violence, threatening the legitimacy of the entire criminal justice system and leading some minority observers to doubt whether the justice system can work for them. An astounding finding Cole reports is that fatal shootings by police have not increased or decreased since Ferguson (Campbell, Nix, & Maguire, 2018). Yet perceptions appear to have been affected, perhaps due to social and other media coverage. Trust in law enforcement among minorities has suffered. What are the implications for jury trials? As Cole suggests, we need to study not only actual police behavior but also how both grand and petit jurors respond to testimony from police officers, both those who are defendants in excessive use of force cases and those who serve in the more common role as hybrid fact and expert witnesses.

I have focused thus far exclusively on racial and ethnic minorities, but they are not the only minority recognized in this volume as potential victims of bias in the justice system. Like racial minorities, members of the lesbian, gay, bisexual, transgender, and queer (LGBTQ) community may face special challenges both outside and inside the courthouse. In Chapter 4 of this volume, Jordan Blair Woods contrasts the substantial advances in legal rights for this community with a continuing social bias that may call for sensitive vetting of potential jurors during jury selection, as well as other efforts to address implicit bias. Despite the paucity of research on juror bias in this area, the available studies do suggest, for example, a greater tendency for jurors to convict defendants they believe to be gay than those they believe to be straight (Wiley & Bottoms, 2009). I share the assessment that empirical research needs to be expanded, but I would go further. Woods reports that prosecutors sometimes show resistance to prosecuting hate crime laws, citing personal skepticism toward hate crime laws and concern that they will not be able to satisfy the jury that the defendant had the requisite hateful motivation. These are very different sources of resistance. Research on jury decision-making might address the second, but it would also be worth probing the sources of prosecutor skepticism toward hate crime laws.

Throughout this discussion of potential juror and attorney bias, we have ignored an important contextual feature of jury trials. We tend to evaluate the jury's performance against the standard of the hypothetical unbiased decision-maker who rationally attends to and appropriately weighs all of the relevant evidence, ignoring any evidence that might be unfair or prejudicial. Although research on the jury shows that it generally performs well (for summaries, see Bornstein & Greene, 2017; Diamond, 2003), experiments do show that bias can infiltrate the proceedings, findings that generate great interest in and concern about who is on the jury. Yet the realistic alternative to the jury is not a machine-like tribunal but instead a human judge. The legal system presumes that the judge will be unbiased, that one judge will be like another. But although the literature on judicial, particularly trial court, decision-making is less extensive than research on the jury, it shows some of the same decision-maker imperfections, including bias, that jury research reveals. In a recent review of the empirical evidence on judicial behavior, Rachlinski and Wistrich (2017) concluded, "judges' personal characteristics influence their decision making" (p. 204) and "in making decisions, judges sometimes rely on factors outside the record, including inadmissible evidence, their emotional reactions, and prejudices" (p. 205). While criminal defendants always have an opportunity to vet potential jurors and juror candidates are subject to excusal as a standard preliminary step in a jury trial, defendants in contrast have no control over the identity of the judge who will preside at their trial (or participate on their appellate panel). Although research on jury selection and composition has revealed substantial limitations in the procedures we use to identify and eliminate potential juror bias, and it offers important suggestions for improving those procedures, we might also consider the value of turning attention to judges.

## The Electronic Context of the Modern Jury Trial

Jurors always come to trials with experiences, beliefs, and expectations that interact with the evidence presented at trial. Indeed, their different backgrounds are a strength of the jury that the single judge lacks. But courts have long recognized, and researchers have documented, that one particular source of those background experiences—exposure to pretrial publicity about the specific trial—can threaten open-minded responses to the evidence presented during trial (Spano, Groscup, & Penrod, 2011). The modern context for jury trials has expanded the sources of pretrial exposure that may influence jurors, both informing them and potentially biasing them. In Chapter 7 of this volume, Jennifer Groscup refers to the influence that popular cultural sources may have on juror decision-making. The line can be thin between the reasonable expectations and accurate beliefs that jurors can form based on media exposure (e.g., new scientific advances in DNA are powerful forensic tools) and the misleading and biasing suggestions that media may convey (e.g., if the prosecution does not provide DNA or fingerprint evidence, the state's evidence for conviction is weak). Thus it is not clear what intervention, if any, is appropriate, and if so, who is in the best position to intervene. Such cultivation effects ought to be susceptible to change if popular cultural sources change. As Groscup discusses, the media studies conducted a decade ago (e.g., Dixon & Linz, 2000) reveal that the media systematically distort the actual world of crime and criminal justice: Media news overrepresented Blacks and Latinos as perpetrators and underrepresented them as victims (again implicating race). It is likely that stereotypic portrayals of minorities reinforce implicit biases in viewers, although it is unclear whether this magnifies or merely reflects already present biases. Yet a more recent content analysis of Los Angeles television news programs showed a significant departure from this prior research (Dixon, 2017). The proportions of Blacks were accurately represented as perpetrators and victims, and Latinos were accurately represented as perpetrators although still underrepresented as victims. Shifts like these may have implications for prejudice reduction both outside and inside the courts. Even so, such changes, because they are external, are not under control of the courts and may be slow to take shape or only temporary.

Other sources of potential cultivation effects, because they can address explicit beliefs rather than unconscious biases, should in principle be easier for judges and attorneys to address. For example, popular fictional crime programs (e.g., *CSI*) portray forensic techniques as unrealistically powerful crime-solving methods. Expert testimony can correct the record. How do these distortions play out in the courtroom? Prosecutors believe that the so-called *CSI Effect* influences jurors (Watkins, 2004), but the evidence for its impact on jurors is mixed. Although some correlational studies show that heavy television viewers are more willing to convict, it is unclear whether exposure to television content is a cause of the association, and Groscup rightly concludes that research has demonstrated very limited effects of viewership on the jury.

Media exposure of course extends far beyond television and video today. The Internet and social media have multiplied the available sources of information and misinformation. As Tarika Daftary-Kapur and Steven Penrod recognize in Chapter 8 of this volume, social networking has exploded and placed a new pressure on the impartial jury. Emerging technologies that facilitate juror access to the Internet and social media (e.g., Apple Watch, Google Glass) are likely to add further pressure. But the explosion has opened a two-way street. Attorneys can learn about juror leanings in the unfiltered arena of social media, potentially uncovering biases that would be difficult to detect during voir dire and perhaps supporting efforts to produce an impartial jury.

Courts have developed detailed instructions warning jurors against use of Internet sources and social media of any kind (Hoffmeister, 2015). They have also sequestered juries and controlled media access in some high-profile cases, and they have removed jurors and on occasion declared mistrials and punished jurors when presented with evidence that court admonitions were violated. Yet, although courts have taken steps to grapple with an increasing number of cases in which juror online research or use of social media has come to light, there is little scholarly research assessing the pervasiveness of juror Internet activity. More importantly, we do not yet have research that provides a good estimate of whether, how much, or under what circumstances the social media search for information affects case outcomes.

Jurors are understandably tempted to seek information on the Internet, just as they sometimes sought outside information before the days of the Internet. The temptation is compounded today because Internet searches can be nearly instantaneous and digital natives are accustomed to going online regularly for all kinds of information. Nonetheless, we have some information from prior to the digital era that reveals what stimulates such searches in the jury context: Jurors recognize that their decisions are important and are motivated to get the "right" answer based on all information that might inform that answer. In one way, that motivation would be consistent with what the legal system also would endorse if the search in fact supplied jurors with an accurate understanding of the relevant evidence and legal standards. If jurors do not understand technical terms used by witnesses or legal terms used by judges, that misunderstanding may undermine fair and accurate decision-making. The difficulty is that when jurors look up definitions on their own, they may or may not receive accurate definitions or explanations. In particular, if a legal definition varies across jurisdictions, a layperson may not uncover the relevant meaning on his or her own.

A second form of search can explicitly undermine the fairness of a trial if jurors, in an effort to learn more about the particular parties or history of the case they are deciding, uncover information that the rules of evidence preclude them from learning about during the trial (e.g., a confession that was ruled inadmissible, a nontestifying defendant's prior conviction). This case-specific form of search is particularly likely to occur in high-profile trials that have attracted media attention.

These two types of searches call for different responses. Permitting juror questions for witnesses and responding explicitly to their questions during deliberations can address the comprehension issues that motivate searches for legally relevant information. When my colleagues and

I studied the questions jurors submitted for witnesses at trial in the Arizona Jury Project (Diamond, Rose, Murphy, & Smith, 2006), we found that some merely sought definitions for terms presented during testimony (e.g., for a testifying physician, "What is a tear of the meniscus?"). And in our 7th Circuit study in which jury questions were permitted, a juror asked "Can I look up to see how [this disease] is transmitted?" The wise judge (after consulting with the attorneys) responded that the juror should not do this search but then permitted the parties to provide the answer. In a criminal case, a juror I interviewed told me that the judge had refused to supply an answer to a juror question about one of the terms used in the juror instructions on the law, so the juror went home and looked it up. All of these questions could have been addressed through official channels and, by supplying the requested information, did remove or would have removed the impetus for conducting outside research.

Searches for case-specific and legally irrelevant information present a more difficult challenge. Some instruction to the jurors may assist, but in an extreme case, juror sequestration may be warranted. Judge Lucy Koh took a different tack. Presiding over the high-profile *Apple v. Samsung* (2012) patent jury trial, she acknowledged to the jurors at the beginning of the trial that the case would be garnering extensive media coverage and promised them that in return for their promise to avoid any media exposure from the Internet or other sources during the trial, the court would supply a notebook of that coverage for each of them after the trial was over. As yet, researchers have not conducted systematic research examining the impact of these various approaches.

Compounding the ambiguity about the extent to which new forms of media have affected the jury is a new cultural phenomenon that may itself become a form of cultivation: the growing belief that fake news is distorting the "information" we receive from the Internet and other media sources. If consumers were to become more suspicious of the accuracy of the information they receive from the media (e.g., is it planted by Russian bots?), it might be easier for courts to convince jurors to ignore or reject media sources and put their trust in courtroom sources. But if consumers (unrealistically) believe they can accurately sort and identify real and fake sources, wide absorption of both real and distorted media information will likely persist. Research on the effect of this changing context is clearly needed.

## The Electronic Content of the Modern Criminal Jury Trial

Technology has brought changes into the courtroom as well. The purely oral trial in which evidence consisted entirely of testimony obtained from witnesses has been dramatically supplemented with electronic evidence.

Attorneys too sometimes use sophisticated visual aids in their opening and closing statements. In 2009, Neal Feigenson and Christina Spiesel published a groundbreaking book, *Law on Display*, tellingly subtitled "The Digital Transformation of Legal Persuasion and Judgment." In it, they showed how attorneys were introducing "visuals" (pictures, videos, or displays used to illustrate or accompany something) to assist in the presentation of evidence. They presented examples from vivid case studies and argued that these techniques can be powerful influences—capable of improving the information judges and jurors obtain from testimony but also potentially manipulating and distorting understanding of evidence. In the nine years that have passed since *Law on Display* was published, visual evidence has exploded with the spread of surveillance video cameras, the advent of police dashboard and body cameras, and the ubiquity of cellphone cameras. In Chapter 9 of this volume, Feigenson and Spiesel describe the important research carried out in the interim and examine the benefits and limitations of these new and increasingly common visuals in the courtroom for assisting jurors in accurately reconstructing events. As the authors describe, viewers may have a false sense of confidence in the judgments they derive from visual evidence. Moreover, they may be unaware of how factors including both prior beliefs and characteristics of the video may influence their perceptions. What should an enlightened court system do with these findings? Are we yet at the point where we can offer useful advice?

The research findings point in multiple directions. For example, experimental evidence shows that slow motion has two effects. It tends to make actions seem more intentional but also less violent. Assuming that finding generalizes, should courts permit slow-motion showing of video-recorded evidence? Is the additional visibility of each action worth the cost? These are tough decisions the legal system has to make. And there are many unanswered questions. Feigenson and Spiesel point out that only two experiments have examined the effects of repeated viewing, which often occurs in real trials when video evidence is presented. Although the two experiments showed few effects of a second viewing on perception and judgment, they leave many important questions unanswered. Does repeated showing reduce the impact of viewing a video in slow motion? Should we thus insist that a video be shown both in slow motion and at regular speed? And what happens to the impact of video evidence when it is embedded in a trial with other evidence? When observers are also shown the video in additional forms (e.g., with freeze-framing or zooming in)? Or when multiple videos taken from different perspectives are presented? Even a judge willing to give a recommended jury instruction would be hard-pressed to come up with advice to the jurors that would provide reasonable guidance beyond somewhat vague warnings that they should be aware that their reactions to the video evidence may be affected by the quality of the tape, the lighting, the use of a frame-by-frame presentation, and so on. It is not surprising that we are not yet in a position to provide a detailed framework for regulating how video evidence should be presented or how jurors should be guided in evaluating it. Feigenson and Spiesel, however, make a compelling case that it is important to conduct the research that will enable us to provide that advice.

A good example of what is possible is provided by Iris Blandón-Gitlin and Amelia Mindthoff who, in Chapter 10 of this volume, address the influence that video recorded confessions can have on jurors, even when the confession is false. One feature of video confession evidence that can influence the believability of a confession has garnered a fairly substantial body of empirical evidence: camera perspective in the interrogation of a suspect. In the traditional interrogation, the camera is focused on the suspect who, after all, is the subject of interest. Yet Dan Lassiter and his colleagues (e.g., Lassiter, 2002; Lassiter, Ware, Lindberg, & Ratcliff, 2010) have provided convincing evidence that the traditional camera focus on the suspect inflates the apparent voluntariness of the confession and is a source of bias that the equal-focus perspective (simultaneously showing both the suspect and the interrogator) can mitigate. Given the current trend toward video recording confessions and evidence that false confessions can be implicated in wrongful convictions, an enlightened criminal justice system would be well advised to insist on an equal-focus camera angle in video recording interrogations.

Further along the cutting edge of new evidence in the courtroom is neuroscience evidence. As we ponder the seemingly impenetrable motivations of Stephen Paddock who killed at least 59 people on October 2, 2017, by firing on concert goers from a 32nd-floor hotel room in Las Vegas before killing himself, it is tempting to search for answers in the growing field of neuroscience. Evidence from the autopsy of another mass killer, Charles Whitman, who shot and killed multiple victims from a tower on the University of Texas campus in 1966, revealed a brain tumor pressing on the amygdala, which may have affected his emotional reactions. We are further along today in understanding the neuroscientific bases of behavior, and neuroimaging has facilitated testing of live human beings, but we are far from being able to use neuroscience to accurately diagnose the sources of behavior in individual living human beings. Yet neuroscientific evidence is increasingly recognized as relevant evidence, at least in the sentencing phase when it is offered as a basis for mitigating punishment. The promise of a new form of diagnostically valid evidence coupled with the ambiguous value of that evidence puts the legal system and jurors exposed to such evidence in a conflicted position. How much should jurors be influenced by neuroscience evidence? The good news is that, in Chapter 11 of this volume, Shelby Hunter, Nick Schweitzer, and Jillian Ware report that while neuroscientific evidence influences jurors, no systematic evidence indicates that its impact is unduly magnified by neuroimages that do not add information. We do not yet understand the conditions under which neuroscience can or should be influential, so a little humility is in order before advising a willing court to implement recommended guidelines for the use of neuroscientific evidence with jurors (or judicial reliance on such evidence).

## Information Processing, Emotion, and the Jury

Many models of jury decision-making (e.g., the story model) simply omit the role that emotions can play in human judgment. Yet jurors (and judges) are humans whose capacity for emotions like anger, disgust, and empathy guide what aspects of the evidence they are likely to focus on and what arguments they are likely to find persuasive. In Chapter 12 of this volume, Colin Holloway and Richard Wiener make a strong case that emotion and motivated reasoning are inescapable aspects of human decision-making and that jurors and judges are not exempt. Although much of the research on emotion in the courtroom to this point has focused on sentencing and punishment decisions, which are particularly likely to evoke emotional responses, the implications of emotions for decision-making reach further. For example, an intriguing set of findings links different emotions to different modes of thinking—anger to heuristic thinking and sadness to analytic thinking (Tiedens & Linton, 2001). This differentiation offers a potentially promising way to understand how jurors experiencing different emotions might bring different ways of reasoning as well as feeling to deliberations. The authors, to their credit, recognize that the next step in this developing area will be to study how the interplay of emotions can influence jury rather than juror decision-making. A similar recipe for next steps could be suggested for many other topics as well, as I discuss later.

The one juror emotion that has received attention from courts to this point is juror stress. Judges consider themselves responsible for the well-being of the jurors who serve in their courtroom, and they sometimes worry about the reactions of laypersons to gruesome evidence or the heavy responsibility of deciding whether to put someone to death. Although Sarah Trescher, Monica Miller, and Brian Bornstein find some evidence for juror stress and suggest a variety of ways that courts can avoid or reduce triggers of stress, the overall picture they present in Chapter 13 of this volume is that jury service is a remarkably positive experience for most jurors. Without minimizing the demands placed on some jurors and the potential costs of inconvenience or loss of privacy, it is worth recalling what John Henry Wigmore, who wrote the classic treatise on evidence, said in 1929 about the jury. He identified only one deficit he could not find a way to cure: the hardship imposed on the jurors in serving. But he swiftly dismissed that deficit as a minor cost to pay in the face of the jury system's four major merits: prevention of popular distrust of official justice, provision for necessary flexibility in legal rules, education of the citizenry in administration of law, and "improved quality of a verdict based on reconciliation of varied temperaments and minds" (p. 171). We should certainly monitor the effects of new technology that may have the potential capacity to harm jurors (e.g., virtual reality tools that may magnify experience with gruesome evidence), but it is reasonable to view jury service as most jurors do: an inconvenient disruption that turns out to be a worthwhile experience. Yet we do have a problem: courts increasingly face a challenge in getting the citizens they summon to appear for jury service (Caprathe, Hannaford-Agor, Loquvam, & Diamond, 2016). We should appreciate the service that jurors provide, and we should make that service as convenient, informative, and stress-free as we can. Research testing innovative ways to stimulate participation will require attention to the factors that produce juror well-being and can pay the dividend of increasing the diversity of the jury pool as well.

## The Future

Despite the massive empirical literature on the criminal jury represented in this volume, questions about the jury remain, and the authors have alluded to many of them. To these I would add that we need to evaluate the size of the effects we have identified in our carefully controlled experiments. And although we can produce statistically significant differences across mock juror responses, what happens to those effects in the context of deliberations—if we study juries rather than jurors? It is tempting to conclude that our research has implications for the legal system if we use a simulated trial as our stimulus and call our respondents mock jurors. But the obstacles to producing relevant evidence also require an appreciation of legal context. I close with one example that I hope will make clear the nature of the challenge we face if we want to not only test theoretical propositions but also to supply the criminal justice system with empirically grounded research that will maximize the quality of jury decision-making.

It is a well-known and persistently replicated finding: If jurors learn of a defendant's criminal record, they are more likely to convict (e.g., Greene & Dodge, 1995; Wissler & Saks, 1985). Admonishing jurors not to use information about a prior record, or to use it only to assist in judging credibility but not propensity or character, tends to be ineffective. This much is clear. But if we want to understand how exposure to criminal records affects the jury, we need to go further. It turns out that we have only an incomplete picture from the studies testing the impact of exposing jurors to the defendant's criminal record because in the outside world, concern about juror reactions to the defendant's criminal record leads defendants to avoid testifying so their records will not be revealed.

What effect does this failure to testify have? It appears that the defendant's resulting silence at trial may itself impose a penalty on the defendant who does not take the stand. Bellin (2018) labeled this the silence penalty and in a recent online experiment showed that, while impeachment with a prior robbery raised a testifying defendant's rate of conviction by individual respondents from 62% to 82% and a prior criminal fraud raised it to 73%, the same defendant who did not testify (and had no criminal record information provided to the jury) was convicted 76% of the time. How should we understand this silence penalty? Laudan and Allen (2011) argue that jurors assume that if a defendant does not testify, he has a criminal record. While that might be a reasonable assumption, there is no evidence that jurors do hold this belief (and if they are permitted to submit questions for witnesses during criminal trials, they sometimes ask if the defendant does have a criminal record, suggesting at least some lack of assurance on this issue). If it were true that jurors believe that nontestifying defendants all have criminal records, we might advise attorneys that choosing not to testify to avoid disclosing at least some (which?) prior offenses is unwarranted.

Alternatively, the silence penalty may arise because jurors simply expect to hear an innocent defendant deny the charge against him. Although jurors are instructed that they should presume that the defendant is not guilty unless the prosecution provides evidence that convinces them of the defendant's guilt, and that the defendant has no obligation to put on any evidence, it is probably difficult for jurors to suppress the feeling that an innocent person would want to deny false charges leveled against him, just as we are inclined to assume that a person would not confess unless he was actually guilty. The point is that we have incomplete information if we focus only on what jurors are told and ignore the potential impact of what they are not told. This provocative experiment is not the last word. We need research to understand the source of the silence penalty. A further complication arises in this example because the experiment, like many others, relies on the responses of individual mock jurors. How would a deliberating jury respond? We need to find out.

Other jury issues too have remained in the background and reflect a context that could enrich our understanding of the jury. Specifically, juries dispose of a diminishing portion of the criminal matters that are filed in American courts. Plea bargaining is the standard method of resolution. The jury is not absent from this process, but we know very little about the role the jury plays in casting its shadow over plea and charge negotiations (for an exception, see Bushway, Redlich, & Norris, 2014). The shape of this shadow is a prime topic ripe for study.

The authors of the chapters in this volume uniquely explore key issues faced by juries in the 21st century, deepening our understanding of how criminal juries behave in the context of continuing and new challenges. If those challenges seem daunting—combatting explicit and implicit bias, controlling the influence of new forms of media, adapting to new technologies, appreciating the role of emotion in decision-making—we can take some comfort in the resilience and adaptability of the jury as we move forward. More to the point, we have a research agenda to study how the jury responds to these challenges.

## References

American Bar Association, Section of Litigation. (n.d.). *Implicit bias initiative toolbox*. Retrieved from https://www.americanbar.org/groups/litigation/initiatives/task-force-implicit-bias/implicit-bias-toolbox.html

Apple Inc. v. Samsung Electronics Co., Ltd., et al., No. 11–1846 (2012).

Batson v. Kentucky, 476 U.S. 79 (1986).

Bellin, J. (2018). The silence penalty. *Iowa Law Review, 103*, 395–434.

Bennett, M. W. (2010). Unraveling the Gordian knot of implicit bias in jury selection: The problems of judge-dominated voir dire, the failed promise of *Batson*, and proposed solutions. *Harvard Law & Policy Review, 4*, 149–171.

Binnall, J. M. (2014). A field study of the presumptively biased: Is there empirical support for excluding convicted felons from jury service? *Law & Policy, 36*, 1–34. doi:10.1111/lapo.12015

Bornstein, B. H., & Greene, E. (2017). *The jury under fire: Myth, controversy, and reform*. New York: Oxford University Press.

Brown, E. G. (2013, October 7). *Letter to the members of the California State Assembly*. Retrieved from https://www.gov.ca.gov/wp-content/uploads/2017/09/AB_1401_2013_Veto_Message.pdf

Bushway, S. D., Redlich, A. D., & Norris, R. J. (2014). An explicit test of plea bargaining in the "shadow of the trial." *Criminology, 52*, 723–754. doi:10.1111/1745-9125.12054

Campbell, B. A., Nix, J., & Maguire, E. R. (2018). Is the number of citizens fatally shot by police increasing in the post-Ferguson era? *Crime & Delinquency, 64*(3), 398–420. doi:10.1177/0011128716686343

Caprathe, W., Hannaford-Agor, P., Loquvam, S. M., & Diamond, S. S. (2016). Increasing jury representativeness. *Judges' Journal, 55*, 16–20.

Charlow, R. (1997). Tolerating deception and discrimination after Batson. *Stanford Law Review, 50*, 9–64.

Chávez, E. (2008). New Mexico's success with non-English speaking jurors. *Journal of Court Innovation, 1*, 303–327.

Cillizza, C. (2017, August 13). Donald Trump's incredibly unpresidential statement on Charlottesville. *CNN*. Retrieved from http://www.cnn.com/2017/08/12/politics/trump-charlottesville-statement/index.html

Cowan, C. L., Thompson, W. C., & Ellsworth, P. C. (1984). The effects of death qualification on jurors' predisposition to convict and on the quality of deliberations. *Law and Human Behavior, 8*, 53–79. doi:10.1007/BF01044351

Diamond, S. S. (2003). Truth, justice, and the jury. *Harvard Journal of Law and Public Policy, 26*, 143–155.

Diamond, S. S., Rose, M. R., Murphy, B., & Smith S. (2006). Juror questions during trial: A window into juror thinking. *Vanderbilt Law Review, 59*, 1927–1972.

Dixon, T. L. (2017). Good guys are still always in white? Positive change and continued misrepresentation of race and crime on local television news. *Communication Research, 44*, 775–792. doi:10.1177/0093650215579223

Dixon, T. L., & Linz, D. D. (2000). Overrepresentation and underrepresentation of African Americans and Latinos as lawbreakers on television news. *Journal of Communication, 50*, 131–154. doi:10.1111/j.1460–2466.2000.tb02845.x

Elek, J., & Hannaford-Agor, P. (2014). *Can explicit instructions reduce expressions of implicit bias? New questions following a test of a specialized jury instructions*. Williamsburg, VA: National Center for State Courts.

Ellis, L., & Diamond, S. S. (2003). Race, diversity and jury composition: Battering and bolstering legitimacy. *Chicago-Kent Law Review, 78*, 1033–1058.

Fed. Evid. Rev. 11 (Dec. 2014).

Feigenson, N., & Spiesel, C. (2011). *Law on display: The digital transformation of legal persuasion and judgment*. New York: New York University Press.

Foster v. Chatman, 136 S.Ct. 1737 (2016).

Green, A. R., Carney, D. R., Pallin, D. J., Ngo, L. H., Raymond, K. L., Iezzoni, L. I., & Banaji, M. R. (2007). Implicit bias among physicians and its prediction of thrombolysis decisions for black and white patients. *Journal of General Internal Medicine, 22*, 1231–1238. doi:10.1007/s11606-007-0258-5

Greene, E., & Dodge, M. (1995). The influence of prior record evidence on juror decision making. *Law and Human Behavior, 19*, 67–78. doi:10.1007/BF01499073

Hoffman, M. B. (1997). Peremptory challenges should be abolished: A trial judge's perspective. *University of Chicago Law Review, 64*, 809–871.

Hoffmeister, T. (2015). Preventing juror misconduct in a digital world, *Chicago-Kent Law Review, 90*, 981–1000.

Lassiter, G. D. (2002). Illusory causation in the courtroom. *Current Directions in Psychological Science, 11*, 204–208. doi:10.1111/1467-8721.00201

Lassiter, G. D., Ware, L. J., Lindberg, M. J., & Ratcliff, J. J. (2010). Videotaping custodial interrogations: Toward a scientifically based policy. In. G.D. Lassiter & C.A. Meissner (Eds.), *Police interrogations and false confessions: Current research, practice, and policy recommendations* (pp. 143–160). Washington, DC: American Psychological Association.

Laudan, L., & Allen, R. J. (2011). The devastating impact of prior crimes evidence and other myths of the criminal justice process. *Journal of Criminal Law & Criminology, 101*, 493–527.

Lockhart v. McCree, 476 U.S. 162 (1986).

Marder, N. S. (1995). Beyond gender: Peremptory challenges and the roles of the jury. *Texas Law Review, 73*, 1041–1138.

Melilli, K. J. (1996). Batson in practice: What we have learned about Batson and peremptory challenges. *Notre Dame Law Review, 71*, 447–503.

Oliphant, B. (2016, September 29). Support for death penalty lowest in more than four decades. Pew Research Center. Retrieved from http://www.pewresearch.org

Peña-Rodriguez v. Colorado, 137 S.Ct. 855 (2017).

Purkett v. Elem, 514 U.S. 765 (1995).

Rachlinski, J., & Wistrich, A. (2017). Judging the judiciary by the numbers: Empirical research on judges. *Annual Review of Law and Social Science, 13*, 203–229. doi:10.1146/annurev-lawsocsci-110615-085032

Skelton, G. (2013, August 28). Noncitizens as jurors? It's not a discrimination issue. *Los Angeles Times*. Retrieved from http://articles.latimes.com/2013/aug/28/local/la-me-cap-jury-20130829

Sommers, S. R. (2007). Race and the decision-making of juries. *Legal and Criminological Psychology, 12*, 171–187. doi:10.1348/135532507X189687

Sommers, S. R., & Norton, M. I. (2007). Race-based judgments, race-neutral justifications: Experimental examinations of peremptory use and the Batson challenge procedure. *Law and Human Behavior, 31*, 261–273. doi:10.1007/s10979-006-9048-6

Spano, L. M., Groscup, J. L., & Penrod, S. D. (2011). Pretrial publicity and the jury: Research and methods. In R. L. Wiener & B. H. Bornstein (Eds.), *Handbook of trial consulting* (pp. 217–233). New York: Springer.

State v. Rico, 52 P.3d 942 (N.M. 2002).

Taylor v. Louisiana, 419 US 522 (1975).

Tiedens, L. Z., & Linton, S. (2001). Judgment under emotional certainty and uncertainty: The effects of specific emotions on information processing. *Journal of Personality and Social Psychology, 81*, 973–988. doi:10.1037/0022-3514.81.6.973

Uggen, C., Manza, J., & Thompson, M. (2006). Citizenship, democracy, and the civic reintegration of criminal offenders. *Annals of the American Academy of Political and Social Science, 605*, 281–310. doi:10.1177/0002716206286898

van Dyke, J. M. (1977). *Jury selection procedures: Our uncertain commitment to representative panels.* Cambridge, MA: Ballinger.

Watkins, M. J. (2004). Forensics in the media: Have attorneys reacted to the growing popularity of forensic crime dramas? Unpublished master's thesis, Florida State University, Florida.

Wheelock, D. (2011). A jury of one's "peers": The racial impact of felon jury exclusion in Georgia. *The Justice System Journal, 32*, 335–359.

Wigmore, J. H. (1929). A program for the trial of jury trial. *Judicature, 12*, 166–171.

Wissler, R. L., & Saks, M. J. (1985). On the inefficacy of limiting instructions: When jurors use prior conviction evidence to decide on guilt. *Law and Human Behavior, 9*, 37–48. doi:10.1007/BF01044288

Wiley, T. R. A., & Bottoms, B. L. (2009). Effects of defendant sexual orientation on jurors' perceptions of child sexual assault. *Law and Human Behavior, 33*, 46–60.

# About the Editors

**Cynthia J. Najdowski** is an assistant professor at the University at Albany. Her research explores how social psychological phenomena shape criminal justice interactions in ways that produce miscarriages of justice for minorities, women, and children. Her work has been recognized with several national grants and awards and published in the top-ranked journals in the field of psychology and law. She also co-edited *Children as Victims, Witnesses, and Offenders: Psychological Science and the Law.*

**Margaret C. Stevenson** is an associate professor at the University of Evansville. She has published over 30 peer-reviewed articles and book chapters related to factors that shape juror decision-making and the nature of jury deliberations. She also explores perceptions of marginalized individuals, including children and minorities, who enter the legal system, either as victims or as perpetrators of crime. Her research has received grants and awards from divisions of the American Psychological Association.

# Index

CPSIA information can be obtained
at www.ICGtesting.com
Printed in the USA
LVHW091313250820
664190LV00003B/443